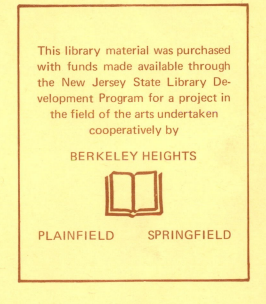

WAGNER: VOLUME II

CURT VON WESTERNHAGEN

WAGNER

A BIOGRAPHY

VOLUME II

TRANSLATED BY MARY WHITTALL

CAMBRIDGE UNIVERSITY PRESS

CAMBRIDGE

LONDON · NEW YORK · MELBOURNE

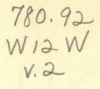

Published by the Syndics of the Cambridge University Press
The Pitt Building, Trumpington Street, Cambridge CB2 1RP
Bentley House, 200 Euston Road, London NW1 2DB
32 East 57th Street, New York, NY 10022, USA
296 Beaconsfield Parade, Middle Park, Melbourne 3206, Australia

© In the English-language edition Cambridge University Press 1978
The translation is based on the second, revised and enlarged German-language
edition © Atlantis Musikbuch-Verlag 1978

First published in English translation 1978

Phototypeset in V.I.P. Bembo by Western Printing Services Ltd, Bristol

Printed in Great Britain at the
University Press, Cambridge

Library of Congress Cataloguing in Publication Data

Westernhagen, Curt von.
Wagner: a biography.

Bibliography: v. 2, p.
Includes index.
1. Wagner, Richard, 1813–1883. 2. Composers –
Germany – Biography.
ML410.W1W55   782.1′092′4   [B]   78–2397

ISBN 0 521 21930 2 Volume I
ISBN 0 521 21932 9 Volume II

CONTENTS

Volume II

List of Illustrations   *page* vii
Summary Bibliography   ix

**Part V (continued). *Tristan* and *Die Meistersinger*
(1857–1868)**

25 Munich   329
26 *Die Meistersinger*   365

Part VI. *Der Ring des Nibelungen* (II) (1868–1877)

27 From Tribschen to Bayreuth   401
28 The First Festival   449
29 Nietzsche in Bayreuth   499
30 The Nation's Thanks   506

Part VII. *Parsifal* (1877–1883)

31 'My Farewell to the World'   527
32 La lugubre gondola   585

Appendices I–V   595
Chronological Summary of Wagner's Life and Work   604
List of works   611
Correspondence of Richard and Cosima Wagner   615
Notes to Volume II   618
Bibliography   629
Index to Volumes I and II   639

ILLUSTRATIONS

between pages 350 and 351

1 Wagner and his circle, Munich 1865
2a Heinrich Porges
2b Hans Richter
3a Friedrich Nietzsche
3b Elisabeth Förster-Nietzsche
4a *Dionysus among the Muses of Apollo* by Bonaventura Genelli
4b Wagner's house Tribschen
5a Mathilde Maier
5b Liszt with his daughter Cosima in 1867
6 Autograph title-page of the *Siegfried Idyll*, 1870
7 Wagner and Cosima, Vienna 1872
8a Wagner: sketch in red pencil by Franz von Lenbach, Munich 1880 (based on photographs of 1871)
8b Judith Gautier
9a Karl Tausig
9b Angelo Neumann
10a The Festspielhaus in Bayreuth: wood-engraving around 1880
10b The Festspielhaus: a modern photograph
11a Heinrich von Stein, Carl Friedrich Glasenapp and Hans von Wolzogen
11b Engelbert Humperdinck

12 Family photograph on the steps of Wahnfried, 1881: Isolde and Daniela von Bülow, the dog Marke, Eva and Siegfried Wagner, Blandine von Bülow, Heinrich von Stein, Cosima, Wagner, Paul Zhukovsky
13a Wahnfried seen from the front
13b Tea at Wahnfried, 1881: Wagner, Cosima, Heinrich von Stein, Paul Zhukovsky, Daniela and Blandine von Bülow
14a Titian's *Assumption of the Virgin* (detail)
14b The Grail scene in *Parsifal*: Zhukovsky's sketch of 1882
15a Paul Zhukovsky
15b Hermann Levi
16a Arthur, Count Gobineau
16b Zhukovsky's pencil sketch of Wagner, Venice 1883: the inscription in Cosima's handwriting reads 'R. lesend 12. Febr. 1883'

Sources

Archiv für Kunst und Geschichte, Berlin: plates 4b, 6, 7, 10a, 10b, 13a

Richard Wagner Gedenkstätte, Bayreuth: plates 1, 2a, 2b, 3a, 3b, 5a, 5b, 8a, 8b, 9a, 9b, 11a, 11b, 12, 13b, 14b, 15a, 15b, 16a, 16b

SUMMARY BIBLIOGRAPHY

With a key to the abbreviations employed in the text

A comprehensive bibliography appears at the end of this volume.

BB   Bülow, Hans von, *Briefe*. 7 vols. Leipzig, 1899–1908

BBL   *Bayreuther Blätter*. Monthly, later quarterly periodical, ed. by Hans von Wolzogen. Chemnitz, later Bayreuth, 1878–1938

CT   Wagner, Cosima, *Die Tagebücher,* ed. by M. Gregor-Dellin and D. Mack. 2 vols., Munich, 1976–7. (An English translation is in preparation. See the Preface and its Postscript, in Vol. I)

CWFN *Die Briefe Cosima Wagners an Friedrich Nietzsche,* ed. by E. Thierbach. 2 vols. Weimar, 1938–40

DMCW Du Moulin Eckart, Richard Graf, *Cosima Wagner. Ein Lebens- und Charakterbild.* 2 vols. Munich, 1929–31

EFWN Förster-Nietzsche, Elisabeth, *Wagner und Nietzsche zur Zeit ihrer Freundschaft.* Munich, 1915

FHKF Herzfeld, Friedrich, *Königsfreundschaft. Ludwig II. und Richard Wagner.* Leipzig, 1939

FWSZ Fehr, Max, *Richard Wagners Schweizer Zeit.* 2 vols. Aarau, 1934–53

GLRW Glasenapp, Carl Friedrich, *Das Leben Richard Wagners.* Definitive edn, 6 vols. Leipzig, 1905–12. (Modern reprint, Wiesbaden and Liechtenstein) (First edn, 2 vols, 1876–7)

JKWF Kapp, Julius, *Wagner und die Frauen.* Final edn, Berlin–Wunsiedel, 1951 (First edn, 1912; numerous subsequent edns)

KLRW König Ludwig II. und Richard Wagner, *Briefwechsel,* ed. by Otto Strobel. 5 vols. Karlsruhe, 1936–9

LJG   Wagner, Richard and Cosima, *Lettres à Judith Gautier,* ed. by Léon Guichard. Paris, 1964

LWVR Lippert, Woldemar, *Richard Wagners Verbannung und Rückkehr 1849–62.* Dresden, 1927

ML   Wagner, Richard, *Mein Leben.* 1st authentic edn. Munich, 1963. (First edn, 1911)

MMCW Millenkovich-Morold, Max, *Cosima Wagner. Ein Lebensbild.* Leipzig, 1937

MWKS Morold, Max, *Wagners Kampf und Sieg, dargestellt in seinen*

Beziehungen zu Wien. 2 vols. Zürich, Leipzig, Vienna, 1950. (First edn, 1930)

NBB   Bülow, Hans von, *Neue Briefe,* ed. by R. du Moulin Eckart. Munich, 1927

NLRW   Newman, Ernest, *The life of Richard Wagner.* 4 vols. New York, 1933–46 (There are some discrepancies between the pagination of the New York printing and the London edn of 1933–47. The author's references are to the New York edn, which is also that reprinted, London and Cambridge, 1976)

RWAP   *The letters of Richard Wagner to Anton Pusinelli,* ed. by E. Lenrow. New York, 1932

RWBC   Wagner, Richard, *Briefe. Die Samlung Burrell,* ed. by J. N. Burk. Frankfurt am Main, 1953. (*Letters of Richard Wagner: The Burrell Collection,* ed. with notes by John N. Burk, was first publ. in New York, 1950, with the documents in translation. The German edn has the documents in the original and the editorial matter in translation. Page references in the present work are to the German edn, and quotations from the documents are newly translated for the sake of stylistic consistency)

RWGB   *Richard Wagners Gesammelte Briefe,* ed. by J. Kapp and E. Kastner. 2 vols. Leipzig, 1914

RWGS   Wagner, Richard, *Gesammelte Schriften und Dichtungen,* vols 1–10. 4th edn. Leipzig, 1907 (Reprint, Hildesheim, 1976)
        – *Sämtliche Schriften und Dichtungen,* vols 11–16. 6th edn. Leipzig, n. d.

RWSB   Wagner, Richard, *Sämtliche Briefe,* ed. by G. Strobel and W. Wolf. Leipzig, 1967– (See p. 617 below.)

SERD   Richard Wagner, *Skizzen und Entwürfe zur 'Ring'-Dichtung,* ed. by Otto Strobel. Munich, 1930

SRLW   Röckl, Sebastian, *Ludwig II. und Richard Wagner,* 2 vols. Munich, 1913–19

TWLF   Tiersot, Julien, ed. *Lettres françaises de Richard Wagner.* Paris, 1935

25

Munich

'I am at the end of the road – I can go no further – I must disappear from the world somewhere.' With these words Wagner greeted Wendelin Weissheimer on Saturday 30 April 1864 in his Stuttgart hotel, whither he had summoned him by telegram, to discuss what steps he should next take. They decided to look for somewhere as remote as possible in the Rauhe Alb, the hill country of southern Württemberg, where Wagner would be able to finish the first act of *Die Meistersinger* in peace. Since he wanted to see a performance of *Don Giovanni* on the Sunday he decided to leave on Tuesday. On Monday evening he went to visit a friend, Kapellmeister Eckert, and there, at already quite a late hour, the visiting card of a gentleman calling himself the 'secrétaire aulique de S. M. le roi de Bavière' was brought to him. Surprised and annoyed that his presence in Stuttgart was known even to people passing through the city, he told the servant to say he was not there. On his return to his hotel he was again told that a gentleman from Munich wished to speak to him urgently. Wagner left a message for him to call again the next morning and passed a restless night, preparing for the worst.

The next morning the Secretary of the Cabinet to the King of Bavaria, Franz Seraph von Pfistermeister, was shown up to his room. He had already been to Penzing and Mariafeld in search of him and, had it not been for Wagner's delay in order to see *Don Giovanni*, he would have missed him in Stuttgart too. Pfistermeister brought him a photograph of Ludwig II, a valuable ring and the message that as the stone in the ring glowed, so the King was on fire to see the author and composer of *Lohengrin*.[1]

'This life, all the poetry and music of which it is yet capable, now belongs to you, my gracious young king,' Wagner replied, 'dispose

329

of it as of your own!' (3 May) One of the not infrequent symbolic chances of his life brought a telegram, as he lunched at the Eckerts the same day, with the news that Meyerbeer had died in Paris the day before. Wagner castigated Weissheimer in his autobiography for breaking into a 'yokelish laugh'.

By 4 May Wagner stood before King Ludwig in the Residenz palace in Munich. 'I should be the most ungrateful of men if I did not tell you at once of my immeasurable good fortune,' he wrote to Eliza Wille the very same day. 'You already know that the young King of Bavaria had sent to look for me. Today I was taken to him.' He went on, prophetically: 'He is so handsome, so great in spirit and in soul, so glorious that, alas, I fear that his life will evanesce in this mean world like a fleeting dream of godhood.' 'My heart is bursting,' he exclaimed to Mathilde Maier, 'I must share my news with someone dear to me. Look at this picture of a marvellous youth, whom Fate has chosen to be my saviour. This is he whom we expected, whom we knew existed, but to find him so handsome fills me with profound amazement . . . He offers me everything I need to live, to create, to have my works performed. All I need to be is his friend: no official appointment, no duties . . . And this now – now – in the darkest, deathlike night of my life!! I am crushed by it!' (5 May)

'If only you could have witnessed how his thanks shamed me', the king told his cousin and future fiancée, Duchess Sophie in Bavaria, 'when I gave him my hand with the assurance that his great Nibelung work would be not only completed but performed as he wished it to be, that I would faithfully see to it. At that he bowed deep over my hand and seemed moved by what was after all so natural, for he stayed in that position for a long time, without saying a word. I had the sensation that we had exchanged roles. I bent over him and drew him to my heart with a feeling as though I were silently taking the oath of fealty: to remain true to him for ever.' (KLRW, I, p. xxxv)

No wonder that the friendship soon passed into legend, for better and, even more, for worse. The publication of the complete correspondence between Ludwig and Wagner, in five volumes between 1936 and 1939, was of all the greater biographical value.

What is immediately apparent from the letters is that the popular conception of a favourite composer and a royal musical amateur does not apply here. A love of music was not the most important motive at work in Ludwig. Was he musical at all? It has been denied and Wagner himself sometimes expressed doubt about it. But he may have meant only that the king had not been properly educated in music; why else should he have encouraged him to let Bülow play Beethoven to him, to improve his knowledge of that master? There was also, from the first, no question of a princely patron condescending to a favourite commoner. Each regarded the other as an equal in his different way. The tone of courtly deference in Wagner's letters does not conceal the fact that he addresses the king as an equal. The king in his turn places himself on the same footing as the artist, in the belief that in realizing the composer's ideas he is only bodying forth his own dreams: he writes of 'our' ideals, 'our' efforts, 'our' work. 'When we have both long since ceased to be, our work will still serve posterity as a shining exemplar, to delight future centuries, and hearts will glow in enthusiasm for art, divinely begotten, immortal art!' (4 August 1865)

In view of the homosexual inclinations that the king was later to reveal, the suspicion was expressed at one time that his friendship with Wagner also rested on that, or a related basis. So far as Wagner is concerned it is of course absurd to suppose that he would have enjoyed an unnatural relationship with the king at the time of his consuming passion for Cosima. He stated his own views on the subject quite unambiguously. 'It is not for me to be to you what the world, your family, your high calling in life, a friend – and one day the woman of your choice can be to you,' he wrote to him on 24 March 1865. And he wrote in his diary in 1873, evidently after reading Plato: 'What we cannot understand in the Greek character, whatever the language we use, is what separates us completely from them: e.g. their love – pederasty.' The king, for his part, as Strobel emphasizes, had far too idealized a conception of his relationship to Wagner to have permitted the intrusion of any such feelings. Newman draws attention to Ludwig's diary, which testifies to his constant but hopeless struggle against his homosexuality, and in which he quotes lines from Wagner's works to strengthen and comfort himself. For instance, he once quotes some lines from Lohengrin's Grail narrative:

> Wer nun dem Gral zu dienen ist erkoren,
> den rüstet er mit überird'scher Macht;
> an ihm ist jedes Bösen Trug verloren,
> wenn ihn er sieht, weicht dem des Todes Nacht,

but alters the last phrase from 'the night of death yields to him' to 'the might of sin yields to him': '. . . weicht dem der *Sünde Macht*. Amen! Amen! Amen!'[2]

It was his idealization of art that drew Ludwig to Wagner, as to Schiller. Growing up in the castle of Hohenschwangau, whose walls his father, Maximilian II, had had decorated with pictures of emperors and dukes, including four of the Swan Knight, the decisive experience of the boy's life had been a performance of *Lohengrin* seen when he was fifteen. Even before then he had already read *The Artwork of the Future* and *Music of the Future*, the word 'future' ('Zukunft') exercising a mysterious fascination on him. He went on to immerse himself in *Opera and Drama* too, and when he came upon the question at the end of the preface of the text of the *Ring* – 'Is such a prince to be found? "In the beginning was the Deed"' – he felt it was addressed to him personally, although he had no idea at the time how soon he would be in a position to respond.

'Rest assured that I will do everything in my power to compensate you for your past suffering,' he wrote to Wagner after their first meeting. 'I want to lift the menial burdens of everyday life from your shoulders for ever, I want to enable you to enjoy the peace for which you long, so that you will be able to unfurl the mighty pinions of your genius unhindered in the pure ether of your rapturous art!

'Unknowingly you were the *sole source of my joys* from my earliest boyhood, my friend who spoke to my heart as *no other* could, my best mentor and teacher.' (5 May)

His first act to relieve Wagner of the burdens of everyday life was a provisional gift of 4000 gulden to meet his obligations in Vienna, followed by another 16,000 gulden in June. He lent him a house on the Starnberg Lake for the summer months, Haus Pellet, just outside Kempfenhausen, from which Wagner could drive over to see him at Schloss Berg in a quarter of an hour. There was not a blot, not the smallest cloud, Wagner wrote to Bülow, but the pure, deep, complete devotion of the disciple to the master. 'I have no other pupil so perfectly dedicated to me as this one.' And he referred to the king for the first time by the name of 'Parzival', as he was to be known to Wagner and his close friends. (18 May)

His experiences in Dresden had taught him that he could expect to meet with envy and rancour in Munich too. His good fortune and his power were now so great, he told Bülow, that his sole care was to avoid attracting the accusation of abusing them. (12 May) But the king had no such suspicions. 'Do you really believe that the composer of *Lohengrin* still has enemies?' he asked once. 'I think it is impossible!'

After the first heady delight had worn off, Wagner became conscious of his isolation in the 'bewitched castle', and it was all the more acute because he was not yet able to collect himself sufficiently to get down to work again. 'Shall I be able to renounce the "feminine" entirely?' he wondered in a letter to Eliza Wille. He plucked up enough courage to appeal yet again to Mathilde Maier: 'Will you come to me and keep house for me? . . . Must I still fear to put you in a fluster if I ask you to come to me? . . . God! God! These eternal petty bourgeois scruples; – and where there is so much love!' He went on, imploringly: 'I'm afraid you will lose me one day, if you do not give me your help entirely.' (22 June) Three days later he followed this: 'I have not yet set eyes on anyone who could take your place. It was not a threat, only the fear that I should be forced to *seek* someone else.'

With this letter he also enclosed a long one for her mother: 'Have you perhaps the courage in the sight of the world and enough confidence in me to entrust Mathilde to me? I know how disturbing, even destructive, a thing this is to ask of you. But I must ask you . . . Do I need to assure you that Mathilde's position in my house will be good and noble and that she will be protected in the most emphatic and energetic manner against every suspicion, every stain? Or may I even go so far, without nurturing an impious wish, as to take the possibility of my wife's death into account and to sue for your daughter's hand in that eventuality?'

Mathilde's answer is missing, but it is clear from Wagner's response that she had not given her mother the letter, for fear that it would indeed destroy her. 'Oh, my dear child! I do not want that at any price!' he exclaimed in horror, 'I can and will endure anything in the world from now onwards, save only new onslaughts of disturbance and strife, such as I now see would inevitably ensue if you were to give the letter to your good mother!' (29 June)

He added incidentally that he was expecting visitors: by a strange coincidence, on the very day that he received and replied to Mathilde's refusal, Cosima von Bülow and her daughters Daniela and Blandine arrived at Haus Pellet. On 30 June he told Eliza Wille that Frau von Bülow had arrived the day before, with two children

and their nurse, and Bülow would be following. 'It makes things a
little more lively, but I am in so peculiar a state that nothing seems
to make any real impression on me any more.' So, instead of the
middle-glass girl from Mainz, his house received the daughter of
the Comtesse d'Agoult, and the eight days that passed before
Bülow's arrival sealed the fate of all three of them.

The letter that Bülow wrote to Liszt on 20 April 1856, asking for
Cosima's hand, ended with the remarkable statement: 'I swear to
you that, however much I feel myself bound to her by my love, I
would never hesitate to sacrifice myself to her happiness and release
her if she should come to realize that she had been deceived in me.
Her will, her very whim, shall be sacred to me.' This almost morbid
sense of his own 'insignificance', as he calls it here, contains the
seeds of the eventual tragedy of his marriage. In the letter he wrote
to congratulate his sister on her engagement in 1862 he confessed
that as a rule it was the office of the husband to play the part of the
protector, but he was painfully aware that in his own case the
relationship was reversed: 'Mine is a nature that verges on the
feminine; my wife has a strong character and has, alas, so little need
of my protection that if anything she gives me hers.' (MMCW, p.
188)

When the Bülows visited the Wagners in Zürich during their
honeymoon, Wagner was taken aback by Cosima's reserve towards
him. Her reticence distressed him. 'If she found my manner too
strange, if occasionally a brusque remark, a word of mockery . . .
offended her, then I should truly have to regret having allowed
myself to go a little too far in my familiarity.' (To Bülow, 18
January 1858) On her second visit to Asyl he again complained that
she seemed more drawn to the Herweghs: 'I dare say she finds me
rather unprepossessing; but we are excellent friends!' (To Liszt, 2
July 1858) It must have startled him all the more, therefore, when, as
she said goodbye, she fell at his feet and covered his hands with tears
and kisses. (JKWF, p. 152) What can she have said in the 'recent mad
letter' for which she asked Hans to make her apologies to Wagner?
(NBB, 5 February 1859) Wagner replied that he wished she would
always send him letters that she regretted. Such regrettable letters
were the only things he had to refresh him. 'Thanks to these
outpourings I suddenly see myself clearly all at once; then a wonderful calm and a deep sense of inner peace take possession of me.
Tell her so! And give her my warmest regards!' (6 February 1859)

When he heard that Hans was worried about her health he ventured the opinion that her temperament was the worst threat to her health: 'Her origins are simply too extraordinary and for that reason it is hard to shield her.' (4 April 1861) 'She's a wild child, is all I can say! But her aristocratic breeding shows.' (19 September 1861)

All this epistolary evidence points to the character of their relationship before her visit to Starnberg. Her tongue-tied and sometimes strange behaviour in Wagner's presence shows what he meant to her. His concern on her behalf was mixed with perplexity and admiration, but no word of love or passion had been spoken between them.

There is, however, a passage in *Mein Leben*, suppressed in the 1911 edition, according to which they had exchanged a vow 'to belong only to each other' on 28 November 1863, on a drive around Berlin during his brief visit to the city. (ML, p. 844) One of Cosima's biographers remarks that this statement was probably composed in the light of later feelings. (MMCW, p. 139) It is understandable that Wagner should have felt a need to give Cosima a place in his memoirs, which finish at the point of his summons to Munich, by thus advancing the date when they confessed their love.

The first direct evidence of the change in their relationship is in a letter she sent from Starnberg to her friend Marie von Buch, later Freifrau von Schleinitz. 'I'm writing to you . . . far from home, far from all disturbance, separated by the lake even from the little village of Starnberg, I feel far away from everything, as if everything has forgotten [me] and as if I have forgotten everything. When I have told you about it all, then you will not misunderstand my words. I have been here three days and it seems to me that it has already been a century and that it will last, how long, I don't know.' (DMCW, I, p. 233)

That was on 2 July 1864. Bülow himself arrived at Haus Pellet on 7 July. The entry for these weeks in Wagner's Annals reads: 'End of July: every day with Hans to the king in Munich. 29 July: Hans's appointment . . . Hans falls ill. 19 August: Cosima to Karlsruhe. Hans to Munich: to the hotel, ill and furious.'

The festival of the Allgemeiner Deutscher Musikverein was due to take place in Karlsruhe from 22 to 26 August. Since Bülow was ill and Wagner unable to get away because of the king's birthday (25 August), Liszt was obliged, against his will, to leave his refuge in Rome and undertake the direction of the festival. He told Princess

Caroline that he had refrained from inviting Cosima, so as not to influence her in any way. But on 19 August, on the same day that Bülow, ill, moved to the Bayerischer Hof hotel in Munich, Cosima went to Karlsruhe. Was it simply to keep her father company? In the light of what was known of the 'Wagner–Cosima–Bülow triangle', Newman felt it permissible to assume that she wanted to tell her father about the crisis that had recently come about and ask for his counsel and help. (NLRW, III, pp. 266ff.) This assumption has since been confirmed by the publication, in 1975, of the full text of Wagner's Brown Book.[3] The entry for 11 September 1865, while Cosima was away with Liszt and Bülow for a time, reads: 'God knows what you'll be like when you return. I know how you were a year ago, when your father brought you back here! It was dreadful: you sleepless, restless, weak, frail, miserable, ravaged!' This leaves no doubt that she went straight to Karlsruhe from Starnberg in order to pour out her heart to her father.

She arrived back in Munich on 28 August 1864, accompanied by Liszt, who visited not only Hans, still on his sickbed, but also Wagner. *'Liszt'*, the latter wrote in the Annals, underlining the name significantly. '(Grey man.) Comes to Starnberg with me for one day and night. Praises my good sense. – Munich again: Bayerischer Hof . . . (Hans!). 3 September, Liszt left in the morning, Hans and Cosima in the evening [for Berlin]. Quiet at Starnberg.'

His 'good sense' consisted in his agreement not to force the situation to a violent resolution. Liszt probably hoped privately that Cosima would be reconciled within herself to returning to her husband. There seem still to have been certain reservations on what Hans had been told. On 30 September Wagner wrote to him: 'The state Cosima is in worries me too. Everything about her is uncommon and out of the ordinary: she has a right to freedom in the noblest sense. She is childlike and deep – the laws governing her nature will always lead her only to what is sublime. Nor will anyone ever help her except herself! She belongs to a special order of creation that we must learn to apprehend through her. – In future you will have more favourable opportunity and greater freedom to observe this and to find your own worthy place at her side. And that, too, consoles me!' Whether this veiled confession was followed by an explicit one is a question to which we shall return.

The week with Cosima at Starnberg found its artistic outlet in the melody – called in German the 'Peace melody' – which Wagner used in 1869 in the third act of *Siegfried* at Brünnhilde's words 'Ewig war ich, ewig bin ich' in E major and then in E minor, and again in 1870 in the *Siegfried Idyll*. He promised her a quartet on the melody, which entered his head during the time that they were together at Starnberg, as he later told her. 'Oh, yes, we know very well where it all comes from!' (DMCW, I, pp. 546, 819) In fact a musical sketch survives of the Peace melody, dated 14 November 1864. Newman points out that the theme that directly follows it in the third act, at the words 'O Siegfried, Herrlicher! Hort der Welt!', which is also used in the *Idyll*, must also have been conceived for the 'Starnberg' Quartet: why else would Wagner have constructed the two themes so that they can combine in double counterpoint, when he makes no use of that valuable attribute in *Siegfried,* but only in the *Idyll*, composed fourteen months later? Both melodies meant so much to him for their entirely personal associations that he was prepared to introduce a slight stylistic discrepancy in the final scene of *Siegfried* for their sake, and even to alter the words, not altogether happily, in order to fit them to the second theme.

The sheet with the sketch of the Peace melody also bears a first version of the World Inheritance motive which is heard in the Wanderer–Erda scene, after the lines

> Was in des Zwiespalts wildem Schmerze
> verzweifelnd einst ich beschloß,
> froh und freudig
> führe frei ich nun aus . . .

In a way it symbolizes the re-invigoration of his creative power as a result of King Ludwig's summons. 'My head is in a whirl!' he wrote to Bülow. 'I need every drop of optimism and energy that I possess: for – seriously – I am now getting down to finishing the *Ring*.' That work was the only thing that was now congenial to him: he was far too tense to bother with Beckmesser and Pogner. (23 September 1864) And a week later he wrote to tell him of his move from Starnberg to Munich: his longing to compose had swelled to a passion. 'I am now wonderfully in the mood for the third act of *Siegfried*: and particularly for the first scene with Wotan: it shall be a prelude, short but – significant.'

He drew up a programme at this time, to show the king:

1865
Spring: performance of *Tristan*
Beginning of the winter season: performance of *Die Meistersinger*
1867–8
Performance of the entire *Ring* cycle
1869–70
Die Sieger
1871–2
Parsifal

Ludwig had asked him for a written account of whether and in what way his views on politics and religion had altered since his writings on art in the early years in Zürich, and Wagner responded with *On the State and Religion*, written in July 1864, in which he developed some of the ideas 'our greatest poet' expressed in *Wilhelm Meisters Wanderjahre* (*Über Staat und Religion*, RWGS, VIII, pp. 3ff.). Never was a king addressed in more worthy or philosophical a fashion, Nietzsche wrote to Gersdorff: 'I was completely exalted and overpowered by the ideality, which seemed to have originated entirely in the spirit of Schopenhauer.' (4 August 1869)

At the same time Wagner was eager to thank his benefactor in words and music. He wrote the *Huldigungsmarsch* (March of Homage) for the king's nineteenth birthday on 25 August, though it was not actually performed until 5 October. Its blend of rapturous idealism and solemn ceremony matches the feelings that he expressed in the poem *An meinen König* ('To my King') in the September.

> es war Dein Ruf, der mich der Nacht entrückte,
> die winterlich erstarrt hielt meine Kraft . . .
> so wandl' ich stolz beglückt nun neue Pfade
> im sommerlichen Königreich der Gnade.

('It was your summons snatched me from the night that numbed my strength in winter's cold. . . Now I tread new paths in pride and joy, in the summer kingdom of grace.' RWGS, VIII, pp. 1f.)

'I have resolved to place all other works on one side for the time being,' he informed the king on 26 September 1864, 'so as to be able to devote myself exclusively and without delay to completing the composition of my major work, the *Ring*.' The following day he began the fair copy of the score of the second act of *Siegfried*, which he had put aside more than seven years before.

A formal ten-clause contract between Wagner and the Court Secretary's office was concluded on 18 October, in which he undertook, for a fee of 30,000 gulden, to compose the music to his drama *Der Ring des Nibelungen* and 'to deliver a complete fair copy into the hands of Hofrat Hofmann within at most three years from today'. For Wagner as for Ludwig this contract was simply a form, to give the work they were doing together plausibility in the eyes of the world.

The king looked forward with impatience to the realization of their hopes. 'I have decided to have a large stone theatre built, so that the performance of *Der Ring des Nibelungen* shall be perfect,' he wrote to Wagner on 26 November. Wagner in turn wrote to Gottfried Semper in Zürich, to find out if he would undertake the project. The famous architect was received by the king on 29 December and commissioned to design the theatre. Shortly afterwards, when the Augsburg *Allgemeine Zeitung* published a report that there was no intention, in the seat of power, of carrying out the plan, Semper's anxiety was stilled by Wagner: 'Have faith – and work for us!' There were in fact two concurrent, alternative plans: a monumental theatre, approached by a new processional way and bridge, to be built on the Gasteig hills on the far bank of the Isar, which it was estimated would cost in the region of 5,000,000 gulden; or a temporary structure in the Glaspalast, the glass exhibition hall, costing about 200,000 gulden.

While the king was all for splendour, Wagner was most concerned to have a functional interior. A letter Semper wrote him on 26 November 1865, after working out the designs in detail, shows what he wanted: an auditorium in the shape of an amphitheatre, its walls articulated by a line of columns, a sunken orchestra pit and, 'in accordance with what we agreed', two prosceniums one behind the other, with the smaller rear one an exact repetition of the front one, only giving a smaller opening. 'This will create a complete dislocation of scale and in consequence everything on the stage will appear enlarged, and we shall achieve the aim of separating the ideal world on the stage from the real world on the far side of the divide represented by the orchestra pit.' In the end this theatre was never built in Munich, but Wagner incorporated these features, which he regarded as his intellectual property, in the Festspielhaus in Bayreuth.

For the moment the building was less important to him than training singers and attracting to Munich the assistants that he would need. 'I have great hopes of Bülow and his help: Peter Cornelius must come soon too. But I still lack a very great deal in spite of those two! In particular a genius of dramatic stagecraft, to look out for people and coach them.' (To Mathilde Maier, 17 December 1864)

Bülow, with his wife and children, had already moved from Berlin to Munich on 20 November. Cornelius and Porges followed after a slight delay. Wagner was less fortunate in his choice of a singing teacher, Friedrich Schmitt, whom he had known as a tenor in Magdeburg. Schmitt, known as 'Blacksmith' for his rough manner, had worked out a method for a kind of German bel canto, which he applied successfully to *Tannhäuser* and *Lohengrin*, but which failed him over *Tristan*. 'Just you wait,' Wagner shouted at him in broad Saxon after one rehearsal, 'when I've finished my *Siegfried*, I'll write another opera specially for you and your pupils in the very best Flotow style!' and threw his velvet cap at him.

Meanwhile Ludwig, in all innocence, had appointed an inveterate enemy of Wagner's as foreign minister and chairman of the council of ministers. Ludwig von der Pfordten, sometime professor of Roman Law in Leipzig, was an old acquaintance of Wagner's from the Dresden days: in 1848 it had been he, as Saxon minister of culture, who had had the last word on Wagner's plan for the organization of a national theatre. Since then he had followed Wagner's career with undisguised disapproval; as late as 1858 he had told the actor Emil Devrient that if the princes stuck together like the democrats none of Wagner's operas would ever get performed anywhere.

From the very first there was an influential circle in Munich, composed of the aristocracy, the civil service and the Catholic clergy, who were suspicious of the parvenu, notorious revolutionary and Lutheran musician whom the king had made his confidant. To begin with they bided their time; indeed it has been claimed that the cabinet would have been quite glad to see the king distracted from the business of government, so that they could pursue their policies with less interference. But when Semper's audience with the king made public the plan to build the new theatre, they made their first attempt, in February 1865, to discredit Wagner with Ludwig. Cabinet Secretary Pfistermeister cannot be absolved of complicity in the scheme. It was a matter of the payment for a portrait of Wagner painted for the king by Friedrich Pecht,[4] and it is obvious that the king was deliberately misled. This was the first occasion on which Wagner experienced Ludwig's capriciousness. Summoned to an audience on 6 February, he was refused admission by the king, who then, a few days later, caused a démenti to be issued, describing the by then widespread rumour that Wagner had fallen into disfavour as 'completely unfounded'. 'Wretched, short-sighted people, who can speak of disfavour,' he assured Wagner, 'who have no notion of Our Love, and can have none.' (14 February)

The enemy faction, who saw the weak point in this denial, launched an attack with an article in the *Allgemeine Zeitung* on 19 February entitled 'Richard Wagner and Public Opinion'. The anonymous author (he turned out to be the poet Oskar von Redwitz, whose *Amaranth* is unlikely to mean much to anybody today) did not scorn to make an issue of such private matters as that Wagner was buying expensive carpets. Wagner replied in sensible, moderate terms on 22 February: he could rightly regard himself not as a royal favourite but as an artist who was being paid a fee commensurate to his work, and he believed he was not obliged to account to anybody for how he spent his salary. (KLRW, IV, pp. 47ff.)

The attack had been fended off. But for all his protestations of love the king still appeared to be avoiding Wagner. The latter therefore put the king's trust to the test in a letter of 11 March, with a direct question: 'Shall I go away? Shall I stay?' '*Stay, stay* here,' Ludwig replied on the same day, 'everything will be *splendid* as it used to be.'

Thus confirmed in his position, Wagner was now able to concentrate on his next major undertakings: the first performance of *Tristan* – for which, at his request, Bülow was appointed kapellmeister – and the composition of a report on the establishment of a national school of music in Munich (*Bericht an Seine Majestät den König Ludwig II. von Bayern über eine in München zu errichtende deutsche Musikschule*, RWGS, VIII, pp. 125ff.). 'It marks a new phase in my life,' he told Mathilde Maier; 'If I find the people who will more or less meet my needs, then I shall have found . . . Archimedes' fulcrum, from which I shall lever the musical world out of its dozy nooks.' (17 March) Unlike the Italians and French, he argued, the Germans possessed no tradition in the performance of their great masters. The first need, therefore, was to evolve an intrinsically German style. What he proposed was a method of instruction that would produce a complete, integrated style: it should be based on singing, as the foundation of all music, but would extend as far as gymnastics and mime. He was conscious from the first that such proposals represented a challenge to 'the whole artisanry of art with its pitiful proletariat'.

Bülow took the first orchestral rehearsal of *Tristan* on 10 April. Wagner's daughter Isolde Josepha Ludovica was born on the same day.

Before the dress rehearsal, which took place on 11 May before an audience of about six hundred, Wagner addressed a few words to the orchestra, in a voice trembling with excitement: 'My work has entered into you, out of you it returns to me again: I can enjoy it in serenity. This is unique happiness. We have achieved the best thing of all, the work allows the artist to be forgotten!'

The first performance was fixed for 15 May. On the evening before, news came from Pusinelli in Dresden that Minna was dying, followed the next morning by the assurance that the danger had passed for this once. Relieved, Wagner wrote a short note to the king, dating it '*Tristan*-day'. 'How I am looking forward to the evening!' Ludwig replied. 'If only it would come soon! When will day yield to night?'

Then all of a sudden a court officer appeared at Wagner's house in the Briennerstrasse, armed with a bill of exchange for 2400 gulden and the authority to distrain the furniture on non-payment. The prehistory of the incident went back to the Paris concerts of 1860, when Malwida had introduced Wagner to a wealthy English widow, Julie Salis-Schwabe, who paid him a subvention of 5000 francs to cover his deficit. Unbidden, Wagner made out a promissory note, and when he applied to Malwida to get it extended for him, she replied that he could save himself the trouble, as Mrs Schwabe had never regarded the sum as anything other than a contribution to the success of the concerts. Wagner was therefore all the more amazed to receive a request for payment of the debt from a Munich lawyer, Dr von Schauss, on 20 March 1865: delay might

lead to an interruption in the execution of his 'ingenious compositions' and hinder his preparations for the production of his 'magnificent opera *Tristan und Isolde*'. This threat proves that the presentation of the bill by Schauss and those who may be presumed to have
been behind him on the very day of the planned première was no
coincidence but a deliberate act of malevolence. Wagner barely had
time to send to the Cabinet Treasury for help, but this was at once
afforded him.[5]

But that was not the end to the day's calamities. At midday
Ludwig Schnorr, who was to sing Tristan, arrived to tell Wagner
with tears in his eyes that his wife had suddenly turned hoarse and
would be unable to sing Isolde that evening. 'My old daemon has
been stirring', Wagner wrote to the king, 'and has frustrated the
work for whose sake friends have made the most arduous sacrifices
in order to get here from great distances.' They had come from all
over Europe, from Paris, London, Vienna, Königsberg. Only a few
of his friends were absent: Cornelius, who was in Weimar preparing the production of his own *Der Cid*; Liszt, who was kept in Rome
by Princess Wittgenstein; and the Willes and Wesendonks from
Zürich. It had been the climax of his life, he told Frau Wille in a
letter, 'and yet it was made bitter by – absences! – Truly, bitter!' (26
September)[6]

The première finally took place on 10 June, followed by three
more performances on 13 and 19 June and 1 July. The house was
full, even the standing room. The king entered the royal box on the
dot of six, greeted by fanfares and cheers. When Bülow raised his
baton, probably no one there realized that he was signalling the
completion of an epoch, not in musical history alone but in the
history of western culture. A century later the literature on *Tristan* is
worldwide, and the work's fascination is as strong as on the first
day. Its epoch-making significance was best expressed by Richard
Strauss, writing to Joseph Gregor after reading his history of world
theatre. Gregor had claimed that in his *Iphigenie* Goethe gave the
theatre of the world a final intellectual and spiritual form that had
never been equalled since. Strauss objected that 'this "final intellectual and spiritual form" is – thanks to the music – not only equalled
but surpassed in *Tristan* . . . *Tristan* is the ultimate conclusion of
Schiller and Goethe and the highest fulfilment of a 2000-year-long
evolution of the theatre.'

According to Schopenhauer, it is impossible for a genius not to

recognize himself and know his worth. This is supported by the
pen-portrait of Wagner at this period of his life by Édouard Schuré,
a young Alsatian who later became well known for his book *Le
drame musical*. In the conversations he had with Wagner at that date
he was overwhelmed by the composer's unshakable faith in himself
and his great ideas: in his blue eyes, which seemed to Schuré to be
fixed immovably on a distant goal, there was a vision that domi-
nated everything else and lent him an air Schuré could only call an
eternal chastity. Now his face was that of Faust, now that of
Mephistopheles, and then again he looked like a fallen angel thinking about heaven and saying 'it does not exist but I shall find a way
to create it'.[7]

The purest realization of Wagner's artistic ideal was achieved, for
him, in Ludwig Schnorr's performance of Tristan's great monologue in the third act. Recalling it, he advised anyone who wanted
to gain some impression of what it had been like to pick up the score
and look first at the orchestral writing alone, the motives restlessly
entering, developing, joining, parting, almost consuming each
other, possessing an expressive significance that required the most
sophisticated harmonization and flexible orchestration, with
instrumental combinations of a richness such as no purely symphonic writing could encompass. And yet, as Schnorr sang, this
whole immense orchestra 'completely disappeared, or – more accu-
rately – appeared to be subsumed in his delivery'. (*Erinnerungen an
Ludwig Schnorr von Carolsfeld*, RWGS, VIII, p. 186) In that one
sentence, too, Wagner concisely defined the performance style he
had in mind for his works.

But the hopes he now entertained of establishing and disseminat-
ing this new style with Schnorr's aid were dashed in a matter of
weeks by the news of the tenor's death of typhus on 21 July in
Dresden. Wagner and Bülow arrived there to find the city en fête to
receive singers pouring in from all over Germany for a festival.
'Yes,' he said to himself, 'but the *one* singer has left us.'

Back in Munich he went for a walk with Schuré in the Englischer
Garten, and they sat down beside one of the streams running
through the park. 'Everyone has his own daemon,' he began, as his
eyes followed the swift flow of the water, 'and mine is a terrible
monster. When he rages round me the air is filled with disaster. The
only time I crossed the open sea I was shipwrecked; and if I went to
America the Atlantic would certainly whip up a hurricane for my

benefit. The world has treated me in exactly the same way, and strangely enough, I keep going back to it. But you could say that the fate that cannot do me down lays its hands on my supporters. No sooner has a man dedicated himself to me unreservedly than I can be sure that destiny has marked him for its own. Today we have lost not just *a* singer, but *the* singer, and now we shall have to build with bricks the house that we had hoped to build in granite.' Suddenly he stood up. 'Let's go! If we are to wage war against fate, we must look not backwards, but forwards!'

The teaching staff at the Munich Conservatory had been given notice for 31 July, but there was no date in prospect for the opening of Wagner's school of music. His plan had been considered by a committee, which finally rejected it on the grounds of expense and made alternative proposals of its own to the king. 'Has the human brain ever hatched a greater piece of nonsense than this?' Ludwig stormed. 'No, this will not do, we must follow a different path to salvation.' But in spite of such emotional outbursts, neither the school of music nor the festival theatre moved a step nearer realization.

Wagner saw very plainly that his opponents hoped to wear out his patience. His suspicion that Pfistermeister was playing a key role in this was not without foundation. Without communicating his suspicions to Ludwig in so many words, he felt obliged to advise the king to limit his cabinet secretary's activities 'to the natural sphere of his original appointment'. He wished that Ludwig would appoint a loyal nobleman of his court to see that the royal directives in artistic matters were not thwarted by self-seeking interests. He confessed in a later letter to his embarrassment at seeming to meddle in administrative matters, but before dropping the subject he had to tell the king what the situation looked like from his point of view. Apart from the school of music and the theatre, he was greatly troubled in his conscience by the distress of the chorus and orchestra; it was all the more difficult for him to close his eyes to their grievances because of his own apparently easy position – though, he hinted, he was going to have to ask for greater independence in his own financial arrangements. (30 July)

The request took the form of a report sent to the king at the beginning of August, in which he suggested that he should be allowed the usufruct for life from a capital of 200,000 florins. Of this sum, 40,000 florins should be assigned to him to manage himself, while the remainder should be administered by the Cabinet Treasury to yield 5 per cent interest per annum, to be paid him in quarterly instalments of 2000 florins. This arrangement would cancel all existing payments already being made to him. (KLRW, I, pp. 146ff.)

Wagner was driven to make this request by the uncertainty of his position. Everything he received from the king, liberal though it was, was bounty, and even the contracted fee for the *Ring* depended on the condition that it would be finished within three years, which he already realized was not going to be possible. Though he was sure he could count on Ludwig's generosity, experience was teaching him that he had no way of knowing what decisions the cabinet might not force upon the king, even against his will.

The intransigence with which this request was discussed by the king and his cabinet can be judged by the fact that their decision was delayed until 19 October. The correspondence on the matter was carried on between Cosima on the one hand and Pfistermeister or the Deputy Secretary, Lutz, on the other, until Wagner himself intervened on 17 October with a letter to Lutz in which he stated roundly that the opposition to his request could not possibly stem from the king, as he had been officially informed. Once that had been delivered Cosima was able to write triumphantly, on 23 October: 'Jusqu'ici Lutz n'a pas répondu. La somme est donnée, le roi n'a pas écrit!!!' (KLRW, IV, p. 94)

In the event Wagner's request was granted only in part. The cabinet refused to make available the capital of 160,000 florins, though they agreed to increase the annual ex gratia payment to 8000 florins; this meant that his income would be what it would have been, but without the same independence. On the other hand he was awarded the lump sum of 40,000 florins and invited to collect it from the Cabinet Treasury.

Since Wagner was not well, as Cosima wrote to tell the king later, she offered to go to collect it herself, with her eldest daughter, in the expectation of being given nothing more onerous than a few large notes. Imagine her astonishment on being told that she could have only silver coins. Since there were no members of the public to witness the event she placed her trust in the clerks' discretion where a lady was concerned, and conveyed the bags of money to Wagner in two hansom cabs. 'He was utterly horrified by the affair, thanked me and came close to scolding me; then he praised my courage and said he was burdened by the thought that it was my friendship for him that had placed me in such a position.' (KLRW, I, pp. lxx f.)[8] The transport of the money went unobserved by passers-by, but the treasury officials made sure that it was adequately publicized later.

Wagner's personal doubts and concerns were the cause of greater anguish to him at this time than that kind of hostility. We must go back to the beginning of August 1865. To restore his health, undermined by the death of Schnorr and even more by his struggle to be united with Cosima, the king placed his hunting lodge on the Hochkopf above the Walchensee at Wagner's disposal: 'Get better in the bracing mountain air!' (29 July) 'And now, in spite of wind and weather, off to the mountains!' Wagner replied. 'My faithful servant [Franz] and my good old dog go with me. An old Indian epic, the *Râmâyana*, comes too: Siegfried in manifold forms shall breathe afresh on the mountain heights.' (8 August) (He intended to work on the score of the second act.)

Cosima, who left for Pest with Hans on the same day, to hear Liszt conduct *St Elisabeth*, had given Wagner a diary, known as the Brown Book on account of its binding. He entered in it everything that was on his mind during their separation.[9]

> *Hochkopf, 10 August 1865.* Late yesterday evening, as we toiled up the path, I looked longingly – dead tired – towards the summit, in the hope of seeing our goal at last: my eye was met above the rim of the mountain by the first shining star: without bothering much about whether it was in the right direction or not, I took it for the evening star and greeted it aloud – 'Cosima'. That gave me courage . . .
> Marvellous morning, the most beautiful weather. A ramble all round the mountain top. All my expectations exceeded: quite incomparable. My sure refuge for the future has been found. Over there is a daybed, and I can already see you lying on it. – Many thanks for your message! Of course, of course! – I love you with my last loving. – And I hope for better health too. Forgetting and remembering!

The view into the depths below inspired him to write a sequence of verses:

> Am Abgrund steh' ich; Grausen hemmt die Schritte,
> der mich geführt, verloren ist der Pfad . . .

('I stand at the abyss; horror slows my steps, the path that led me here is lost.')

But everything that he experienced came to have a symbolic meaning for him:

> Was mich dem steilen Gipfel zugetrieben,
> hält jetzt gebannt mich an des Abgrunds Rand:
> verlassen mußt' ich, die zurück mir blieben,
> dem Druck entglitt wohl manche Freundeshand;
> wo einst ich mich gesehnt nach letztem Lieben,
> der Nebel deckt mir manches Heimatland.
> Und darf ich zögernd nicht mehr rückwärts schauen,
> wie späht' ich in den Abgrund nun mit Grauen?

('What drove me to the sheer summit now holds me spellbound on the brink of the abyss: I have had to leave those who remained behind me, full many a friend's hand has slipped from my grasp; where once I yearned to find a last love, more than one homeland is hid from me in mist. And if I may no longer hesitate and look back, how is it that I now look into the abyss with dread?')

The summer heat gave way to cool, rainy weather.

> *13 August.* Ill and wretched. A very bad cold: high temperature. Lonely here . . . I thought I would at least write something in the book: complaining to you ought to help me. We'll see! I hope it will . . .
> *14 August.* Oh, my dearest woman! The world is appalling! I would choose to read Hugo's abominations[10] when I've got a temperature: trust me to do something clever like that . . . Immense talent! I had to shout that aloud several times. But why go on about these horrible things all the time, right up to old age, like Hugo? They should be left to the police, the chamber of deputies, boards and councils and so on. Plain statistical reports can say it all better, anyway. Surely a poet is nothing if not someone who knows all that without ever having made a study of it and, just because it is so obvious and easy to understand, doesn't waste any more words on it but concentrates on finding and preserving the ways of

redemption from the evil. It's true! there are some
sublime passages even then: e.g. the erstwhile Jean
Valjean's internal struggles before giving himself up are
masterly. Oh, what ghastly stuff! What a beautiful
world! . . .

15 August. Was so worn out that I had to leave the two
letters from you that both arrived together today lying
there – opened – but unread for several hours: I saw at
first glance that I wouldn't be able to bear them . . . In
the end, though, I read them. And now – I am
speechless! I stare blankly in front of me and I think I
shall give up speech altogether again. What madness,
what madness!! And that idiot Hans, not to let you go
to Penzing,[11] and to show you the shops of Vienna
instead! Is it to be believed? Is it to be believed? And *he*
is now my only friend! – Oh, cloddish hearts! blind
eyes! Ah, but how beautiful, how beautiful you are, my
dear woman! – Yes, you are mine and only *you* have any
claim on *me*. Nobody else knows anything about me.

God in heaven, how long shall we have to go on
tormenting ourselves in this manner of existence? But –
what am I saying? didn't we find each other in it?

What else can I do but read a book again? –
Râmâyana![12] Adieu!

16 August. Good morning, dearest woman! I feel better
again . . . The *Râmâyana* is a great poem and getting
more beautiful as I read! – Truly, just to get into the
right mood for something like this, one has to be able to
withdraw from all the trash of the present day . . . What
a world it is, and how it is constructed and realized! It's
an astounding work of art . . . everything is alive,
resounding and moving round me . . .

Râma is godlike!! Everything seems grander and more
spacious, simply from having to do with such people! –
A magnificent drama, unlike any other, takes shape
before me. But who could write it? . . .

17 August. Good morning! Slept very well. – Today at
last I shall get down to the score of *Siegfried* again.
Perhaps I shall have a letter too? . . .

There is a letter! – –

> That was a sad letter! a real letter of separation . . .
> To make up for it I worked hard at *Siegfried*: the spell
> has been lifted! – Good night, dearest woman!

His friendly relations with Mathilde Maier had by no means been severed after her rejection of his plea to come and keep house for him and his talk of the possibility of marriage after Minna's death. (22 June 1864; see above) He did not omit, however, to give her some hint of the change that had since arisen in his situation: 'Your coming to me on the only conditions that are possible now . . . would be a source of nameless, now quite unbearable anguish for my heart; no silence or concealment on your part, however tender or loving, could shield me from it.' (19 July 1864)

Cosima evidently made his continuing correspondence with Mathilde the cause of understandable, though unjustified, reproaches in the 'letter of separation' mentioned above (cf. Bergfeld ed., *Das Braune Buch*, pp. 37ff.). The following entry is one that Eva Chamberlain pasted over:

> *18 August*. Good morning, you wicked child! What a
> nasty letter that was you wrote me yesterday! Just how
> horrid it is, is still sinking in. Really what you say in it
> is that you were wrong to love me so much, and on the
> other hand to treat your father so badly, when he's the
> only person who loves you . . . And now unlucky M.
> M. must bear the brunt: my God, the plans I have for
> her – no! what haven't I already been up to with her –
> what endearments I lavish on her! and so on – That's all
> very nicely put, and looks exactly as if you wanted to
> make a 'break' with me. Just keep it up! – Well! Well! –
> And all this, while you are afloat in joy and happiness,
> and I am wasting away up here in the mist and clouds,
> sick and sad.

The next three pages in the Brown Book had not been published before 1975. Wagner writes about his future and his future work. Bergfeld takes what he says as fantasies brought on by his illness, but in my opinion it is a conscious flight into illusion:

> I can and must live only in a kind of cloud. Since I am
> solely an artist, the only kind of life I can lead is an
> artificial one . . . Cosima must always be with me –

1. Wagner and his circle, Munich 1865
From left to right: Friedrich Uhl, Richard Pohl, H. von Rosti, August Roeckel, Auguste de Gasperini, Wagner and his dog Pohl, Hans von Bülow, Adolf Jensen, Carl Grille, Franz Müller, Felix Draeseke, Alexander Ritter, Leopold Damrosch, Heinrich Porges, Michael Moszonyi

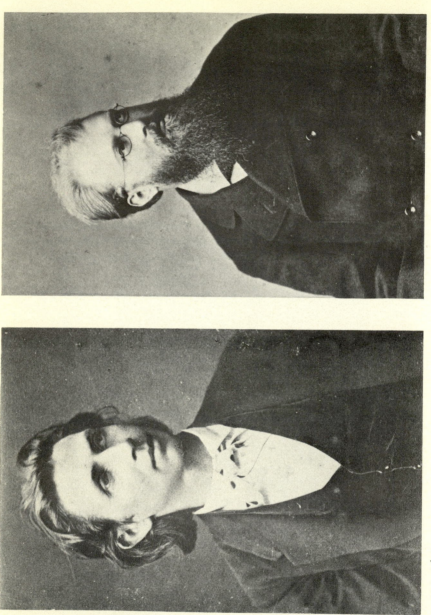

2b. Hans Richter

2a. Heinrich Porges

3a. Friedrich Nietzsche

3b. Elisabeth Förster-Nietzsche

4a. *Dionysus among the Muses of Apollo* by Bonaventura Genelli

4b. Wagner's house Tribschen

5a. Mathilde Maier

5b. Liszt with his daughter Cosima in 1867

6. Autograph title-page of the *Siegfried Idyll*, 1870

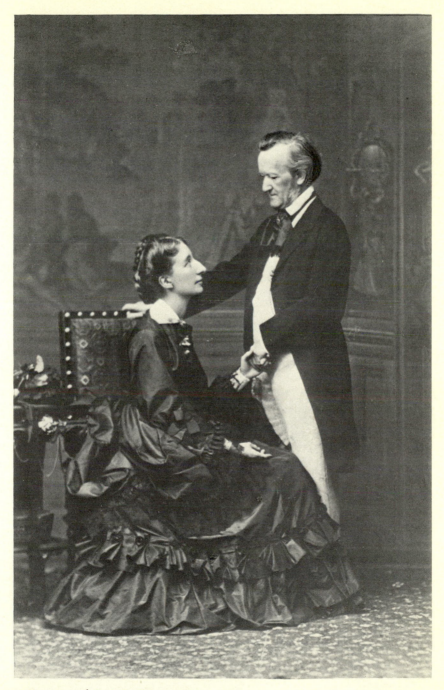

7. Wagner and Cosima, Vienna 1872

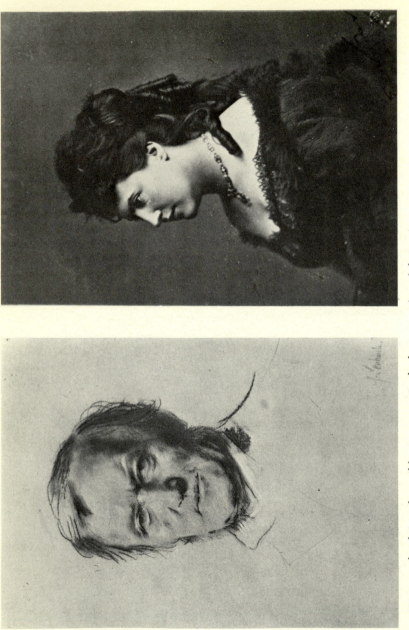

8b. Judith Gautier

8a. Wagner: sketch in red pencil by Franz von Lenbach, Munich 1880 (based on photographs of 1871)

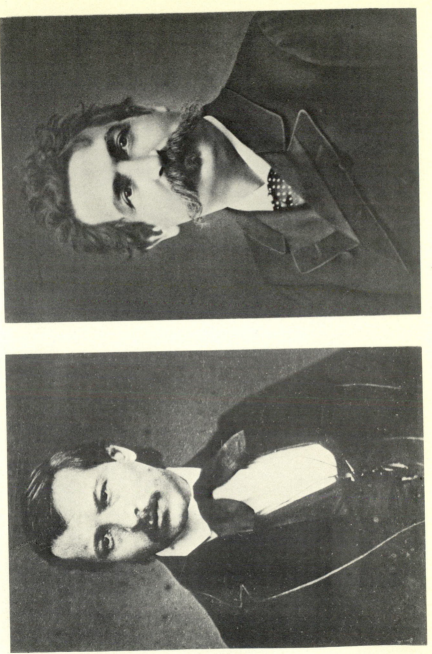

9b. Angelo Neumann

9a. Karl Tausig

10a. The Festspielhaus in Bayreuth: wood-engraving around 1880

10b. The Festspielhaus: a modern photograph

11a. From left to right: Heinrich von Stein, Carl Friedrich Glasenapp and Hans von Wolzogen

11b. Engelbert Humperdinck

12. Family photograph on the steps of Wahnfried, 1881
Front row, from left to right: Isolde and Daniela von Bülow, the dog Marke,
Eva and Siegfried Wagner
Back row, from left to right: Blandine von Bülow, Heinrich von Stein, Cosima,
Wagner, Paul Zhukovsky

13a. Wahnfried seen from the front

13b. Tea at Wahnfried, 1881

From left to right: Wagner, Cosima, Heinrich von Stein, Paul Zhukovsky,
Daniela and Blandine von Bülow

14a. Titian's *Assumption of the Virgin* (detail)

4b. The Grail scene in *Parsifal*: Zhukovsky's sketch of 1882

15b. Hermann Levi

15a. Paul Zhukovsky

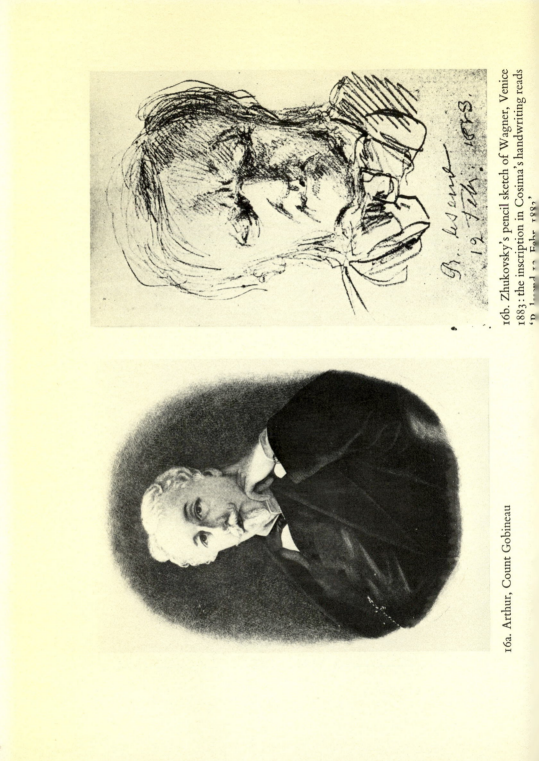

16b. Zhukovsky's pencil sketch of Wagner, Venice 1883: the inscription in Cosima's handwriting reads 'R. I. ...d 12 Febr. 1883'

16a. Arthur, Count Gobineau

always: there's no other way . . . Given that, then, I believe, I shall still achieve the full earnest of my works: but my work is the only place where there must be any earnest, everything else must be light-hearted and joyous.

19 August. What useless babble all this is; as if you could answer me! –

Strange! How shall I feel when I am sitting again, entire and single-minded, at that miraculous loom. It is the only thing that is right for me. The world that *I* cannot shape I must just forget; that is the only possible relationship I can have with it.

There is one really bad thing! The fact that the imagination is filled in the end with the essential image of the world, and that there's no longer much that can be changed in it, nor anything new that can be added, engenders a kind of disgust with existence.

No matter what thoughts I have, finally I turn away from it with a kind of satiety, because I feel that I've thought it all before. Everywhere I keep coming upon ideas I've already had: the thrill of discovery has entirely vanished.

He drew the following conclusion:

There remains nothing absorbing any more except – the processes of form, the pure artistic joy of perfecting the portrayal. It is my hope that I shall find great satisfaction in that again.

But he had an important reservation:

All the same, it will be distracting to be forever casting an imperceptible[13] sideways glance at the realism of the portrayal to be expected from most performers.

20 August. Good morning, my soul! – Hearing nothing more from you at all is dreadful. To put an end to feeling so ill, too, I have decided to return to the lowlands again tomorrow. – I am really ill. Nothing can help me except – – God knows? Since what will help may still not be said aloud. But – for the time being let us call it – work!

. . . You can still draw my work out of my very soul. But, oh, give me peace as well! Stay with me, do not go away again. Tell poor Hans plainly that I cannot do without you any more. God in Heaven, if only you could simply be my wife in the eyes of the world!

21 August. Now a last good morning from the forest lodge! – It's grey. Everything is packed. Except not the book yet. – I'm coming closer to you. Tomorrow I shall already be able to send you a telegram. – There you have ten days from my life . . . Far away from you, I've been coming closer to you all the time! I feel sure of it!

Adieu, mountain-top forest! . . . 5 a.m.

Munich, 22 August. When I was crossing the Walchensee in the boat yesterday I saw something beautiful.

The shallows: how clear, how light everything on the bottom was; the water was just glass: lovely white sand bottom, every individual stone, there and there and here a plant, there a stem – everything distinct. Then it was deep: the water dark, dark, all clarity gone, all closed over; but instead suddenly the sky, the sun, the mountains – all bright and clear enough to touch in the mirror – – shallow souls, deep souls! I have seen to the bottom of many shallow souls: how few deep souls there have been who have mirrored the world for me!
. . .

I found everything in order at home in the evening.

My clean, polished rooms make me laugh: – that will last, or at least it *can* be made to last! Lovely weather and everything else that gives me such swift and strong delight disappears so swiftly and leaves such long, dull days behind. Curious, how we bring ourselves – or our daemon brings us – to endure it.

The following day, 22 August, Wagner went to visit the children, who had remained behind in the Bülows' house. The baby Isolde had woken up at once and was about to start crying: 'then she laughed up at me instead . . . How much longer will you be away? I suspect a very, very long time.'

He went on to refer to a letter Cosima had sent him from Pest:

I didn't like the sound of those gypsies. Artificially polished barbarians: not entire nature, not entire art. Their music, half arranged, mutilated in a barbaric-cum-dilettante way. Not everything that rouses our enthusiasm, in our disgust with German philistinism, is worth it. It's good enough to intoxicate us, but we ought to be beyond intoxication. Your father as much as I. Those Eljen, Rakoczy etc. are very nice – but they lead nowhere, or only backwards, that's a weakness: it's not that I don't feel the attraction, but I steer clear of it . . .

Oh, I'm very different from all the rest! – Where can I expect my joys to spring from?

24 August. I am more reluctant each time I turn to the Brown Book. I feel as though I ought to be deprived now even of being close to you. No letter for three days. – I can understand why!! But I cannot and never shall be able to understand these pious worldlings! God alone knows how genuine they are! To me most of it is alien and incomprehensible! Good morning!

The next day, 25 August, was King Ludwig's twentieth birthday. After some lines celebrating it:

Kanonen dröhnt! Hallt laut und hell ihr Glocken!
Mich will dem Gram der frohe Tag entlocken! . . .

('Cannons roar! Ye bells ring loud and clear! The joyful day will rescue me from grief!')

the following lines for Cosima were written sideways across the page:

Vom fernen Ost, vom Land der Magyaren,
kam morgens mir ein Traumbild bang und wüst:
dem Liebchen ist groß' Freude widerfahren,
mein Weib ward dort viertausendmal gegrüßt.
'Mein Weib?' Du Tor! Frag' erst bei kund'gen Leuten,
was solcher Freudentraum Dir mag bedeuten!

('From the far east, from the land of the Magyars, a wild and fearful vision came to me this morning: great joy has befallen my darling, four thousand came to greet my wife. "My wife"? You fool! Just ask those who know what such a dream of joy can mean to you!')

He wrote to Bülow on the same day. 'The 4000 Magyars would have been the last straw for me. Give Liszt my dearest and warmest regards! What he can do is beyond my power: – from Rome to Pest and then still to be relaxed and in good spirits – I cannot do that. Above all – not *now*! God knows what's wrong with me. I am a bull that has been stunned but hasn't died of it.'

While he was in this mood of recoiling from the world Wagner received a request from the king: 'Tell me something of your plans for "die Sieger" and "Parcival"! I am longing to hear about them!'

> *26 August.* How wonderful! – The king longs passionately to hear something about *Parzival*.

The very next day Wagner began to write the first detailed prose scenario, which fills twenty-eight closely written pages in the Brown Book. At the end he wrote '*30 August 1865*. There! That was help in the hour of need!!' It was in the same mood that he was to write the text and music of his 'work of farewell to the world' twelve years later, and this mood – even more than the work's subject – is what conveys the sense of withdrawal from the world. But already on 31 August he was back with Tristan:

> 'Das Schiff – siehst Du's noch nicht?'
> As long as I was sitting over *Parzival*, my imagination was a wonderful help: – whenever the red curtain over the door moved, my heart trembled: – she is going to come through it! –
> Now the tension of my ideas has dispersed. –
> Reality is back, entire and unvarnished, to be mastered. Tomorrow she is going to Szegźard [the country house of Liszt's friend Baron Augusz] for four days, – then to Venice, wherever they take her. – And she doesn't understand me! . . .
> Dearest woman! I know that you are suffering in all this! But that you can't even imagine what my suffering is like!

The next page is one that Eva Chamberlain pasted over.

> *1 September.* No! It's only tomorrow that she's going to Szegzárd. – 'Father says we'll stay in Pest until Saturday.' 'Father says "I need a holiday".'[14] – And all

the time she's persuading herself that I meant to hurt her
feelings; I probably don't love her any more! Her father
was right in the end, – he told me a year ago – 'that's
how it will be – he will treat me despicably!' . . . And
there will be more letters from Rome.

Here Wagner was referring to Princess Wittgenstein, who was
using her influence with Liszt against Wagner and Cosima.

All this Catholic rubbish is repugnant to me in the
depths of my soul; whoever takes flight in that must
have a great deal to do penance for.

Wagner returned to *Parsifal*, and sketched two alternative versions of lines about the spear, then asked (2 September), as though
she could answer him, 'Which is the better, Cos?'

Oh, anything, anything is better than to be so
God-forsaken as I was yesterday! . . . Oh, if only a
magic word could be found to explain you completely
to your family!

After entries made on 3, 4 and 5 September, that for 9 September
is another that was pasted over and proves informative:

A shock: Semper is here! Unfortunately Franz told him
that I was not away. I am in such a state that Semper's
visit is very unwelcome. God, what do I care about a
temporary theatre, or a definitive festival theatre, what
do I care about all the architecture in the world! . . .
How I hate this theatre project, indeed – how childish
the king seems to insist so passionately on the plan.

In the next day's entry, Wagner quotes an old proverb, that
everything in life repeats itself. He speculates that in the end it will
turn into a 'life-art-form' [an art-form for the art of living], and goes
on to reflect on the incredible power of music to express this: canon
is a representation of the life of ordinary people, but then there is
fugue: the theme remains always the same, but the free counter-
points which accompany it make it appear in a perpetually new
light.

There is nothing richer or greater in life than the theme
of a beautiful fugue by Bach: unless perhaps a beautiful

countersubject: that then is the greatest triumph, and
when a double fugue displays both themes all the time
with equal clarity and significance, then it achieves the
most beautiful course life can take . . . We two live in a
beautiful Bachian double fugue like that. –

In this same vein of fantasy he essayed an evaluation of Liszt:

Your father's career strikes me as being in 'variation
form'. There is nothing there except the one theme,
repeated afresh over and over again, but slightly changed
each time, ornamented, decorated, refurbished, now the
virtuoso, now the diplomat, now bellicose, now
spiritual, always the artist, always endearing, always
himself . . . I have nothing against variation form, I
think Beethoven used it to the most wonderful creative
ends . . . I r lf am simply at a loss with it: I can't
write so much as one variation on any theme!

On 11 September he read a report in the Leipzig *Illustrierte
Zeitung* on the jubilee of the Students' Association of the University
of Jena.

The three Nestors of those founder-members who are
still alive include a Pastor Riemann: his picture made a
deep, deep impression on me. I should like to make that
man's acquaintance . . . You must see Riemann's head.
That is *German* ideality . . .
    You can keep Rome – and Hungary! – that's all
galimatias!

Then he pondered the meaning of 'German'. It was to be the
subject of the 'diary' of 14–27 September 1865 that he wrote for
King Ludwig.[15] The king was so fired with enthusiasm that he had
copies of these impromptu notes distributed among his various
ministers 'for implementation' of the ideas contained in them,
as Wagner wrote to Constantin Frantz. 'I hardly need to describe
to you the almost farcical confusion this caused!' (19 March
1866)
    The next part of the entry for 11 September was pasted over. It
refers to a letter of Cosima's that had just arrived, and demonstrates
the whole conflict of her emotions.

> Your letter, my dear! Pure madness again! Madness and
> no end to it! Surrounded by unalloyed bliss, love,
> adoration, nature, music, enthusiasm – and full of terrors
> and fears, shrieking and swooning! – There is nothing
> more that I can say about it. If it must be, then let it be:
> I submit to it. Perhaps it is necessary to you.

Then follows the passage already quoted, about her return from the
Karlsruhe festival the year before:

> God knows what you'll be like when you return. I
> know how you were a year ago, when your father
> brought you back here! It was dreadful: you sleepless,
> restless, weak, frail, miserable, ravaged! There's nothing
> to which I can compare the pain I felt . . . It will be the
> same again now . . .
>
> If you go off adventuring again, I shall take charge of
> the child, and you . . .

The entry breaks off here, because the next two pages – four sides –
were cut out by Eva Chamberlain.[16]

The Bülows returned from Budapest on 13 September. 'She has
survived it bravely,' Wagner wrote to Mathilde Maier, 'and completely astonished me. He was ill when they arrived, and still is.
They are dining with me tomorrow again for the first time.' (22
September) Cosima was now able to resume the running of
Wagner's household, as well as her own. Above all, they now
embarked together on a literary project that was to occupy them for
years to come.

'You would cause me inexpressible happiness, if you were to give
me a detailed account of your intellectual and spiritual development
and of the external events of your life as well,' the king had written
to him on 28 May. 'May I nurture the hope of seeing this wish of
mine fulfilled one day?' When he asked again on 19 July, Wagner
replied: 'What do you think I was doing when your letter of
yesterday reached me? To save you guessing, I will tell you: – I was
dictating my biography! Friend Cosima does not cease reminding
me of our king's wish. So now the opportune hours of the day are
occupied with my faithfully telling my tale to our friend, while she
diligently writes it down.'

The growth of the autobiography, virtually under the king's

eyes, can be traced in their correspondence. Thanking Wagner for the first part, Ludwig wrote: 'Ah, continue with it, I beg of you.' Even during the unhappy time of the Prusso-Bavarian war he looked forward longingly to the arrival of each new instalment, and continued to do so through the years until a telegram from Siena, dated 24 August 1880, announced that Wagner had sent off the last part, in the hope that it would reach the king in time for his thirty-fifth birthday.

He amazed Cosima by the fluency with which he dictated, as if he were reading from a book, making it difficult for her to keep up, skilled as she was. He was helped by the notes he had started to make for his 'future biography' at the age of twenty-two in Magdeburg, in the Red Pocket Book: set down while his impressions were fresh, they kept his recollection clear.

Meanwhile Cosima had completed a work of her own: she had copied in her own hand a large number of Wagner's earlier shorter writings and presented this 'Wagner Book' to the king on 25 October. 'I would not wish anyone but Your Majesty to see this book. One must have known Wagner entirely and seen into his inmost depths to be able to mount these steps of his development retrospectively with joyful understanding.' 'How absorbing and profoundly moving every word is , that comes from the pen of our great friend,' the king replied, and he enclosed a ring as a small token of his gratitude. 'May the blue of the sapphire . . . be to you a symbol of firm faith and unshakable confidence.' (KLRW, I, pp. lxxi f.)

Seeing that they were on the point of losing the game, Wagner's opponents thrust the king's grandfather on to the field as a last resort. Returning from a trip to Switzerland, the young Ludwig found a letter from ex-King Ludwig I waiting for him, 'full of coarse reprimands'. His response was to invite Wagner to spend a week with him at Hohenschwangau. (To Julius Fröbel, 28 November; to Mathilde Maier, 30 November) The Indian-summer weather, the freedom from constraint between himself and the king, the beauty of the little castle's setting among lakes, woods and mountains all made the visit an unforgettable experience for him. But already on the second day he wrote presciently in the Brown Book: 'My Cosima! Who takes thought today, that the daemon will have to be paid for this beauty!'

In conversation with the king he raised the subject of his relation-

ship with the cabinet, which had become untenable. He showed
him a document which reflected badly on Pfistermeister. An old
Viennese friend, Julius Fröbel, whom Wagner had recommended as
editor of a journal to publicize the purpose and outlook of the new
school of music, had received a letter dated 4 October 1865 from
Police Assessor Pfister, a confidant and colleague of Pfistermeister,
urging him in the strongest terms not to accept the appointment,
since Wagner's stay in Munich, in spite of everything, would be
only temporary and his fall would bring down all his 'creatures'.
(KLRW, I, p. 212)

'There is only one person, namely your king, to whom you
should show this letter,' Fröbel wrote when he forwarded this
document to Wagner. (KLRW, IV, p. 102) The king read this
unambiguous evidence of an intrigue with anger, but, as usual,
drew no conclusions from it and soon appeared to have forgotten
about it.

In order to understand the process leading to Wagner's
prophesied fall, we must go back to the events of the preceding
February. He received an offer of help in that crisis from an unexpected quarter. Prince Maximilian of Thurn und Taxis had conceived an ambitious plan to found a kingdom for his eldest son,
consisting of Rhineland–Westphalia and half of Belgium. Feelers
had been put out to Berlin and Munich, to ensure the non-
intervention of Prussia in the north and Bavaria in the south. The
plan was backed by ultramontane circles, as it contributed to their
strategy of manoeuvring the Prussians out of western Germany. In
order to render the parliaments of the German Federation tractable,
a banking enterprise was to be founded, which would gain control
of German agriculture and so control elections. This part of the plan
was in fact realized, with the foundation of the notorious Lan-
grand–Dumonceau Bank in Antwerp, the liquidation of which is
believed to have cost the Taxis family millions.

In Bavaria those party to the plan wanted above all to use
Wagner. On 12 February he received a visit from his old acquaintance Councillor Klindworth of Brussels and Baron von Gruben
from Regensburg, the Thurn und Taxis estate manager. At table the
two hinted to Wagner that the prince had authorized them to cut
him in on a banking venture.

'I played the innocent,' Wagner recounts. But the two agents
came again, this time accompanied by the lovely Agnes Street-

Klindworth. This time the three put their cards on the table: Wagner was to use his influence with the king to have Pfistermeister replaced by Klindworth; in return he – Wagner – would be given capital to finance his plans in the form of bonus shares in the new bank.

'Once more I failed to understand,' Wagner says. 'The Jesuits wanted to give me two festival theatres, two music schools, and as many villas and securities as I wanted,' he told Mathilde Maier, 'all I had to do was show myself compliant.' And to August Röckel he wrote: 'The Jesuits . . . made my path to everything I could desire so smooth that really I betrayed my artistic ideal by not showing myself at all compliant.' (KLRW, IV, pp. 116f.)[17]

Even if he did not seize the opportunity of benefiting directly from the intrigue, it nevertheless brought him, though only temporarily, a certain relief in his own difficulties, without his seeking it. The king's adjutant Prince Paul of Thurn und Taxis, a younger son of Prince Maximilian, got wind of the plot and warned Pfistermeister he was threatened, as Pfistermeister noted in his diary on 19 February. In the circumstances he thought it prudent to adopt a more moderate attitude to Wagner. He not only now shook the hand of friendship Wagner offered him but also took the initiative in showing him 'favour and flattery', arranging for the purchase of the house in Briennerstrasse from the Civil List, presenting Wagner with the possibility of 'unlimited credit', and above all rendering him every assistance in the preparation of the performance of *Tristan*. 'Pfistermeister is clinging passionately to Wagner, who has kept his footing but has been unfortunately under severe attack,' Bülow wrote to Carl Bechstein on 4 May.[18]

But as Pfistermeister saw his own danger recede, so his good will was replaced by a hostility of which Wagner remained unaware for a time.

Another temptation to busy himself with politics came to Wagner from a strange quarter. We read in the Annals for 22 February: 'Frau Dangl; "the care of Bavaria".' Fröbel's diary contains the explanation: Wagner had told him of a curious incident with a mysterious old woman, with a humble Munich background, who came to his house one evening and said she had to talk to him about the young king and his destiny. The king was destined for great things, she said, it was written in the stars. 'Do you believe in the stars?' she asked, in a loud, solemn voice. 'I want tranquillity for

my king and you, Herr Wagner, must protect him.' Even repeating
it to Fröbel, Wagner had become extremely excited again. (SRLW,
II, p. 217)

Just how greatly he was stirred by this appeal to a belief in the
stars that he in fact held is demonstrated by what he wrote the very
next day to Mathilde Maier: the fate of this young man was placed
in his, *his* hands. To leave him to be the prey of intrigues was a
treason for which he had no excuse. An almost miraculous experience had revealed to him his duty to the king. 'Now I ask myself:
Why this cup to me? I, who expected to find only rest, rest,
obligation to myself alone? I, now holding in my hand the fate of a
people, of a glorious, uniquely gifted king?' (23 February) Three
days later he wrote to Eliza Wille in almost exactly the same terms:
he had to shudder at the idea of thinking only of his own peace and
quiet while abandoning the king to the mercy of his entourage. 'I
feel dread in the depths of my soul, and I ask my daemon: why this
cup to me?' (26 February)

In spite of these feelings he still tried to restrain himself, but when
he had to fight the cabinet for the sake of his artistic goals he was
drawn unwillingly ever deeper into politics. ' "New age", "new
principle" mean – "new men",' he declared to Ludwig. 'They will
be found just at soon as the "old men" have been driven out.' (26
November) With alarm his friends watched him assuming the
Schillerian role of a Marquis Posa, attempting to influence the
policies of Ludwig's Philip II.

More than ever Pfistermeister and his colleagues felt their position threatened. 'Now – in the twelfth hour – Lutz had to ask me in
plain language at Hohenschwangau to lend my support to their
precisely delineated reactionary plans, "for the love of the king, the
enhancement of whose authority is at stake",' Wagner wrote to
Röckel. 'How easy it would have been for me to say "yes, yes – of
course!" for the sake of peace and my own advantage!' And he went
on presciently: 'And I am afraid that if they do not get the upper
hand over him . . . they will kill him!' (18 December, KLRW, IV,
pp. 116ff.)

Wagner later revealed the cabinet's 'reactionary plans' in a letter
to Dr Schanzenbach, the confidant of Prince Chlodwig Hohenlohe.
During his stay at Hohenschwangau in November 1865, the deputy
Cabinet Secretary, Lutz, had made him privy to the trend of
cabinet thinking, with the unconcealed intention of winning his

co-operation: namely, that negotiations were afoot to come to an agreement with Bismarck, which would enable them to restore the Bavarian constitution to what it had been before 1848. 'Since this would mean the restoration of full monarchical powers, as the king's particular friend I would surely – so Herr Lutz surmised – go along with the government of the day. All I said to this was that these confidences were completely useless, as I had nothing to do with politics and in particular knew nothing whatever about the interests of the kingdom of Bavaria.' (17 January 1867) Newman is right when he comments that the politicians were only trying to trick Wagner, so as to bring him down later: his downfall had long been decided upon. (NLRW, III, p. 486)

'Now they've finally set the dogs on me,' Wagner wrote to Mathilde Maier, 'I've grown tired of it and have denounced the brutes fairly publicly.' (17 December) On the face of it the cause was remote. A democratic newspaper in Nuremberg had criticized the institution of a Cabinet Secretariat in Bavaria as 'thoroughly unconstitutional', to which the Munich *Volksbote* had responded on 26 November with a sharp attack on Wagner: 'Pfistermeister and Hofmann . . . are to be removed, so that certain desires anent the plundering of the royal treasury can obtain easy satisfaction.'[19]

The article, inspired by the Cabinet Secretariat, was quite obviously calculated to draw Wagner out of his covert. He stepped into the trap, with an anonymous open letter that appeared in the *Neueste Nachrichten* on 29 November, and whose authorship was easy enough to guess. It concluded: 'For there is one thing of which you may be sure: it is not a matter of some principle or another, of some partisan policy to which Wagner is opposed, it is simply a matter of the *shabbiest personal interests,* and these can moreover be traced back to an uncommonly small number of individuals; I dare to assure you that the removal of two or three persons, who do not enjoy the least respect among the people of Bavaria, would rid the king and the people of Bavaria at one stroke of these tiresome disturbances.' (KLRW, IV, pp. 107ff).

At last the cabinet had the lever to topple Wagner that they had so long sought. The first to make use of it was the minister of state, Ludwig von der Pfordten, who levelled an imposing charge against Wagner.

'Your Majesty stands at a fateful crossroads and has to choose between the love and respect of your loyal subjects and the friend-

ship of Richard Wagner. This man . . . is despised by every class of
the people . . . despised . . . for his ingratitude and betrayal of
patrons and friends, for his arrogant and dissolute self-indulgence
and squandering, for the shameless way he exploits the undeserved
favour he has received from Your Majesty.' (FHKF, p. 143)

How painfully this letter touched the king, and how powerless it
was to alter his trust, is demonstrated by his letter to Wagner,
quoting Schiller, two days later: 'Oh, my beloved friend, "great
was the agony of these last days",' and concluding: 'Take comfort,
your friend will never desert you.' (3 December) He returned to
Munich and was besieged by visitors on the morning of 6
December: the cabinet threatened to resign if Wagner was not sent
away, the Queen Mother and the Bishop of Munich—Freising supported the demand, his great-uncle Prince Karl spoke of the threat
of a revolution, which the military would join. The young king was
not strong enough to withstand this concerted onslaught. 'His
imagination ran away with him,' Wagner told Röckel, 'he saw
me as the victim of a popular uprising, wanted to save me and
asked me to leave Bavaria for a few months.' (KLRW, IV, pp.
112f.)

It gave the deputy Cabinet Secretary Lutz a peculiar satisfaction
to convey this message personally to Wagner in the afternoon of 6
December. The king confirmed it the next day in a brief note: 'It is
not for ever, of course. Until death, your faithful Ludwig.'

'I am sure that you, too, do not deceive yourself as to the length of
my absence,' replied Wagner, who had made up his mind never to
return. 'My child! it was no longer endurable,' he confessed to
Mathilde Maier. 'One day, riding four-in-hand with a king, the
next, torn to pieces by the priests – and trying to find peace to do
some work in between. It was madness!' (17 December)

The most astonishing thing about this whole astonishing episode
is that in the midst of all the events that have filled the pages of this
chapter, Wagner found the spirits to orchestrate his heroic fairy tale,
the second act of *Siegfried*. Unlike his other creative periods he
referred only rarely and fleetingly to this occupation at the time, by
word of mouth or in letters: for instance, when he and the king used
'Mime' and 'Fafner' as nicknames for Pfistermeister and the
treasury minister Hofmann.

In spite of his emotional turmoil and all that weighed on his
mind, Cosima told the king on 2 December, he was at that moment

in the act of writing the jubilant orchestral passage that ends the act, with the bird first teasing Siegfried and then leading him off:

> So wird mir den Weg gewiesen:
> wohin du flatterst
> folg' ich dem Flug!

And the instruments – flutes, oboes, clarinets, cor anglais, trumpets, violins – play tag with each other, chasing the Woodbird's motive up and down imitatively, with the effect that earned Richard Strauss's praise, the *single* 'ting' of the triangle falling on the strings' pizzicato like a ray of sunshine through the leaves.

The end of the first draft of the score is dated '2 December 1865 (still on board the ship)'. 'The ship' was what they called the house in Briennerstrasse, because it 'was always swaying', as Cosima told her daughter Daniela: 'Uncle Richard can tell you about it, we were on the ship together.'

Wagner asked the king for a few days to put his affairs in order. Porges and Cornelius went down to the station to see him off at five in the morning of 10 December. 'At last the carriage arrived,' Peter recorded in his diary. 'Wagner looked like a ghost; pale, distraught, his long lank hair looking quite grey. We accompanied him to the train . . . Cosima had broken down completely. When his carriage disappeared beyond the pillars, it was like the fading of a vision.'

26

Die Meistersinger

'Lake Constance again,' Wagner noted in the Annals for 10 December 1865. He went on, via Berne and Vevey, to Geneva, where he found a temporary haven nearby in the Campagne aux Artichauts. It was a large villa, furnished in a 'mesquin' fashion, just for appearances, he told Cosima, 'still – it was a port in the storm: I am undisturbed here, as if I had left the world . . . The view is wonderful, Mont Blanc right in front of me, when I look out from my seat at the piano.' (5 January 1866) By 10 January he was ready to resume the composition sketch of *Die Meistersinger* at the point where it had been interrupted at Penzing two years previously, at Beckmesser's words, as he holds out his slate covered with chalk marks, 'Seid Ihr nun fertig?'

The fact that he did not go on with *Siegfried* at this date shows that the belief that he would see the *Ring* performed, revived by the call to Munich, had once again deserted him. Much as the king and Cosima hoped he would return, he was determined never to go back to Munich. On 1 January he asked a French friend, Monsieur S. (probably Schuré), to commission an agent to find a house in the country for him to rent for five or six years, somewhere in the south of France between Avignon, Arles and Perpignan. His main concern was to settle somewhere away from the world and to sever all the ties that still linked him to his dreadful past. 'C'est le seul moyen pour moi de sauver mes oeuvres conçues, qui seront perdues, si je passe encore une année dans des convulsions du genre de mon ordinaire.' (TWLF, pp. 267f.) His income appeared to be assured, even though Lutz, informing him of this, made the following reservation: 'unless some completely unforeseen circumstance should compel His Majesty the King to act other than His

Allhighness would wish to act when following the dictates of His Allhighness's heart and enthusiasm for art'. (KLRW, IV, pp. 113ff.)

Wagner's most difficult task was breaking the news of his decision to the king. 'I cannot yet bring myself to write to Parzival,' he told Cosima. 'Every day what I have to tell him seems to take on a different form. I am becoming increasingly unsure of myself on this point.' Ludwig poured out his heart to her in a profoundly moving letter: 'Oh, I had hoped, hoped, and that enabled me to suppress my pain; but now the enemy star is in the ascendant, it rends me violently from my friend, hurls me towards a future full of torments, robs me of my hope, my life, my all!' (2 January 1866)

It was a genuinely tragic situation: the young king believing that even in his friend's best interests no other course of action was open to him; and Wagner seeing that the king had been the victim of a conspiracy. At last, on 8 January, he found the courage to write a long and affectionate letter, which could leave Ludwig in no doubt of the irrevocability of his decision: 'Two questions on which our fate depends, my king.' Did Ludwig still believe that his subjects had been stirred by their relationship to an anger that could be appeased only by Wagner's departure? In that case he must keep Wagner at a distance from himself for ever. But if he saw now that he had been shamefully deceived and lied to – what should be the offender's punishment? If Pfistermeister and Pfordten were not dismissed, then, to spare the king and himself further humiliations, Wagner had no alternative but voluntary self-banishment.

He would submit to the decree of fate, Ludwig replied, if he could be sure that this was the only way for Wagner to find happiness and peace of mind. For, as he added in a second letter, the dismissal of those persons was at present out of the question. (15 and 28 January)

The king was the only person to whom the political background to the plot was not becoming daily more obvious. The *Neue Freie Presse* of Vienna declared openly that Wagner had been the victim of a reactionary palace revolution. It was a fact that the liberals had pinned their hopes on his opposition to the unconstitutional Cabinet Secretariat, but their behaviour after his fall aroused his contempt. 'Look at those sheep and foxes washing their hands of anything to do with me, I'm nothing to them but that voluptuous musician!' (To Röckel, 16 December 1865)

For his part he no longer hesitated to give the king political advice. 'I wish you suitable, genuinely valuable guidance in the serious career you must now follow,' he wrote at the end of his letter of 8 January. He implored him to read without delay two books by Constantin Frantz, *Thirty-three Propositions concerning the German Federation* and *The Restoration of Germany*. 'His is the most competent, truly statesmanlike brain that I have yet encountered among Germans. The second and larger book, in particular, expounds what I, too, have felt to be the right, truly German policy; the author has written to me that my harmonies revealed the future of Germany to him.'

Frantz was a political publicist who did not owe his reputation to his pen alone, and whom Bismarck, on coming to office in 1862, had tried in vain to win for his party. He first approached Wagner in November 1865. On his return from Hohenschwangau a letter was waiting for him, in which he made the discovery of a new person, Wagner had told the king. He was going to find out who Constantin Frantz was. A few days later: 'Frau Cosima knew more about him: she describes him as one of the "famous unknown". He is supposed to be significant, profound and completely unflawed.' He was to exercise a formative influence on Wagner's political views similar to Schopenhauer's on his philosophy.

A fire in one of the rooms at Les Artichauts, necessitating redecoration, lent urgency to Wagner's decision to find somewhere to live in southern France. Then a telegram from Cosima arrived on 20 January, asking him to wait just a few days, and when he replied refusing, a second telegram followed: 'Wanted to travel to you tomorrow . . . May I still come?' 'Will my friend please not disturb my resolve,' he replied; 'it must be!' His fears of an attempt to make him change his mind were not unjustified. The same evening he sent her a 'musical letter', direct from the stage he had reached in the *Meistersinger* composition sketch: after the bars from 'Singt dem Herrn Merker zum Verdruß' to 'Ade! Ihr Meister hienied!', with the stage direction 'The masters greatly scandalized: you know!', he scribbled a few lines: 'Nothing more about *Munich*: last hope of deliverance! Do not misunderstand me! You see! merely to write about it is really almost impossible for me!'

He reached Lyons on the evening of 22 January. In a dire mood he had stepped out on to the balcony, he confided to the Brown Book. 'Night, slender crescent moon. On the left Orion's sword with the point to the north-east. Slash, slash, my sword, that a royal heart may feel what true sorrows are!'

The next day he was in Toulon and the following in Hyères. 'Nothing in Hyères,' he telegraphed Cosima. But for the pure chance of not being able to find a suitable haven in the south of France, *Meistersinger* and the *Ring* would have been completed under the halcyon Mediterranean skies that Nietzsche, in his later alienation from Wagner, used to imply would greatly have benefited his outlook!

So he returned to Marseilles. Scarcely had he gone to sleep when he was woken with a telegram from Pusinelli, announcing Minna's sudden death. Since it had been forwarded from Geneva he could not even be sure what was meant by 'last night'. After all the shocks that had assailed him, he confessed to Pusinelli, he had sensed that the next bad news to reach him would either make him break down completely or rouse almost no sensation at all. 'So far, this morning, after a weary night, I can describe my condition in no other way than as one of complete numbness, in which I dully brood – brood – without knowing what, if anything, I have got to think about . . . I am sure that in your friendly solicitude you showed the body of my poor unhappy wife the same honour in my name that I would have shown her, if she had departed from life happily at the side of a husband to whom she gave happiness.'[1]

Minna's letters had become more and more of a torment to him, till in the end he told her on 5 October 1865 that he had not read her most recent one: 'Since the letter I had from you last spring, which depressed me so shamefully, I have decided not to embitter my heart and my memories unnecessarily.' (RWBC, p. 565) An undated draft of a letter, written in a shaking hand, perhaps her last sign of life, begins conciliatingly: 'You *are* good, at the bottom of your heart; I have always known it, it is only in your head, where there is so much that is beautiful and splendid, that sometimes there sprouts much that hurts those closest to you' – and then she goes on to rehearse all the old complaints and accusations. (RWBC, pp. 563ff.)

Just how out of sympathy she had remained with his development as an artist emerges with horrifying clarity from a letter to a friend, dated 14 October 1864: 'It looks as though he won't be writing anything very enjoyable in future, if he's already composed all he had in him and has to force it out now. It's a very poor outlook

– compared with what a Meyerbeer wrote, every one in his own style, he left whole crates whose contents the world still does not know.'[2]

In the will she made in 1865 she left no memento to her husband but bequeathed everything to her 'sister' Natalie. But it was destined that her last act should be one of reconciliation. When the Munich *Volksbote* sank to asserting that Wagner was content to let his wife starve and depend on the charity of strangers, she published a denial on 15 January, ten days before her death, declaring that she received sufficient support from her husband to live a decent life, free from care.[3]

'In great love she endured much sorrow and little joy at my side,' Wagner told a friend later, in Bayreuth, and Glasenapp's unfavourable depiction of her met with his disapproval.[4]

Now, in Marseilles, he took refuge from the recent turmoils in the world of the imagination. A book published by the French railway company had reminded him of the tale of the death of Roland. He drafted a short sketch of it in the Brown Book ending: 'The horn goes unheard – the traitor remains at the king's side – the hero perishes – only love redeems.' He was so filled with the immediacy of experience of the legend, that he wrote to tell the king about it the same day. 'What a sad and dreadful allegory,' Ludwig commented to Cosima.

Wagner got back to Geneva from his wasted journey on the evening of 29 January. 'I am too tired for everything and anything,' he wrote to Cosima. 'Perhaps this condition will be my deliverance. I have two months in front of me that I shall really be able to spend in the same place – here. What I can do for the good of my soul in those two months is the only thing that occupies me at the moment . . . I have rented this place for another two months. Nobody has the right to drive me away for another two months: – methinks life is at my feet, the knowledge is so reassuring.' (KLRW, I, p. 261)

What he could do for the good of his soul was work. And so he settled down to *Die Meistersinger* as if the two remaining months in Les Artichauts were a lifetime. Already in the sketch he worked out the first-act finale on fifteen staves in careful detail. When he received a letter from Cosima on 21 February, bringing him reassuring news that he had been greatly hoping for, he was able to tell her by telegram: 'That did the old shoemaker good. In return the act finale was finished today. Sachs.'

As so often before, his literary imagination was stimulated while he was composing. The thoughts he committed to the Brown Book on 7 February about the holiness of night-time are a fine example. He referred to the performance of the *Oresteia* in the Greek world, when its grim tale of bloodshed and vengeance was begun in broad daylight, only to finish in reconciliation as night fell, whereupon the tragedy was followed by the satyr play. 'The night induces a sense of holiness that sanctions comedy and light-heartedness as well . . . The world sheds its solemn burden in foolery.'[5]

He had been expecting Cosima on 3 March, but she delayed her journey for a few days for an important reason. The king had encouraged her to seek an interview with Pfordten, in order to gain his approval for Wagner's return. His response had been that either the matter was a private concern of the king's – in which case he had nothing to say – or it was an affair of state – in which case it was not proper for him to discuss it. 'Honourable and blinkered' was the impression he made on her: 'truly he thinks our friend is a menace to the state!' (KLRW, I, pp. 262f.)

She arrived at Les Artichauts with Daniela on 8 March, and he resumed dictating his autobiography to her the next day. But above all he devoted himself to orchestrating the first act of *Meistersinger*, which he finished on 23 March.

At this time, too, he wrote a long letter to Constantin Frantz (19 March), which is especially interesting for what he has to say about King Ludwig: he believed his abilities to be exceptional, even though the question of how his capacities as a ruler might develop was still open; a senseless education had succeeded in imbuing him with an insuperable reluctance to concern himself with affairs of state, and this unrealistic attitude made Wagner anxious lest he decline into weakness of character. Representations and reasoning with him would do no good at all, but on the other hand he, Wagner, was in a position to make the king 'lucid and clear-sighted' by means of his art.

All the same he recognized the limits to the influence a king could wield, and the need to seek out supporters among the educated people scattered throughout the nation, who would strive with him to further his artistic undertakings. He thought of writing an occasional series of open letters to Frantz, who he hoped would advise him on the moderate and discreet treatment of any personal topics. His experiences in Bavaria had convinced him that nothing could be accomplished without the concerted action of like minds against the 'so well-organized phalanx of the common sort'. 'My artistic ideal stands and falls with the weal of Germany.'

Cosima went back to Munich on 31 March. Before she left they searched in vain for a new 'Asyl', while making a round trip through Lausanne, Vevey, Berne, Interlaken and the Lake of Lucerne. She reported to the king that she had found their friend changed, restless and unquiet. He had been so pale, so gaunt, so depressed. As they were parting in Romanshorn he had said he supposed he would have to move into a hotel. 'But *Die Meistersinger*?' she had had time to exclaim. He had just smiled sadly as her steamer pulled away from the shore. (KLRW, IV, p. 140)

Without hesitation the king offered to lend him his hunting lodge in the Riss as temporary accommodation, even though it was in Bavaria. 'He must be saved, though it destroy me!' But the very next day, 5 April, Cosima had a telegram from Wagner, telling her he had taken a year's lease on a large villa on the Tribschen peninsula just outside Lucerne, which they had noticed when they were crossing the lake. A fortnight earlier the king's letter would have changed everything, everything, he wrote to her on 7 April, but now it was too late. 'And so: welcome, fate! Let Asyl be Tribschen!' (KLRW, IV, p. 141) Ludwig accepted this turn of events, probably with some relief, and also undertook to defray the expenses of the move and settling in. 'Let us allow him to go his way in peace,' he agreed with Cosima; 'he will surely find what is right for him.'

On 15 April Wagner moved into Tribschen. Two days later he wrote to Cosima:

> Today, Tuesday, glorious morning, market day. Boat after boat from Ury, Schwyz and Unterwalden going to Lucerne market: a delightful sight, quite unspeakably beautiful – especially against this background, on the lovely smooth surface of the lake, where every boat is lapped round by a radiating silver circle. A hard month of winter is not too great a price to pay for a morning like this. Now I can understand the choice I have made and the winter that lies in front of me: Walther has already sung about it, 'am stillen Herd zur Winterszeit, wenn Hof und Haus [sic] mir eingeschneit', and so I shall remember the spring morning, how I shall love the

winter here! Truth, the highest truth be our dogma! See, there is only one other person I can admit to this alliance! Only Parzival [King Ludwig]. And let him be our guardian angel. Once more, let no one disturb us here, let holy peace reign here. These are the last years of a difficult, tormented life, which shall now find their goal, their crown.

Nothing has moved me so greatly for a very long time as renewing my acquaintance with the legend of Melusine. Oh God – Melusine, departing, returning as a ghost in future ages. A fever made me tremble: melancholy and pity threatened to dissolve me into atoms. God! what poetry the human race has produced in its exploration of the fearful riddle of existence – and it's all useless, they play with their immense poems like silly children. What is there for me in this world?

I am sending you *Melusine*, read it, and give it to Parzival to read too.

This mystery of enchantment! By an evil chance Raymond kills his uncle in the forest at night – moonlight – wild flight; a wonderful voice calls to him: Melusine, in sore need of release from enchantment – woos him, brings him boundless happiness, is betrayed by him. On moonlit nights she tends the youngest children – then nothing more is known of her. Night – the elements. Guilt – magic: disbelief – doubt – the breaking of the spell. A long lament through the night – through the air. Moonlight! The birds are undaunted and sing merrily . . .

I have just finished reading *Melusine*, ah! ah God! My heart is breaking!

Have you ever heard starlings rattling and chattering? There are beautiful cows in the meadows all round. Day and night you can hear their bells ringing. That ringing is lovelier than any sound I know. The arbitrary alternation of the sounds, the beauty of the bells, the pride of their owners, possess an indescribable magic. I would give all the bells of Rome for them. (DMCW, I, pp. 279f.; KLRW, V, p. 150)

Cosima wrote to the king on 20 April: 'I take the liberty of sending you *Melusine*, as I was asked to do so.'

The prospect in Wagner's heart was less smiling than the view from his window. His faithful housekeeper Verena Weidmann saw how depressed he was. He was not well, he complained, he was going to settle who was to have his things after his death. '*May*: great distress; provision for my death,' he wrote in the Annals. One evening, Verena recounted, he stayed out unusually late, night fell and to her alarm the dog Russ came home on his own. Accompanied by the groom Jost, she set out towards the town with a lantern. They met Wagner along the road. 'Why, I thought no one cared about me any more; even Russ, who has always been faithful, abandoned me.' (GLRW, IV, p. 174)

What was upsetting him were his hopes and fears concerning Cosima. 'You are invited, with wife, children and servants . . . to come and stay with me in the villa and enjoy my humble hospitality,' he implored Bülow. 'If you fulfil my request you will be making the greatest, the only effective contribution to my well-being, to the well-being of my work – and of my future work.'

Cosima and her daughters arrived at Tribschen on 12 May; Hans was kept in Munich by his duties. In *The Women in Wagner's Life* Julius Kapp writes that, immediately after Cosima's departure, an ardent love letter from Wagner arrived for her, which Bülow opened in the belief that it might contain something urgent that he would have to telegraph after her. 'It revealed the whole bitter truth to him! The great lie of the last two years suddenly stared him implacably in the face.'

When Kapp's book was published in 1912 this story was generally accepted without question, until Ernest Newman poured cold water on it: why, he asked, would Wagner have sent Cosima a letter that would in all probability not arrive until after the time at which he knew she would be leaving home? And, above all, why would Bülow think he might need to telegraph Cosima the contents of a letter from Wagner, when she was already on her way to Tribschen?

Kapp based his story on a letter Peter Cornelius wrote from Munich to his fiancée on 13 May 1866.[6] 'We discussed serious matters at Bülow's yesterday. He had written a very firm letter to Perfall [the intendant of the Munich theatre], complaining bitterly about the bad performance of [Liszt's] *Elisabeth*, demanding four new violinists for *Lohengrin*, etc. Bülow thought it depended on these things whether he might not refuse his cooperation at the last minute. Just after his family had left he had opened a letter, something he normally never does, but he thought he might have to telegraph his wife immediately. The letter was such that he was horrified by it. He is very much afraid that nothing will come of the Conservatory or anything else, and perhaps he will take his leave and go to Italy.'

No mention there of an ardent love letter, or any other kind of letter, from *Wagner*, let alone any of Kapp's sensational deductions. Both Newman and Cosima's biographer Max Millenkovich-Morold held the view that it would hardly have needed an accidentally opened letter at this late date to open Bülow's eyes. His friend Cornelius told his fiancée six months earlier that a 'full-blown affair' was going on between Wagner and Cosima, and wondered whether Bülow might not have completely surrendered his wife to Wagner 'in a highly romantic agreement'. 'Was Wagner's embrace at the station [when leaving Munich] his thanks for it? The actual marriage between Hans and Cosima has probably been only a marriage of appearances for some time now. There's no other explanation for Hans's behaviour.' (10 December 1865)

We know what the reasons were that stood in the way of a solution to the marital deadlock: regard for public opinion and, perhaps more important, for the king, who, as events were to prove, had no comprehension or sympathy for such infringements; Liszt's disapproval; the fact that the Bülow marriage had been celebrated in the Catholic church; and finally the opposition of Bülow himself, who wished to preserve appearances at least – and who would have lost, as well as his wife, the friend to whom he clung in spite of everything.

Elucidation of the mysterious letter may lie in quite a different direction.

On 15 May Wagner had just started the composition sketch of the second act of *Meistersinger* when a horrifying telegram (well over a hundred words long!) arrived from the king, disclosing his intention, 'if it is my Dear Friend's wish and will', to renounce the throne and come and live with him in Switzerland. 'I cannot endure any longer to remain separate and *alone*.' (KLRW, II, pp. 34f.)

The growing threat of war between Prussia and Austria, in which Bavaria could not escape involvement, had been worrying Ludwig for some time. On this particular 15 May, as Pfistermeister told the king's doctor, he had been very agitated, and had spoken of abdicating on grounds of his mental health so as to be able to go and live in Switzerland. (KLRW, II, p. xv)

And suddenly light dawns: the letter to Cosima that Hans opened was *from the king*. He wanted to inform *her* of his intention to abdicate, as he did again two months later, after the Austro-Prussian war had run its unhappy course. Then, on 21 July, he wrote that he had not written directly to Wagner about his decision, once again, to abdicate, 'the shock might have been harmful to him; I ask you to convey to him the content of this letter in your own words.' (KLRW, II, p. 75)

Now we can understand why Bülow was 'horrified' by what he read in the letter he opened on 12 May, and why he feared that it was all up with the school of music and everything else, and that he would have to leave Munich. This letter had crossed with a letter Cosima sent to the king on 10 May, telling him that she would be leaving 'tomorrow morning'[7] with the children to spend some weeks in Lucerne. On receiving that, Ludwig sent her a telegram at Tribschen on 13 May. 'Now you, my friend, will be united with our dear friend, I am with the two dearest ones on earth in spirit. I too dream of future happiness and have every hope that the dream of blissful hours on the shores and waters of the Lake of Lucerne will be fulfilled.' The final sentence, 'I long for news soon', proves that the telegram must have been preceded by another missive to which the king had not yet received an answer: namely the letter opened by Hans. (KLRW, IV, p. 145)

The reference to a 'dream', which only Wagner and Cosima would have understood, even enables us to guess what was in the letter. 'I had a vivid dream about you today,' Ludwig had written to Wagner on 12 November 1865; 'we were talking together on the shore of the Lake of Lucerne, when we heard music on the approaching steamer, we had to part; the ship carried me far away.' Three months later he had a very similar dream, as he wrote to Cosima on 4 February. 'We were sailing on the Lake of Lucerne, our friend was telling me about his plans and talking about his works. It was an elevating dream.' 'The dream . . .' Cosima replied; 'sometimes I feel as though it must come true, but in what worlds?' (KLRW, I, p. 211)

'In what worlds?' On 15 May Ludwig made up his mind that the dream was going to come true here and now. He did not wait for the answer to his telegram of 13 May, but sent off the telegram informing Wagner of his decision to abdicate at 6.40 a.m. Pfister-meister's letter to the king's doctor tells us that he spent an hour and a half with the king that same morning persuading him that in view of the political situation he ought not to go away but stay and open parliament in person. (KLRW, II, pp. 35f.)

In his despair Ludwig sent Wagner a letter like a single, sustained 'cry of pain'. He implores his friend to come to him; he would easily find a suitable house close to Schloss Berg, where he himself was then living. 'You cannot ignore this entreaty; otherwise the strength of my ardent enthusiasm . . . will be shaken to its very foundation and "madness" will overcome me!' (KLRW, II, pp. 35f.)[8]

Wagner's reply was a psychological masterpiece, demonstrating to the full his sympathetic understanding of the king. He appealed to Ludwig's love for himself. '*Six months' patience*!! You must make this sacrifice – for my sake, who stand for ever on the brink of the abyss, tormented by worry, sensing that my future creativity, my very life, depend on these six months, if they allow me the peace to create, undisturbed; – for your own sake, who would fail in your high calling, if you did not steel yourself in these fateful six months for the whole of your life.' (15 May)

But the king's impatience to talk everything over with his friend was no longer to be controlled. On the morning of 22 May, after sending Wagner a birthday telegram, so as to pull the wool over his household's eyes, and listening as usual to the report from Cabinet Secretary Lutz, he rode, accompanied only by a groom, to the railway station at Biessenhofen, caught the express to Lindau, crossed Lake Constance on the steamer to Rorschach in Switzer-land, and arrived at Tribschen during the afternoon, to Wagner's complete surprise. His journey did not go unnoticed in Munich for long, however, and in the very tense political climate of the time it aroused general anger. The blame was wrongly placed at Wagner's door, and a flood of abuse burst over him, Bülow and 'Madame Hans the carrier pigeon'.

On Wagner's advice the king opened parliament in person on 27 May, but he was conscious of the deputies' disapprobation. 'Parliament opened today,' he telegraphed to Tribschen, 'reception ice-cold! Press disgraceful!'

As the stormclouds of war thickened Wagner drew up a 'Political Programme' early in June, though it is not known whether it was actually printed at that time. It reflects Constantin Frantz's conception of a Germany united as a 'triad' or 'trinomium', in which the central states should stand together under the leadership of Bavaria, between the two giants, Prussia and Austria. War between the two latter automatically meant that both would leave the German Federation, and it was incumbent on the remaining member states to form their own independent policy without delay. The King of Bavaria, as head of the oldest state, should summon the other princes to Nuremberg, with the exception of the King of Prussia and the emperor. This reduced Federation, backed by their own armed forces, should then negotiate with Austria and Prussia and prescribe to them the terms for a new federation.

Though the programme rested on a false estimate of the relative military strengths of the different states, it nevertheless shows that what Wagner had in mind was not Bavarian particularism. The idea of a united Germany inspired him so profoundly that he thought of using music to win support for it. Frantz had already asked him in the spring if he would not give a musical expression to the idea of the German cause and compose a morning song to rouse the German nation from its slumbers, and now a Count Enzenberg appealed to him: 'Write the German national anthem that our great banner still lacks, and give it the eloquence of Demosthenes!'

The count's letter was rather formal and old-fashioned, Wagner told the king, but it betrayed a strong, warm heart, such as he rejoiced to find still beat in a manly breast in those sorry times. 'This is the language through which Germany speaks to me.' He wrote back to the count that he, too, dreamed of an earnest German anthem 'that may inspire our will to act with its simple, solemn gravity'. The right idea would come to him, not after days spent pondering on it but in the moment of fervour, of crisis, of inspiration: 'The days of greatest danger are at hand: may the princes apprehend them.' (15 June)

Wagner had started the orchestral sketch of the second act of *Meistersinger* on 8 June, and the exuberant woodwind trills and string figurations are prefaced by the sombre heading 'Still on the brink – as usual'. Things were now so bad that the pressure on Bülow, who was now accused of making one in the 'tricksy race to the treasury', made it impossible for him to stay in Munich any longer. After suing the *Neuer Bayerischer Courier*, and challenging the editor of the *Volksbote* to a duel, he asked the king to accept his resignation and arrived at Tribschen on 10 June. Four days previously Wagner had already drafted a letter, as from the king to Bülow, vindicating Bülow's honour, and sent it to Ludwig with a covering letter urging him to sign the document. 'I fall to my knees before my king,' Cosima added, 'and pray in humility and distress for the letter to my husband, so that we need not leave in shame and disgrace the country where we desired only good.' (DMCW, I, p. 290)

The king yielded to his friends' urging and Bülow hastened to publish the letter – with a foreseeable lack of effect, in view of the fact that the Austro-Prussian war had broken out on 14 June and Bavaria's fate was in the balance.

Wagner had hoped that the new Progressive Party, to which he was close through Röckel, would succeed in blocking Pfordten's policies in the Landtag. In this hope he had implored the king to listen to the voice of the people and follow the majority will of the chamber of deputies, but – 'what does the chamber do? Almost without debating the matter it gives Pfordten a more glowing vote of confidence than scarcely any minister has ever received.' (To Röckel, 23 June) The outcome was that Bavaria abandoned the neutrality Wagner had argued for in his 'Political Programme', and joined the war on Austria's side.

He wrote to the king on 18 June of his regret at seeing that the latter had not found the right man, that 'incompetence, short-sightedness, weakness of character' had led the statesman, who was now at the head of the government, to the ruinous half-measures to which the present sorry state of German affairs was due. Wagner's opinion of Pfordten was shared by Bismarck, who referred to him in his memoirs as 'an honourable and learned German professor of no political acumen'.

The Bavarian army suffered a decisive defeat on 10 July at Kissingen. 'For days I have been wondering how to begin still being something to you now,' Wagner told the king. There must, he thought, be some deep-seated and perhaps painful reason why he should have regained his most carefree creative powers at a moment of national crisis. 'World destiny, unable to realize the glory of the German spirit in the political life worthy of a great nation . . . created the two of us to realize what is too beautiful for life in the eternal mirror of art and – perhaps to preserve it there for posterity, so that one day people will recognize beyond all doubt that the nation that created something like that must have truly lived!' (14 July)

God grant, Ludwig replied, that Bavaria's independence would be preserved; 'if not . . . then away, I will not be a puppet king'. (18 July) This hint of abdicating became passionately explicit in a letter to Cosima three days later: 'Gain for me my dear friend's consent! . . . It is not the difficult political circumstances that drive me to this decision, that would be cowardice – but the thought that my true destiny will never be reached along this road!' (21 July)

Once again Wagner knew what to say to him. He did not stipulate any fixed term for reconsideration, but asked the king whether the world would always appear to him as it did at the present time. When he grew to maturity he would find the world a larger place; and his sense of manhood would also make him aware of his capacities for the exercise of royal power. A king believed in himself, or was no king. What if he should become conscious of his belief in himself only after resigning his rights? If he should ever regret it?

Completely under the spell of the atmosphere of *Meistersinger* himself, he suggested to Ludwig that he should move the seat of government to Nuremberg, 'the heart of Germany': 'Nuremberg, the old, true home of German art, original German inspiration and splendour, the vigorous, ancient imperial city, preserved like a noble diadem.' One can almost hear the words accompanied by the music he had just written to Pogner's lines:

> Nürenberg, die ganze Stadt,
> mit Bürgern und Gemeinen,
> mit Zünften, Volk und hohem Rat . . .

And then he went on to mention Bayreuth. A short while before, in dictating his autobiography, he had described a journey to Nuremberg in 1835 and how he had seen Bayreuth for the first time, bathed in the light of a lovely summer evening. Now, in this same letter, he pictured to the king how Bayreuth could turn out to be his 'best-loved residence'. (24 July)

But while he seemed to lose himself in building such castles in the air, in reality he retained an astonishingly cool head for the changed political situation. 'Send for Prince Hohenlohe-Schillingsfürst at once,' he advised the king on 26 July. He followed up the advice the next day with a long letter justifying it: 'I implore you on my knees: send for Prince Hohenlohe at once . . . new men! new men! You are betrayed if you do not!'

Hohenlohe was known to be opposed to the ultramontane party and to favour an alliance with Prussia, and for that very reason he did not enjoy the king's confidence, as Ludwig informed Wagner through his adjutant, Prince Paul of Taxis. (29 July) However, he bestirred himself to make two ministerial changes: the Treasury Secretary Julius von Hofmann was asked to resign in August and Cabinet Secretary Pfistermeister in October. It was exactly as if the Emperor of Austria had kicked out Metternich, Wagner wrote to Mathilde Maier: all at once the whole pack of baying hounds was silent. He took the opportunity to recommend Prince Hohenlohe to the king again: 'if you could bring yourself to have confidence in Prince Hohenlohe, I think it would be a great advantage.' It was necessary to adopt a dignified and circumspect attitude towards Prussia, and that called for a man possessing rank and the free deportment of a prince. On 31 December the king appointed Prince Chlodwig zu Hohenlohe-Schillingsfürst Minister of Domestic and Foreign Affairs and Chairman of the Council of Ministers, in place of Pfordten.

While Wagner lived in a state of permanent tension and, as he put it, was frightened to death once a fortnight, he nonetheless managed to finish the composition sketch of the second act. Taking refuge from the 'miserable world of experiences' in this occupation was what kept him alive. (To Heinrich Esser; RWBC, p. 806) '6 September 66, 11 p.m. Good night, Cosima!' he wrote on the sketch, after the full moon had risen over the rooftops of Nuremberg and the Night Watchman had called eleven o'clock. It is interesting to see that he originally sketched the Riot scene (which Alfred Lorenz describes as a chorale fantasy in form, with Beckmesser's serenade as a cantus firmus) as an orchestral piece, and then fitted the text to it quite freely, writing each part on a separate stave, with the orchestral part on three staves. He finished the orchestral sketch on 23 September and, without losing the impetus, went straight on to start the composition sketch of the third act on 2 October.

He described his day to Mathilde Maier, that 'dear, loyal soul': up at seven, breakfast between eight and nine, work until one. At three in the afternoon a long walk, returning between five and six, half an hour with the children in the nursery, teaching little Isolde to walk. Work, while Cosima gave the two older girls a French lesson. At eight tea in his room, nine to ten-thirty dictation of his autobiography. 'And that was that! Every day is like this. It's beginning to do Cosima some good, which she needed. Meanwhile the mastersingers are making progress . . . My finest work: everything is turning out well: I weep and laugh over it.'

'Is there anything more you would like?' he concludes. 'I can't think of anything. I cannot write you my music. We live in the air, out of the world – and – have earned it . . .

Wagner was working with a quite unusual application and vigour, Bülow wrote to Jessie Laussot. Overpowering though the effect was of witnessing the work at such close quarters, he did not think he was deluded in forming the opinion that *Die Meistersinger* would be Wagner's 'most classical (please forgive the banality of the word), most German, ripest and most *generally* accessible work of art . . . You cannot begin to imagine its wealth in terms of absolute music, the Cellini-workmanship in every detail. It is unshakable dogma with me: Wagner is the greatest composer, absolutely the equal of a Beethoven, of a Bach – and much more besides. He is the incarnation of the spirit of German art, its most enduring monument even when German, and perhaps music too, may have become a "dead" language.' (14 August)

There was a new shock in store for Wagner, when Ludwig Schnorr's widow Malvina arrived at Tribschen in November. She brought with her her pupil Isidore von Reutter, who was in nightly communication with the spirit of Schnorr. He had told Isidore that she was to marry the king, and Malvina was to marry Wagner – 'all on express ghostly command'. They had led him a fine dance, he told Mathilde Maier, especially as he had realized that the Reutter girl was an impudent fraud, whom he had had to forbid his house. Frau Schnorr had departed in fury and was now stirring up all kinds of trouble. 'Once again it was like an abscess growing in perfectly healthy flesh, when you've no idea what caused it! In short, there's always something pestering my poor mastersingers.' (15 December)

Frau Schnorr was a friend of Cosima's, but she saw to the bottom of her relationship with Wagner, whereupon her feelings changed to raving jealousy, and she denounced the pair to the king. At first Ludwig simply refused to believe the tale, but later grew puzzled. He wrote to Court Secretary Düfflipp, expressing surprise that the latter should think there was something 'not kosher' (in Ludwig's phrase) about the business of Wagner, Frau von Bülow and Frau Schnorr: 'Can the sorry rumour be true after all? I was never able to bring myself to believe it, but can it really be a question of adultery? – Then alas for it!' (KLRW, V, p. xlix)[9]

Coming to the prelude of the third act Wagner referred to the sketch he had made on the morning of his forty-ninth birthday. 'I was the lonely man then,' he told Cosima later. (BBL 1937, p. 2) A second sketch survives showing the reworking of the original 'profoundly melancholy' 'Wahn' motive, so that we can trace how the diatonic descent of the melodic line came to acquire the expressive inflexion it needed.[10]

The Prize Song, too, in the version Walther sings in Sachs's workshop, was conceived before Wagner actually started the composition sketch of the third act. The sheet of paper is dated '28 September [1866], afternoon, because waiting for C[osima]', while the Abgesang is hastily scribbled in 3/4 time on the back of the sheet (it had figured in the prelude in common time). He wrote the text of the song after the music and gave it to Cosima at midnight on Christmas Eve as a birthday present. It had been granted to him, Cosima told the king, at a time when the world outside had nothing but ugliness and evil for them.

In another letter she told him: 'Today Beckmesser was given his musical entrance after the incredibly beautiful scene between Walther and Sachs. When our friend was playing me the words he had just set, and sang "das waren hochbedürft'ge Meister, von Lebensmüh' bedrängte Geister", we both burst into tears. If only I could send you the music our friend has written for these words.' (DMCW, I, pp. 312f.) Beckmesser's musical entrance had a special significance. The ghostly doings with Malvina Schnorr had prevented Wagner from working for a week, and he had picked the sketch up again at the Marker's enraged outburst 'O Schuster voller Ränke'. Cosima had to laugh out loud when he played her the passage.

He often felt his heart was breaking over the sad, dreadfully disturbing times that lay behind him, Wagner wrote to the king on 11 January 1867. 'And – in the midst of all the turmoil – I am near to finishing *Die Meistersinger*! Who will believe it?' Barely recovered, he had been thinking about a curious dream he had had and suddenly laughed aloud, for at that instant the tune for the Tailors' song on the festival meadow had come to him. The strange, really quite unique character of the work itself had helped him once again: Sachs and Walther had been his doctors.

He had a lot of difficulty with the Prize Song. He decided it was impossible to have the same song twice in the one act: it had to be the same and yet different. Moreover it would have been out of character for Walther to repeat the very personal song, in which he had recounted his dream to Sachs and Eva in the privacy of the workshop, in exactly the same form before the masters and the crowd in the festival meadow. So Wagner changed the text in such a way that the second version of the song interprets the dream. His solution to the musical side of the problem is a stroke of genius. In place of the workshop version with its three stanzas (each in Bar-form)[11] the festival-meadow version consists of only one stanza, but its three sections are expanded so skilfully that the listener is under the impression that there are again three complete stanzas. In fact, if we compare just the first Stollen in each version, we find that only seven bars are the same, and no fewer than sixteen are new in the festival-meadow version; nevertheless, as Alfred Lorenz emphasizes, the listener is perfectly satisfied by the similarity. It was the work of a master to shape the two musical periods so that, although not the same, their relationship is evident.

At last, early in 1867, after so many interruptions and grave crises, Wagner came to the composition of Sachs's final monologue, where he was suddenly overcome with doubts. Cosima told the king she had spent a whole day talking about the ending; Wagner felt that Walther's song concluded the drama and Sachs's speech had nothing to add, but was rather a direct address to the audience by the composer: he would do better to leave it out altogether. 'I pulled such a horrible face at that, and said besides that "Will ohne Meister selig sein" was completely in character for Walther – so he thought it over, although he naturally held to his own opinion. It would not let him rest at night, he wrote the new lines, crossed out [his other version] as I had proposed, and sketched the music as well in pencil.'

The passage in question was that beginning 'Habt acht! Uns dräuen üble Streich' '. The sketch Cosima referred to is in the Wagner Archives in Bayreuth, dated '(at night) 28 Jan. 67'. There is no doubt that the lines, like the essay *German Art and German Politics* written shortly afterwards, reflect something of the political feeling of the period 1866–70. But besides its ideological significance, the new stanza performs a dramatic function as well. Wagner recognized that the original ending was static and did nothing to raise the dramatic temperature. Sachs's prophetic warning here adds a new, stirring emotional element that gives the action – which would otherwise float out on a wave of lyricism induced by Walther's song – a last surprising, dramatic upbeat.

One may indeed make a further observation about this ending that touches on the nature of comedy as a whole. Comedy, Schopenhauer remarks, resolves the sorrows and adversities of human life in pure joy. 'But then it must make haste to let the curtain fall at the moment of joy, so that we do not see what comes after.' That is why every happy ending is slightly unsatisfactory for those who see further and deeper than the majority. By changing the focus of attention, in the last moments of *Die Meistersinger*, from the joys and sorrows of the protagonists to something higher than purely personal concerns, the fate and the mission of art, Wagner found an incomparable means of avoiding the dangers of a customary happy ending. The added lines remind us of the realities of life once again, but only in order to raise us to a higher ideality.

With the dismissal of 'Pfi' and 'Pfo' and the appointment of Prince Hohenlohe, all obstacles to the king's artistic plans seemed to have been removed. He was determined to usher in a new Periclean age. 'On the very day that von der Pfordten left the Foreign Ministry in Munich a royal decree created me "kapellmeister in extraordinary to the Bavarian court",' Bülow wrote to Raff. 'That is, hofkapellmeister in partibus infidelium. I solicit your silent commiseration.' Semper was permitted to show the king the long-awaited model of the festival theatre and was appointed architect in charge of the project with the 'royal word and handshake'. The plan for a journal, to be the organ of the new political and artistic movement, also moved nearer realization: in May the Foreign Ministry opened negotiations with the Viennese publicist Julius Fröbel, whom Wagner had recommended as editor.

But it soon became apparent that the obstacles had not only lain in external opposition, but were also rooted in the king's own complex personality. As long as he was talking enthusiastically about his plans in the abstract, he was with Wagner in heart and soul; but when it came to their practical execution he allowed 'all matters of energy and of principle, everything that goes beyond purely personal amiability' to be set at naught by officials. (Wagner to Röckel, 29 January 1867) It has been conjectured whether the king was merely weak or devious, but this schizoid contradictoriness combined with a perfectly clear conscience points rather to a psychopathic element in his character. Wagner did not express any views on it, but he wrote in the Annals on 17 March, after seeing the king: 'Physiognomic change.' (KLRW, II, p. 6)

He was delighted at the news of Ludwig's engagement to his cousin Princess Sophie, of which the king lost no time in informing him by telegram. (22 January) When he made the princess's acquaintance in Munich he was impressed by her unpretentious nature, and by the obvious love and concern she felt for the king. 'If only you could be wholly united with her soon, soon,' he wrote to the king with foreboding. (16 March) Liszt, who was able to observe the young couple during a performance of *Tannhäuser*, remarked: 'Les ardeurs matrimoniales de sa Majesté semblent fort tempérées. Some suspect that the wedding will be postponed for ever.' The termination of the engagement 'by mutual agreement' was announced officially on 11 October. In explaining to Cosima how the engagement had come about and how he had suffered under it, Ludwig showed a clarity in self-analysis that is almost uncanny in so young a man. (DMCW, I. pp. 379ff.)

Wagner discovered that the governmental changes still did not mean an end to his difficulties as early as 6 January, when the king, at Hohenlohe's instigation, asked him to postpone a planned visit to Munich: 'A large faction claims that there is a very close connection between Hohenlohe's appointment and your visit.' Hohenlohe's personal physician of many years' standing, Dr. Schanzenbach, undertook to explain the minister's reasons to Wagner in a letter, to which the latter replied on 17 January with a comprehensive review of the political events before and after his departure from Munich.[12]

At the end of January Schanzenbach went to Tribschen in person, to acquaint Wagner with Hohenlohe's political plans and to recruit Wagner's powerful influence on their behalf. The prince does not mention this mission in his memoirs, and it has been questioned whether it actually took place, but it is confirmed by a letter Wagner wrote to Röckel, swearing him to 'ignorance' of the visit. (KLRW, IV, p. 181) Obviously Hohenlohe would not want the help an opera composer could give him to become common knowledge.

A few weeks later Schanzenbach had to report new scheming against Hohenlohe in circles close to the king. 'Stand by Prince Hohenlohe in preference to anybody, to anybody,' Wagner implored Ludwig. 'If he succumbed to the plotting against him I should regard the misfortune as immeasurable. For once, just this once, stand firm. Whatever may be said against him, for once at last you *must* stand by the man of your choice, or you are lost.' (21 February)

Having finished the composition sketch of the last act of *Meistersinger* on 5 March, he would have preferred to get on with the scoring of it 'unmolested and forgotten', but he made the long-postponed journey to Munich at last. While he was there he paid a call on Hohenlohe. The prince set the ball rolling by remarking that they were united by their devotion to the king and by the hatred of the ultramontanes. Wagner spoke of the way the king had been tormented to the point of twice contemplating abdication, then moved on to Bavaria's role in German affairs, to his own art and finally to the Cabinet. He stressed the importance of Hohenlohe's remaining in office. The prince replied that that did not depend on himself; he could not guarantee that the king's confidence in him would not be undermined by someone else; his uncertainty was the greater because, according to custom, the king communicated with him only through the Cabinet. To Wagner's objection that that could not be allowed to continue, Hohenlohe reminded him of the grave danger of issuing a challenge to the Cabinet: he – Wagner – knew that better than anyone![13]

The situation in foreign affairs all too soon gave Wagner occasion to urge Hohenlohe's policies on the king. Louis Napoleon attempted to assuage French disappointment over the outcome of the Austro-Prussian war by annexing Luxemburg at virtually no cost to France. Prussia prevented this, though without exercising her right to occupy Luxemburg herself. While the negotiations were still in the balance Bismarck put out feelers in Munich to discover the likely Bavarian reaction in the event of a Franco–Prussian war (April 1867). An important letter from Wagner to the king dates from this time, urging that it was obvious that every sympathy in

Bavaria was turning towards Prussia, while the Austrian party was still working hard to maintain its influence. If that went on then eventually Austria would simply annex Bavaria, and there would be no more question then of Germany or of Bavaria. 'Therefore, firmly and honourably, an alliance with Prussia.' That would preserve the integrity of Germany and would still permit Austria to join the alliance later. When he had told Prince Hohenlohe of his ideas, Wagner assured the king, the unemotional minister's face had lit up. 'Forwards! Forwards! Now is the time to throw the weight of Bavaria into the scales with Prussia: thus you will make yourself the leader of southern Germany, and Austria – must follow you – must! – There: that was my last will and testament!' (25 April)[14]

Of the king's plans for the arts, his favourite project, the festival theatre, was the first to go by the board. When Röckel told Wagner of the strong opposition in Munich to the clearance that would be necessary along the proposed route of Ludwig's processional way, Wagner answered that the last thing he had on his mind was a Wagner Theatre, let alone a Wagner Avenue. In any case he was used by now to keeping calm when heated resolutions were passed, and waiting until natural developments damped the fire down and poured water over it. Court Secretary Düfflipp had told him recently that the money would be found, by 'economies etc.', at least to start building the theatre and keep it going 'doucement' for five or six years. (29 January) The 'economies', however, failed to be made, as all available monies were swallowed up in the preparations for the king's marriage: the wedding coach alone was said to have cost a million gulden.

Ludwig's second project, the school of music, was almost ruined by Bülow. When his appointment as court kapellmeister and director of the Royal School of Music was at last officially confirmed, the terms of his contract were expressed so vaguely that he felt obliged 'to answer the allhighest proposals with his simple refusal'. He was only able to serve a king who also thought and acted like a king and did not merely have the sensibilities of an artist, he told Raff. In discussing the matter face to face with Düfflipp, he must have referred to himself as a 'Prussian nobleman', an expression Wagner deplored in a letter to the king. The latter had been gracious enough not to pay any attention to Bülow's insane behaviour. 'I could not treat it so lightly and my decision to break with him completely . . . had really already been taken.' (20 February)

On the morning of 17 February Cosima gave birth to Wagner's second daughter, Eva. When her labour started Wagner sat in the next room and softly played Walther's Dream Song.[15] Bülow arrived at Tribschen in the afternoon. According to his second wife, he stood at Cosima's bedside in tears and said 'Je pardonne', to which she replied, 'Il ne faut pas pardonner, il faut comprendre.' Max Morold, her biographer, adds: 'Bülow had long understood, and *because* he understood he also forgave her from the bottom of his heart.' The child was christened Eva Maria three days later in Lucerne. Driving home from the church, Wagner told the king, he had sung to himself Sachs's lines (with some minor alterations obviously to relate the words to himself):

> gar manche Not in Leben,
> manch ehlich Glück daneben –
> Kindtauf', Geschäfte, Zwist und Streit: –
> wem's dann noch will gelingen,
> ein schönes Lied zu singen, –
> seht, Meister nennt man den!

A great misfortune had misfallen the king's faithful servants, he went on in this veiled confession, and if they should recover from it, it would be of no little significance. (20 February)

In order to preserve the appearances of the Bülow marriage in the eyes of the king and the world, Cosima had to leave Tribschen on 16 April and go back to Munich with her husband. En route she telegraphed Wagner:

> Es ist bestimmt in Gottes Rat,
> daß man vom Liebsten, was man hat,
> muß scheiden.

('It is determined in God's counsels that we must part from what we hold most dear'; see above, vol. I, p. 253.)

He wrote in the Brown Book that evening: 'I have probably never been so sad in all my life as at this moment!! – How easy it is to say that, and how inexpressible it is! I went home on foot and sank down exhausted. A short leaden sleep . . . dredged up all the misery of my life as if from the bottommost depths of my soul. I yearn for a severe illness and death. I do not want any more – will not have any more! Would it but have an end, an end!' (KLRW, II, pp. xxi f.)

It was the king's dearest wish that Wagner would spend his birthday with him at Starnberg. Although Wagner's own instinct warned him against it, rightly, and he excused himself on the grounds of needing to work on *Meistersinger*, Cosima, fearing Ludwig's displeasure, persuaded him to change his mind, in a vigorous exchange of telegrams. 'Come here . . . otherwise complete break. Take last wish to heart, will write no more.' (19 May) So Wagner arrived on the morning of his birthday at Starnberg, where the king had rented the Villa Prestele for him, so as to have him nearby. They spent the afternoon together at Schloss Berg. As the villa was not yet ready for him to move in, he went to Munich to stay with the Bülows for a few days. In the evening various events were put on to celebrate his birthday, including a concert in the Westendhalle of excerpts from *Tannhäuser* and *Lohengrin*, and *Das Liebesmahl der Apostel*. Public interest was so great that hundreds had to stand in tight-packed rows.

He moved into Villa Prestele on 30 May – and the king left on 31 May on a sightseeing trip to the Wartburg. Then, late at night on 6 June, there was a knock at Wagner's door. It was Ludwig, who stayed with him for several hours, discussing the model performances of *Lohengrin* and *Tannhäuser* that Bülow was to rehearse under Wagner's supervision. Unfortunately Wagner had recommended his old companion-in-arms from Dresden, Tichatschek, for the role of Lohengrin. It then occurred to him that this might have been a mistake, and he tried to prepare Ludwig for the ageing tenor by telling him that he would be seeing a Holbein rather than a Dürer. He embraced his old friend after the dress rehearsal, greatly moved and delighted that his voice still possessed the same firm, silvery timbre that he remembered. But the king was appalled: this 'knight of the dolorous countenance' was so far from his ideal of the Swan Knight that he dismissed Tichatschek, in spite of Wagner's pleas.

He could not help but feel humiliated by this, Wagner wrote to Ludwig the next day, and in order to get over it he had no choice but to return to Tribschen. 'Farewell, deeply beloved friend!' He heard nothing from the king for a fortnight, then a long letter arrived: 'Lord of my life . . . I kiss the hand that has chastised me!' (21 June)

Ludwig's third project, the newspaper, got under way more auspiciously. After Fröbel had acquainted Hohenlohe with his editorial programme, a state subvention of 20,000 gulden for fifteen months was approved. Wagner and Fröbel were agreed that the paper should be run in a spirit of 'humane patriotism'. Wagner himself was to contribute a series of articles on cultural policy, but otherwise his artistic standpoint was to be represented by Heinrich Porges, 'this diligent, truly industrious, good young man of refined feelings'. That Wagner should have chosen a Jew for this task is an interesting reflection on his alleged anti-Semitism. He hoped that Semper might be persuaded to write something about the spirit of his style of architecture and its application to the crafts, but he advised Fröbel to take his time over finding the right man to deal with literature: on no account should battalions of 'intellectual' collaborators be allowed to draw up in too much of a hurry in this field. (2 September)

The first, trial issue of the *Süddeutsche Presse* appeared on 24 September, and Wagner's articles on German art and German politics began publication in the evening edition. 'By God, anyone who is not delighted, who is not persuaded and won over by the magic of the discourse, the profundity of the spirit that manifests itself therein, does not deserve to live,' the king exclaimed. (21 November) Relations between Wagner and Fröbel were soon clouded. 'Wagner says "beauty serves no end",' Fröbel wrote to Cosima on 10 December, 'but I say, what serves no end is useless, good for nothing, should not exist.' 'What you say about the theory of beauty', she replied, 'surprised me all the more because I thought that since Kant (and Goethe and Schiller after him) the principle of beauty as something that is an end in itself was established beyond question.' This illustrated a division between the artist and the politician that was to prove impossible to bridge in the long run. 'If Fröbel believes the world will be saved by the Americanization of Europe . . . we should appear very strange neighbours in the future,' Wagner commented. He felt inclined to withdraw from the *Süddeutsche Presse* at once, without fuss, simply in the name of common sense, and edit an independent paper, *Der deutsche Stil*, but he would first publish the last two articles in the series on German art and politics.

'Decide for yourself,' Cosima wrote to Fröbel on 19 December, after hearing this from Wagner. 'Do you think it possible to go on together? Wagner *can no other*. That is his strength, but also the danger, in his dealings with the world.'

However, the matter had already been decided in another quarter. That same morning a government official presented himself at the editorial office with an order from the Ministry of the Interior, commanding in the king's name the immediate cessation of the appearance of Wagner's articles. 'His Majesty regards these articles as suicidal.'

'Of course: I write all of it for you alone in reality,' Wagner had admitted in a letter to the king of 30 November, 'I might almost say as a substitute for our conversations at Hohenschwangau . . . I have great hopes of the impression my insights will make on the better sort of those who are themselves active in the theatre; perhaps that ought to be our chief hope.' And he went on percipiently: 'Those honoured gentlemen, the officials of the court and government, will probably be the last . . .' His instinct did not deceive him. The government official, Otto Freiherr von Völderndorff, still boasted in 1900 of the success he had once had in 'executing an express royal command which was the beginning of the end for that tapeworm'.[16] (KLRW, II, p. 209)

Another important event took place in the autumn of that year. Liszt, who had come to Munich to attend the model performances, took the opportunity to see his daughter as well and attend a party in celebration of her nameday at the house of their friend the painter Wilhelm von Kaulbach, where his attitude towards her was affectionate and attentive. This gave the lie to the rumour current in Catholic circles that the Abbé still condemned her behaviour. From Munich he went incognito to Tribschen, where he arrived on 9 October, to have a serious discussion with Wagner.

'Liszt's visit: dreaded but a pleasant relief,' the Annals record. It is not hard to guess the subject of the six hours' private conversation they had together. Wagner sent Cosima a telegram the next morning: 'One word only. Agreeably pacific guest left early today. Completely sleepless but hopeful.'

The two friends had sat up till past midnight, with Liszt's travelling companion Richard Pohl and Wagner's 'apprentice' Hans Richter. Liszt played *Die Meistersinger* from the manuscript, while Wagner sang all the voice parts. Liszt's sight-reading from a score he had never set eyes on before was a unique experience, Pohl recalled. 'I have never heard a finer performance of *Die Meistersinger*. The truth of the expression, the beauty of the phrasing, the clarity in every detail was thrilling . . . The third act delighted him most of all – nobody could have written anything like that except

Wagner, he said when he stopped in delight and admiration to play a passage over again.'

Wagner was greatly changed in appearance, Liszt wrote to Princess Wittgenstein. He had grown thin and his face was deeply furrowed. But his genius was as vigorous as ever. Liszt went back to Munich for another week and while he was there told people he had been to see Wagner. 'That was the best thing I did. I feel as if I had seen Napoleon on St Helena.'

The 'apprentice' mentioned above, Hans Richter, a horn-player in the orchestra of the Vienna opera, had become Wagner's amanuensis a year earlier, when he was barely twenty-four. He had a room on the first floor of Tribschen, and while Wagner was scoring *Meistersinger* downstairs in his study Richter was making a fair copy of the completed pages for Schott's. Once Wagner asked his advice over the point in the finale of the second act where the horn takes up the melody of Beckmesser's serenade: was it possible to play it at that tempo? It was possible, Richter replied, but it would sound very odd and nasal. Excellent, Wagner exclaimed, that was exactly what he wanted. In all other respects, Richter recorded, he always knew exactly how the score was going to sound.

What Richard Strauss admired most about the *Meistersinger* orchestra was its moderation: although it was approximately the same as that of Beethoven's C minor Symphony, with the addition of valve horn, a third trumpet, tuba and harp, yet it produced quite different and original sound-combinations in every bar. He mentions Wagner's writing for the string section, the five parts often reduced to four by the omission of the double basses, which makes full use of the range of registers in the part-writing, so that all the upper partials are heard, for instance, at the words 'Das schönste Weib' in the Prize Song; or producing a fortissimo pizzicato chord to express Beckmesser's nervous start when he thinks he hears mocking laughter; or, finally, making the effect of distant organ-playing with the whole section playing pianissimo. Wagner's treatment of the clarinet throughout its four different registers also wins Strauss's praise: when David is complaining of Lene's not giving him any supper because of Walther's failure in the singing trial, the solo clarinet dives out of its cantabile region and down by two octaves to where it suddenly takes on a cold, menacing timbre. Strauss quotes any number of examples of the valve horn's 'Protean nature', from the Riot scene, where it is the ringleader of the wildest parts of the fighting, to the warm-hearted solo accompanying Sachs's 'Schön Dank, mein Jung . . .'[17]

'This evening on the stroke of eight the last C was written. I solicit your silent concelebration. Sachs,' Wagner telegraphed Bülow on 24 October. The end of the autograph score is in fact inscribed: 'End of the *Meistersinger*. Tribschen, Thursday 24 October 1867, 8 p.m.'

After his recent exertions and emotional disturbances, Wagner felt the need for a brief holiday. Snow had already fallen in the Alps, and getting to Italy would take too much time, so he decided to spend six days in the 'old, strange nest of his fate, Paris'. But this time he found that the interest he could muster in the 'curio' was significantly diminished. The streets he had once known so well had been torn up and he hated the new buildings so much that he could hardly bring himself to look at them. He lived quietly, away from the public eye, in the Grand Hôtel and looked up only one friend, Charles Truinet.

In the Annals he wrote two catchwords: 'schoolchildren; butter-flies'. On the final day of the Universal Exhibition he bought a collection of large, brightly coloured Indian butterflies from an impecunious dealer, which later adorned the study in Wahnfried. The other experience made so indelible an impression on him that he was still gripped with emotion when he recalled it in the last year of his life. Trying to leave the exhibition hall he was prevented by the entrance of thousands of schoolchildren. He stood for nearly an hour watching this youthful horde who represented an entire future, and saw prefigured in it every vice and misfortune that could befall the population of a metropolis. His description recalls Balzac's portrayal of the population of a great city in *La fille aux yeux d'or*. Wagner went on: 'All this was under the supervision of teachers, most of them members of religious orders, wearing the grotesquely elegant habits of the newfangled priesthood; themselves without a will of their own, stern and strict, but obeying rather than commanding. All completely soulless' – except for one young sister in a teaching order, who was in charge of a file of girls, and in whose face he read an inexpressibly beautiful concern for others which was the very soul of her life. She symbolized for him the spirit of a 'nation vraiment généreuse', as he described the French in a letter to Catulle and Judith Mendès, governed under the Second Empire by a rigid, soulless educational system.

Wagner travelled to Munich on 23 December, to spend Christmas with the Bülows, loaded with all sorts of 'Parisian toys' for the children. He suffered another unpleasant surprise. Fröbel had told the king that Cosima was involved in political machinations, and Düfflipp was sent to warn them on 27 December. 'I am thunderstruck,' Ludwig told his minister; 'the refined, intelligent Frau von Bülow is devoting herself to gutter journalism, writing these infamous articles! Truly, I would not have thought the cultivated Cosima capable of such a knavish trick!' 'The next day to the king,' Wagner wrote in the Annals. '$2\frac{1}{2}$ hours of reconciliations and apologies to C.' 'One thing I implore of you, beloved friend,' Ludwig wrote to Cosima, 'forget the last conversation with Düfflipp . . . I gladly take everything back; it was a passing wisp of fog.' It was a matter of the utmost urgency that Fröbel should leave Munich for good now that the king had seen into his 'black soul'.

All the same, Wagner thought it prudent not to take the initiative in resuming his correspondence with the king, and it was not until 9 March that Ludwig broke the silence: 'I cannot go on like this any longer, with no news of you!' The reserve with which Wagner replied drew a further outburst: 'I will tear, tear with all my strength at my friend's heart, until the wall that keeps us apart collapses.'

In the meantime Wagner had again come to Munich, on 17 March. Two days later a city-court writ was served on him, demanding the payment of a total of 2197 gulden 32 kreuzer to Advocate Simmerl acting on behalf of Widow Klepperbein of Dresden. The document, which is kept in the Wagner Archives as a curiosity, authorizes the court messenger to arrest Wagner, if he does not at once settle the principal and the interest on the debt, and 'to bring him to the New Tower'. Wilhelmine Klepperbein was a motherly friend who had lent him money in Dresden in 1847. God might know, Wagner wrote to Düfflipp, under what pretext the old lady had been persuaded to issue the document. For his part, in the letter covering an advance on Wagner's allowance from the Cabinet Treasury, Düfflipp could express only repugnance at yet another proceeding carried out in the shabbiest fashion. (KLRW, II, p. 9; IV, p. 260; V, p. 76)

Another financial settlement claimed Wagner's attention at the same time. Since the plan to build a festival theatre, which the king had entrusted to Semper three years before, and confirmed with word and handshake only the previous year, now seemed to have been abandoned for good, Semper presented the Treasury, through his lawyer Dr von Schauss, with a bill for 42,305 gulden in payment for his plans and models. At the same time Schauss asked Wagner to ensure that the settlement was made in a way that would not harm Semper. While Wagner was still toying with the idea of acting personally as go-betweeen with his old friend in Zürich, he learned that the king had broken with Semper and would not permit his name to be mentioned in his presence. It was ten months before the architect's account was finally settled, and yet another ambitious scheme ended in discord.

Wagner returned to Tribschen on 22 April 1868, without having seen the king once in the five weeks. He occupied himself with minor literary projects: a preface to the second edition of *Opera and Drama*, which he dedicated to Constantin Frantz, and his *Reminiscences of Ludwig Schnorr von Carolsfeld*, from which I have already quoted. (RWGS, VIII, pp. 195ff.; 177ff.) His prevailing mood was of an enervating melancholy. He noted in the Annals: 'Buddhism: rethought *Sieger*'; and he outlined a mythological and philosophical background for the work in the Brown Book: 'Creation of a new world: the beings from the Dhyana descend to the world again . . . Paradise is lost. The music of the Brahman world recalls it as memory: it leads to truth.' (KLRW, V, p. 159) He also wrote the opening of a Funeral Symphony to *Romeo and Juliet*, with a melancholy A♭ minor melody as principal theme.[18]

Cosima and her children arrived for a short visit in the middle of May. The jottings in the Annals illustrate his feelings: 'Great emotional turbulence: continual new difficulties. Inexpressible pangs of love. Am tempted to flight and disappearance.' Then all at once: 'Continual rapid change: blissful solace. Deliverance essential.' Their need for a decision to be made, once and for all, grew more and more urgent, set aside only for the sake of *Die Meistersinger*, which was soon to be performed.

On 21 May Wagner returned to Munich to stay with the Bülows and supervise the rehearsals. 'A present: my mother's portrait! Great, profound happiness!' he noted on his birthday; 'Lunch with the king on the Roseninsel.' 'What a day! What a life! What a memory!' he wrote to Ludwig in the evening after his return from Schloss Berg. Evidently he talked to him about *Die Sieger* on that occasion, for a few days later he sent him the copy of Burnouf where he had found his source material twelve years previously.

But as with the Volsunga saga he realized how much his imagination had shaped and developed the material in the interim. (31 May)

Meanwhile rehearsals had started. Wagner insisted on a faithful recreation of old Nuremberg: the sketches for the sets had been drawn 'on location' a year before. The street fight, too, was to be arranged by Madame Lucile Grahn 'with the utmost choreographic precision'. 'Singers good,' he recorded, 'but management [Perfall] evasive in everything.' His greatest anguish was caused by an obscure, heavy sense of 'profound hostility and alienation from Hans'. His friends Cornelius and Weissheimer had no idea of what it was, apart from the exhausting rehearsals, that was oppressing him and making him irritable and impatient in those weeks. '*Now* association with him is not exactly enjoyable,' Draeseke wrote, 'but later, perhaps in thirty or forty years' time, we shall be *envied* by the entire world, because he is so gigantic a phenomenon, and his stature will only grow and grow after his death.'[19]

When Schott's published Tausig's superb piano score of the work, Wagner did not forget to send two copies to Editha von Rhaden in St Petersburg, for herself and Grand Duchess Helene: 'If you are kind enough to keep it, then I may hope not to be forgotten by you, just as you, noble lady, are unforgettable to me.' (7 June)

Gradually visitors began to assemble in Munich for the première. In the Annals Wagner mentions, among others, Mathilde Maier – and Jessie Laussot, with whom he wanted to run away to the Far East eighteen years before. 'Nobody can write like I can,' he noted after her name, evidently recording something she had said after seeing a rehearsal. '[*German*] *Art and Politics* written to her from the heart.' He took particular note of a group of French friends: curiously enough it was they, he wrote, who pounced on the popular element in the work and acclaimed it. 'French enthusiasts: German detraction.'

After the last ensemble rehearsal, attended by a considerable audience, he spoke a few cordial words to his artists: the moment of performance, upon them at last after so much hard work, was of decisive importance; for it was their task to show the eminence and dignity to which German art could rise, if people would dedicate themselves to its service in all seriousness. This simple speech profoundly moved all who heard it. There could have been few among them, Newman remarks, who did not realize that with Wagner a new day had dawned for German art. (NLRW, IV, p. 141)

The king attended the dress rehearsal on 19 June, which was in effect a full performance. After he had written to Wagner that same evening saying that it had exceeded his highest expectations, Wagner replied: 'I knew it: He understands me!! Impossible that He should not have sensed and clearly recognized, behind the comic wrappings of popular humour, the profound sadness, the lamentation, the cry of distress of the enchained poetry.' (20 June)

He had sworn in a dark hour not to attend the first performance of *Die Meistersinger*, but in the event, out of consideration for the king and his artists, he was there in the theatre on Sunday 21 June. He was sitting with Cosima at the back of a box and the prelude had already started, when the king sent for him to join him in the Royal Box. 'Had to hear *Meistersinger* at his side, under the public gaze. Very tired and exhausted. Cosima sad that I didn't stay with her.' In vain the audience called for the work's creator at the end of the first act. After the second, at the king's insistence, he advanced to the parapet of the box and acknowledged the applause without speaking, deeply moved, and again after the third act. A murmur ran through the audience: 'Horace at the side of Augustus.' And a newspaper reported that one involuntarily looked up at the ceiling to see if it was not about to collapse.

'Took my leave of Parzival after the performance,' Wagner goes on in the Annals. Presciently he told Ludwig that they would not see each other again for a long time. (KLRW, III, p. 79) It was another eight years, in fact, in Bayreuth. In the ancient republics deserving citizens were accorded royal honours for a day, he wrote to the king: 'The purple mantle was permitted to rest on their shoulders. The next day, humbly, they retired again into the quietness of their private life.' On 24 June he arrived back at Tribschen, whence he wrote to Bülow, to thank him once more for his conducting: Wagner thought it 'incomparable', a view shared by a number of conductors who had come to Munich specially to hear the performance. He also expressed a few wishes with regard to the remaining performances, above all concerning the 'discretion', the 'conscious restraining of the orchestral volume', in the symphonic accompaniment to the musical dialogue on the stage. 'Lucky for us, that we have nothing more to face!' And he signed himself 'Lykurgos, far from Sparta'. (25 June)

Cosima gave the king the autograph score of *Meistersinger* as a Christmas present in 1867 (it is now in the Germanisches

Nationalmuseum in Nuremberg). For his birthday on 25 August 1868, Wagner gave the king a dedicatory copy of the engraved score. (KLRW, V, p. 207) The poem of dedication ends:

> Nun lasse demutsvoll das Glück mich büßen,
> daß ich so herrlich hoch Dir nahe stand:
> hat ferne Dir der Meister weichen müssen,
> drückt' er zum Abschied Dir die Freundeshand;
> nun lieg' sein Werk zu seines Königs Füßen,
> dort wo es Schutz und höchste Gnade fand.
> Und durft' ihm wonnig eine Weise glücken,
> die mög' ans Herz nun hold der Freund sich drücken!

('Now may fortune allow me humbly to repay the honour of having been so close to your glory; when the master had to go far away from you he pressed your hand in friendship and farewell; now let his work lie at his king's feet, where it was accorded protection and highest grace. And if a melody gave him pleasure, may his friend now press it to his heart in happiness!' KLRW, II, pp. 240f.)

Otto Wesendonk attended two of the later performances. Hearing Pogner's address to the masters, he will have remembered Wagner once writing to him that when he read the text to the Grand Duchess of Baden, the particular warmth in his rendering of the part of Pogner gave her the impression that the character had associations with some beneficent experience in his own life. 'I was quite delighted [by her comment]. I really do feel that in the love with which I have created this part – musically, too, now – I have set up a monument to a friend.' (26 July 1862) Though we must deplore the fact that that friend is not treated as he deserved in *Mein Leben* – for which we may blame the coolness of Easter 1864 – Otto Wesendonk's abiding *musical* memorial is in the figure of the art-loving goldsmith:

> Was wert die Kunst und was sie gilt,
> das ward ich der Welt zu zeigen gewillt.

Part VI: *Der Ring des Nibelungen* (II) (1868–1877)

27

From Tribschen to Bayreuth

I

'Mood: Siegfried's exultant theme . . . recurred, persisted,' Wagner telegraphed Cosima on his way back to Tribschen. But he soon fell prey to depression, aggravated by a feverish cold. 'Ensuing great clarity as to my condition and the state of our affairs,' he wrote in the Annals. 'Too deeply despondent to make any move: in the fate of my relationship with Cosima and Hans recognized the reason for the impotence of all desire. Everything null; Munich experiments complete failure. Seemed essential never to return there.' He was determined to force a decisive issue in his relations with Cosima and with Munich alike, even though it meant new struggles and disturbances on both fronts.

He had realized during the *Meistersinger* rehearsals, when he had had to fight for every one of his wishes against the opposition of Perfall, the theatre intendant, that any future collaboration with the Munich opera, even as guest producer, would be impossible. It was time now to take the last step on the long road to the realization of his idea for a festival, and to take it in the direction of his original idea of a theatre of his own where, even if it was built of wood, he would be master under his own roof.

Where the requests from other theatres to perform *Die Meistersinger* were concerned, he had to resign himself in advance to the impossibility of protecting the work from distortions and to the prospect of its at least surviving as an 'ordinary theatrical success'. He proposed not to worry any further about it, he told Schott. 'The work itself . . . will live on; but how?' (To King Ludwig, 14 October 1868)

Nevertheless *Die Meistersinger* made the general public begin to realize, for the first time, that what was at stake here was not just the career of one operatic composer but German art itself. Wagner was all the more angry, therefore, when the friend of his youth, his 'discoverer' Heinrich Laube, published a scurrilous article about it in the Vienna *Neue Freie Presse*, Hanslick's paper. Laube had applied for the post of intendant at the Munich opera in 1867 and blamed Wagner for his failure to obtain it. In reality it was the king who turned him down, being reluctant to have a commoner in the post, while Wagner took some pains to find an acceptable alternative for his friend. 'Read Laube's letter,' he wrote to Bülow. 'Believe me, you could do a lot worse than him. If Perfall was appointed, he could hardly ask for a better chief producer or technical director.' (3 October 1867)

Wagner vented his feelings at Laube's attack in three sonnets. (RWGS, XII, pp. 373f.) In the meantime Laube had become director of the theatre in Leipzig. 'Dear Laube,' Wagner wrote on 6 March 1869, 'You would give me cause for sincere gratitude if you were to use your position at the Leipzig Stadttheater to ensure that my operas were absolutely never given there again.'

Cosima had promised Wagner in Munich to follow him a week later. Her departure was delayed, and before she could leave her relationship with Wagner was once again denounced to the king. Röckel's gossiping was to blame, and the incident led to a complete rupture between the two old brothers-in-arms, but it also hastened the decision that had to be taken: Wagner sent for Cosima to come to him at once. 'She comes 22 July. Welcoming the children,' he noted in the Annals. 'Reports difficulties over decision: Plutonic and Neptunian solutions! – Agreed on the main issue.'

Peter Cornelius, who spent five days at Tribschen in August, was impressed by the patriarchal life Wagner led in surroundings that were a standing invitation to dreaming and composition. And when, during his stay, the Parisian impresario Pasdeloup made enquiries about *Lohengrin* and *Meistersinger*, while Signora Giovanna Lucca, the wife of the Milan music publisher, arrived in person with an offer of 50,000 francs for the Italian publishing rights to his works, Peter could not restrain his astonishment over the way 'Wagner's stock is now rising insanely'. Wagner himself was to be amused by Lucca's announcement of the forthcoming score of *Rheingold*. 'Who would have thought it?' he wrote to Schott. 'The barber of Seville sings about the "prodigious, omnipotent metal", but it's intriguing to see it turn into *Oro del Rheno*!' (Autumn 1870)

A passage in the Annals reveals his private mood: 'Melancholy and passionate days.' On 19 and 22 August he drafted a scenario in the Brown Book of a drama on the subject of Luther's marriage, in which the character of a wholly personal confession is more pronounced than in any other of his dramatic conceptions.

The first scene is set in the Wartburg, where Luther took refuge after the Diet of Worms. Dreadfully disturbed at this turning point in his life's work, he has opened the window, and the mildness of the air, the view over green countryside, the song of a bird and a draught of Einbeck beer all help to calm him. Then he is suddenly visited by the memory of the enigmatic look of a woman, containing the peace of ignorance, refreshing gentleness, certainty and moderation. But would it not be a humiliation, if the man in whom a whole world is in ferment submitted to the yoke of a woman? Is it not a trick of the devil? It is something other than the solace of nature. The words that he now has to pronounce to himself are spoken by the hand that gives him the drink, the lips that bless it: 'Brother, forget and remember!'

But if Catharina's blonde plaits fall over the pillow, will they not also fall across his desk? 'Exactly! That would be worth trying . . . It's there, in the priest's pride, that the devil lurks: I must drive him out! I'll take a wife, and it shall be Catharina.'

The sketch contains only a few sentences outlining the final scene, the wedding celebrations, but they indicate the general tenor of the whole. The chorus to the words 'Wine, women and song' harks back to Wagner's reflections on Buddha and Luther in the dark spring of 1864, on the shores of the Lake of Zürich. And if Lucas Cranach figures far more prominently among the guests than Philipp Melanchthon, then it shows Wagner is invoking Protestant *art* as the living testimony to the spirit of Luther.

As in *Die Meistersinger*, the limits of the stage are transcended at the end and attention directed away from the characters of the drama to the life of the nation. 'Genial indication of the goals of the German "rebirth" through philosophy, poetry and music – prefigured in the evolution of Protestantism and given popular expression in Luther's marriage.'

Wagner was to return to the sketch again, notably at a significant point in the writing of *Parsifal*. On 1 September, again in the Brown Book, he sketched a 'comedy in one act' to follow it, which satirizes the theatrical tribulations he had to contend with all his working life; the setting, in a third-rate touring company, is vividly reminiscent of his description of the Bethmann troupe in Lauchstädt. 'Counter to serious depression', he wrote beneath it.

Though Wagner and Cosima were agreed on the 'main issue', the necessity of her divorce, they were now faced with the task of overcoming public and private obstacles and the choice of a 'Plutonic or Neptunian' solution. They thought they would arrive soonest at a clear view if they had a complete change of scene. On 14 September, accompanied by Wagner's servant Jakob Stocker, the faithful Verena's husband, they set off for a holiday in northern Italy.

In Genoa – 'wonderful Genoa, loved from earlier days' – Wagner took Cosima to the street with the palazzos of the nobility where, fifteen years before, alone in the world, he had first felt the spell cast by an Italian city. 'Great joy. Cosima full of life,' he noted in the Annals. In Milan, where they called on the Luccas, heavy rain began to fall and as they started back they heard reports of flooding. 'Bellinzona. Wait or turn back?' After two days they continued their journey. From Biasca onwards the Ticino was swollen to a lake, bridges were down and further progress was possible only on foot. Stepping out from Giornico they were surprised by a dreadful thunderstorm: 'A most terrifying hour.' In the Lavorgo valley with its waterfalls they began a long trek through the mud: 'Lanterns! Broken bridges: through the water.' In this manner they reached Faido, whose woods and orchards had been turned into a watery waste. They found accommodation of a sort in the Hôtel de la Poste: 'Sharing one room with Cosima. Noah's Flood continues: further advance by carriage impossible. Three foul but profound days. 3 October (Saturday): very low spirits. Cosima writing. Close to death.' What Cosima was writing was obviously the letter in which she informed Bülow of the decision she had taken. 'Sunday, 4 October, still pouring . . . indecision: the road increasingly difficult. Post-chaises in caravans. Midday, decide to go on. Off at 1.30. Cosima in oilskins. Pouring with rain. Terrible march: four hours to go the same number of post-hours. Arrival in Airolo. (Coupé!) Spent the night. 5th, morning, posted over the Gotthard (with difficulty) . . . 6th (Tuesday) arrived home. What did our fate mean by it?'

'I've never met a woman with courage like that,' Jakob Stocker declared, 'sharing the most awful hardships without a word of complaint.'

An entry in the Annals betrays that Wagner and Cosima were not yet agreed about everything. 'Understanding and agreement. Melancholy, most important days. Cosima's promise.' On 14 October she set off back to Munich to talk things over with Hans once and for all. Wagner went with her as far as Augsburg. Before leaving he wrote to the king, admitting for the first time what he had hitherto kept from him.

On 14 September he had undertaken a journey to Italy for a holiday, he wrote. A stroke of fate, whose meaning he was still striving in vain to guess, had delayed his return journey, so that he had been caught among the landslides and floods of the Ticino and had had a forewarning of his end. His incredible exertions had been shared by a suffering woman, their mutual friend, to alleviate the grievous state of whose soul he had conceived the idea of this journey. 'On the brink of the abyss, illuminated by long lightning flashes, life revealed itself to us once more with its fearful earnest. Deception could no longer stand its ground! To see death face to face is to turn one's back on all deceit.'

Cosima had now returned to Munich, to set her position to rights and carry out her decisions. 'My blessing went with her: I have reason to honour her as the purest witness for truthfulness and inexhaustible deeps that life has yet shown me: she is the most perfect being I have encountered in my human experience. She belongs to another order of existence.'

Back in Tribschen Wagner endured several days of suspense. Evidently Cosima won Bülow's consent to the divorce without any delay, for on 16 October he was already writing to Carl Bechstein that his wife had been advised to try a change of climate and he would probably have to be separated from her for a considerable length of time – 'in several respects that is very hard for me'. But at the same time he wanted her to promise to go to see her father in Rome first, and move into Tribschen only later, after the divorce had gone through.

'To Rome?' Wagner exclaimed aghast in the Annals; 'bewilderment and passionate concern.' He feared that Liszt would shake her resolve. In desperation he turned to Cosima's half-sister Claire Charnacé, asking her to go and see Cosima in Munich and dissuade her from the idea of going to Rome. He had not foreseen Cosima's anger at this interference in her freedom of decision: 'Cosima beside herself.' She sent him a telegram: 'Wilful interference makes existence intolerable. Bitterly hurt by play with peace of the weary.' And after her sister's arrival in Munich she sent another: 'Claire's arrival has most disagreeable effect, opposition to Rome the saddest thing.'

'Great despondency,' he mourned in the Annals, 'decide to leave' – for Munich, where Cosima had gone to stay with a couple who were former servants of Wagner. After crossing Lake Constance by moonlight Wagner arrived in Munich on 2 November, but went on to Leipzig that same afternoon to seek the relaxation and sense of security that he had found in his sister Ottilie's house in the old days. One disappointment was still in store: he sent a plea to King Ludwig for an audience on his return journey – 'de profundis clamo' – but the answer, sent through the Cabinet Secretariat, was a refusal on a transparent pretext. The king could not get over Wagner's deceiving him as to the true nature of his relations with Cosima.

Wagner returned to Tribschen on 11 November, where he was joined by Cosima, with Isolde and Eva, on 16 November: this time for good. She arrived in Lucerne at night. Bülow wanted to preserve appearances to the last possible moment and she had had to promise him that her presence at Tribschen would be kept a secret for the time being. 'Distress over Hans,' the Annals note significantly.[1]

It was from this time forward that Cosima kept a diary, which she prefaced with a note to her children. 'You shall know about every hour of my life, so that one day you will be able to know me . . . Thus you will help me to fulfil my duty – yes, children, my duty. You will see later what I mean by that . . . 1868 is the most important turning point of my life: it was in this year that it was granted to me to enact what had been my inspiration and hope for five years. This action was not sought, not procured, fate willed it upon me.' (DMCW, I, pp. 422f.)

'She did not share the opinion that many of my friends were content to hold about me, to the relief of their consciences, namely that I was past helping,' Wagner wrote to Madame Muchanoff-Kalergis. 'She knew where and how I could be helped once and for all and did not hesitate for an instant to offer me that help in the possession of herself.' (24 August 1869)

Nevertheless, joy and a sense of guilt were at war in her heart. 'I will bear the world's abhorrence gladly and lightly, but Hans's suffering robs me of all happiness.' It could be thought of Wagner that he demanded and accepted this sacrifice from his friend with the naive egoism of genius, but a comment he made to Cosima after reading the text of *Tristan* to her reveals his inner feelings: he could only depict his relationship to her in Tristan's words in the second act. 'How long I grieved for Hans's sake, until I recognized that in our case, as in *Tristan*, something was at work which nothing else in the world could withstand.' (DMCW, I, p. 542)

Bülow himself was fully aware of the deeper consequence of his sacrifice. 'If Wagner writes but *one* note more,' he admitted to Klindworth, 'then it will be due to Cosima alone.' He and Wagner even began to write to each other again early in December 1868: he signed himself 'in steadfast admiration,' and once used one of his uncomfortable puns, 'With all my head, your sincere Hans von Bülow.'

'Little from without,' the Annals record of Wagner's life in the winter and spring of 1868–9. 'Within: dictation of the biography, score of *Siegfried*.' There were other, minor, literary activities, 'parentheses': his good-natured *Reminiscences of Rossini* and his less good-natured 'censures', his attack on Eduard Devrient and his *Clarifications of Jewry in Music*, an open letter to Marie Muchanoff-Kalergis, which formed the preface to a new edition of *Jewry in music*. (*Aufklärungen über das Judentum in der Musik*, RWGS, VIII, pp. 220ff.) Why he chose to publish something of that sort at that time is rather a mystery. Bülow may have had an inkling of the true reason when he wrote that the 'maestro' was now very isolated and by his action had 'to a certain extent severed the possibility of associating with the world'. (To Jessie Laussot, 13 April 1869)

Having completed the fair copy of the score of the second act of *Siegfried* on 23 February 1869, Wagner at last began to sketch the third act on 1 March. It was a peculiar characteristic of his creative personality that a period of passionate stress and disturbance in his personal life was on each occasion transmuted, sublimated, in renewed, heightened artistic creativity, and in this way was accorded a justification before which all moralizing must fall silent.

Reading Homer and the Edda with Cosima in the evenings revived in him once more the fundamental spirit of his myth, born as it was of the conjunction of ancient Greece and ancient Germany.

Work on the score of the second act restored his familiarity with the mass of motivic material, which he now set about developing further. 'A break of twelve years in a work must be without precedent in the history of art,' he wrote to King Ludwig, 'and if it transpires that this break has in no way impaired the vitality of my conception, then I can probably cite it as proof that these conceptions have an everlasting life, they are not yesterday's and not for tomorrow alone.'

In the same letter he reflected on his compositional technique. The realizing of his initial inspiration demanded long, wearisome labour. One reason why so little was wholly perfected in the world was that true genius manifested itself not only in the speed with which a great plan was conceived, but more specifically in the passionate, even painful perseverance required if the plan was to be realized in full. 'Nothing will come of scribbled jottings in a case like this; from an artistic point of view what transfixes us like a flash of lightning is a miraculously linked, delicately articulated piece of jewellery, in which every stone, every pearl, every link in the chain has to be fixed in its proper place with painstaking diligence, like a work of art in its own right.'

His creative imagination now concentrated on the scene between the Wanderer and Erda. It was already in his thoughts five years before, when he wrote to Bülow: 'It shall be a prelude, short but – significant.'

Now, in his letter to the king, he went on: 'If I wanted to tell you more about *Siegfried* today, I should have to speak of the dark, sublime, aweful dread with which I enter the world of my third act. We come here, like the Hellenes at the steaming cleft in the earth at Delphi, to the heart of the great cosmic tragedy: a world order is on the brink of destruction; the god is concerned for the rebirth of the world, for he himself is the world's will to become. Everything in this scene is instinct with a sublime terror that can be invoked only in riddles.' Since his return to Munich from visiting the king at Hohenschwangau in 1864, when he had put his fearful question to fate, he had been haunted by the theme that greets us as the curtain rises:

'Awe has prevented me until now from writing down what has often flared up in me as brightly as lightning when I have been walking alone in a storm.' (23–4 February 1869)

The music he was now sketching is developed out of motives that are already familiar: but what a change has come over the musical structure compared with the preceding parts of the work! The texture has become denser, the part-writing more polyphonic, and the melos surges irresistibly forward. The technical profit from the composition of *Tristan* and *Meistersinger* is manifest. If he set Wotan's words 'Um der Götter Ende grämt mich die Angst nicht, seit mein Wunsch es will' as recitative it would create an extraordinary theatrical effect, Wagner told Cosima; 'but', he added in a tone of great seriousness, 'then it would cease to be art'.

The consequence is that when the new motive of 'World Inheritance' is introduced at the climax of the scene it is thrown into all the greater relief. It is the motive that he had once conceived in connection with *Die Sieger*:

During the rehearsals at Bayreuth in 1876 Wagner asked for this to be taken 'a little faster' than what immediately preceded it and 'very clearly projected': 'It must sound like the proclamation of a new religion.' The slight increase in tempo has the effect of the illumination that has suddenly burst upon Wotan himself.

On their headland, encircled by the snow-covered mountains, Wagner was living entirely in this world of the gods evoked in his music, and despair seized Cosima when he gave way to doubt about his contemporaries and brooded on the futility of his work: 'This great, passionate work for this mean, petty age of Puritans!'

The king's silence worried her and it began to seem not unlikely that either he would cancel Wagner's allowance, or Wagner would have to renounce it. 'We discuss the possibilities of life in a garret in Paris in the future. A living room and two bedrooms for ourselves and the children. God knows what fate has in store for us.' But on 10 February a letter arrived from the king, couched entirely in the old, warm tone, to which Wagner replied with the long letter about his progress that has been quoted above. It is true that Ludwig had a particular motive in writing, which was to plead for performances of *Tristan* and *Rheingold*. 'I *implore* you, do what you can, beloved friend, to make this possible; ah, I need such pleasures if I am not to be overwhelmed in the whirl of everyday life.'

Although Wagner, believing Heinrich and Therese Vogl not up to the title roles, advised Bülow to throw away his baton rather than have anything to do with the 'botching of a work like *Tristan*', Hans nevertheless did not spare himself or his artists in carrying out the king's wish: 'First and foremost I could not but consider it my duty, and I was satisfied, too, that the reverence your work deserves was consistent with that duty. There was no question of botching or profanation, I do assure you.' (21 June)

It was his own farewell to the Munich theatre. The performance of *Tristan* would see him directing this orchestra for the last time, he told Cosima in a letter written four days earlier. 'Mon séjour à Munich finira par où il a commencé – cela lui donnera une espèce de "Abrundung" ["rounding off"] (cercle plus fatal que vicieux!).' He believed it would make it easier for him eventually to look on the whole sequence of events and suffering – 'la punition de mes fautes envers toi' – contained between the performance of one and the same work at an interval of four years, as a nightmare. 'Truly, without intending any reproach to its mighty creator – *Tristan* gave me the coup de grâce.' (17 June 1869, NBB, pp. 477ff.)

Ludwig's other desire, to see *Das Rheingold*, was to lead to the profoundest disaffection between the king and the composer.

But before that took place, several notable events happened at Tribschen. Friedrich Nietzsche paid his first visit there on 17 May; Wagner and Cosima's third child, Siegfried Helferich Richard, was born on 6 June; and Judith, the daughter of Théophile Gautier, and her husband Catulle Mendès stayed in Lucerne 16–25 July.

Nietzsche, then twenty-four years old, had first made the acquaintance of Wagner, whom he already admired, on 8 November in the previous year in Leipzig, in the house of the composer's sister, Ottilie Brockhaus. 'At the end . . . he pressed my hand very warmly and invited me in a very friendly tone to visit him, to talk music and philosophy.' (Nietzsche to Erwin Rohde, 9 November 1868) Newly appointed professor of Classical Philology at Basel University, he set out on foot from Lucerne to Tribschen on Whit Saturday, 15 May 1869. He stood outside the house for a long time, and heard an anguished chord played over and over again. 'It was, as my brother later discovered,' Elizabeth Förster-

Nietzsche wrote, 'the passage from the third act of *Siegfried*, "Ver-
wundet hat mich, der mich erweckt".' (EFWN, p. 9) Thus at the
very start we come across an example of Nietzsche's predilection
for embellishing his experiences: it would require an uncommon
musical memory to recognize that 'ominous' but motivically not
especially individual passage again.

He was invited for the Monday, when he arrived at midday and
spent the afternoon with Wagner and Cosima. From the walls of the
drawing room, papered in a faded red with gold arabesques, flanked
by portraits of Goethe, Schiller and Beethoven, Genelli's *Dionysus
among the Muses* presided over this fateful meeting. When Nietzsche
wrote at the end of 1871 to announce that *The Birth of Tragedy* was
very nearly finished, Wagner referred to the picture in his reply:

> Only the other day, when I was looking at Genelli's
> *Dionysus among the Muses*, I experienced true amazement,
> as if suddenly understanding an oracular pronouncement
> about your latest work . . . In your ideas, as from that
> picture, I read a remarkable, even wonderful coherence, I
> venture to say, of each part of my life with every other.

When Nietzsche wrote to Erwin Rohde six months later about
the essential, underlying idea of his book (which was proscribed by
the academic establishment, though Rohde for one championed it),
saying that that world of purity and beauty had not dropped from
heaven, but had been preceded by an immense, savage struggle to
escape from darkness, crudity and cruelty, he added: he had been
thinking of Genelli's watercolour of the Muses gathering around
Dionysus, which he had seen in Wagner's house Tribschen.

Obviously the picture, which possessed a deep significance for
both, was the point of departure for their discussions at that first
visit. A kind of intuition enabled Nietzsche to grasp the symbolic
significance of the moment. He did not come unprepared: he had
been a Wagnerian since Bülow's vocal score of *Tristan* had come his
way while he was still a schoolboy. Now the *Dionysus* was the key
that unlocked the problem of the Greeks and the problem of
Wagner for him and simultaneously presented new, unfamiliar
problems.

Nietzsche's French biographer, Charles Andler, remarks that
contemporary classicists would have been less taken aback had not a
badly taught generation forgotten the works of their predecessors:

Otfried Müller, Creuzer, Welcker. Nietzsche's attention was drawn to these forgotten works not by his colleagues but by Wagner himself. A comparison between the dates of his visits to Tribschen and the record of his borrowings of these authors from the library in Basel supports the conclusion. He filled his notebooks with extracts from these books, and their basic ideas take shape in his preparatory work for *The Birth of Tragedy*.[2]

But what were intellectual stimuli compared with the direct personal experience of the problem of the Apollonian and the Dionysian in the art and personality of Wagner! It is greatly to the credit of the young classicist that he recognized the question of Greek culture as being one and the same thing as the question of the phenomenon of Wagner. Thus he was able to speak of the Greeks not like those classical scholars who knew them only by hearsay, but as one who had walked among them; and to refer to Wagner not like contemporary writers who looked at him from the narrow angle of the nineteenth century, but as to a contemporary of Aeschylus.

'What I learn and see, hear and understand there, is indescribable,' he confessed to Rohde, 'Aeschylus and Pindar are still alive, believe me.' (3 September 1869) The fruit of his experiences was one of the most remarkable books ever to have come from the pen of a classical scholar: *The Birth of Tragedy from the Spirit of Music*.

Meanwhile Wagner was continuing to work on *Siegfried*. The letter to the king that has already been quoted included an account of his daily round, though omitting any mention of Cosima's presence in the house. His rule, religiously kept, was 'Nulla dies sine linea!' In the morning, after a cold wash, a light breakfast and a quick look at the newspapers; then his letters, of which he sometimes got large numbers, the great majority nonsense or idiotic imputations. At ten he got down to his score, which gave him three beautiful and profitable hours before lunch every day. His principal concern, in furnishing his green study, had been with the library, which was now gradually increasing again after sustaining so many depredations. At one Jakob summoned him to a not too luxuriously or elaborately prepared meal, at the end of which the dogs generally joined him. Then he withdrew to his salon for coffee, after which he took a short nap or played the piano a little. At three he placed upon his head the mighty Wotan hat that struck fear into the hearts of all beholders, and in the company of Russ, the Newfoundland, and

Koss, a rough-haired terrier – 'Falstaff and his page!' – he set off on his constitutional, which in bad weather was usually confined to a walk to Lucerne, where he sometimes browsed among the books in a second-hand shop and had recently found four volumes of Schiller's *Die Horen*. He returned to Tribschen at five, and went back to his score again. The evenings were devoted to reading, in which he constantly returned to the great spirits, Schiller, Goethe, and Shakespeare; sometimes Homer and Calderón, too, less often scholars like Winckelmann. 'And that gives me my blessing for the night; I am in good company and know which of my friends deserve my loyalty.' (24 February 1869)

It was with the celebrated first-violin unison passage that Wagner led Siegfried up on to the 'blessed desert on blissful height' where he recreated in sound the 'sublime impression of the holiness of the empty waste' he had received sixteen years before on his way to the Roseg glacier. There is a daemonic moment when the earth seems to open when Siegfried 'as if dying' presses his lips to the mouth of the sleeping woman, while Freia's motive is heard very softly rising out of the depths. 'The kiss of love is the first intimation of death, the cessation of individuality,' Wagner said to Cosima; 'that is why Siegfried is so frightened.' With Brünnhilde's greeting to the sun, Siegfried's key of C major is asserted with an almost physical brilliance: true religion is when the human being, forgetting self, surrenders everything to the universe, Wagner commented on another occasion. It is again characteristic that this high point of musical expression is simultaneously an outstanding example of musical form: the whole period, as Lorenz has shown, represents a potentiation of Bar-form so that the intensification rests not only on the quality of the sound but above all on a formal, intellectual principle.

The use of the two themes from the 'Starnberg' Quartet in homage to Cosima has already been mentioned in Chapter 25. But the themes of the close of the act, where the pair exclaim their joy aloud, as it were 'to the high Alps, so as to bequeath it to eternity in the undying echo', had also long been in Wagner's mind. Nevertheless, the work on the 'crystallization of the jewel that is intended to be the cornerstone' made such demands on him that he decided against celebrating his birthday in any special way. How wonderful it was, he mused, that Siegfried's exultant theme, 'Sie ist mir ewig, ist mir immer, Erb und Eigen, Ein und All', fitted itself so naturally to the motive of 'Heil dem Tage, der uns umleuchtet' to provide a contrapuntal accompaniment, which continues on its jubilant way in the horns.

'Safely delivered, 14 June 1869', he wrote at the end of the composition sketch, and when he showed the finished pages to Cosima she said: 'Only now has our child been born.'

But their joy in the completion of *Siegfried* was clouded by the prospect of the impending performance of *Rheingold* in Munich. Wagner wrote to Düfflipp that he had no right to oppose his benefactor, if the latter wished to see his works, and as far as he reasonably could he would gladly advise on the production. (18 May) The producer Reinhard Hallwachs and the machinist Karl Brandt had been to see him in April, to receive his instructions. In the middle of August it was the turn of Hans Richter, who was to conduct at Wagner's wish, to arrive at Tribschen with the singers who were to take the parts of Wotan, Loge and Alberich. In the evening Wagner complained that he was like Falstaff, he had lost his voice with singing of anthems, Cosima wrote to Nietzsche: 'he gave the good people a demonstration of everything'. (19 August)

The dress rehearsal took place on 27 August, and an alarming telegram from Richter arrived the next day, urging Wagner to prevent the première at any price, because of the inadequacies of the scenery. Hot on its heels came a letter from the Wotan, Franz Betz, which spoke of a 'crime against the work' and an 'insult to the public'; the root of the trouble, he said, was that the intendant, Perfall, had not given Hallwachs and Brandt the freedom to act as Wagner's plenipotentiaries. Wagner at once sent a telegram to the king, begging him to postpone the performance, following it up with a letter explaining the reasons for the request: in spite of everything he was still confident, he wrote, that if his suggestions were followed they would result in improvements that would salvage the production. It was of course essential that Richter should remain the conductor. (30 August)

For Richter, in order to lend weight to his demand, had refused to conduct a public performance, which Perfall countered by declaring he was seeking a replacement as quickly as possible. In his letter to the king Wagner affirmed his belief that his name commanded enough respect in every musician to deter any conductor from consenting to the act of infamy he was asked to perform. And in fact, with Bülow having already left Munich, Lassen of Weimar, Herbeck of Vienna, Levi of Karlsruhe and Saint-Saëns of Paris all refused.

The king was beside himself: 'The way "Wagner" and the theatrical rabble are behaving is truly criminal and quite shameless,' he raged to Düfflipp. '"Richter" is on no account to conduct again, and is to be dismissed forthwith . . . Pereat the theatre pack! With my usual thoughts and good wishes for yourself, but with curses on the coterie of chicanery and impudence!' (30 August) The next day he sent a telegram after the letter: an end must be put as soon as possible to the disgraceful intrigues of '"Wagner" and accomplices'. 'If W. dares to object again, his allowance is to be stopped for good, and no work of his is ever to be performed in Munich again.' (31 August)

As Wagner had let it be known that he was coming to Munich to supervise the rehearsals himself, the king instructed Düfflipp to try to prevent it. 'But there is no need for him to know that this is my wish, or there will be the devil to pay!' (31 August) Wagner arrived in Munich nonetheless on 1 September, and Ludwig, who had fled to his hunting lodge on the Hochkopf, wrote to, of all people, Pfistermeister: 'The last straw in the insufferable *Rheingold* affair is that completely against my wishes R. Wagner has come to Munich; it will serve him right if there is a hostile demonstration against him, now, when the Bülow scandal is au comble. J'en ai assez!' (KLRW, II, p. 286) Unable to come to any agreement with the intendant, Wagner left the next day with nothing accomplished, but he implored Düfflipp once more to persuade the king to postpone the performance: there was a point, he wrote, 'beyond which no more demands can be made on a man of my sort: or else the reserve of strength I have for creation will be exhausted once and for all'. (3 September)

But the affair ran its course. When finally the Munich kapellmeister Franz Wüllner agreed to conduct, Wagner could not restrain himself from telling him 'in plain German' that he was not up to it:

> Keep your hands off my score! Take my advice, Sir, or the devil take you! Go and beat time for choral societies and glee clubs, or if you must have opera scores at all costs, get hold of the ones your friend Perfall has

written! . . . You gentlemen are going to have to take a lot of lessons from a man like me, before you realize that you have no understanding of anything. (September 1869)[3]

The Augsburg *Allgemeine Zeitung* published an article instigated by Perfall, which represented the whole affair as an intrigue of Wagner's, and drew a reply from him. (*Das Münchener Hoftheater*, RWGS, XII, pp. 304ff.) It seemed, he wrote to Schott, that his name and his fame served only to draw a whole pack of hounds after him. 'I believe that this time I have stood my ground against this sort of agitation for the last time.' (21 September) The first performance of *Rheingold* took place under Wüllner on 22 September. All the published comment agreed in finding the performance splendid but the work itself insupportable, Cosima told Nietzsche: 'But some beautiful, profound words of great congeniality were written à propos of *Rheingold* by Heinrich Porges (a Jew).' (29 September)

Wagner wrote the epilogue to the whole affair in verse:

Spielt nur, ihr Nebelzwerge, mit dem Ringe,
wohl dien' er euch zu eurer Torheit Sold!
Doch habet acht: euch wird der Reif zur Schlinge;
ihr kennt den Fluch: seht, ob er Schächern hold!

('So play with the ring, you foggy dwarves, may it repay you well for your folly! But beware: the ring will trap you; you know the curse: see if it will do rogues any good!' RWGS, VIII, p.338)

Among those who travelled to Munich from far afield to attend the performance was Judith, the beautiful and intelligent daughter of Théophile Gautier and the Italian singer Ernesta Grisi, together with her husband Catulle Mendès and the poet Villiers de L'Isle-Adam. Wagner had thanked her in 1868 for sending him three articles about himself. However, when she invited him in the following year to attend the Paris production of *Rienzi* at the Théâtre Lyrique, he declined in a letter she published in the *Liberté*: people would think, if he came, that he was trying to win back with *Rienzi* what he had lost with *Tannhäuser*. 'Therefore I refrain, so as not to make stonier the stony path my French friends have chosen to tread in attempting to naturalize in France "une individualité essentiellement germanique". If such naturalization is possible, they will clear the road for it without my help.' (RWGS, XVI, pp. 114ff.; LJG, pp. 41ff.)

Thenceforward she had but a single thought: to visit Wagner and hear his works in Munich. When he asked her, on her enquiry, to extend her stay in Lucerne a little, she arrived on 16 July with Catulle and Villiers for a stay of ten days. They spent the days at Tribschen: swimming in the lake, arguing about literature and philosophy, Villiers reading his poems, Wagner organizing excursions and playing to them from the *Ring*. One evening as dusk fell and they sat in the salon looking out over the garden, Villiers broke the silence by asking Wagner without any preamble whether it was by an act of conscious deliberation that he had imbued his works with the sublime, mystical spirit that proceeded from them: in short, whether he was a free-thinker, and a Christian only insofar as the material of his lyric dramas required it. There was one particular circumstance that justified his question, he felt: that is, the fact that the name of God is not once invoked in *Tristan*.

In his own account of the incident Villiers goes on: 'I shall never forget the look Wagner turned on me from the depth of his exceptionally blue eyes: "If I did not feel in my soul the light and the love of the Christian faith you mean, then my works, which all testify to it, would be those of a liar, a jackanapes. My art is my prayer. And believe me: every true artist sings only of what he believes, speaks only of what he loves; for liars betray themselves by the sterility and worthlessness of their work. So far as I am concerned, since you ask, you should know that I am a Christian before all else, and that the accents that impress you in my works are inspired at bottom by that alone." '4

By the time the French visitors left for Munich on 25 July they were all firm friends, Judith and Cosima having become particularly intimate. They attended the dress rehearsal, and Judith lost no time in sending a report, 'un tableau très vivant': it was impossible, she wrote, for *Rheingold* to be presented in that form. Ill will and stupidity had formed an alliance. The singers and orchestra were very good, but the sets and machines were impossible: the shabbiest fairground booth would blush to own them. There was nothing to choose between the producer and the intendant: 'je crois que je vais mourir de rage. . . 27 août 2 h du matin.' She had had a good look at the king in his box: 'Féminin et volontaire, candide et dominateur.'

Judith also had a confidential message for Cosima, who was grieving at the thought that it was her father who was influencing Bülow against their divorce. Judith discussed the matter with Liszt during her visit to Munich, and he empowered her to assure his daughter that he, more than anyone, desired the legal resolution of the crisis.

'You have done me a great deal of good,' Cosima replied. She had wept all night long, and then the letter had come and acted like balm. She knew that she and her father were agreed in those areas where the clamour of the world did not penetrate, and she understood that he had to keep silent about her situation. 'If I sleep tonight, then I shall have you to thank for it. I embrace you with my whole heart and the Meister kisses your hand.' (28 August)

But the stresses of the last few weeks had told on him: Judith would find him looking ten years older, 'he is not working so regularly any more, and that worries me now more than anything else'. (7 September) Even so, he had started to 'paint' the score of the third act of *Siegfried* on 25 August, and swore that it was not tiring him in the least. On 2 October he began the composition sketch of *Götterdämmerung* with the first bars of the Norns' scene.

It was nearly twenty years since he had written down the first sketch of this scene, mentioned in Chapter 16. The change in his style since then is plainest to see in the following scene, Siegfried's leavetaking from Brünnhilde. Here, the fact that the words in the two versions are identical and the melodic lines of the vocal parts are also basically similar makes the difference in the outcome all the more prominent. The note values are now doubled, so that the singing is further removed from recitative and elevated to a kind of German bel canto. Syncopations and wider intervals enhance the vigour of the melody; individual notes are changed, an ordinary triad is replaced by the *Tristan* chord; a repeated phrase is raised by a third on repetition, so that it undergoes sequential intensification and gains mediant colouring. Everything is more plastic and more colourful. Above all the inner tension which keeps the flow of the infinite melody in motion has become far stronger:

Siegfrieds Tod, composition sketch (1850)

Götterdämmerung, full score (1873)

It is interesting to see that Wagner did not begin to sketch the short orchestral prelude to the Norns' scene until three months later, on 9 January 1870. 'My preludes must all be elemental, not dramatic like the *Leonore* overtures,' he once said, 'for then the drama is superfluous.' After the 'elemental' preludes to *Rheingold*, *Walküre* and *Siegfried*, that to *Götterdämmerung* evidently caused him trouble. The choice of the chords that had accompanied Brünnhilde's awakening and greeting of the world shows how instinctive, rather than rational, his own apprehension of his motives was. Certainly the motivic combination is incomparably successful in creating a mood of tense, uneasy expectation, and the return of the chords at Siegfried's death means that the whole of the intervening musical and dramatic action is enclosed within a huge frame.

The 1850 sketch contains no hint of the orchestral passage between the first and second scenes: first light, sunrise, full daylight. This owes its existence not only to the growth of Wagner's compositional technique, but also to the experience of a natural phenomenon: the crescendo of the triplets in the strings depicts mist dispersing as sunlight breaks through, as Wagner could see it looking out from Tribschen towards the Rigi.

While he was 'weaving at the Norns' rope', he also composed his essay *On Conducting,* a truly classic piece in its mixture of earnest and irony. (*Über das Dirigieren,* RWGS, VIII, pp. 261ff.) Cosima wrote to Nietzsche that he wanted to set down on record the whole of his experience in the musical life of the day. In a free adaptation of Goethe he apostrophized his fellow-conductors:

> Fliegenschnauz' und Mückennas'
> Mit euren Anverwandten,
> Frosch im Laub und Grill' im Gras,
> Ihr seid mir Musikanten!

('Buzzing flies and whining gnats and your kinsmen the frog in the undergrowth and the cricket in the grass, you're the musicians for me!')

He used a series of examples, mostly from Beethoven, to expound his own method of interpretation, and also revealed its fons et origo: the inspired singing of Schröder-Devrient, and the performance of the Ninth by the Paris Conservatoire orchestra. The right tempo can be judged only by approaching the music as song, and grasping the thread of the melos. Wagner was the first, Furtwängler wrote, to draw attention to the slight but continuous variation of tempo required by Beethoven's works, which is the only thing that turns a piece of classical music in performance from the notes printed on a page into a living process, something that comes into being and grows as it is heard.[5]

'It's all gold – wonderful,' Bülow exclaimed after reading the essay, of which he at once ordered several more copies. (To E. Spitzweg, 11 May 1870) It was in fact he who schooled a new generation of conductors on the Wagnerian model.

As Christmas approached Cosima began to prepare her surprises. Nietzsche was commissioned to look in Basel for a copy of Dürer's *Melencolia* and a puppet theatre for the children. 'My warmest thanks for undertaking all this, if the king is not as kingly or the devil as black as one might wish, it doesn't matter, children's imaginations are satisfied with an approximation to the real thing.' (9 December) 'Please do not lose patience over the Christ-child at all costs! Yet another request – some tulle with gold stars or spots on it . . . You see, we want to dress a Christ-child and cannot find the proper heavenly clothes anywhere in Lucerne! When I ask you for things like this I cannot help forgetting that you are Professor and Doctor and a classical philologist, and just remember that you are twenty-five and a good friend to us Tribscheners.' (15 December)

When the puppet theatre arrived she sent a telegram: 'Marionettes heavenly. Greetings and thanks.'

Nietzsche was of course invited to spend Christmas at Tribschen. In another letter Cosima told him of Wagner's instructions that he was to arrange things so that he could spend the whole holiday period with them. '*Ifthikar* has already arrived,' she went on mysteriously, 'but I shall only tell you who or what Ifthikar is if you are a good twenty-five-year-old and get here a little earlier to help me gild apples and nuts. But perhaps you will guess what Ifthikar is if I tell you that you will not see it shining where it was intended to, but on the proscenium of our puppet theatre.' (18 December) It was, in fact, the 'Order of Fame', the Nischân el Ifthikar, which the Bey of Tunis had awarded Wagner, and which the latter hung on the theatre in an access of high spirits.

Something doctrinaire about Nietzsche had grated on Cosima, but he made a better impression on Christmas Eve, when she read him the detailed prose scenario of *Parsifal*. 'Dreadfully impressed,' she noted in her diary. Wagner had 'a sublime discussion' with Nietzsche about the philosophy of music, expressing ideas that she hoped he would develop further. (DMCW, I, pp. 472f.) These are two facts that should be remembered, since they contradict certain assertions of the Nietzsche legend: namely that *Parsifal* later took him completely by surprise, and that he played a formative part in Wagner's metaphysics of music.

'J'en ai assez,' the king had written to Pfistermeister on 1 September, but he proved unable to endure silence for long either. 'Is it not so, my beloved friend, you never mistake me!? . . . Oh, God, the desire to hear your divine work was so powerful, so uncontrollable! If I erred, be lenient and forgive me . . . Are you writing *Götterdämmerung*? Will you soon be starting the text of *Parcival*? A thousand greetings to our beloved friend [Cosima]; I shall never lose faith in you, in any respect, you understand me.' (From Linderhof castle, 22 October 1869)[6]

Wagner told Cosima on 1 November that he had decided to write and tell the king that he could not write to him. He read her the restrained letter he had composed, which she would have wished even more reserved. (KLRW, II, pp. 288f.; CT, I, p. 166)

But the matter did not rest there. On 13 November he told her he was going to reproach the king with what they had had to suffer, emphasizing at the same time that, on the other hand, he owed him everything and would not have been able to work at all without him, and asking him finally not to have anything performed for the time being, to have nothing to do with the theatre for a while. She advised him to wait before doing so.

'Still worried about Richard, who looks ill,' she wrote in her diary on 18 November. 'This morning he wrote to the king; I asked him to alter some things that might cause offence and he said he would.' 19 November: 'He will not post his letter to the king because it is Friday.' 20 November: 'Richard read me his letter to the king and posted it.' (CT, I, pp. 169ff.)

'My noble friend and gracious benefactor! . . . The head wars with the heart, emotion with reason, and in the end what is established all over again is what we are and cannot help but be. When I received and read your last, quite unexpected letter, the first thing I said to myself was "we have had all this before", and that depressed me: the last thing I wanted was that it should all be repeated in exactly the same way . . . There is one question I must put to you, and your answer will determine our whole future: Do you want my work as I want it to be – or do you not?' (KLRW, II, pp. 290ff.)

Overjoyed by Wagner's expression of his 'trust' in a letter of New Year greetings, Ludwig wrote: 'Ah, I knew we could not misunderstand each other! I may say I deserve it.' (6 January 1870)

And yet it was from a newspaper that Wagner learned on 12 January that the king had ordered *Die Walküre* to be put into production. 'Greatly alarmed at it; once again his will to work completely halted.' (CT, I, p. 187) His young king was once again causing him the greatest distress, Wagner wrote to Schott: 'You will soon learn that the *Rheingold* shambles is going to be repeated with *Die Walküre*. This is the price I have to pay for enough peace and quiet to be able at least to finish composing my works.' (4 February)

He had already written to the king on 12 January, begging 'put my works on, but not without me', and had listed the conditions on which he would be ready to take part in preparing model performances of *Rheingold* and *Walküre*: the king was to give his absolute authority, the performers were to be at his exclusive disposal, the theatre to be closed for six weeks, the intendant to be given leave of absence.

He had read the entire letter to the king, Düfflipp wrote to Tribschen, but had gained nothing by it, except that the king had finally called him 'Richard Wagner's advocate'. Düfflipp also wrote to Bülow appealing for his help, and giving the significant information that 'it is impossible for His Majesty to approve a formal appointment for Wagner in the prevailing regrettable circumstances' – meaning Wagner's relationship with Cosima. When he had asked for other, more acceptable suggestions, Frau von Bülow-Liszt had replied that the Meister was not in a position to make any others. (BB, IV, pp. 364ff.)

Bülow excused himself on the grounds of his health: 'I regard a return to Munich as tantamount to suicide.' Levi, too, again refused an invitation, which earned him Wagner's undying respect.

As 3 May approached, the anniversary of his first summons from Ludwig, he wrote him a poem:

> Noch einmal mögest Du die Stimme hören,
> die einstens aus Dir selber zu mir sprach . . .

('May you hear once more the voice that once spoke to me from you'; KLRW, II, pp. 303f.)

Under the draft in the Brown Book he wrote '(dernier effort!)'. This last effort to dissuade the king from his purpose was as unsuccessful as the rest: the first performance of *Die Walküre* was given on 26 June, conducted by Wüllner.

II

In the meantime a new avenue had opened for Wagner. 'I really would not know what to balance against the infamy of the present production of *Die Walküre*, if it were not for the Bayreuth hopes,' Cosima wrote to Nietzsche on 24 June 1870. Wagner had never forgotten the pleasing impression the town had made on him on the occasion of his one visit thirty-five years before, but it was only when he looked it up in an encyclopedia on 5 March that he learned of the existence of the old Margraves' Opera House with its unusually large stage, which he at once thought might make it suitable for the *Ring*. As Glasenapp emphasizes, however, it was not what might be called the physical or topographical considerations that constituted the new element in the idea of Bayreuth which was born at that moment, but the fundamental rejection of the modern civilization of the large cities.

Nietzsche was one of the first to be told of the idea, since Wagner was confident of gaining his support for it. Early in 1870 Wagner read Nietzsche's paper *Socrates and Greek Tragedy*, which attributes the decadence of Greek drama from Aeschylus to Euripides to the decline of the lyric and the proliferation of dialectic – an idea he himself had expressed twenty years before in connection with the artwork of the future.[7] He wrote to assure the author of his own conviction as to the correctness of the theory. 'But I am worried about you, and pray with my whole heart that you won't ruin yourself. I would advise you, if I may, not to handle such very implausible views in short papers, with an eye to making an easy effect for considerations that will prove fatal in the long run, but . . . to gird yourself to write a larger, more comprehensive work on the subject.' (4 February 1870) 'Turn your paper into a book,' Cosima agreed; 'certainly it is too good for just a nibble.' Reading the paper had wrought a change in the gloom that had been affecting Tribschen, she went on. The pilgrimage to the finest age of human history had had such a beneficial effect that the next morning Wagner had got his Siegfried as far as the Rhine, blowing his high-spirited theme accompanied by the boldest and most exuberant violin figure; hearing it the Rhinemaidens were filled with joy and hope and let their own song be heard, broad and strong. (8 February)

'I now have no one with whom I can discuss things so seriously as with you – except for the one and only Cosima,' Wagner confessed to Nietzsche. But he was concerned from the first that his young friend should not permit himself to be distracted from his true calling for his sake. 'If you had become a musician, then you would be approximately where I would be if I had stuck to the classics . . . Remain a classicist now, so that, as such, you may let yourself be guided by music . . . Show what classical studies are for, and help me to bring about the great "renaissance", in which Plato embraces Homer and Homer, now imbued with Plato's ideas, at last becomes great Homer indeed.'

'Pater Seraphice,' Nietzsche wrote, to greet Wagner on his birthday, 'if what you once wrote – to my pride – is true, and music shall guide me, then you at all events are the conductor of this my music.' He signed himself, continuing the allusion to the last scene of *Faust*, 'one of the blessed boys'. (21 May) He brought his friend Erwin Rohde to stay at Tribschen from 11 to 13 May. Rohde, later to be famous as the author of *Psyche*, a two-volume work on the Greek belief in the immortality of the soul, amazed Wagner and Cosima by his apparently inexhaustible knowledge of the Greek world. Cosima thought him more impressive than Nietzsche himself. For his part, Rohde told Nietzsche that the visit to Tribschen had been the climax of the fifteen months he had spent in Italy; he had left the house with a respect and admiration for every aspect of the life lived there that bordered on the religious. Reporting this to Cosima, Nietzsche went on: 'I understand how the Athenians could erect altars to Aeschylus and Sophocles, and give Sophocles the heroic name of "Dexion", because he entertained the gods in his house. This presence of the gods in the house of genius creates that religious atmosphere of which I write . . . In the matter of Bayreuth, I have been thinking that the best thing for me would be to suspend my professional activities for a few years and join your pilgrimage to the Fichtelgebirge.[8] Those are just hopes, to which I gladly surrender.' (19 June)

Cosima replied that they had been finding out all they could about Bayreuth from their bookseller, who came from Wunsiedel, and the auspices sounded very favourable. 'You shall write your book in Bayreuth, and we shall do honour to your book. And if they are castles in the air . . . I shall tend them and make them more productive than any real estates have ever been.' (24 June)

The Bayreuth plan, even if it was only a castle in the air, was what saved Wagner at this time from a paralysis of his creative powers. All the same, as he wrote to Schott, he postponed completing the score of *Siegfried* deliberately, having learned that his Most Serene patron, after 'executing' the *Walküre,* was bending his bow at the next score, so as to lose no time in performing the same experiment on it. He was now quietly working on a counter-plan of his own, to produce the entire *Ring* according to *his* wishes, and it was that that had encouraged him to get on with the composition of *Götterdämmerung*. (Autumn 1870)

Exuberantly, he went on with the composition sketch of the first act: 'Family council', he wrote above the scene in the Gibichungs' Hall, where the plot against Siegfried is hatched. (7 February) By 25 March he was writing to Judith Mendès that on the previous day Siegfried had drunk Gutrune's fateful potion; 'I wager that will bring about some misfortune that I shall have to set to music.' And when he had written the final scene of the act, which Cosima found almost unbearable in its cruelty, he wrote below that 'Fidi', their own small Siegfried, 'thinks it's funny!!' (5 June) But on the back of the sheet of manuscript paper he wrote down his first notes, evoking the names of Schiller and Goethe, for the commemorative essay on Beethoven.

The committee set up in Bonn to celebrate the centenary of Beethoven's birth pointedly made no approach to Wagner. From Vienna, on the other hand, there came an invitation to conduct the Choral Symphony, but as the signatories of the letter included his old adversaries Eduard Schelle and Eduard Hanslick he had regretfully to reply that any document that appeared over those two names belonged necessarily to the category of what was barred to him. (To N. Dumba, 24 June)

The first rumours of war had reached Tribschen, when Wagner, Cosima, the two eldest girls, a student named Schobinger and the servant Jakob set out on 10 July on an expedition that had been planned for a long time, to climb the Pilatus. In spite of her weariness, Cosima was impressed by the sublime quiet and solitude, the more so as Wagner reminded her that experiences like this in the past had inspired his representation of the gods' existence in the *Ring*. 'While we were up there we read the *Parerga* diligently,' she wrote to Nietzsche, 'since recently the Meister has taken up Schopenhauer's aesthetics. You will soon be able to read his – the Meister's – ideas on the philosophy of music in an essay on Beethoven.' (16 July)

Their return to Tribschen on 15 July heralded a rush of events. The marriage of Hans and Cosima was legally dissolved in Berlin on 18 July, France declared war·on Prussia on 19 July, and on the same day their French friends, their ranks swollen by Camille Saint-Saëns, Henri Duparc and René Joly, arrived in Lucerne, on their way home from 'model' performances in Weimar and Munich. The declaration of war touched Cosima in a very personal way, for it was her brother-in-law Emile Ollivier, now president of the French Council of Ministers, who issued it, 'le coeur léger'. At Tribschen they agreed not to mention the burning questions on which they would not be able to agree, but to keep to the subject of art, where they all agreed so well. Judith sensed Wagner's passionate excitement at the events. 'I admit', she wrote, 'that I would not have liked him so much if he had not succumbed to patriotic enthusiasm like the rest of us at that moment of decision.'

There was music. Wagner sang passages from *Walküre* and *Siegfried* and, from *Götterdämmerung*, the Norns' scene, of which he had just finished the orchestral sketch. Saint-Saëns, who accompanied him, reading admirably at sight, was so carried away that at the end he cried: 'You owe it to the French to write them a *Charlemagne*!'

The Mendès and Villiers stayed until the end of the month before going on to Paris.

The fact that King Ludwig mobilized the Bavarian army and took the side of Prussia helped to turn away Wagner's wrath from him. For his birthday on 25 August, Wagner sent him a copy of the orchestral sketch of the prelude and first act of *Götterdämmerung*, with a topical poem of dedication:

> Gesprochen ist das Königswort,
> dem Deutschland neu erstanden . . .

('The royal word has been spoken to Germany, newly risen . . .' RWGS, VIII, pp. 339f.)

On the same day Wagner and Cosima were married in the Protestant church in Lucerne. Messages of congratulation and good wishes arrived from far and wide. Mathilde Wesendonk sent a wonderful bouquet of edelweiss, the flower which is to be found only on dangerous mountain slopes.

While following the events of the war with growing interest, Wagner continued to work at the essay on Beethoven which he had started while their guests were with them. Throughout the essay, ideas inspired by the events of the time, on the relationship of the German artist to his people and the national spirit, chime in among the reflections on the metaphysics of music. 'So let us celebrate the great pathfinder in the wilderness to which Paradise degenerated!' the essay ends. 'But let us celebrate him worthily – no less worthily than the victories of German courage: for he who enriches the world with joy has precedence over him who conquers the world!' (RWGS, IX, pp. 61ff.)

'The voice of the prophet in the desert,' Rohde wrote to Nietzsche, when it was published at the end of the year, 'an elevating reminder of the existence of a better life in the midst of this time when one is daily driven ever further from one's true life. The book is a true revelation of the inner meaning and purpose of music, a revelation which no one could make as profoundly or as convincingly as this genius.' (29 December)

A private Beethoven festival also took place at Tribschen during the winter of 1870–1, with a cycle of the quartets, which Wagner rehearsed with three players from Zürich and Hans Richter on the viola. One of them left a memoir of the sessions, remarking that they soon recognized Wagner's calibre. 'His blue eyes flashed, he jumped up, now just beating time gently, to indicate a nuance with a graphic gesture. But then when the pieces were played again in their proper context everything came together as if fashioned in bronze, and the most easily overlooked phrases acquired life and consequence.' (FWSZ, II, pp. 318ff.)

Nietzsche, who had been taken ill while serving as a volunteer medical orderly, was invited to come and hear the quartets when he recovered. In her letter Cosima referred to E. T. A. Hoffmann's fairy tale of the Golden Pot: Wagner was Lindhorst, the archivist with magical powers, Nietzsche the dreaming student Anselmus, and she herself the Orange Lily. 'The Archivist wishes me to invite you to the quartet recital, which I hereby do. If you come you will find the Isle of Spirits in its usual dream state and as always concerned about you and your dreams.' (21 January 1871)

Alluding to Goethe's praise of German courage,[9] Wagner wrote in his *Beethoven*: 'Let the Germans now be courageous in peace as well; let them cherish their true merit and cast false appearances away; let them not aspire to seem something that they are not, and let them on the other hand recognize what is uniquely theirs.' Is he to be blamed if for once he relaxed and shrugged off a troublesome subject that had depressed him for days at a time with a sudden burst of laughter? In the middle of November 1870 he wrote in the Brown Book the outline of 'The Capitulation, Comedy by Aristop Hanes'. The point of the piece is that what it ultimately mocks is not the Parisian capitulation to the German army, but the German surrender to Parisian opera and operetta. So that there should be no doubt as to his intention, when he came to write the play he changed 'The' to 'A' in the title – *A Capitulation: Comedy in the Antique Manner*. 'My subject inspects no other aspect of the French but the one in the reflection of whose light we Germans truly show ourselves more ridiculous than they, who, in all their follies, are always original, while we, in our sickening imitation of them, sink far below the ridiculous.' (RWGS, IX, pp. 3f.)

As German writers seem to take pride in misunderstanding this comedy, a Frenchman should be allowed to speak. In reality it is a play on words, G. Leprince writes, it is about a German capitulation in the world of the theatre. What else does the indefinite article in the title mean, if not that the word 'capitulation' is to be understood as having been transferred? 'Admittedly, one can be mistaken as to that, if one has read only the title. But if one is going to make the comedy the grounds for a destructive condemnation of its author, then one has the duty at least to read it and take all its allusions into account. Otherwise one is open to a charge of bad faith.'[10]

Without revealing his authorship, Wagner asked Hans Richter to write some incidental music for it: 'it ought to parody Offenbach's parodies'. (28 November) After the play had been turned down by the Berlin Vorstadttheater, where it had been sent anonymously, Richter admitted to great relief, as it would have been impossible for him to compose à la Offenbach.

Astonishingly, while Wagner was writing this revue piece, he was simultaneously engaged on the composition of his most personal piece of music. On 4 December he completed the score of the 'Tribschen Idyll with Fidi-Birdsong and Orange Sunrise, a symphonic birthday greeting to his Cosima from her Richard'. 'The first Christmas Eve when I have given Richard nothing and had nothing from him,' she wrote in her diary. But when she woke the next morning a sound fell on her ears that grew richer as she listened: 'I heard music, and what music! When it had died away, Richard came in with the five children and gave me the score of the symphonic birthday composition.' He had rehearsed the *Idyll* in secret with his fifteen players, and they had performed on the stairs. Richter had learnt to play the trumpet for the occasion and played the birdcall so lustily that it was a joy to hear.

This was the only one of his compositions, Wagner said, that he could write a programme for, down to the last 'and'. A sequence of experiences – 'our whole existence', as Cosima put it – is woven together and transformed into absolute music in such a way that no programmatic exposition is needed. At the same time this occasional piece opens completely new paths for symphonic music. Wagner confessed to the king that he felt a little vain about it, and he told Cosima that it was his favourite composition.

The brazen notes of world events still penetrated into the idyll of Tribschen. 'It is right that we should be silent in the face of this awesome greatness, no boasting about victories, no complaining about sufferings,' Wagner said, 'silent, profound recognition that the god disposes.' The same thought is expressed in his poem *To the German Army before Paris*: 'In ernstem Schweigen schlägst du deine Schlachten' ('In solemn silence you fight your battles') (RWGS, IX, pp. 1f.). He wanted to express gratitude for the army's achievements and sacrifice in a Symphony for the Fallen, but when he made discreet enquiries in Berlin he was told that he should not imagine he had a monopoly of the German spirit, and moreover they did not intend to make special arrangements to furnish unpleasant impressions for themselves. His proposal for a festive march, with a chorus to be sung by the people as the troops returned home, also failed to gain approval. So he contented himself with writing a concert piece, the *Kaisermarsch*, a piece of strength and tenderness, its symbolism a happy blend of patriotism and humane sentiment. While he was writing it, he at last, on 5 February 1871, accomplished the long-deferred task of finishing the score of *Siegfried*. The last page of the composition sketch of the march shows clearly enough how the descending fourths of Siegfried's and Brünnhilde's rejoicing were the inspiration of the melody of the closing chorus:

> Feind zum Trutz,
> Freund zum Schutz,
> Allem Volk das deutsche Reich zu Heil und Nutz!

('Defying foes, defending friends, the German Empire is for the good of all people'; RWGS, XII, p. 376)

Nevertheless, the idea of a Funeral Symphony, based on the grave A♭ minor theme he had originally conceived in connection with *Romeo and Juliet*, was to recur constantly in the years to come.

If judgement is to be passed on Wagner's four 'occasional' pieces of 1870–1, then they must all be taken as a whole: the Beethoven essay, as serious and impassioned as the first movement of a symphony, the burlesque scherzo of *A Capitulation,* the Andante con moto of the *Siegfried Idyll,* and the Allegro maestoso of the *Kaisermarsch*. It is only together that they reveal the whole Wagner – and we must also remember that his principal concern throughout the whole period was always the *Ring*.

Wagner's and Cosima's reactions to the events of the war, which ran through the whole gamut of conflicting emotions, from approval of the bombardment of Paris to concern for their French friends, is reflected in their correspondence with the Mendès. On 5 September 1870 Wagner wrote to Catulle: 'Your letter, my dear Catulle, touched me profoundly. Thank you! Yes, happily there is a realm of existence where we are, and shall always be, united . . . For we are in perfect accord on these two great principles: Love and Music. Those are the two lights, shining from the same hearth, that, when placed behind the bad painting of this earthly life, render it transparent and reveal it to us as a mirage!. . . . If only you had stayed with us! I would have made you prisoners. Not of war. Solely in all honour, but in love and in music above all.'

The entry in Cosima's diary for 12 September reads: 'Letter from C. Mendès, very elegiac, he thinks he will die below the walls of Paris.' Catulle had enclosed a 'proclamation from Victor Hugo to the Germans', 'the sort of pure nonsense', Cosima commented, 'that the French find sublime'. (CT, I, p. 284) It stirred Wagner to sit down the same day and write both the Mendès a 'vigorous' letter, running to four pages in print: 'My dears, I do not need to tell you how sad your letter made me. It is truly a tragedy that is taking place between us.' When he had been in a similar situation, it was a 'hydropathic cure by philosophy' that had helped him. But they fortified themselves with 'a kind of false poetry' – referring to Hugo – 'which, for quite a long time, has been upheld as true poetry by a propitious chance which flattered the spirit of a sanguine nation'.

He recommended them, instead, to try 'to find a true statesman . . . capable, above all, of explaining to the French nation what the German nation is, and what its intentions are'.

In his closing paragraphs Wagner rehearsed his theory of the danger of this 'nation vraiment généreuse' becoming too centralized in Paris, in combination with his own disappointments in trying to win the city's favour. 'I see myself – in your place – on the ramparts of Paris, and I say to myself: should this enormous capital city fall in ruins, perhaps!

'But not perhaps! Rather, assuredly! It would be the point of departure for the regeneration of the French people . . . Blessings from your friends! We are with you! Au revoir! Ever yours.'[11]

Communications into and out of Paris were cut directly after this, but as soon as they were re-opened Catulle lost no time in sending a seven-page letter to his 'bien-aimé maître' on 3 July 1871: 'I regret your not having received my letter all the more because in it I said a host of things, in complete disorder, which . . . would be singularly meaningless by now. One of them, however, remains eternally true, it is something that you know: that events do not undo the ties joining people's spirits, the sword does not exist that can cut through that kind of Gordian knot, and our friendship, composed of your kindness and my gratitude, exists without end, and has not even been threatened.'

The prophecy proved false nevertheless. Wagner's inclusion of A

Capitulation in Volume IX of his collected writings in 1873 ('he didn't have enough manuscripts', Cosima wrote; CT, I, p. 698) offended Catulle, 'who was especially disgusted by the gratuitous insult to Victor Hugo'. He attended the Bayreuth Festival of 1876, but did not set foot inside the gates of Wahnfried.[12] In all probability, too, he wanted to avoid running into Judith, from whom he was by then divorced.

In May 1869 Wagner had been elected a corresponding member of the musical section of the Royal Academy of Arts in Berlin. In the spring of 1871, as he girded himself for his first visit to the new empire, to inform himself as to the practical and personal preconditions for realizing his idea for a festival, he wrote a paper entitled *On the Destiny of Opera*, which he hoped to deliver to the Academy. The difficulty, he was to write in the preface, lay in treating at length for the second time a subject that he had already discussed in detail years before in *Opera and Drama*. But a glance at the text is enough to see that he gave the subject a quite new turn, in the emphasis on an 'improvisatory' element in drama and in music, which ought to be more successful in blending the two into a whole than the rigid formalism of opera had so far managed to be. It should be like the difference between a 'scene in nature' and a 'work of architecture'. (*Über die Bestimmung der Oper*; RWGS, IX, pp. 127ff.)

Nietzsche arrived in Tribschen on 3 April, on his way from Lugano. He had applied for a chair of philosophy at Basel, and since he still had to demonstrate his qualifications as a philosopher, he had used his holiday to write an essay on the 'origin and aim of tragedy', based on his lectures on Greek music drama, Socrates and tragedy, and the Dionysian world view, and intended to be the first part of his 'major book on the Greeks'. 'I live in a state of derisive alienation from classical philology, and can think of nothing worse,' he wrote to Rohde from Lugano on 29 March. 'So I am gradually getting accustomed to my philosopherhood, and already believe in myself.' His principal reason for breaking his journey back to Basel at Tribschen, his sister tells us, was to read the piece to Wagner. 'But my brother must have suffered a slight disappointment. Being so sensitive, he probably noticed that Wagner had hoped that the new essay would serve in some way to glorify his own art. Great as my brother's enthusiasm for Wagner and his music was, his conscientiousness as a scholar at first refused to associate two very disparate things in the essay, which was at that time entitled "Greek Gaiety".

But regard for his friend won, for as soon as my brother was back in Basel he set to with the greatest enthusiasm to rework it, cutting some chapters and restricting himself now to the subject of Greek tragedy, so as to be able to refer to Wagner's art.' (EFWN, pp. 71f.)

The genesis of the book and the papers that had preceded it had been stimulated by Wagner's ideas and art, under the aegis of the Genelli *Dionysus*, and the six days Nietzsche spent at Tribschen at this stage in its writing will have played a decisive role in its reworking. But his sister's inference that moral pressure was brought to bear on him, by either Wagner or Cosima, and that the reworking was a 'burnt offering on the altar of his friendship', is completely unconfirmed.[13]

'I shall devote tomorrow to packing,' Cosima wrote to Nietzsche on 13 April, 'and I want to get a last letter from Tribschen to you today.' On 15 April she and Wagner started their journey to the 'empire'. In Augsburg they were met by Düfflipp, who conveyed the king's wish to have the first two acts of *Siegfried* performed. Wagner replied that he would sooner burn them and go a-begging than consent. The next day they arrived in Bayreuth. 'A charming edifice,' Cosima commented after they had seen the Margraves' Opera House, 'but the theatre is not in the least suitable for us. Therefore, build, so much the better.' In Leipzig their friends and relatives gathered for a festive reception. His sister Luise Brockhaus found he had become benign and fatherly, and thanked Cosima for having the courage to marry him. In Dresden he had a joyful reunion with the faithful Pusinelli. Then he took Cosima on a tour of the streets and the secluded corners of his boyhood and told her of the impressions the Brühl Terrace, the Frauenkirche and so on had made on him then.

All the preparations for their stay in Berlin, where they arrived at the Tiergarten Hotel on 25 April, had been made by Karl Tausig and Countess von Schleinitz, the wife of the Minister of the Royal House [Internal Affairs]. 'The lecture at the Academy . . . was a curious proceeding,' Cosima reported to Nietzsche. 'The "Scientific" has nothing to do with its sister institution, so the scholars were absent, and our Meister delivered his paper at the conference table to Dorn, Joachim, Taubert and a few, admittedly very well-disposed, painters.' (12 May)

On 5 May Wagner conducted a concert in the Royal Opera House in aid of the King Wilhelm Association. While the emperor had assured him of every facility, Hülsen the intendant told the orchestra to pay no attention to Wagner: the man was there to wave his baton, he said, not to give orders. Only Frau von Schleinitz's last-minute intervention frustrated another high-handed act by the intendant, who had forbidden the decoration of the conductor's desk and the admission of any people carrying flowers: asked by her for an explanation, he excused himself by saying it had been a misunderstanding. Every seat in the house was filled when the emperor and empress entered their box. The concert began with the *Kaisermarsch,* followed by Beethoven's C minor Symphony, the *Lohengrin* prelude, Wotan's Farewell and the Magic Fire music, and the finale of Act I of *Lohengrin*. In response to tumultuous appeals from the audience, after some hesitation, Wagner played an encore of the *Kaisermarsch*.

The emperor declared that he had never heard anything so accomplished as this concert, and his opinion was confirmed by what the leader of the orchestra said to Wagner, apropos of the symphony: 'You have no idea of the casual attitude they take here to things like this.'

In the week before the concert he had had an interview with Bismarck, a historic meeting. At the beginning of the year Cosima had sent Wagner's poem *To the German Army before Paris* to the German headquarters, addressing it to the chancellor's confidant, Lothar Bucher. Bismarck thanked Wagner in a cordial letter written in his own hand, concluding: 'You, too, have overcome the resistance of the Parisians after a long struggle, with your works, in which I have always had the keenest interest, although at times inclining towards the opposition party; it is my belief and my hope that many more victories will be granted them, at home and abroad.' (21 February 1871)

Even before the end of the war Wagner had told Cosima of his wish to pay homage to the great man, the founder of the empire, who continued to be the subject of controversy even in court circles. At the special instigation of Bucher, on arrival in Berlin he left his card at the chancellor's residence, and received an invitation to call on the evening of 3 May. Bismarck received him in an intimate family circle with as much exquisite courtesy 'as if he were greeting perhaps the minister of an allied state'.

'You know something that none of us know,' Wagner said, meaning the secret of the political strength of the nation. 'The only thing that can be said in my praise', the prince replied with a subtle smile, 'is that now and then I have managed to procure a signature. I have found the hole in the crown' – 'in the spiked helmet' according to another version – 'that lets the smoke through.'

The subject of books arose, but Bismarck was dismissive, saying that nowadays he only ever saw their spines. To Wagner's regret the conversation dwindled into diplomatic and parliamentary gossip.

He had never encountered such self-confidence, Bismarck told Bucher after the meeting. Wagner himself acknowledged the foundations on which his confidence rested, when he said in his *Review of the Festival of 1876* that his faith in the secret artistic strength of the nation had truly required a courage to match it. (RWGS, X, pp. 103ff.)

For his part he was delighted by the prince's genuine amiability. 'No trace of reticence or reserve. Easy of speech, cordially interested in others, inspiring complete confidence and sympathy. But', he added, 'we can only watch each other at work, each can act only in his own sphere. I would not so much as try to win him for me, or ask his support for my cause. The meeting remains something that I value very highly.' (GLRW, IV, pp. 355f., 451; DMCW, I, p. 561)

Cosima wrote to Eliza Wille, mentioning the fact that François Wille and Bismarck had been students at Göttingen together: Wagner would be delighted to see her and her husband again. 'He would have a lot to say to the latter about his princely friend, who made the most significant and agreeable impression on him.' (June 1871, FWSZ, II, pp. 461f.)

There are thus no grounds for the interpretation that has been put on the meeting, to the effect that Wagner sought it in the hope of gaining Bismarck's support and, on being refused, turned against the chancellor. On the contrary: when he wrote the preface to his collected writings shortly afterwards he came out firmly against those self-appointed critics of the founder of the empire, who expected 'a statesman to justify his successes to those who previously had had no idea that such things were even possible, and to subject his measures to the approval of people who first have to have explained to them what is at issue'. (RWGS, I, pp. iii ff.)

His other important activity while in Berlin was to discuss the Bayreuth Festival with Karl Tausig. As the provisional business manager of the undertaking, under the patronage of Countess von Schleinitz, Tausig, 'undeterred by Wagner's fulminations against the Jews', as Newman comments, 'threw himself wholeheartedly into the Bayreuth scheme'.

Leaving Berlin for home, they stopped again in Leipzig, and it was in the town of his birth, on 12 May, that Wagner made the first public announcement of the festival, to take place in 1873. The patrons and benefactors who raised the necessary financial means would receive 'the title and rights of Patrons of the Stage Festival in Bayreuth, while the realization of the undertaking itself will be entrusted to my experience and skills and to my endeavours alone'.

Wagner had written to tell King Ludwig of his plan on 1 March. The king's comment to Düfflipp had been 'I do not like Wagner's plan at all' (19 April), but he now wrote to Wagner himself: 'The gods have inspired your plan for performing the "Nibelungs" in Bayreuth.' (26 May)

One of the last stops on the way back to Tribschen was in Heidelberg, which they reached on 15 May. Absorbed in the view of the castle bathed in the evening sunlight, Wagner's attention was caught suddenly by a puppet show set up on the street, and they watched to the end as the hero, Kaspar, outwitted the foppish count, kept just out of reach of every representative of the law, cocked a snook at devil and priest alike, vanquished death and hell and took his leave of the enthralled audience with a saucy bow: 'Spit out the lights!'

'It was the best moment in the whole trip,' Cosima thought, and, not least, the most instructive in Wagner's view. He could not remember when he had last had so forceful a reminder of the living spirit of the theatre. What a daemonic being that puppeteer was! By creating a world of characters from nothing and animating them with his own breath, he demonstrated in the plainest possible way that mimetic genius consists not in 'affectation', however polished, but in the intrinsic ability to forget one's self and enter into other souls and bodies. At the same time he confirmed what Wagner had said so recently in his paper to the Berlin Academy: that this mimic capability originates in the art of improvisation. And so the unknown puppeteer of Heidelberg was commemorated side by side with Schröder-Devrient in Wagner's essay *On Actors and Singers* (RWGS, pp. 157ff.)

'Unique happiness at being in his own world again,' Cosima

confessed as they at last ended their journey on 16 May. But Wagner did not have the chance to spin himself back into his cocoon. In the twelve months between then and the laying of the foundation stone of the festival theatre, he brought off the incredible double feat of writing the composition sketches of the second and third acts of *Götterdämmerung* at the same time as he was organizing the preparations for the Bayreuth Festival.

When he read Cosima his pamphlet *On the Performance of the Festival Drama 'Der Ring des Nibelungen'*, he remarked: 'As for us, we can do without it. Our pleasure lies in the idea.' He foresaw that the realization of the idea would bring struggles and disappointment in its wake. 'I curse the music that puts me to this torture, that will not let me enjoy my good fortune for a moment,' he exclaimed when one such crisis was upon him. 'It's a madness, or I ought to have been made fierce like Beethoven. It's not true, what you think, that this is my element. To spend my life improving my mind, to enjoy my good luck, that was my spur. It was different once. Oh, I feel as though I was trying to build a house on a catalpa flower. I should have to fill the world with airy vapours first, to separate me and my art from the human race. Idylls, quartets, I should like to write some before I die – and all the while there's this bother about performing the *Ring*!' (DMCW, I, pp. 578f.)

The single response to his appeal had come, in the meantime, from a complete stranger, the Mannheim music publisher Emil Heckel, who wrote to Wagner asking what contribution he could make to the success of the great undertaking. (15 May) Wagner sent him a letter of cordial good wishes and referred him to Karl Tausig, to whom Heckel explained the idea he had had of founding a Wagner Society, with branches in various towns: the purpose of these would be to finance the festival by purchasing patronage vouchers corporately, and so give people of modest means the opportunity to buy a share of a voucher.

'Your Wagner Society is an excellent idea,' Tausig replied, and Wagner pronounced his readiness to conduct a concert in Mannheim, in spite of his commitments: 'Be prepared . . . for me to announce my arrival – perhaps in the autumn – at short notice, and then do you see to it that everything is done decently.' (21 June)

He began the composition sketch of Act II on 24 June 1871: '*Midsummer Day!!!*' he wrote at the head of the introduction to the blackest nocturnal music ever written. There is no sign that the composition had been interrupted for a year: for all its motivic complexity the 'ghostly, dreamlike duologue' between Hagen and Alberich, which he later described as one of the high points of the entire work, was written straight down without any corrections or emendations either while he was writing or inserted later.

Then came the news of Tausig's death of typhus in Leipzig on 17 June. Again, as with Schnorr, he felt with daemonic force that fate, unable to touch him, had laid hands on one of his faithful friends instead. He reflected on the tragedy of Tausig's life, his precocity, a Schopenhauer at sixteen, suffering under his Jewishness, taking no pleasure in his immense virtuosity, since Liszt was greater and he was himself too great to be Liszt's pupil. And now this 'stupidity of fate', that snatched him away at the very moment when a great occupation would have given him inner joy and satisfaction. Wagner wrote him an epitaph:

> Reif sein zum Sterben,
> des Lebens zögernd sprießende Frucht,
> früh reif sie erwerben,
> in Lenzes jäh erblühender Flucht,
> war es Dein Los, war es Dein Wagen –
> Wir müssen Dein Los wie Dein Wagen beklagen.

('To be ripe for death, to harvest early the shyly sprouting fruit of life in the frenziedly blooming flight of spring, was it your fate, was it your daring – we must mourn your fate and your daring together.' *Grabschrift für Karl Tausig*, RWGS, IX, p. 324)

Obtaining the king's approval was another cause for anxiety: if he insisted on his contractual right to have the *Ring* performed in Munich then Bayreuth would be in jeopardy. Rumours were beginning to circulate that Ludwig's new enthusiasm was architecture, that he was going to have his hunting lodges gilded and furbished in the style of Louis XIV. 'My thoughts are heavy,' Wagner complained, 'I shall never be happy or well. This disgrace, being dependent on the king, it's unheard-of and insupportable.' He discarded what he had written of Hagen's summoning of the vassals, because it was 'over-composed' – blaming it on external circumstances. But he greeted Cosima with the new version on their wedding anniversary, 25 August. He started the composition of the vassals' scene with contrapuntal studies on 'Was tost das Horn?' When Cosima looked in on him, he clapped his hand to his head:

'My thoughts are itching'; but the next morning he was able to play her the wild chorus, 'Der Hagedorn sticht nun nicht mehr . . .'

In the end his faith always triumphed: 'I expect a miracle, you will see, it will come, how and where I don't know, but it will come.'

He finished the sketch of the second act on 25 October, in exactly four months. On 1 November he wrote to the banker Friedrich Feustel, the chairman of the town council of Bayreuth, and a friend of Wagner's sister Ottilie Brockhaus, asking for a site for the theatre. 'Let me say at once, too, that as a site for a house for myself I was much taken with a longish piece of meadow land, lying between the left side of the palace garden and also [like the proposed site for the theatre] towards its far end, and the road out to the Eremitage.'

After the council had agreed to the proposal, Wagner went to Bayreuth on 15 December to look at the site for the theatre again, and from there to Mannheim, where Cosima and Nietzsche joined him. 'Herr Jesses, I'm not a prince!' he exclaimed in the purest Saxon, when he was greeted at the station with a resounding three cheers from the members of the Mannheim Wagner Society.

The historic 'Mannheim Concert' took place on 20 December: the *Kaisermarsch*, which he interpreted as a dramatic representation of a military procession; the overture to *Die Zauberflöte*; Beethoven's A major Symphony; the *Lohengrin* and *Meistersinger* preludes; and the prelude and close of *Tristan*. In the morning of the same day he had performed the *Siegfried Idyll* to a small circle of friends.

The concert attracted not only Wagner's supporters but also drew his enemies into the open. He referred to this at the banquet after the concert when he spoke of the people who were assisting his undertaking – 'and then there's Heckel here, who is annoying people', shaking his hand heartily as he spoke. Subsequently a Munich professor, W. H. Riehl, cultural historian, author of novellas and composer of salon music, bestirred himself and gave public lectures in Mannheim, calling for the foundation of Anti-Wagner Societies. Wagner got his own back on Riehl, who, he said, had broken out of his retreat in order to stir up 'all kinds of petty but malicious mischief', by having an article he had written on Riehl's collection of novellas reprinted with a new satirical afterword. (RWGS, VIII, pp. 205ff.)

Nietzsche wrote to Rohde that he felt wonderfully confirmed in his ideas about music by what he had experienced in Mannheim that week. 'If only you could have been there! Other artistic memories and experiences are nothing, compared to this latest one! I was like a person who has had a premonition, at the moment of its fulfilment. For music is precisely that and nothing else. And that, and nothing else, is precisely what I mean by the word "music", when I am writing about the Dionysian!' (21 December)

Nietzsche sent his new book to Tribschen on 2 January 1872. To please Cosima he had had their copy printed on paper in a yellowish shade she particularly liked. 'May my book be to at least some degree worthy of the interest you have taken in its genesis until now, really to my shame,' he wrote to Wagner. 'And if I myself think that I am right in the main argument, it means no more than that *you* with *your art* must be eternally right.' (2 January)

Cosima's letter thanking him took off in a flight of lyrical eloquence: 'How beautiful your book is! How beautiful and how profound, how profound and how audacious! . . . In this book you have conjured spirits that I had believed obeyed the bidding only of our Meister; there are two worlds, one we do not see because it is too remote, and one we do not recognize because it is too close to us, and you have thrown a brilliant light upon them both . . . I have read this book like a poem which reveals to us the essence of the deepest problems, and I can no more tear myself away from it than the Meister can, for it answers all the unconscious questions of my inner being.' (18 January)

On the same day Wagner wrote an important letter to his nephew Clemens Brockhaus, in which he refuted the latter's criticisms of *Socrates and Greek Tragedy*, and at the same time gave his own opinion of *The Birth of Tragedy*: 'It is a truly godlike thought that the profoundly significant rebirth of art under the influence of the German spirit has been seen by this mind as simultaneously the rebirth . . . of the essence of Greek art. If it is my influence that has guided him in this, then certainly none can judge better than I how deeply and inwardly my thought has become the property of this man who is academically so formidably well equipped with everything that I have had to leave uncultivated in myself.' (CWFN, II, pp. 94ff.)

An incident shortly before, of little significance in itself, appears in retrospect as an early symptom of the way the friendship was to develop. In November Nietzsche had completed a composition for piano duet, twenty minutes in duration, entitled *Echo of a New Year's Eve, with processional song, peasant dance and midnight bell*. 'Now I am copying it', he wrote to Gustav Krug, 'in order to make a birthday present of it to my excellent and honoured friend Frau Cosima W.' (13 November 1871) It was a matter of so much importance to him that he also let his friends Karl von Gersdorff and Erwin Rohde into the secret: he was agog to know what Tribschen would think of his music, since he had never yet heard a competent opinion of it. (To Rohde, 21 December 1871)

Just as Wagner had dedicated the *Siegfried Idyll* to Cosima for her birthday in the previous year, so now Nietzsche dedicated his *New Year's Eve* to her. But he sent it to her through the post instead of presenting it in person, refused her cordial invitation on the grounds that he needed time and solitude to think about his lectures, and spent Christmas on his own in Basel.

He left his friends in no doubt that he regarded himself, for all his devotion to Wagner, as his equal as a cultural critic and innovator. 'I have concluded an alliance with Wagner,' he wrote to Rohde on 28 January 1872. 'You can have no conception of how close to each other we now are, and of how our plans coincide.' And his piano duet and its dedication to Cosima was a cautious attempt to put himself on the same footing as Wagner as composer and as Cosima's confidant.

Wagner resumed work on *Götterdämmerung* on 4 January 1872 with the composition sketch of the last act. 'You ought to hear the Rhinemaidens' second song!' Cosima exclaimed in her letter to Nietzsche. (18 January) But only a few days later she was lamenting that their song had been rudely interrupted. Hagen's horn itself would not have intruded so harshly as the 'ruthless summons of the world' to discuss business in Berlin and Weimar. On his return journey Wagner stopped in Bayreuth and on 1 February set up the festival management committee, consisting of the mayor Theodor Muncker and the lawyer Käfferlein, as well as Feustel. Feustel and Muncker had previously visited him at Tribschen, after the negotiations to buy the piece of land on the Stuckberg had fallen through and it had become necessary to find another site. Wagner had been inclined to give up the idea of Bayreuth after all, but Feustel's persistence and Cosima's diplomacy persuaded him at the last moment to approve of the present site.

He was back in Tribschen by 5 February and was at last able to get on with the composition sketch, which he finished on 10 April. 'He has been working less than we had hoped,' Cosima wrote to Judith. 'He has been ill and then there have been many distractions. I don't know when he will find the leisure to devote himself to his work again, for a whole ocean of affairs, conferences, journeys etc. lies before us.' (22 April)

That he was able to complete the composition sketch – thereby fixing the music in all its essentials and most of its details – in this relatively short period, in spite of all the calls on his time and energies, was due once again to the fact that it had long been prepared and waiting in his mind. We know indeed that he had already written down a version of Siegfried's Funeral March. Cosima noted in her diary on 28 September 1871, her nameday, 'Richard refuses to celebrate St. Cosmas's day. My father expressed his good wishes and Richard said: "He's a Catholic, that comes between us," which made us laugh.' But in fact he did have a late surprise for her. The next morning he called to her: 'I have composed a Greek chorus, but one that is, as it were, sung by the orchestra. After Siegfried's death, while the set is being changed, Siegmund's theme will be heard, as though the chorus is saying: that was his father; then the Sword motive, finally his own theme, then the curtain rises and Gutrune comes on thinking she has heard his horn. How could words ever evoke the impression that these serious themes do, newly recreated. Yet the music expresses the immediate present, too.' (CT, I, p. 444)[14]

On the eighteen staves that it occupies on a half-sheet of manuscript paper in the composition sketch of 1872, this powerful passage appears as a delicate tissue of fine pencil lines that can be taken in at a single look. When sketching purely instrumental music Wagner preferred to use this kind of shorthand notation, which enabled him to oversee the musical form with the eye as well as the mind.

He had been uncertain all along as to what Brünnhilde's final words should be, and had drafted more than one set of lines. He had settled on one of these versions, including the lines:

> Nach dem wunsch- und wahnlos
> heiligsten Wahlland,
> der Weltwanderung Ziel,
> von Wiedergeburt erlöst,
> zieht nun die Wissende hin.

('To the holiest chosen land, where striving and delusion are unknown, the goal of world-wandering, thither, absolved from rebirth, she will go who now knows all.')

Now, when he was starting to set her final monologue, Cosima asked him to leave out this conclusion altogether, because it struck her as 'rather artificial'. He must have been alluding to this debate in the cheerful marginal note on the orchestral sketch: 'Enough! Anything to please Cosel!'[15]

The orchestral finale appears in the composition sketch approximately as we now know it. The only major difference is that the sketch lacks the two bars in which the motive of the Gods' Downfall is played fortissimo by the strings and woodwind, so that Siegfried's theme runs directly into that of Redemption through Love.

At the end the sketch is inscribed: 'So enacted and accomplished, seven years from the day on which my Loldchen [Isolde] was born, 10 April 1872. R. W.'

It was Wagner's intention to leave Tribschen for good on 22 April, and go and live in Bayreuth. A curious encounter took place on the eve of his departure. Early in March he had received a letter which began: 'I am a Jew. By telling you that I tell you everything.' The writer went on to describe how he had dragged out his whole life in complete dispiritedness until the day when Wagner's works had first come to his knowledge, whereupon he had immersed himself in this new world and had been able to forget the other, the real world. It had been the happiest period of his life, but it too now lay in the past. Now he found himself once more in a state of the greatest desolation and had already made one attempt to take his own life. 'Perhaps you can help me again. Of course I do not mean help me from sheer pity . . . But could I not be of some use to you in the production of the "Nibelungs"? I believe I understand the work, even if not perfectly yet. I look to you, then, for help, for the help I urgently need. My parents are rich. I would have the means to go to you at once. I look for an answer as soon as possible. My address is as follows . . . Joseph Rubinstein, c/o Isaac Rubinstein, Kharkov . . .'

Before Wagner had made up his mind how to respond to this, Rubinstein arrived at Tribschen in person, in a state of complete demoralization. 'The extraordinary Russian I mentioned before has been here,' Cosima wrote to Nietzsche, 'on the evening before Wagner left, a strange, disturbing incident.' (24 April) Wagner was kindness itself and offered Rubinstein the opportunity to see him often in Bayreuth. In order to avoid seeming to help him 'from sheer pity' he took him into what was called the 'Nibelung Chancellery', where several young musicians were employed in copying parts. (See also Appendix I.)

Cosima's letter to Nietzsche, quoted above, also said she had just had a telegram announcing Wagner's safe arrival in Bayreuth. They would have been very happy to have seen Nietzsche in Tribschen just once more, and had expected him the previous Sunday. A letter would reach her there up to 29 April. 'And so, auf Wiedersehen in Bayreuth.'

Instead of a letter, Nietzsche himself arrived on 25 April for a final visit lasting two days. 'Last Saturday we bade a sad and deeply felt farewell to Tribschen,' he wrote to Gersdorff. 'Tribschen has now ceased to be: we went about as if among actual ruins, the emotion was everywhere, in the air, in the clouds, the dog wouldn't eat, when you spoke to the servants they couldn't stop sobbing. We packed all the manuscripts, letters and books – oh, it was so miserable! These three years which I have spent close to Tribschen, during which I have visited it twenty-three times – what they mean to me! If I had not had them, what would I be! I am glad that I have conserved that Tribschen world for myself in my book.' (1 May)

Cosima too left Tribschen on 29 April – 'le coeur gros, et moi l'esprit inquiet', as she wrote to Judith. Wagner met her and the five children and Russ at Bayreuth and drove with them to the Hotel Fantaisie, which stood in a romantic park seeming to stretch away for ever, in the nearby village of Donndorf. 'The journey was strange and very fatiguing,' she wrote to Nietzsche, 'and here, suddenly, a dream world, a fairyland!'

They had only a few days in which to relax, for on 6 May they were off again to Vienna to rehearse a concert for the Vienna Wagner Society, which took place on 12 May in the concert hall of the Musikverein, whose two thousand seats had been sold out long in advance. The way Wagner was cheered on his appearance, after every item and at the end was without parallel in the annals of concert-giving, an eyewitness wrote. One laurel wreath after another came hurtling down from the gallery to the platform, putting the players in some anxiety for their instruments.

During the performance of Wotan's Farewell, at the words 'Herauf, wabernde Lohe, umlodre mir feurig den Fels!', a thunderstorm broke out. Wagner alluded to it at the end, as he thanked his audience: 'When the Greeks had a great work in mind, they appealed to Zeus to release his lightning as a sign of his approval. Let us, who are all united in the desire to found a home and a hearth-fire for German art, interpret today's lightning as a favourable omen for our national work − as a sign of blessing from on high!'

The foundation stone of the festival theatre was due to be laid at a ceremony on 22 May, Wagner's fifty-ninth birthday, and messages poured in from far and wide from artists and other well-wishers intending to be there. But there was one person who Wagner feared would be absent.

'My great, dear friend,' he wrote to Liszt on 18 May, 'Cosima insists that you would not come, even if I invited you. If so, then we shall have to bear it, as we have had to bear so much! But I cannot *not* invite you. And what do I declare when I say to you: Come? You entered my life as the greatest man whom I have ever been permitted to call my intimate friend; you slowly withdrew yourself from me, perhaps because you could not feel the same intimacy towards me as I towards you. In your place, your reborn, innermost being came to me and fulfilled my longing to enjoy the closest intimacy with you. And so you live within me and in my sight in complete beauty, and we are as if wedded till death and beyond. You were the first person whose love ennobled me; now I am married to her, for a second, higher life, and am able to do what I could never have done alone. Thus you have become everything to me, while I have had to remain so little to you: how immense my advantage is over yours!

'If I now say to you: Come! I am saying: Come to yourself! For you will find yourself here. May you be blessed and beloved, however you decide! Your old friend, Richard.'

But as ever Princess Wittgenstein stood between him and Liszt and sought to prevent a reunion by claiming that Wagner and Cosima had renounced Christ in word and deed.

'Dear, sublime friend!' Liszt replied on 20 May. 'Deeply moved by your letter, I cannot thank you in words. But I hope ardently that all the shadows, the considerations, that keep me far away will disappear and we shall see each other again soon . . . God's blessing be with you both, and all my love. F. L.' He shrank from the idea of putting such a letter in the post, and gave it to Baroness Meyendorff to hand to Wagner in person.

It had looked, in March, as though another crisis was threatening in Wagner's relationship with King Ludwig. The latter had conveyed, through Düfflipp, another request to deliver the score of *Siegfried*, reminding him that, according to the contract of October 1864, it was the king's property. Wagner had no alternative but to deny that he had yet finished scoring the work, though he had in fact done so on 5 February 1871. He wrote back to Düfflipp that a contract had indeed been concluded at the time, but purely as a form, to placate public opinion. 'I sincerely regret that it has occurred to somebody to revert to this contract which has been completely superseded in the meantime by His Majesty's own most unequivocal, gracious assurances.' (27 March 1872)

But on 22 May a telegram arrived for the 'poet–composer Herr Richard Wagner', in which King Ludwig expressed his sincere good wishes for the occasion. 'Felicity and blessings be upon the great undertaking in the next year! Today, more than ever, I am with you in spirit.'

In spite of the rain a dense crowd gathered on the hill. Twenty-one giant flagstaffs marked out the conformation of the future building. The stone was lowered into place to the strains of the *Huldigungsmarsch,* enclosing within it a capsule containing both the king's telegram and a verse by Wagner:

> Hier schließ' ich ein Geheimnis ein,
> da ruh' es viele hundert Jahr':
> so lange es verwahrt der Stein,
> macht es der Welt sich offenbar.

> ('O may the secret buried here
> rest undisturbed for many a year;
> for while it lies beneath this stone,
> the world shall hear its clarion tone.')

Then Wagner took up the hammer: 'Bless you, my stone, long may you stand and firm may you hold!' As he turned round again he was deathly white and there were tears in his eyes.

'On that day in May in the year 1872, when the foundation stone had been laid on the hill in Bayreuth in pouring rain and under darkened skies,' Nietzsche wrote in *Wagner in Bayreuth*, 'Wagner drove back to the town with some of us; he did not speak and communed long with himself with an expression on his face that words cannot describe. He began the sixtieth year of his life on that day: everything that had gone before had been preparation for that moment. We know that at instants of extreme danger or at any decisive turning-point in life people concentrate everything they have ever experienced in an immeasurably accelerated inner vision, and review both the most recent and the most remote things with the rarest clarity of perception. What may Alexander the Great have seen at that moment when he caused Asia and Europe to be drunk from the same cup? But what Wagner inwardly reviewed on that day – what he has been, what he is and what he will be – we, the nearest to him, can also review to a certain degree: and it is only from Wagner's own viewpoint that we shall be able to understand his great deed ourselves – *in order to ensure its fruitfulness through this understanding*.'

The ceremony continued in the Margraves' Opera House, where Wagner made a speech. It had been suggested to him, he said, that he should describe his undertaking as the foundation of a national theatre, but he had no right to use such a term. Where was the 'nation' that erected such a theatre for itself? 'I had only you, the friends of my particular art, of the work and creation that are peculiarly my own, to whom I could turn to find sympathizers for my plans. And it is only in this almost personal relationship that at present I discern the ground on which we will lay the stone that shall support the whole edifice of our noblest German hopes, which as yet hover before us, an audacious vision. Though it is now but a provisional structure, it shall be so only in the same sense that for centuries all outer forms of the essential German nature have been provisional. But the essence of the German spirit is that it builds from within: the eternal god truly lives in it before it builds itself the temple in his honour.' (RWGS, IX, pp. 326ff.)

In the afternoon, again in the rococo Opera House, Wagner conducted Beethoven's Ninth Symphony, the work that had always had so significant a resonance in his life from his earliest youth. A hand-picked orchestra had assembled at his invitation from all over Germany. 'There are no programmes, no announcements, nothing tucked away in corners,' Wagner told them cheerfully at the last rehearsal. 'We're not giving a concert, we're making music for ourselves and only want to show the world how Beethoven should be played, and anyone who criticizes us can go to the devil!'

'Our ceremony is over,' Cosima wrote to Judith, 'and it was, in spite of the atrocious weather, marvellous. What Beethoven sings, "Alle Menschen werden Brüder", became a reality during these four or five days in Bayreuth, whither all our friends, known and unknown, hastened from the ends of the earth, united in one thought, one belief.' (29 May)

She wrote to Nietzsche, too, on the same day. 'The last lamps of our ceremony are now extinguished, it is quiet about us, but not yet quite peaceful within us . . . The bells are ringing – it is Corpus Christi – and the savage screech of the peacocks can be heard from time to time, the children are singing . . . and it is all, all a dream! . . . Farewell, dear, best of friends, may you be proof and steeled for ever!'

28

The First Festival

I

'I have hopes that the Meister is gradually sinking into the peaceful, twilight mood that he needs for creation,' Cosima wrote to Nietzsche on 14 June 1872; 'yesterday he took up the second act with relish and now I can hear him playing Siegfried and the Rhinemaidens.' After an interruption lasting two months, Wagner was getting himself into the mood to go on with the orchestral sketch of the third act, which he resumed on 15 June at Hagen's line 'Finden wir endlich, wohin du flogest?', and finished on 22 July. 'I lack the power', Cosima confided to her diary, 'to describe the emotion that overcame me when Richard called me to tell me the sketch was finished. He played me the ending, and I do not know whether I am more deeply moved by the sublime music or by the sublime deed.' (DMCW, I, pp. 616f.)

But Wagner's creative quiet was under constant attack and had to be fought for. The act of laying the theatre's foundation stone seemed to unleash a flood of assaults, of which two must be mentioned here, as the retaliation to which they gave rise made them in a sense historic.

The first was an attack on Nietzsche by a former fellow-student, Ulrich von Wilamowitz-Moellendorff, in a pamphlet with the aggressive title: *Philology of the Future! A Rejoinder to Friedrich Nietzsche's 'Birth of Tragedy'* (Berlin, 1872). The Meister had received, read and answered the pamphlet, Cosima told Nietzsche, 'the last in a letter to you, dear Professor, which you will receive any day now'. She would have preferred not to touch the object with a pair of tongs, she added in her impetuous manner. (14 June)

Wagner's answer was his *Open Letter to Friedrich Nietzsche* (RWGS, IX, pp. 295ff.), published on 23 June in the *Norddeutsche*

Allgemeine Zeitung. In it he wrote that he had not believed that things were conducted so crudely in the 'service of the Muses' and that their 'favour' could result in such lack of cultivation. 'What can things be like in our German educational institutions?' He put this question to Nietzsche precisely because he had dared, young as he was, to point out with a creative hand the harm that had been done.[1]

The other attack was of a medical nature. A Munich doctor, Theodor Puschmann, published a pamphlet with the title *Richard Wagner: A Psychiatric Study* (Berlin, 1872), purporting to give 'scientific' proof that Wagner suffered from manic delusions, which had already had a malign influence on his mental condition. One can only hope that not too many unfortunates fell into the hands of this 'priceless imbecile', as Newman calls him, who described himself on his title-page as a 'practising physician and psychiatric specialist'. (Cf. NLRW, III, pp. 564f.) But there could be no more striking illustration of the climate of the time than that such a pamphlet could be not only published but also seriously discussed in the press and reprinted three times within a year.

This time it was the disciple who sprang to his master's defence. When the weekly *Im Neuen Reich* published a leader in its issue for New Year 1873, exhorting 'self-examination and the return to the old simplicity', and commending Puschmann for having pointed the finger at the 'guiltiest' in his theoretical demonstration of Wagner's megalomania, Nietzsche's patience snapped and he pilloried the 'scientific-sounding cries of this huckster' in the *Musikalisches Wochenblatt* for 17 January.

Although Liszt, who since 1869 had again been spending part of each year in Weimar, had not attended the foundation-stone ceremony, Wagner was not deterred from extending the hand of friendship again. 'Will our visit be convenient for you and will you be glad to receive us?' he wrote on 29 August, and Liszt replied: 'From what is holiest in my soul I give you thanks and welcome.' Wagner and Cosima stayed in Weimar from 2 to 6 September. They saw Liszt in the Englischer Hof and in his house in the idyllic setting of the palace gardens. Wagner was in an effervescent mood, but Cosima was distressed by her father's 'weariness of soul'. Liszt, who was fully aware of Princess Wittgenstein's hostility towards his daughter, could not refrain from telling her: 'Cosima really is "ma terrible fille", as I once called her, an extraordinary woman and of very great merits, far above every commonplace standard of judgement and certainly worthy of the admiration she arouses in all who know her – beginning with her first husband, Bülow. She has completely and enthusiastically dedicated herself to Wagner, like Senta to the Flying Dutchman.' (DMCW, I, pp. 622f.)

It says much that Liszt even reconciled himself to Cosima's reception into the Evangelical church, which took place on 31 October.[2] She embraced Protestantism with all the fervour of her Catholic heart. 'My entire soul trembled, our dean spoke with a full heart. Richard deeply moved.' 'How beautiful it was after all in that little vestry!' Wagner confessed. 'How powerfully the dean's voice resounded! What could take the place of the feeling aroused when one hears the unspeakably stirring words: "This is my body"?' Still working on *Götterdämmerung*, he had already entered the world of *Parsifal*. He was studying the Grail legend, and was delighted with the idea that in his treatment of it he displayed an affinity to the Greeks, whose mystics were likewise ignorant of a creator.

As well as composition and all the activities involved in organizing the festival, Wagner also found time to continue the series of essays on music and the theatre which had begun with *On Conducting*: no longer fired with the partisan passion of the earlier Zürich essays, they bear witness to the superior achievement of a now unlimited experience.

'The Meister has now settled down to the work he has been planning for a long time, *On Actors and Singers,* which gives a place of honour to our Heidelberg puppeteer,' Cosima told Nietzsche on 22 August. 'It's yet another way of getting to the heart of the matter,' Wagner commented, 'this time directly, through the actors.' Nietzsche replied that after his study of the choreography of Greek tragedy the essay had struck him 'like a revelation', and he longed for someone to take the aesthetic principles that Wagner had established as the basis for a comprehensive demonstration that traditional 'aesthetics' was now a thing of the past.

What was new about Wagner's thesis was that he developed an aesthetic of the drama out of the art of improvisation, the primeval phenomenon of the psychology of the mime. (*Über Schauspieler und Sänger*, RWGS, IX, pp. 157ff.) Similarly, in his subsequent *Letter to an Actor on Dramatic Art* he advised the actor to practise improvising scenes and whole plays: the basis of all mimetic art lay in that. The author who was unable to imagine the full power of his work in performances he improvised in his own mind had been denied the true vocation to drama. (*Brief über das Schauspielerwesen an einen Schauspieler*, RWGS, IX, pp. 258ff.)

Finally, the most illuminating article of all, though only a few pages long, is *On the Term 'Music Drama'*. From criticizing the misleading implications of the expression, Wagner went on to explain the true relationship of 'music' and 'drama' in his works. Revising the view expressed in *Opera and Drama*, he now admitted the primacy of music, 'the constituent that was everything at the beginning'. Music reveals the sense of its sounds to our eyes by means of the 'scenic parable', 'as a mother explains the mysteries of religion to her children by telling them the legends of the saints'. For that reason he was almost inclined to describe his dramas as 'deeds of music made visible' – certainly a high-sounding category of aesthetics for future Poloniuses to add to their lists! While he had once believed that its outcome would be an 'artwork of the future', he no longer thought he had created a genre that all and sundry would be able to adopt. His colleagues should continue to use the term 'opera' for their works: 'It makes their position quite clear, does not make them sail under false colours, raises them above any kind of rivalry with their librettists; and if the ideas they have for an aria, a duet or even a drinking chorus are good ones, then they will please their audiences and produce a respectable piece of work, without unduly exerting themselves to the extent, perhaps, even of spoiling their agreeable little ideas.' (*Über die Benennung 'Musik-drama'*, RWGS, IX, pp. 302ff.)

At the beginning of November 1872 Wagner prepared to set off on a journey of inspection 'hither and thither among the theatrical staging posts', hunting for artists. When his faith in the success of his undertaking faltered, Cosima rallied him: the author of works like his could be allowed to attempt the impossible. And he too decided that in the end it was his vocation to set examples. 'If the light is there it cannot be extinguished, it must go on shining.' But Cosima felt the touch of despair one day, when he said he thought there was something wrong with his heart.

In five weeks, from 10 November to 15 December, they made a round trip that took in Würzburg, Frankfurt, Darmstadt, Mannheim, Stuttgart, Strassburg, Karlsruhe, Wiesbaden, Mainz, Cologne, Düsseldorf, Hanover, Bremen, Magdeburg, Dessau and Leipzig. 'I have already bolted down four theatres and have had to get through a regrettably large number of banquets and dinners,'

Wagner wrote to Feustel from Darmstadt. 'The only certain prize I have captured so far is *one* singer,' and he added with a sigh: 'If there had been anyone who could relieve me of this journey, I would gladly make him a Christmas present of all the honours and festivities!' (20 November)

Cosima excused herself from the banquet in Cologne and used the time to write to Nietzsche. In among her chatter of Lenbach, of the Rhenish school of Old Masters, of the churches of Cologne, she scattered throughout the letter, in parentheses, a commentary on the noises coming up to her from the banqueting room below, which gives a more vivid account of the evening than any formal report: '(They're beginning – a military band – *Tannhäuser* overture; poor, poor Meister, everywhere the same torment, the same wrong tempos)' – '(My God! they won't stop, now they're playing the Soldiers' Chorus from *Faust*. You see, "more appetite than taste", my head is reeling!)' (4 December)

But at the same time the journey took Wagner back into the past and into his own youth. A thousand memories were revived as he roamed through the narrow streets of Würzburg with Cosima. The little house next to the Residenz still stood, where he had lived on his chorus master's pay of ten gulden a month and had written the closing bars of *Die Feen* to the ceremonial accompaniment of all the bells in the city. On the Breiter Weg in Magdeburg he pointed out a fourth-floor window to her: 'Up there we kept our brilliant household, with love, the poodle and the summonses for debt.' The theatre where *Das Liebesverbot* had received its first performance was unchanged, and he told her how he had conducted wearing a sky-blue frock coat with gigantic cuffs and felt himself in heaven.

Wagner cast up the artistic accounts of his journey in his essay *An Insight into Opera in Germany Today*. It is filled with pain and irony: he knew beforehand that he could expect to hear his own works disfigured and he had steeled himself to endure it with the resignation born of long practice. But in every field of opera, from Mozart to Meyerbeer, he had encountered an inability in conductors to do anything right which had far exceeded his worst expectations. It cut him to the quick, as an entry in Cosima's diary shows: the performance of Auber's charming *Le Maçon* in Darmstadt had made him feel sorry for the singers and the composer, to whose memory he had dedicated a warm-hearted reminiscence a year before,[3] and weep for the decline of the theatre.

'In opera,' he appealed to conductors, 'if you are good musicians in other respects, pay attention solely to what is happening on the stage, whether it is a soloist's monologue or a scene of general action; your essential concern should be that that episode, intensified and spiritualized beyond measure by the part taken by the music, is as clear as it possibly can be; if you manage to attain that clarity then you may be sure that you have found the right tempo and the right orchestral delivery as a matter of course.'

He ended by singling out for praise the production of Gluck's *Orpheus* in Dessau: never had he experienced a nobler or more perfect realization of a work as a whole. Everything – grouping, decor, lighting, every movement, every entrance and exit – had been in perfect harmony, and so had achieved that ideal illusionism that envelops us like a 'prohetic dream of something we have never actually known'. 'But this happened, as I say, in little Dessau.' (*Ein Einblick in das heutige deutsche Opernwesen*, RWGS, IX, pp. 264ff.)

On his return to Bayreuth he heard from the festival management committee the sorry news that the Wagner Societies, of which they had had such high hopes, had raised far less than even the most modest estimates had predicted. His own concerts had been the only successful enterprises. Wagner's appalled reaction was that he could not possibly subject himself to the strain of giving a concert for every thousand talers they still needed: it would mean another two hundred or so concerts! But since Feustel and Muncker hesitated to issue new contracts for the building work in these circumstances he had to accept the necessity of doing something of the kind, deciding this time to concentrate his efforts on Berlin and Hamburg.

'It's a bad end to the year,' Cosima wrote to their friend Malwida, 'and a bad beginning to 1873. Richard is tired to death, and I can only follow him, only suffer with him, but I cannot help him!'

As a late gift for Christmas and her birthday, Nietzsche sent *Five Prefaces to Five Unwritten Books*, 'written in a cheerful mood over Christmas 1872 for Frau Cosima Wagner in sincere respect and in answer to oral and epistolary questions'. Worried as they were, Wagner and Cosima were particularly distressed that he did not come himself. Writing to thank him for the *Five Prefaces* on their return from their second tour, on 12 February 1873, she felt obliged to tell him candidly the reason for her delay: Wagner had been hurt by his not coming and by the way he chose to announce the fact. She had been torn between telling and not telling him so, and so she had left it to long-suffering time to erase the minor sense of grievance and allow the purity of their true feelings to flower again. 'Now this has come to pass, and when we talk about you I do not hear the slightest note of offended friendship but only pleasure in what, once more, you have given us.'

'I simply cannot imagine', Nietzsche wrote to Gersdorff, 'how anyone could be more loyal and more deeply devoted to Wagner in every matter of importance than I am; if I could imagine it then I would be it. But in small, less important, subsidiary points, and in the matter of a certain abstention from frequent personal intercourse, which is necessary to me, I might almost say for "sanitary" reasons, I must preserve my freedom, really only in order to be able to sustain that loyalty on a higher plane.' (24 February)

Cosima wrote in her letter of 12 February that they had been particularly struck by the ideas he had aired in the 'Preface to Homer's Contest'. But they will not have read it as we do today with the wisdom of hindsight. The Greek concept of the 'contest', he writes, is inimical to the modern idea of the 'exclusivity' of genius; it presupposes 'that in the natural order of things there are always *several* geniuses, who reciprocally stimulate each other to new achievements and at the same time restrain each other within the bounds of moderation. That belief lies at the heart of the Hellenic idea of the contest: it abhors monocracy and fears its dangers, and as the means of defence against genius it requires – a second genius.' It was typical of Nietzsche's 'paper courage', when he was asserting a new claim, not to do it face to face.

Wagner and Cosima set off on their second tour on 12 January 1873. 'With a heavy heart I ask myself what we think we can accomplish in this iron age of industry,' she confessed as they travelled through the industrial belt, 'the last and highest cry and upward reach of art as it lies stretched in the dust.'

Apart from the concerts in Berlin and Hamburg, the most memorable event was Wagner's reading of the text of *Götterdämmerung* in the house of Count von Schleinitz on 17 January. In Cosima's view there could seldom have assembled so select a company from all walks of life for a single purpose: princes, ambassadors, university professors, the emperor's adjutants, and captains of finance like Strousberg and Bleichröder. 'Then I saw Moltke, too, much older than his pictures, stooping with flashing eyes . . .

The more select and important the people there, and the more interested and sympathetic they showed themselves, the more profoundly one felt the isolation of genius.' (DMCW, I, pp. 647f.; CWFN, II, p. 46)

Wagner used to read his own verse texts as he read Shakespeare, without histrionics but with thrilling effect. Cosima found words inadequate to describe him while he was doing it: his face transfused with light, his eyes visionary, his hands magical, whether gesturing or still, his voice gentle, all soul, but penetrating into the depths and to the furthest horizons. (BBL 1938, p. 11)

He prefaced the reading with a short introduction: whereas in opera, in the usual sense of the term, only those passages of lyrical reflection inserted into the action were considered suitable for musical realization, in his works his dramatic dialogue itself provided the stuff of the musical realization. He believed that the dialogic composition of his text justified him in presenting it to his audience 'naked as it is'. (RWGS, IX, pp. 308ff.)

'We really are back in Bayreuth,' Cosima told Nietzsche in her letter of 12 February, 'though for how long is something we cannot tell.' Wagner used the interval to write another of the short essays for which he drew on the wealth of his artistic experience: *On the Performance of Beethoven's Ninth Symphony*. In it he rehearsed once again all that contributes to clarity in the delivery of the work. (*Zum Vortrag der Neunten Symphonie Beethovens*, RWGS, IX, pp. 231ff.) He also worked on the collected edition of his writings, hoping to have the eighth volume ready before embarking on another concert tour.

One moonlit night he and Cosima went to inspect their new house, which was still in the process of being built, and he showed her the spot he had chosen for their grave. 'Mood serious and light-hearted together', she recorded. The worthy Muncker was very alarmed when Wagner discussed the grave in the garden with him, 'but Richard explained to him the serenity with which we look forward to our eternal rest'.

A telegram from Nietzsche and Rohde announced their intention of arriving for a visit on 6 April. The former confessed to Gersdorff that he himself had not yet grasped quite how it had all suddenly come about. Even on the point of departure he was moved at the thought that the two of them were about to arrive at the railway station of *that* place, where every step would arouse a memory.

They had been the happiest days of his life. 'There was something in the air that I have never sensed anywhere else, something quite outside the scope of verbal expression but full of hope . . . I hope my visit will repair what was damaged by my failure to go there for Christmas, and I thank you from my heart for your simple and potent encouragement, which has cleared my vision and shooed away the stupid "midges" that sometimes trouble me.' (5 April)

He brought another manuscript with him, *Philosophy in the Greek Tragic Age*, which he read aloud to them over three evenings. (CT, I, pp. 668f.) However, his sister's claim, in her biography, that Wagner did not disguise his disappointment at Nietzsche's occupying himself with such remote matters, instead of with the Bayreuth undertaking, is yet another of her pet distortions of the truth. Only a short time before, Cosima had referred in her diary to the 'new Nietzsche essay' – probably one of the *Five Prefaces* – saying that for all its profundity it sometimes betrayed a boorishness that made her and Wagner wish he would concentrate on Greek subjects. (DMCW, I, pp. 644f.)

The deep impression Wagner made on his young friend in his ceaseless struggle for Bayreuth is revealed in Nietzsche's letter to him of 18 April: 'It's true, every day I grow more melancholy, feeling so acutely how gladly I would help or benefit you in some way, and how completely incapable I am of doing anything of the kind.' 'Or perhaps I shall have done something', he went on, 'when I have dealt with what I have in hand.'

This was a reference to a book by David Friedrich Strauss, *The Old and the New Belief*, whose intention seemed to be to get rid of 'redemption, prayer and Beethovenian music'. Wagner and Cosima had discovered great enthusiasm for it wherever they went on their recent tour, and it had been the topic of much concerned discussion during Nietzsche's visit. Back in Basel he lost no time in settling to the task of showing the famous historian up as a specimen of the German 'cultural philistine'. 'Emotional tension while working on the first of the *Unseasonal Meditations,*' he recorded, 'anxiety for genius and works of genius, contrasted with the sight of Straussian complacency.' His intention was that it should be the first of a series of essays supporting Wagner in his fight for a German culture, and his original title for them was 'Observations of the Horizon from Bayreuth'. But the expression 'unseasonal' ('unzeitgemäß'), which he now decided to use, was one that he had first thought of in connection with Wagner and what he stood for: in 1869 he had written to Rohde that Wagner stood on his own feet, firmly rooted by his own strength, his eyes fixed far above all ephemerality and not of this age – 'unseasonal in the best sense'.

'I swear to you before God,' Wagner exclaimed after receiving the first of the *Meditations*, 'I believe you are the only person who knows what I want to do!' But he could not suppress the premonition that a time would come when he would have to defend the book against Nietzsche himself. (21 September 1873)

Having received assurances that a concert in Cologne would make a good profit, he agreed to give one in the Gürzenich hall on 24 April. He began a conversation with his agent in Cologne by telling him the story of the Emperor Alexius Comnenus, who, on the eve of battle, asked his commanding general the number of his soldiers. ' "An immense army," the general replied, "a mass of troops reaching as far as the eye can see." The emperor: "I want to know the exact number." – "Ten thousand." – "I am satisfied with that, they will be enough." – Now tell me, my friend,' Wagner went on, 'how much will today's concert make?' – 'Three thousand talers.' – 'Very good, then I am as satisfied as the emperor, and you have done your job well.'

On his way back to Bayreuth Wagner made another trip into his past by breaking his journey at Eisleben, where he had stayed with his step-uncle the goldsmith half a century before and fought the 'autochthonous boy population'.

Now he hoped for three months without disruption in which to orchestrate *Götterdämmerung*. He began the prelude on 3 May, with the chords already heard in Brünnhilde's greeting of the sun from *Siegfried*, not only transformed by being a semitone lower and in 6/4 instead of triple time, but above all darkened by the use of tubas instead of trumpets and trombones, so that they now present not day but night. Here in the Norns' scene he achieves an orchestral sound that in its ebb and flow recalls the swell of an organ. The accompaniment is so symphonic in its treatment that at a concert in Vienna in 1875 he risked performing the whole scene without the vocal parts.

When he came to score the transition leading into Siegfried's Rhine Journey he wished that he could have a second complete orchestra so as to be able to express the state of Brünnhilde's feelings as he would have liked. It was not the desire to make effects for their own sake and play virtuoso games, but the need to enable different instruments to enter and alternate with each other. (BBL 1936, p. 1)

Meanwhile Cosima had begun to prepare in good time for his sixtieth birthday. She enquired of Judith about French translations of the standard works of Indian literature, and gave him the four volumes of the Rig-Veda in Alexandre Langlois's translation.[4] But the most important celebrations took place in the Margraves' Opera House. She arranged for the company temporarily in residence to perform Ludwig Geyer's *Der Bethlehemitische Kindermord*. Peter Cornelius was commissioned to write a play he called *An Artist's Dedication*, in which the painter Genelli introduced the youthful Wagner to the Dramatic Muse. The evening began and ended with two of Wagner's juvenilia, the Concert Overture in C major and a New Year Cantata written in Magdeburg. Wagner listened to the overture very attentively; it was strange, really, he remarked to Cosima, it could not have been written by either Beethoven or Bellini. He left the theatre where these youthful memories had been revived deeply moved.

Wagner had sent a presentation copy of the score of *Rheingold* to King Ludwig, with the dedication:

Conceived in faith in the German spirit,
Completed to the glory of his noble benefactor
King Ludwig II,
by Richard Wagner.

Ludwig thanked him in a birthday telegram: 'Completed the eternal work! I exulted at the news.'

Nietzsche's birthday letter still reflects the distress caused by his visit to Bayreuth the month before: 'What should we be if we could not have you, and what else, for instance, should I be (as I feel at every moment) but stillborn! I tremble every time I think that I might perhaps never have met you: and then life truly would not be worth living and I should not know what to do with myself from one hour to the next.' (20 May)

But the letters and celebrations could do nothing to relieve Wagner of his worries and sometimes he felt like following the advice an old soldier gave Frederick the Great after the battle of Kolin: 'Now, Your Majesty, just let the battle be.' In order to keep his friends informed of how the undertaking stood, he had an essay printed, *The Festival Theatre at Bayreuth*, illustrated with architect's drawings. (*Das Bühnenfestspielhaus zu Bayreuth*, RWGS, IX, pp. 322ff.) He sent a copy to Bismarck, with a covering letter in which he said that some people might think it a regrettable omission if he failed to acquaint the restorer of German hopes with the cultural idea that inspired him. If his enterprise had to be realized without the participation of the only truly beneficial and ennobling authority, then he would have to comfort himself with the thought of the fate that befell the renascence of the German spirit through the agency of the great poets of the second half of the previous century, which Frederick the Great, although the true hero of that renascence, persistently regarded with cold antipathy. (24 June)

He received no reply.

The theatre was topped out on 2 August with due ceremony, attended, to Wagner's joy, by Liszt. They climbed up to the top of the shell of the building on a swaying ladder, accompanied by the children. The world took on the appearance of a dream from up there, Cosima wrote, an artist's dream that had become reality. The foreman carpenter began to recite some verses by the Evangelical dean, asking God to keep the roof on the building, but Wagner cut the final lines, which were addressed to himself, and replaced them by a cheer for the 'German spirit'.

As the funds were increasing only very slowly during this summer, Feustel recommended applying for a loan, for which they would have to find a highly placed guarantor. In the circumstances, Wagner wrote to the king on 11 August, he ventured to ask his only true patron and benefactor to send Secretary Düfflipp to Bayreuth to investigate the financial position for himself. Receiving no answer to that, Wagner addressed himself directly to Düfflipp, telling him that Feustel was coming to see him. Düfflipp replied that the king had not been prepared to give the guarantee Wagner had asked for. He had raised the matter again after Feustel's visit, but in vain. The king was wrapped up in his own plans and he had no interest in anything that might possibly hamper or delay them. (KLRW, IV, pp. 210f.) Those plans centred on the building of Neuschwanstein.

When one thread broke, Wagner commented, he tried to spin another. He discussed with Heckel the idea of launching an appeal representing the festival as a matter of national concern, to capture the interest of those who might not actually want to attend it but could spare ten or twenty talers for a great cause. A conference of Patrons and delegates from the Wagner Societies was called for 31 October in Bayreuth to debate the matter. 'If you take the step of a *manifesto*,' Wagner wrote to Heckel, '. . . then I ask you, if I may, to consult *Nietzsche* in Basel about writing it . . . I have very special confidence in him, specifically, for the task.' (23 September)

But the conference rejected Nietzsche's *Admonition to the Germans* as inopportune, and Cosima, too, felt that if the infant undertaking was capable of survival, then it was too severe an instrument. Instead Professor Adolf Stern of Dresden was entrusted with the composition of an appeal to be sent, with subscription lists, to every book, music and art shop in Germany. 'The whole session was an extraordinary occasion,' Nietzsche told Gersdorff, 'half elevated, half very down to earth; but powerful enough overall to silence all talk of lotteries or anything of that kind . . . The evening ended with a harmless, jolly and very successful banquet at the Sonne, at which Frau Wagner and Fräulein von Meysenbug were the only ladies present. I had the place of honour between them and so was given a nickname from an Italian opera, "Sargino, the pupil of love".'

The four thousand dealers in books and music who received the appeal kept the subscription lists under the counter. Only in Göttingen did a handful of students put their names down for a few talers. An Englishman like Newman cannot restrain himself, in the circumstances, from commenting ironically on Wagner's faith in the 'German spirit'.

Since Düfflipp thought a request coming directly from Wagner might perhaps help, the latter sat down to write to the king on 6 November, reminding him that it had been he who had once adjured him: 'Complete your work: mine be the concern of presenting it worthily to the world!' He also said that he intended to visit Munich with his trusted friend Feustel before the month was out, in the hope of obtaining an audience of the king.

An answer came through Düfflipp. Unfortunately an audience could not be arranged, as 'His Majesty is on the point of moving to Hohenschwangau, and wishes to be undisturbed there'.

Wagner replied that he had almost foreseen the refusal of an audience, but it was essential for him to know very soon whether his request was also to be refused or not. If the *Ring* was to be performed at Bayreuth in 1875, then they must have the security for the credit they needed by the end of the month, so as to be able to give contracts to machinists and scene–painters. (14 November 1873, KLRW, III, p. 25)

On 21 November Wagner saw Düfflipp in Munich, and his hopes were raised that the guarantee might be given. But on 6 January 1874, when more than a month had passed without any confirmation, he asked for a definite decision. It came: His Majesty refused. (SRLW, II, pp. 133f.)

Instead of a guarantee Wagner had received the Order of Maximilian from the king on 12 December, which he was tempted to return when he heard that it had also been awarded to Brahms. 'His Bavarian Majesty sends no word,' Cosima wrote to Countess von Schleinitz, 'but the Order of Maximilian has come instead . . . I besought Wagner to accept the honour in silence, but I thought of Falstaff and his tailor: "I looked a' should have sent me two and twenty yards of satin and he sends me security" – we asked for a guarantee and have been sent an Order.' (DMCW, I, p. 681)

On the morning of her birthday she asked Wagner to drive her to the theatre. The stage was awe-inspiring: 'The whole towers like an Assyrian palace and the pillars are aligned within it like sphinxes, the wings stretch to each side like mysterious passages . . . From the stage we then went into the auditorium. At the moment of entering it, it makes a sublime impression. No amount of instruction can do this for the spectator, but to enter this room prepares him for the mysteries in an instant.'

'Now we must be many things at once,' Wagner warned her, 'cautious, clever, truthful and well bred. You shall hear *Der Ring des Nibelungen* yet.' He had conceived yet another plan in their apparent impasse: the emperor should commission him to produce the *Ring* in the summer of 1876, to celebrate the fifth anniversary of the peace, for the sum of 100,000 talers. He asked Heckel to approach the Grand Duke of Baden to act as intermediary, but the duke, anticipating refusal, advised against the scheme.

In the meantime Wagner had by chance found out why King Ludwig was annoyed with him. Some time earlier the poet Felix Dahn had sent him an ode to King Ludwig with the demand that he set it to music. Finding it impossible, Wagner had simply refused. He could very well understand Dahn's desire to have one of his poems set by himself, who had hitherto set only his own words, he wrote to the king; but he had dismissed Dahn's claim that it was

Ludwig's own wish as just another of the boasts he had heard so often. (9 January 1874)

The king replied that Dahn had indeed expressed the wish that Wagner would set the ode, at an audience he had given him the previous summer; 'I didn't want to put him out, so I agreed rather than disagreed with the idea, voilà tout . . . Thank God that through your genius you are called to higher things than to provide musical illustrations to fulsome odes!' (25 January)[5]

This frank explanation cleared the air. 'No, no, and again *no*! It shall not end thus!' Ludwig exclaimed in the same letter. 'Something must be done. Our plan must not be allowed to come to nothing!' 'Everything is all right with His Majesty,' Wagner reported to Heckel on 9 February; 'the undertaking in which you take so laudably serious an interest is assured.' And referring to his other idea for celebrating the peace of 1871: 'I *knew* that would all lead nowhere; my cause requires a "wise fool".'

And so on 20 February 1874 a contract was drawn up between the festival management committee and the Court Secretary's Office, guaranteeing the committee an advance of 100,000 talers from the Cabinet Treasury. One unwelcome condition was that the entire income from the patronage vouchers was to go to the treasury from thenceforward, and Wagner did everything he could to get round it. But it was not until 27 September 1875 that the king gave his authorization for the Cabinet Treasury to take only 315 gulden out of the 520 brought in by each voucher. Then, as the date of the performances grew closer and rehearsals began, current expenditure began to rise steeply – to 2000 marks a day – and Wagner was forced to ask for a stay in the repayments. 'I received no news! My artists were on the point of coming: I was bold enough to interpret the silence in my own favour . . . So I crossed the Rubicon: I let my players and singers come.' 'Remain favourably inclined towards me,' he begged the king, 'and may you be eternally blessed for it!' (12 June 1876)

On 29 June Düfflipp informed Wagner that the repayments could be suspended until a total of 800 patronage vouchers had been sold, but there was once more a qualification: the Cabinet Treasury would make no further advances over and above the 216,152 marks, 42 pfennigs that had already been indented for of the 300,000 marks guaranteed.

'It is glorious, after all, to have been forsaken by everyone!'

Cosima had declared one evening early in January 1874, after a stormy day of crisis, and Wagner replied: 'It is the only honourable state.'

They had no suspicion then that their most eloquent disciple had also forsaken them. Returning to Basel, Nietzsche found dismaying news from Bayreuth waiting for him. 'Things were in a bad state, without a single ray of comfort, from the New Year onwards,' he wrote to Rohde on 15 February, 'from which I was only able to rescue myself in the end by the strangest method: I began, as coldly as I could, to investigate the reasons why the undertaking had failed; in doing so I learned much, and I believe I now understand Wagner far better than I used to.'

What Nietzsche noted down in the month of January 1874 amounted to the whole of his philosophy of failure. He looked for the causes, not in the uncomprehending obstruction of the world but in Wagner's character: the composer was, Nietzsche decided, an actor and a tyrant; he sought to achieve tyranny through the massed forces of the theatre; he brooked no other individual personality within his own ambit; in respect of musical form he possessed all the crudity for which Germans were notorious; his art was a kind of Counter-Reformation; 'what do we care for a Tannhäuser, a Lohengrin, a Tristan, a Siegfried!' In short, in sixty-nine aphorisms, Nietzsche not merely questioned the worth of Wagner's personality as man and as artist, he roundly denied it.[6]

Nor did he confine himself to private note-taking: Overbeck recalled that Nietzsche spoke to him about Wagner at that time in terms that anticipated *The Wagner Case*.[7]

At all events the condemnation is so complete and so fundamental that even Charles Andler, who was sympathetic to Nietzsche's point of view, had to admit that it was astonishing how Nietzsche managed to continue regarding himself as Wagner's friend, claiming his hospitality and supporting his cause, when he found so many deficiencies in his character, and so many dubious aspects to his cause. 'His silence on the subject of his doubts was an act of great and culpable hypocrisy towards Wagner.'[8]

It is only human, all too human, that an enthusiastic disciple should try to dissociate himself from a cause that he gives up as lost. There is no need to attribute disreputable motives to it. To be forced to watch the downfall of a cause, or a person, to which one has privately and publicly subscribed is painful and humiliating. 'It is hard to recover from this waiting and fearing,' Nietzsche wrote to Rohde on 19 March, returning to the same topic; 'there were times when I gave up hope completely.'

And so he 'rescued' himself by distancing himself 'as coldly as he could'.

By an irony of fate, immediately after writing that, he received the long letter in which Cosima thanked him for sending them the second of the *Unseasonal Meditations, Of the Uses and Disadvantages of History for Life*. 'What has made a particularly deep impression on me personally in your book is the certainty, which it makes even clearer, that the suffering endured by genius in this world illuminates the whole order of things for you, and that you see not with the eyes of the intelligence alone, but with the more penetrating vision of the heart as well . . . Thus you have been enabled to form an overall judgement on the cultural world of today by your compassion for the suffering of genius, and this gives your work its marvellous warmth.' (20 March)

During the anxious months of the desperate struggle to save Bayreuth, Wagner finished the score of the first act of *Götterdämmerung* and gave it to Cosima for Christmas. He also had two encounters with works of contemporary music, each significant in its own way. He had already gone through Liszt's oratorio *Christus* at the piano with Cosima in 1872. 'That anyone can so relinquish the hard-won skills of a great art in order to imitate the droning of priests is an impoverishment of the spirit,' she wrote in her diary. 'We are saddened by this development of Father's, for which Princess Wittgenstein is undoubtedly the most to blame.' They could not, however, avoid attending the first complete performance of the work in the Stadtkirche in Weimar on 29 May 1873, under Liszt's direction. 'Richard passed through every phase of transport to downright rage,' she remarked, 'finally achieving a state of the most profound, loving fair-mindedness.' (DMCW, I, pp. 612, 622)

Anton Bruckner, who visited Wagner in 1873, had first been introduced to him when he was in Munich to hear the première of *Tristan* in 1865, and in 1868 he obtained permission to perform the final chorus of *Die Meistersinger* with the Frohsinn choral society in Linz, two months before the work's première. He recalled his first visit to Bayreuth in a letter to Hans von Wolzogen after Wagner's death:

It was about the beginning of September 1873 . . . when
I asked the Meister if I might show him my No. 2 in C
minor and my No. 3 in D minor. The Thrice-Blessed
refused because of lack of time (theatre-building) and
said he couldn't look at the scores now, since even the
'Nibelungs' had had to be laid on one side. When I
replied: 'Meister, I have no right to rob you of even a
quarter of an hour, and I only thought that with the
Meister's powerful perception, a single glance at the
themes would suffice for the Meister to know the
substance of it.' Thereupon the Meister said, slapping
me on the shoulder, 'Come on, then,' went with me
into the drawing room and looked at the Second
Symphony. 'Very good,' he said, but he seemed to find
it rather tame (for they originally made me very nervous
about it in Vienna), and picked up the Third (D minor),
and exclaiming 'let's see, let's see – well – ah!' he went
through the whole of the first section (the exalted one
singled out the trumpet part) and then said: 'Leave this
work here with me, I will take a closer look at it after
dinner' . . . I thought to myself, shall I make my
request, when Wagner asked me what was on my mind.
Very shyly, my heart pounding , I then said to my
dearly beloved master: 'Meister! I have something in my
heart, that I do not trust myself to say!' The Meister said
'Out with it! You know how much I like you.'
Thereupon I made my request, but only in the event of
the Meister's not disapproving, since I did not want to
profane his thrice-famous name. The Meister said: 'This
evening, at five o'clock, you are invited to Wahnfried, I
shall be there, and after I've had a chance to look at the
D minor symphony properly, we'll talk about this
matter again.' I had been up to the theatre site
immediately before I went Wahnfried at five o'clock.
When I arrived the master of masters hurried to meet
me with open arms, hugged me and said: 'My dear
friend, the dedication is quite all right. The work gives
me uncommonly great pleasure.' For two and a half
hours I had the good fortune to sit beside the Meister,
while he talked about musical affairs in Vienna, offered

> me beer, took me out in the garden and showed me
> his grave!!! Then I had, or rather, was permitted,
> blissfully happy, to accompany the Meister into his
> house.

The sculptor Gustav Adolf Kietz, who was working on a bust of Cosima and had set up his studio in the villa, which was still not completed, was also present during this conversation. According to him, Bruckner kept on trying to talk about Viennese enthusiasm for *Lohengrin*. 'Oh, never mind about that,' Wagner replied, 'I know that, there's a swan comes, bringing a knight, it's something a little different, it makes a change – here, have a drink instead, this is a wonderful beer, Weihenstephan, your health!' – 'For God's sake, Meister, I mustn't, it would be the death of me, I've just come from Karlsbad!' – 'Nonsense, it's good for you, drink it!'

And in spite of his protests, which hilariously punctuated his musical conversation, Bruckner was obliged to drink one glass after another, with the result that the next morning he did not know which symphony Wagner had accepted. Fortunately Kietz, who was staying at the same hotel, remembered that they had talked about a symphony in D minor; at the time he had thought they meant Beethoven's Ninth. To be quite sure, Bruckner wrote to ask Wagner again, if it was to be the symphony 'where the trumpet introduces the theme'. 'Yes! Yes! Cordial greetings!' Wagner scribbled at the bottom of the note, and 'Bruckner the trumpet' became a kind of leitmotiv with him.

Wagner's conscientious study of the score shows that accepting the dedication was no empty act of politeness on his part, as indeed one would hardly expect of him. Cosima's diary tells us that early in 1875 he went through the symphony at the piano with her; the dedicatory copy of it is still in the Wagner Archives. Meeting Bruckner in Vienna in May of the same year, he spoke of performing his symphonies, according to Heckel, and in the letter to Wolzogen Bruckner went on to say: 'Anno 1882, already sick, the Meister took me by the hand and said "Rely upon it, I will myself perform the symphony and all your works." ' In his biography of Bruckner Peter Raabe questions the sincerity of this promise and wonders where and when Wagner thought he would carry it out, but it is obvious that he was thinking not of concert tours, but of the Bayreuth 'school', the project nearest to his heart after the festival, where he intended that the performance style of the widest possible variety of works should be taught and practised.[9]

Wagner also had this to say about Bruckner during the 'Parsifal summer' of 1882: 'I know of only one who approaches Beethoven, and that is Bruckner.' His behaviour towards the Austrian composer rebuts the legend that he had no time for his contemporaries, but above all it proves that he had completely discarded the theory he had advanced in *The Artwork of the Future* of the 'end of the symphony with Beethoven's Ninth'.

Moreover, while he was scoring *Götterdämmerung* in 1874, he conceived the desire to compose orchestral works himself, 'each having the dimensions and significance of a large-scale overture', 'because truly, while I have been toiling on the large scores of my dramas,' he wrote to Schott, 'a large number of embryo ideas and outline schemes have leapt into my mind for orchestral compositions of the kind that I have now offered you; I have suppressed and ignored them, but when I have finished that last, immense score, I think that it would be a true recreation and pleasure to return to them and realize them'. (23 and 31 January 1874) Although the offer was dictated at that particular time by the hope of obtaining an advance of 10,000 gulden, so as to pay for the final stages in completing the new house and garden, nevertheless the wish kept reviving, showing that he was perfectly serious in seeking a channel for the expression of this side of his nature, too. After he had finished *Götterdämmerung* he talked to Cosima about these new orchestral works, and told her that he would call them 'wavering shapes' ('schwankende Gestalten') from the first two lines of Goethe's *Zueignung*, which he would quote as their motto:

> Ihr naht euch wieder, schwankende Gestalten,
> Die früh sich einst dem trüben Blick gezeigt.

('Once more you approach, you wavering shapes, which appeared to my sad gaze in years gone by.')

These symphonic plans revived in an altered and more definite form while he was working on *Parsifal*.

Work on the house was sufficiently advanced by 28 April for the family to be able to move into it.[10] 'At last – the move into the house. It's not ready yet, but we shall get the better of it,' Cosima wrote in her diary. At four o'clock it was consecrated by a meeting

of the festival management committee and Wagner's assistants.
'Richard told me the meeting had a beautiful atmosphere, they had
all been filled with a single spirit of dedication to the cause. There
could have been no better way of consecrating the house.'

It had been on the very first occasion that Wagner was passing
that he had suddenly stopped the carriage, gone for a walk across
the site and decided on the position and outlines of the drive, the
house and the garden within half an hour.

The drive is an avenue lined with chestnut trees, now replanted,
leading up to and encircling a round rosebed with the twice-lifesize
bronze bust of King Ludwig by Zumbusch. The plain façade of the
house beyond is timeless, its sole ornament the sgraffito by Krausse
depicting the 'Artwork of the Future'.

The purely functional character of the lobby and stairwell means
that one passes without pause into the hall, a lofty room reaching
the full height of the house, with a gallery running round at first-
floor level and lit by a skylight. It was intended as a music room.
The Pompeian red walls set off the marble statuettes of Wagnerian
characters and Kietz's busts of Wagner and Cosima. Cosima's lilac
sitting room used to lie to the left, the dining room to the right of
the hall. On its far side double doors lead into the great drawing
room (destroyed by bombing on 5 April 1945 and restored in 1976),
with a huge bay window overlooking the garden. The walls are
lined to half their height with the three thousand volumes and more
that make up the library of masterpieces of world literature, from
the Upanishads of India to Wagner's own contemporaries. In
Wagner's day portraits of Goethe, Schiller, Beethoven, Liszt, King
Ludwig, Adolf Wagner, Ludwig Geyer, Johanna Wagner, the
Comtesse d'Agoult, Wagner and Cosima were hung above the
bookcases. Round the edge of the coffered ceiling, and added at a
later date, runs a row of the coats of arms of the German towns
where Wagner Societies were formed. The taste of the nineteenth
century was ennobled and raised wellnigh to timelessness by the
genius who lived in this house. This drawing room was where
Wagner sat among his family and friends in the evenings, often
reading aloud to them, flanked by a grand piano and his desk. It was
here, too, that he received visitors, but, except during the first few
weeks in the house, the popular idea that he worked in these opulent
surroundings is quite without foundation: it was in a simply decorated room on the upper floor, the walls hung with grey satin, its

only ornament a portrait of Cosima by Lenbach, that he finished the score of *Götterdämmerung* and wrote *Parsifal*.[11]

When Wagner had resumed his work and was ruminating on a name for his house, he remembered a village in Hessen that he had come across on his travels, called Wanfried, a name which had struck a mystic chord in him for its conjunction of two words, 'Wahn', meaning illusion, delusion or even madness, and 'Fried', meaning peace. Like a poem in Goethe's *Diwan*, recited only to the wise because the mob would at once deride it, 'so only the meditative nature will have any idea of what we mean by it'.

The king gave 25,000 talers towards the house. (His other substantial contributions towards the Bayreuth undertaking were loans and were repaid in full.) But since building a house always costs at least as much again as the original estimate, as Wagner complained, he had to make shift to find the additional sums himself, as we have seen.

'You wish to know the pattern of my daily life?' he wrote to the king. 'Splendid! Because it is the key to the direction of the life that is the sum of my days.' His principle was to wrest as much spiritual tranquillity and cheer as possible from the daemon of earthly existence, so as to be able to perform his duties in the service of genius. His only regret was that he was not ten or fifteen years younger: so much had come to him very late. The fact that destiny had granted him a son had given his life a totally new meaning: property, a home, rights as a citizen, fortune, all now had a significance they had never had for him before. And his wise wife had relieved him of the pressure of daily life and stood guard over his peace.

After his morning bath he took breakfast with Cosima, and then devoted the hours before lunch to work. Unless illness or business worries put him out of the mood for it, 'children's familial lunch' was always a cheering occasion. Then he took coffee in the garden, leafed through the *Bayreuther Tagblatt* – the only newspaper he would now have in the house – and usually discussed some interesting topic with Cosima. After a short rest he looked at his post, considering himself lucky if there was no bad news, but only poems sent for him to set, treatises on the philosophy of art and offers of costumes and suits of armour for the *Ring*, or, the most frequent of all, requests for his autograph from English and American music-lovers. If all was well he did a little more work, perhaps scoring another page of *Götterdämmerung*, then a walk or a drive in the carriage they hired from the landlord of the Sonne to the Eremitage or the Fantaisie, where the children explored the park. At seven in the evening a simple meal with the children. At eight he and Cosima settled in the drawing room for the evening, where they read to each other, or made music with the young men from the Nibelung Chancellery; there were now four of them: a Saxon, Hermann Zumpe; a Hungarian, Anton Seidl; a Russian, Joseph Rubinstein; and finally, of all things, a Macedonian, Demetrius Lalas. These, his journeymen, asserted that they learned more from such evenings than in the conservatories and music schools they had paid such high fees to attend. (To King Ludwig; 1 October)

Like each individual day, all his time was carefully planned. That was the secret of how he accomplished so much work of so many different kinds: scoring, business and private correspondence, supervising the construction of the Festspielhaus, contracting for machines, sets and costumes, engaging players and singers, coaching the principals in their parts, concert tours – and all that in the shadow of not knowing where the next day's money was coming from. He hoped, he wrote to Schott, that fate had good health and great age with unimpaired intelligence in store for him, 'so that for once one person may accomplish and experience all that in Germany takes two lifetimes'. (9 February)

II

No sooner had Wagner received the king's assurance of a guarantee than he wrote, on 6 March 1874, to his 'foreman', Hans Richter, who in the meantime had been appointed musical director at the Pest opera. He had the following tasks for him: to take charge of the female singers, of whom Wagner had completely lost track, to follow them from place to place, listen to them, report on them, correspond with them and so on; to select the wind players, which would also involve travelling, and also to get the string section in order with the help of the leader, August Wilhelmj; to hear the singers individually with him that summer in Bayreuth. 'How about it? Can you manage it?'

Richter set off on his tour of inspection on 23 May, and from the end of June onwards was assisting Wagner with the preliminary coaching of the singers. These early rehearsals had strengthened his confidence in the success of the whole venture in the most gratifying way, Wagner reported to the king, but the labour and worry involved had made the most extreme demands on his strength and absolutely exhausted him.

Repetiteurs specially trained by him were then to follow the singers to wherever they were working that winter, to continue assisting them to learn their parts. Wagner envisaged rehearsing in the theatre itself in the summer of 1875, with the orchestra and with the major pieces of scenery in place. The months of June and July 1876 were to be devoted to general rehearsals, first of the acts individually, then of the dramas as a whole, and then finally three cycles would be performed in August.

There could naturally be no question, as he had emphasized from the first, of any of those taking part gaining any financial advantage, so he was regretfully obliged to dispense with the services of any prima donnas who performed only for such-and-such a fee. He had fixed the sum of 500 talers a month as the maximum reimbursable to each of the twenty singers he needed, for their travelling and accommodation expenses, in the hope that some of them would manage with less. (To Franz Betz, 8 March 1874) 'And thus you find yourselves called upon, perhaps for the first time in your careers, to dedicate your powers and abilities solely to the one purpose of achieving an ideal artistic end.' (*To the Singers*, 14 January 1875)

The musical demands the *Ring* made on its performers were new and testing. Wagner was able nevertheless to point to a familiar precedent on which he had built to meet his needs. During the 1875 rehearsals he spoke of it to Julius Hey, the singing teacher: 'Didn't Mozart himself bequeath us the basic form of German bel canto in *Die Zauberflöte*? The dialogue between Tamino and the Speaker will stand as the model for all time. What else do you suppose I am trying to achieve in the dialogue between the Wanderer and Mime in the first act of *Siegfried*?'

But the demands made by the staging of this drama drawn from Germanic myth were not only new, but also completely without precedent or model. From the first Wagner knew he could not entrust the task to any run-of-the-mill designers: he would have to have designs by real artists to lay before the very best scene-painters to inspire them to achieve something of a higher order. Cosima would have very much liked to engage the services of Arnold Böcklin, whom she knew from Basel, and she sounded him through Lenbach. But Böcklin declined and, troubled, she wrote to

Lenbach: 'It is sad that the theatre and the fine arts are so separated that when a dramatic artist comes on the scene he finds himself without support.' On the other hand it is not true that Wagner approached Makart. The latter had in fact designed a front curtain with figures from the *Ring*, but Cosima had her doubts as to 'whether a theatre curtain should be painted, whether a picture is the best thing to have in front of another, and whether a beautiful fabric falling in heavy folds does not answer the purpose better'. This idea was the origin of the Bayreuth curtain, which is not raised, but drawn to either side. (MMCW, pp. 298f.)

Through the medallist Anton Scharf, for whom he sat on the occasion of the laying of the foundation stone, Wagner got in touch with Joseph Hoffmann, the landscape and history painter, then forty-one years old. Hoffmann had attended the Vienna academy, travelled extensively, as far afield as Greece and Persia, and studied under Rahl in Vienna, Genelli in Munich, Cornelius, Overbeck and Preller in Rome. He had come to public notice, too, for his beautiful sets for *Die Zauberflöte* and *Der Freischütz*, and his reputation was such that the Uffizi in Florence had bought his self-portrait. His general culture, his sense of the poetic, his gift for landscape in the heroic style with Hellenic and Homeric traits, all these recommended him to Wagner. 'My attention has recently been drawn. . . quite particularly . . . to your exceptional work, the character of which seems already very close to what I need.' (28 July 1872)

Hoffmann submitted his designs, based on studies made in the mountains, by late November 1873. Wagner was surprised and delighted, and had no fault to find with them except for the occasional neglect of the dramatic requirements of a scene in favour of a picturesque effect. The rich decoration Hoffmann gave the Gibichungs' Hall was the subject of lively discussion: it was for that very reason, Wagner declared, that he had got away from the period of the knightly Middle Ages represented in *Tannhäuser* and even *Lohengrin*, in order to do without irrelevant visual splendour and display the characters without conventional clutter.

At first he had thought of letting Hoffmann build the sets too, but then, with his consent, commissioned the Brückner brothers of Coburg. Hoffmann retained the right of supervision, and in the event considerable differences arose between him, the Brückners and the machinist Brandt, who had also worked on the Munich *Rheingold*. A meeting was called in Bayreuth on 5 October 1874, in the hope of persuading Hoffmann to relinquish his supervisory rights; it was a stormy occasion at which Wagner, according to Muncker, displayed admirable restraint. There was something positively sublime about the moment when he averred that if Hoffmann could not win and inspire those who worked under him, as he could his musicians, then he was simply incapable of carrying out the commission assigned to him. It was not his *wish*, Wagner wrote to Hoffmann on 12 October, that the latter should have no further part in it; he had proved as much by his attempts to bring about an understanding between him and his co-workers. 'My only real wish is that you and I, two honourable men, part in peace – for the time being.'

Hoffmann was invited to the festival in 1876, and criticized the sets severely. But Wagner himself was so little satisfied with them that he said he would want to start again from scratch for another production.[12]

How the production was to be costumed presented far more problems than the scenic and architectural aspects. Wagner had objected to the costumes of the Munich *Rheingold* in 1869, which were copied from the series of frescoes based on the *Ring* painted for the king by Michael Echter, because, what with the Greek *peplos* and so on, they suggested almost everything except Germanic gods. The best painters and archaeologists would have to be consulted, and research made into Germanic dress in Roman times, based on Tacitus: 'Just a slight suggestion will give an intelligent and inventive brain all it needs to come up with analogous forms, which then provide the basis for further ideas. Then I wish for *less nudity* and more true clothing, and I don't want the giants replaced by the green men from the Prussian coat of arms . . . No golden ornaments of any kind! That stands to reason in a piece in the course of which gold becomes available for the first time to the gods themselves.' (To Hans Richter, summer 1869)

He commissioned designs in 1874 from Professor Emil Doepler of Berlin, in the hope of his observing these principles: he believed, he wrote, that the commission offered rich opportunities to the imagination. Basically he wanted nothing less than a realization in the form of separate figures of a 'painting' representing personal events from a cultural epoch remote from every known realm of historical experience. The illustrations by Cornelius, Julius Schnorr and others of scenes from the medieval *Nibelungenlied* were to be

ignored completely. More recently artists had attempted to represent Nordic mythology by reference to classical antiquity, with
suitable modifications. As yet no one had thought of pursuing the
clues offered by those Roman writers who had come into contact
with the German peoples. 'And so it seems to me that an artist who
is willing to adopt my suggestion will find he has the run of a unique
field, both for intelligent compilation and for the exercise of his
own imagination.' (17 December 1874)

The outcome was discouraging. Wagner did not like Doepler's
designs, which were overladen with archaeological minutiae and
lacked the grand simplicity of the tragic myth. During the 1876
rehearsals Cosima commented that 'the costumes look like nothing
so much as Red Indian chiefs, and apart from the ethnographic
nonsense they bear the stamp of petty theatrical tastelessness'.

Immediately before the preliminary sessions with the singers
were due to start, on 26 June 1874 Wagner completed the scoring of
the second act of *Götterdämmerung*. The instrumentation, spanning
the utmost extremes, from Brünnhilde's 'Heilige Götter, himm-
lische Lenker' to the almost chamber-music-like 'Nicht eine Kunst
war mir bekannt', often changing from one bar to the next, represents a peak in his achievement. He began the score of the third act
while the rehearsals were in progress, on 10 July. 'I háve had to
work on the instrumentation of this concluding work amid incessant interruptions, labouring in torment,' he wrote to King Ludwig
on 1 October, 'and I have often cursed myself for having designed it
so prodigally; it is the pinnacle which will tower above the whole
Nibelung structure, reaching high up into the clouds!' He told
Cosima that the fearful work would occupy him for a long time yet,
just as the whole undertaking was growing too big for him to cope
with. At about midday on 21 November he called to her, asking her
to bring the newspaper; assuming that he was too tired to go on
working, she did not dare to look at the score on his desk and,
thinking it would distract him, she gave him a letter from Liszt that
had just arrived. Hurt, he told her that he had just finished the work,
but of course a letter from her father banished all interest in him.
When he repeated this bitter complaint after lunch, she burst into
tears. 'That I have dedicated my life to this work, at the cost of great
pain, has not won me the right to celebrate its completion with joy,'
she wrote in her diary, 'and so I celebrate in pain.'

That evening, after she had written those lines, Wagner came and put his arms round her, and said he thought they loved each other too much, and that was the reason why they suffered.

For her birthday in 1873 his surprise for her had been a question-and-answer game on the name 'Cosima', set for girls' voices. This year he composed an accompaniment for this 'Children's Catechism' for small orchestra, and concluded it with the last seven bars of *Götterdämmerung*.

'Our Christmas Eve was very jolly,' she wrote to Nietzsche. The tree in the hall had reached as high as the gallery, so that she had had to function as the 'dear Lord' on a real Jacob's ladder, while the Nibelung Chancellery had played the part of angels, flying to and fro, passing her the nuts and apples; the Meister had sat quietly at the foot, not asleep, but deep in Gfrörer's history of early Christianity, which he was reading for the sake of *Parsifal*. (31 December)

On Christmas Eve, to make up for what had happened on 21 November, she found the complete sketches for *Götterdämmerung* on the table with her other presents. On the morning of Christmas Day the *Idyll* was performed and the girls sang their 'catechism', 'Sagt mir, Kinder, was blüht am Maitag?', accompanied by the town orchestra from nearby Hof, which Wagner had secretly engaged. On New Year's Eve, as she walked out on to the terrace to hear the bells ringing, he greeted her with the Indian saying asserting the unity of all life, 'tat tvam asi' – 'that, too, you are'. He had had the snow cleared from the grave, and food scattered for the birds.

A late Christmas present came for him from Lenbach, who sent him his portrait of Schopenhauer. Wagner thanked him for the ' "Idea" of a Schopenhauer' realized in it. 'It expresses the whole of your latest *Unseasonal* [*Schopenhauer as Educator*],' Cosima told Nietzsche, 'a wonderful expression, full of clarity, discernment, concern and melancholy.' (16 January 1875) The picture was hung ceremonially in the library–drawing-room. He did not belong with Goethe, Schiller and Beethoven, Wagner felt: 'the philosopher must stand apart.' So he was given the place high above Wagner's desk.[13]

In retrospect, 1874 was a year that gave Wagner much to reflect on and warned him to make haste. Death had carried away a number of his friends and relatives. His sister Luise Brockhaus had died in February, followed in May by Franz Schott and Madame Muchenoff-Kalergis, and in October by Peter Cornelius, his brother-in-law Heinrich Wolfram and his brother Albert.

Their relationship with Nietzsche was also giving him and Cosima some concern. They knew nothing of his secret disaffection, but they sensed that in some way his friendship had lost its innocence. They had planted three saplings from Tribschen in the garden of Wahnfried, Cosima wrote to him, and the previous day she had got Daniela to read *Der goldene Topf* to them. 'It brought our home at Tribschen back to me all at once, and the curious life that you, too, shared in. Things are different now, and yet not so very different, the bond of trust remains between us, do not let it waste away.' (20 April 1874)

Nietzsche's notes in February 1874 include the observation, again, that the 'tyrant' acknowledged no other individuality beside his own, and that Wagner would be in great danger if he did not acknowledge Brahms etc. He heard Brahms's *Triumphlied* on 9 June and took the vocal score to Bayreuth with him in August, laid it on Wagner's piano and would not leave him in peace until it had been played through. 'Handel, Mendelssohn and Schumann swaddled in leather', Cosima commented in her diary. Wagner had got very bad-tempered and talked about his longing to meet a musical equal, and the superiority of Liszt's *Christus*, which did at least bear witness to a creative urge and sincere emotion.

As usual when there is no other corroboration of Elisabeth Nietzsche's version of an incident, one can take it or leave it. But as Newman craftily points out, when Elisabeth said it had '*since* occurred to her' that the score in its red binding was 'a sort of experimental object', she unwittingly gave her case away. (DMCW, I, p. 705; NLRW, IV, pp. 432ff.)

The year 1875 began with the negotiations for another detested concert tour. The contract with the king contained another disagreeable condition, besides the clause requiring repayment: namely, that the guarantee covered only the cost incurred for sets, machines and gas installations, which would become the property of the Cabinet Treasury in the event of failure to repay; it did not extend to the structural work, which necessarily could not be confiscated. So Wagner had to give concerts in Vienna and Budapest, to pay for the building work. There is no need here to go into the problems that made it necessary for him to change his original programmes. In the end he gave two concerts in Vienna including the first performance of excerpts from *Götterdämmerung* and one concert in Budapest, in which both Liszt and Wagner took part, for the first and only time since a concert at St Gallen in November 1856. Wagner conducted excerpts from *Walküre, Siegfried* and *Götterdämmerung,* and Liszt, 'with his poor ten fingers', played Beethoven's E♭ Concerto. As usual, the concerts were sold out and the audiences wild with enthusiasm. On 3 March Makart gave a fancy-dress party in his studio in Wagner's honour, with the theme of the court of Catharina Cornaro, in fifteenth-century Venice. Amused rather than greatly impressed by the costumes and play-acting, Wagner moved among the guests, chatting in his homely Saxon dialect. When the playwright Adolf Wilbrandt assured him that the German public had warmed to him as to no other great man in his lifetime, Wagner replied, 'Oh, yes, the Sultan and the Khedive of Egypt bought patronage vouchers.' In homage to Wagner, Hellmesberger and his colleagues came to play Beethoven's C♯ minor Quartet, which he was known to value highly, but the noise the guests made, crowding into every room, made serious listening impossible. At the end of the first movement, Wagner shook Hellmesberger by the hand gratefully: 'No more now, all the same, let's not – scatter the pearls any further, but keep them for ourselves, shall we?'

One ray of light came with a reunion with his old friend Gottfried Semper, who had blamed Wagner for the turn taken by the theatre project in Munich. Now he admitted candidly that he had been wrong to trust those who did not deserve it and to withdraw his trust from those who did.[14]

After a short rest, Wagner went to Berlin at the beginning of April to conduct two more concerts. At both of them Siegfried's Funeral March made so enormous an impression that it had to be repeated. After the second concert Wagner and Cosima were invited to the house of Hermann Helmholtz, the physicist, who had listened to 'the godlike music in unceasing tears'. When they visited Adolf Menzel's studio one evening they were greeted by his brother-in-law playing something from *Götterdämmerung.*

Wagner returned to Bayreuth at the end of April, before setting off to give a third concert in Vienna at the beginning of May, and during this brief halt his Newfoundland, Russ, died. The faithful Verena had bought him the dog out of her savings nine years before. 'One has to know from one's own experience how rare unconditional loyalty and affection are among people,' Cosima wrote to her two elder daughters at the Luisenstift boarding school in Dresden, 'to appreciate the friendly wagging tail, the faithful eyes, the unconditional devotion of a dog. Our old friend will be buried tomorrow at the foot of our own grave.' (2 May 1875) A small stone tablet still marks the spot: 'Here Wagner's Russ rests and keeps watch.'

Hagen's Watch was heard for the first time at the third Vienna concert. From the orchestral colouring, you might have thought the strings of the instruments had been spun from ravens' feathers, was Cosima's vivid description of the string syncopations accompanying the eerie tritone in the tubas and double basses. The manner in which Wagner conducted the Allegro introduction (the passage following 'Du, Hagen! Bewache die Halle!') impressed itself on Heinrich Porges's memory: the first two crotchets of the sequence were, so to speak, hurled out, while the downward-swinging triplets dashed onwards exultantly. This drastic rendering, which might be described by the Italian *incalzando*, created an effect that brought the listener to the edge of his seat.

While Cosima was away with Wagner on his concert tours, Elisabeth Nietzsche was at Wahnfried, looking after the children. 'In the last resort it will be a kind of higher education for you,' her brother had written approvingly. And indeed, the future guardian of the Nietzsche archives learned something from observing the mistress of Wahnfried. 'It has often been said to me', she wrote to Cosima on 12 November 1900, 'how remarkable it is that it should be two women who, deputies to a certain extent, stand at the head of both the dominating intellectual trends of the modern world.'

Some light is shed on the inner conflict Nietzsche was experiencing at this time by the letter he wrote Wagner for his birthday in 1875:

> Truly, beloved Meister, writing to you on your birthday is always no more than wishing *ourselves* happiness, wishing *ourselves* good health, so as to interest ourselves in you as we should. For I should think really it is illness, and the egoism that lurks in illness, that force people always to think of themselves: while genius, in its abundant health, always thinks only of others, involuntarily bestowing blessing and health wherever it happens to lay its hand. Every sick person is a

scoundrel, I read recently: and what human condition
isn't sickness! . . . Farewell, honoured Meister, and enjoy
what we do not: good health. (24 May 1875) [15]

His friends seemed to find something thrilling, Wagner
remarked in a letter to the king, in the sight of him busily engaged in
activities that were almost beyond the strength of even a young
man, at an age when everyone thinks only of enjoying the fruits of
toil. And why was he not content with the fruits of his toil, he
wondered; why did he constantly hazard them by devoting all his
endeavours to something for which the world about him had no
desire? But so be it! Schopenhauer had pointed a very fine distinction between talent and genius: while the former hits a target all can
see but cannot themselves reach, the latter hits a target that others
cannot even see. 'That's how it is with me too, and my great work!
At best . . . people substitute for the target perceived by me a target
they all think they can perceive, while mine lies far beyond theirs.'
(30 May)

The preliminary series of rehearsals began on 1 July, using piano
accompaniment until 1 August, and an orchestra from 2 to 12
August. Wagner conducted rehearsals regularly every morning and
afternoon, singing every line and performing every action for the
singers' benefit. Moreover he met the expenses for the 140 people
these rehearsals involved in various capacities – a sum of 12,000
talers, of its nature not covered by the royal guarantee – out of the
profits from his recent concerts.

At the first orchestral rehearsal Hans Richter took the beginning
of the second scene of *Rheingold*. When Wagner arrived he was
greeted by Franz Betz singing Wotan's salute to Valhalla, 'Voll-
endet das ewige Werk'. Deeply moved, he thanked the musicians:
'Opinions about our great enterprise may vary considerably, but I
believe that everyone taking part in it will be convinced that it is a
work of art of great significance, and not a "bag of tricks".' Then he
walked up a gangway on to the stage, near the edge of which stood
his small table, with a box on it supporting an oil lamp and against
which he propped his copy of the score. Richter conducted and
Wagner followed the score, continually waving his arms and legs
about in his excitement.

We owe the description of this scene, recorded by Menzel in a
well-known drawing, to the sculptor Kietz, who had been present

at the first reading of the text of *Siegfrieds Tod* in Dresden in 1848.
His memoirs are supplemented by those of two of the people
assisting in the production, the singing teacher Julius Hey from
Munich and the choreographer Richard Fricke from Dessau.[16]
Wagner had asked Hey to come to Bayreuth to administer 'singing
therapy' to the tenor who was to take the part of Siegfried. He had
discovered Fricke on the occasion when he had seen Gluck's
Orpheus in Dessau; in his letter inviting him, Wagner told him that
he needed not a 'producer' but a 'plastic choreographer', who
would clarify his wishes to the performers by visual example.

Hey had ample opportunity to learn to appreciate Wagner's quite
unique manner of preparing the realistic stage presentation of his
music dramas. 'He spoke, sang and mimed like the most experienced of actors. All his physical movements – even when expressing
the most extreme emotions – were governed by the surest instinct
for beauty. Always certain of his aims, which he conveyed by
suggestion to all the performers . . . his direction was nothing other
than the outpouring . . . of his overflowing creative abundance –
the emanation of his artistic being as such.'

No less admirable was his skill in coaxing the artists to work
together harmoniously, where so much depended on the good will
of each one individually. Only Albert Niemann, the Paris Tannhäuser, whom he had cast, not without misgivings, as Siegmund,
introduced a discordant note. During a rehearsal of Act I of *Die
Walküre* in the hall of Wahnfried, Niemann's intonation became
increasingly insecure; growing conscious of it, he walked up to the
accompanist, Rubinstein, from behind, seized hold of him by his
narrow shoulders and shook him violently, venting his anger on
someone who was in no way at fault. As Hey recorded, Wagner was
so shocked that for a moment he could find no words with which to
resolve this dissonance. He looked at the singer with disgust and
finally said, after a general oppressive silence: 'Please, let us go on.'
At the informal supper following this rehearsal Niemann assumed
the role of the one who had been offended, refusing anything he was
offered by the servant, until one of the female singers placated him
by giving him food from her own plate. Cosima took her on one
side and privately reproved her behaviour, and this so enraged
Niemann that he resigned his part and left Bayreuth. At once the
press seized on the incident, the artists began to form camps, and it
was rumoured that others would follow Niemann's example. None

did. 'Niemann was the only one who did not grasp the seriousness of our position.'

At the end of the series of rehearsals Wagner invited everybody to a party in the garden: lights were hung everywhere and the children led a procession along the leafy paths with brightly coloured paper lanterns. Then the trumpeters blew a fanfare to call everyone to the foot of the steps leading from the house, and Wagner addressed them: in performing all the music of his four dramas in a manner rising to virtuoso heights, his singers and orchestral players had accomplished something unbelievable; but they had achieved something far higher still: they had shown the world 'that the only truly vital art now was music'. (KLRW, III, pp. 64f.)

Among those who came to sit in on the rehearsals was the new director of the Vienna court opera, Franz Jauner. As the person with the last word on whether or not Amalie Materna would be free to sing Brünnhilde at Bayreuth, he used this position of strength to angle for Wagner's collaboration in preparing revivals of *Tannhäuser* and *Lohengrin* and, above all, to gain his consent to a production of *Walküre* in isolation from the rest of the *Ring*. 'No *Walküre* in Vienna, then no Valkyrie Amalie Materna for Bayreuth.' 'The haggling over *Die Walküre*,' Wagner remarked, 'that was a black page, and altogether unworthy of our friendly relations.'

For the present he hoped the plans for *Tannhäuser* and *Lohengrin* would be dropped, as he had stipulated that all the customary cuts must be restored. He wanted to devote his energies now not to new productions of his earlier works, nor even to seeing the *Ring* itself performed: even with that the 'Idea' would have sufficed him personally. 'We have sunk ourselves deep into *Parzival*,' Cosima wrote early in September to Countess Schleinitz. One thing emerged with reasonable certainty: that the Grail was an expression of the longing of the Christian soul to confront the Saviour directly, without the church and its hierarchies intervening – not a protestation but a counter-creation. They had read some of the poetry of Kiot de Provins, the author of a lost *Perceval*, and the first line, 'En ce siècle puant et horrible', had become Wagner's motto.

But to no avail: since Jauner agreed to all his conditions he had to keep his word and on 1 November he moved to Vienna with the whole family for six weeks. He wrote to Feustel complaining of great weariness, and of the exhausting rehearsals, where he had to show them how to do everything.

Whereas in Paris he had had the conclusion of the *Tannhäuser* overture played as well, here in Vienna he went directly from the central section into the Bacchanale, so that, in addition to the Dresden and Paris versions, there is a Vienna version as well. When he appeared on the stage at the end of the performance to acknowledge the enthusiastic applause he promised the audience that he would continue in his efforts to make his works more familiar to them, 'so far as the forces available permit'. Although this qualification quite unmistakably referred to the selection of which works might be performed next, the press represented it as criticism of the artists. On the morning of the day of the second performance, Wagner collected the singers together to thank them and clear up the misunderstanding. It had never entered his head, he assured them, to denigrate the artists who had contributed to the success of the work. If they insisted on public satisfaction, he would ask Jauner to publish the letter of acknowledgement he had sent him. But in that case he would have to abandon his cooperation with them, since he could interpret such a wish on their part in no other way than as mistrust in him. 'I repeat that you are free to publish my letter to the management. . . I myself cannot have any contact with the press.' And he added vehemently: 'For I despise the press' – which was then reported in the newspapers as 'I detest the press'.

The two principals in *Lohengrin* were poorly cast. He wrote to Hey after returning home that his recent survey of tenors in Vienna had profoundly depressed him, 'so that I had to keep on asking myself whatever possessed me to write all the principal parts in my works, where the character's soul is important, for the tenor voice!' (3 January 1876)

The only thing he enjoyed was working with the chorus, which he coached not only to sing as beautifully as possible, as if each member was a soloist, but also to act so intelligently that their personal involvement in the action was credible. Wagner repaid them by returning to Vienna to conduct a performance of *Lohengrin* himself, for the chorus's benefit, on 2 March 1876.

During his stay there in November 1875 he had the opportunity to hear Verdi's Requiem and Bizet's *Carmen*. What he thought of the former is unknown ; Cosima thought it hailed from the regions where Spontini had directed all his compatriots. *Carmen* wrung from her the admission that the French were now the only nation with talent: even this 'unpleasant work' showed talent. Later, of course, in *The Wagner Case*, Nietzsche was to play Bizet off against Wagner. In September 1888 Nietzsche wrote to Gast that Gersdorff had witnessed an angry outburst against Bizet by Wagner: 'On that basis . . . my malice will be even more keenly felt at a certain important passage.' But this is contradicted by the testimony of Joseph Rubinstein, who told Paul Vidal, a professor at the Paris Conservatoire whom he met in Rome in 1884, that Wagner had often asked to hear passages from *Carmen*, especially the first-act duet; the phrase 'Ma mère, je la vois', particularly delighted him; he felt that this naive freshness could be the starting point for a renewal of French dramatic music, drawing new vigour from popular melody.[17]

On the whole Wagner did not enjoy his stay in Vienna. 'Do you suppose those six weeks in the winter of 1875 have lingered in my mind as an agreeable memory?' he asked Jauner as much as three years later. 'No, my dear friend! When I parted from you after your lavish supper on the last evening I was certain that I would never enter Vienna again! There every scoundrelly dog can fall on a man like me and empty his pisspot over me with impunity, but, thank goodness, I need never show my face there again. Never! Never! – Give my respects to Councillor Hanslick and Speidel and all the rest of that crew; I don't blame them for what they do, since it seems to earn them a living in Vienna: consequently the public seems to prefer them to me. Therefore, they have my blessing!' (MWKS, II, p. 184) In fact, the reason for the ferocity of this attack on Vienna lay in an experience of 1877, to which we shall come in due course.

But those Vienna productions of *Tannhäuser* and *Lohengrin* have an enduring importance for posterity because of the chroniclers they found. One of the members of the court opera at the time was a young baritone, Angelo Neumann, who later became world-famous as the director of the touring Wagner Theatre. In his memoirs he wrote that during the rehearsals he gained the indelible impression that Wagner was not only the greatest dramatist, but also the greatest director for the stage and the greatest actor. Fortunately for us Neumann did not content himself with this generalized approbation, but gave a detailed account of Wagner at work with the singers, singing and acting their parts for them to show them how he wanted everything done.[18]

Of even more value are the notes on Wagner's tempos made by a student at the Vienna Conservatory who became a great Wagner conductor, Felix Mottl. While performance styles are tempered more or less by the taste of the time, Wagner's tempos, so far as they can be ascertained, had a sublimity transcending the fashion of any period. At least, they should have had. In Vienna, bad habits had crept in under Richter's predecessor, Esser: 'too fast in the lyrical music', 'too little ardour in dramatic dialogue – too much emphasis on crotchets, instead of a dashing alla breve'. (MWKS II, p. 170) Mottl recorded all Wagner's oral remarks about tempos in his diary, and later used them in the vocal scores of *Tannhäuser* and *Lohengrin* that he made for the Leipzig publishers, Peters, who in turn incorporated them in their editions of the full scores.[19]

Wagner and Cosima got back to Bayreuth on 17 December 1875. 'We are seriously worried,' he wrote to Heckel, 'and when it comes down to it, I have to admit that the idea of holding the festival this year as planned is downright foolhardy. We are up to 490 with the patronage vouchers, but according to the latest calculations we need 1300. So really the original project has totally failed. Now all we can do is hold our breath and see what curiosity will bring in in the end. Even Feustel is inclined to take the risk . . .Otherwise we are putting a good face on things here. Everything will be ready on time (on credit!)' (4 February 1876)

The only really grave fear was that they would not have the ready cash when the singers and players arrived in June and wanted to see the colour of their money. Having heard that the German Emperor was in charge of a fund set up to further enterprises of national interest, Wagner had applied to him directly in October 1875, asking for a loan of 30,000 talers. He was informed that the emperor had approved the request without hesitation, and recommended it to the Imperial Chancellery where, however, it had been refused by Delbrück, the president of the ministry. Bismarck himself had known nothing of the request, Wagner wrote later in the *Review of the Festival*, but Delbrück had acted entirely on his own initiative. (RWGS, X, pp. 106ff.) Instead the Chancellery had advised him to apply to the Reichstag. 'To this suggestion I replied merely that I had thought to apply to the emperor's bounty and the insight of the Imperial Chancellor, but not to the views of the right honourable members of the Reichstag.'

But this version of the story put out for public consumption, namely that Bismarck had known nothing about it, was not true. At the New Year, when they were still waiting to hear the decision,

Wagner said to Cosima that only a man like Bismarck could help, 'otherwise we are lost'. The suggestion that he should apply to the Reichstag arrived a fortnight later. His friends were divided over the likely outcome of such a step. Wagner himself, as he told King Ludwig, felt that a petition to the Reichstag would be 'quite improper'. In the meantime he did not abandon all hope in Bismarck.

All the same he persisted in helping himself by his own endeavours. He started negotiating to give a series of concerts in Brussels. Then he was approached by Theodore Thomas of New York to write something for the centenary of American independence, and replied that he would write something in a broad march form, although it was a long time since he had written a note, and he had got completely out of the habit of composing, as it was called. He expected that the Americans would treat him well, meaning that they would patronize the festival. (See also Appendix II.) He gave the march a motto from Goethe: 'Nur der verdient sich Freiheit wie das Leben, der täglich sie erobern muß' ('the price of liberty, as of life, is daily reconquest'), which gave rise to a comic misunderstanding when the delegates who came to take delivery of the march translated the word 'erobern' ('conquer') as 'rob'. In the gentle passages, Wagner explained, he had been thinking of the 'beautiful and industrious women of North America', who were to be envisaged as taking part in the triumphal procession. As so often when his musical imagination was once roused, it was stimulated in respect of another work altogether. He had shown her his latest album piece, Cosima wrote in her diary on 16 February 1876: it was the song the Flower Maidens sing to entice Parsifal. The sheet of paper was inscribed at the top: '*Parzival*. Act II. *Women*. (Schöner Knabe komm' zu mir)', and at the bottom: '(wanting to be American!)' The remarkable thing about the gentle middle section of the march is a melodic figure which sounds more like Richard Strauss than Richard Wagner:

When a telegram arrived from America, reporting the work's great success, Wagner commented: 'Do you know what the best thing about the march is? The money I got for it.' He had 5000 dollars for the American performing rights, and he asked Schott's for another 9000 marks for the European publishing rights – which they paid.

On 4 March he went to Berlin, in response to an invitation to prepare a performance of *Tristan*, the proceeds of which, by imperial decree, were to go to the festival funds. In his letter to Heckel of a few weeks previously he had said that he wanted to see if he could still do anything about the loan he had requested, but he had no sooner arrived than he learned from Countess Schleinitz that no help was to be expected from the Chancellor.

Tristan was sung by Niemann, with whom Wagner was again reconciled. 'Where else, at the moment, would we find a better Siegmund?' he had asked Hey. 'I know of none. The fact of the matter is that in spite of a certain lack of self-control – or perhaps precisely because of it – he is a fully developed masculine personality. And it is only someone like that who will be capable of entering fully into the role, so that there is not the least vestige left of those all too often pomaded, simpering drawing-room and chamber tenors. Although his acting of a part is always on broad, sweeping lines, he does not display that all-purpose, unintelligent pathos that I so detest and that in the case of the majority of opera singers nowadays turns into a mindless, artistic pose, robbing every performance of the realistic lineaments of dramatic truth.'

Hülsen, who had refused to see Wagner on business thirteen years before, on this occasion gave a glittering dinner party in his honour. Frau von Hülsen, in her memoirs, wrote that she still entertained the most vivid recollection of the festive board, and Wagner at her side, and she still remembered how she involuntarily gave a little start whenever one or other of the singers addressed him as 'Meister'. Hülsen himself behaved like a thorough gentleman towards Wagner. *Der Fliegende Holländer* had proved to be a cast-iron success over the years, and in view of this Hülsen had arranged for Wagner to be paid a retroactive royalty stretching right back to the first Berlin performance in 1844. After deduction of the fee that had been paid at the time, this now amounted to 818 talers and 16 silver groschens. In the case of the new production of *Tristan* it was he who suggested to the emperor that the net proceeds of the first performance should be dedicated to Bayreuth. 'It is a fact that the only operas popular enough to sell out at virtually every performance at the present time are certain of Wagner's.'

The première on 20 March was rapturously received. During one of the intervals Wagner was presented to the emperor, who expressed his admiration and promised to come to Bayreuth for the festival. The net profits amounted to 14,000 marks, which were paid to the festival funds.

But Hülsen made no secret of his opinion that *Tristan* had no future: only *Tannhäuser* and *Lohengrin* would last, *Tristan* and the *Ring* would be forgotten in fifty years' time – according to Julius Kapp, though according to Glasenapp he said fifteen – but either estimate was proved wrong long ago; by 1933, fifty years after Wagner's death, *Tristan* alone had been performed 250 times at the Oper unter den Linden.[20]

King Ludwig replied to Wagner's message on the twelfth anniversary of their first meeting on 3 May with one of his rhapsodic telegrams: 'Wonnemond des Nibelungen-Jahres!'[21] But he did not refer in any way to the request Wagner had by then submitted to suspend the payments on his loan. On 26 May Wagner wrote to Düfflipp that on the very eve of the realization of his undertaking the only remaining means of ensuring it lay in the king's bounty, namely his consent to suspend the repayments as of that moment; otherwise there would not be a pfennig in hand to pay the instrumentalists and singers who would be arriving on 1 June, and he had no alternative but to conceal the whole thing publicly. Nevertheless he crossed the Rubicon, allowed the artists to come and implored the king, once more, to come to his aid. 'The day is nigh when I shall once again behold you, for the first time since I parted from you on the evening of *Meistersinger*, and told you of my profound premonition that we would not see each other again for many a long day. It was fully eight years ago!' (12 June) At last, on 29 June, Düfflipp wrote to tell him that the king had consented to the suspension of the payments, on the conditions already mentioned.

This biography is not the place for a detailed chronicle of the rehearsals and the eventual performances of the *Ring* in 1876. Starting with Glasenapp, the tale has already been told often and adequately. Of greater importance to us are some individual events and personal testimonies which throw light on Wagner's personality, on his work and on the performance of it. In addition to the records

by Hey and Fricke, the eyewitness accounts of Felix Mottl and
Heinrich Porges are especially valuable.[22]

'Send Mottl immediately!' Wagner telegraphed Richter in
Vienna on 20 May. 'I arrive on the Meister's birthday, throw myself
into tails and white tie and present myself at Wahnfried for
Wagner's great Gaudy! He greets me with a cry of "Enter Count
Almaviva!" My forehead was bathed with anxious perspiration, the
more so when he said, apparently in all seriousness, that they must
be careful in front of me, I came from Vienna and would report
everything to Hanslick . . . In the evening, in the Meister's presence, inauguration of the restaurant on the Festival Hill . . . Wagner
makes a comic speech about the proprietor, offering to waive his
own fame in his favour. Later he appears on the gallery in the
restaurant with pike and lantern and sings the Night Watchman's
song from *Meistersinger*, producing a hilarious imitation of the F$\sharp$
on the steer-horn.'

Mottl was placed in the Nibelung Chancellery to begin with,
before being brought into the rehearsals as offstage conductor. His
impromptu notes are a first-rate reflection of Wagner's changing
moods, his directives on acting – 'Never come down to the front of
the stage!' – and singing – 'No "recitatives", there's no such thing in
my music! Nothing but "arias"!' – his informal remarks about art
and artists in general and his own work in particular: 'When I am
composing and need something, it is always to hand.' During a
rehearsal of Act II of *Die Walküre* with the orchestra, at the passage
'Gefallner Helden hehre Schar umfängt dich hold mit hochheiligem
Gruß' tears came to Mottl's eyes, whereupon Wagner gave him a
cheerful nudge and said, to hide his own emotion, 'How about that
for sentimentality! Here on the stage we know it's all make-believe!
People out there will be duped, but we can stay quite unmoved!'

'I not only respected the Meister deeply, but loved him ardently,'
Mottl confessed spontaneously after describing a rehearsal of *Siegfried*. 'If he had wanted it, I would have jumped into the fire for him.'

An article Porges had written about the Bayreuth performance of
the Choral Symphony in 1872 gave Wagner the idea at the time of
asking him to perform 'an office of the very greatest future importance' to the festivals, 'to follow all my rehearsals very closely . . .
and to note down everything I say, even the smallest details, about
the interpretation and performance of our work, so that a tradition
goes down in writing'. (6 November 1872)

Porges devoted himself to the task conscientiously and with amazing insight and perception. He was not only thoroughly familiar with the score of the *Ring*, but also, thanks to his education and culture, fully able to appreciate its literary and philosophical content. We sense the fresh air of first-hand experience in his descriptions of how Wagner transformed himself into each character, placed himself in each situation, and so inspired all his colleagues, as we might imagine Shakespeare doing, by his playing of the whole drama in his one person. His manner of musico-dramatic delivery impressed as being fundamentally sound, possessing a thoroughly positive vital energy, which was the source of the definitive realism of all his creative directives. For all that, everything he said seemed impromptu, as though what he asked of the performers had only that moment occurred to him.

The distinguishing characteristic of Porges's record is his ability always to locate the endless detail of Wagner's individual instructions to his performers in an overall intellectual context. Thus at the very start, he does not content himself with reporting Wagner's insistence that, as the curtain rises, the violin figurations accompanying Woglinde's 'Weia Waga!' should suddenly be played as softly as possible, but adds that this unexpected reversal after the powerful crescendo of the orchestral introduction, similar in method to Beethoven, is of outstanding stylistic significance: it is a direct expression of the form mastering the material, which Schiller defined as the highest function of art. When, at the end of the second scene, Loge was told to articulate the words 'erstirbt der Götter Stamm', accompanied by pianissimo trombone chords, with temperate but incisive emphasis and quite without personal emotion, it was because at that moment he is the herald of cosmic destiny. 'I shuddered with a feeling as if the spirit of classical tragedy was abroad on the stage.' When Erda appears it should create the impression that as Wotan's lust for power erupts with a daemonic strength it wakens a hidden subterranean force, which normally exercises its sway under the mysterious cover of darkness. The veiled tonal colour for which Wagner asked and the masterly deployment of the verbal accentuation both contributed to this effect: in the passage beginning 'Wie alles war', the next two words, 'weiß ich', marked 'ritenuto', should be sung very slowly and expansively, as if Erda's spirit is sinking back into itself like light fading; on the other hand, the final words, 'meide den Ring', should be sung with an intensity that cuts right through the soul. It is this order of insight that makes Porges's notes on the performance of the *Ring* simultaneously an authoritative commentary on the work per se.

Nietzsche had not come to Bayreuth during the 1875 rehearsals. 'I have just passed through a *very bad* time, and perhaps an even worse one is to come,' he wrote to Gersdorff at the time. 'Will you break it to them in Bayreuth that I am not likely to come in July? Wagner will be thoroughly angry, I am myself.' Nonetheless, with the 'miracle' in which he had ceased to believe on the point of realization after all, he was compelled to make his own contribution in the form of a kind of 'Bayreuth festival sermon'. Having written most of it, in the autumn of 1875 he suddenly claimed that he could write no more. This one of his *Meditations* would not go to the printer, he told Rohde in a letter of 7 October. It was almost finished but he had come nowhere near the standard he set himself.

Elisabeth Nietzsche, on the other hand, claimed to remember his replying to her at the time, asking him if he would continue the essay, 'Oh, Lisbeth, if only I could!' To this Newman adds the ironic comment that there were far too many occasions on which Elisabeth conveniently 'remembered' a little remark of her brother's that came in pat to confirm whatever she happened to be saying at any given moment.

Fortunately we have Peter Gast's account to set against hers. When he urged Nietzsche to go on and complete it, Nietzsche gave no hint of inner reluctance or scruples of conscience, but merely said that it was too personal for publication. It was Gast's enthusiasm after reading the manuscript that finally persuaded him to add the last three of the eleven sections and to publish the book as a 'Festschrift' in July 1876.

The letter he sent Wagner for his birthday a few weeks earlier is enough in itself to refute the later legend that he wrote the fourth of his *Unseasonal Meditations* in despite of his own inner nature: 'It is almost exactly seven years since I first visited you in Tribschen, and I can think of nothing else to say to you on your birthday except that I, too, since then, celebrate my spiritual and intellectual birthday in May each year. For since then you have lived in me and work incessantly as a completely new drop of blood that I certainly did not have before.' (21 May)

The legend, however, not content with representing the book as an offering on the altar of friendship, interprets it as a kind of autobiography. He initiated the process himself in *Ecce Homo*: he would not deny that the fourth *Unseasonal Meditation* is basically about himself alone: '*Wagner in Bayreuth* is a vision of my future.' But, as Newman says, the reading of the composer's nature and character is too penetratingly accurate in most respects not to rank as a painting from life, and the line Nietzsche took twelve years later was 'at once brazen and naive'. And even Andler has to admit that it was 'une construction faite après coup'.

In order to establish his claim that the portrait of the dithyrambic artist in *Wagner in Bayreuth* was in truth that of the 'pre-existent poet of *Zarathustra*' and did not impinge for a moment on the 'reality of Wagner', Nietzsche asserted in *Ecce Homo*, as the acid proof, that Wagner himself had understood it in that light: 'He did not recognize himself in the text.' In reality Wagner wrote to him immediately after reading it: 'Friend! Your book is prodigious! How did you get to know me so well?' How indeed? The answer should have been, from the intimacy of their friendship in the years at Tribschen, and from Nietzsche's acquaintance with Wagner's autobiography.

When Wagner was planning a private edition of his *Life* in 1869 he entrusted it to Nietzsche to deal on his behalf with an Italian printer, Bonfantini, in Basel, and to read the proofs. 'I am committing an act of the most stupendous confidence in you', he wrote to Nietzsche, 'in sending you with these lines quite a tidy quantity of the most valuable manuscript, namely the first part of my autobiography.' Before long, however, he gained the impression that he had perhaps given Nietzsche rather more than he could cope with: 'I . . . now ask you most sincerely to regard yourself as absolutely relieved of this trouble . . . You can be confident that I shall never prevent you from seeing these pages, the more so, I expect, since you know that you are foremost among those I have appointed to continue to watch over these souvenirs of me after my death.' (4 June 1870)

Even if Nietzsche read no more than the history of Wagner's early life on that occasion, it is precisely the knowledge of a person's youth that gives a psychologist the code with which to decipher the adult.

'Come soon, won't you,' Wagner wrote on 12 July 1876, 'and let the rehearsals accustom you to your impressions!' In the first cycle of rehearsals (3 June to 12 July), each act was assigned three working days, but in the second (14 to 26 July) only one. It was a time of hard work and great excitement: the builders were still working on the fabric, the sets were still being painted and repainted, shortcomings in the stage effects had still to be eliminated, and in addition, almost every day there were the usual theatrical tantrums, so that every morning Cosima had personally to seek out whoever happened to have taken offence. And the whole was accompanied by the chorus of the press, which spared no effort to discredit the festival in advance and as far as possible to ruin it. The worst thing of all for Wagner and Cosima was their recognition that the performances would fall as far short of the work as the work itself was remote from the age.

One evening she found him standing at the window. 'He was talking to the stars, especially the Pleiades, his lifelong friends, which were very bright. And he said: "Protect my wife and my children, you good star! With me, do what you like!" He was thinking of his death, he told me.'

Cosima herself had an additional source of distress in Bülow. According to Du Moulin, who presumably learned it from her diary, he had been offered the musical directorship of the festival, and later a tactfully expressed invitation to attend had been sent him. In order to remove himself from the scene entirely he had undertaken an American tour. 'I nurture the warmest wishes – have no doubt on that score – may providence award you the fullest satisfaction in the success of the greatest musical event of the century. Believe me, Madame, that the equal impossibility for me to be there, and not to be there, was the major reason for the irrevocable decision that I took,' he wrote to her from Chicago on 6 February. Now she learned that he had fallen ill and returned to Germany, and was in a sanatorium in Godesberg. 'I have difficulty in overcoming a sense of shame at having come to such decrepitude', he wrote to Richard Pohl, 'and it had to happen of course, in anno Bayreuth, the year I was determined to spend in America because of the, to some extent, two-headed moral impossibility for me . . . not to attend the festival as a Wagnerian de la veille. It is really the bitterest blow in the whole business.'

On 3 August, a rest-day between the first general rehearsals of *Siegfried* and *Götterdämmerung*, after entertaining guests in the evening, Cosima confided to her diary: 'The news is like an overwhelming shadow, engulfing my soul; the very thought of any joy is now impossible, only patience and work.' (DMCW, I, pp. 769f.)

Meanwhile friends wishing to attend the rehearsals were arriving from far and near. When Wagner entertained them at home in the evenings he was friendly and in good spirits, and it troubled him to see Nietzsche, who arrived on 24 July, silent and gloomy. Schuré, who was meeting him for the first time, wrote that 'en présence de Richard Wagner, il était timide, gêné, presque toujours silencieux'.

King Ludwig was expected to arrive for the final dress rehearsals (6 to 9 August). 'To receive . . . the various royal personages, all of whom I detest in some degree or other, and to listen to their idle chatter, to do them the honours there, instead of immersing myself in your sublime, godlike work, is something that I would never ever be able to bring myself to do,' he had written to Wagner back in January. He had decided to stay at the Eremitage palace just outside the town, rather than at the margraves' Neues Schloss in the centre. But the flags and decorations that the townspeople put up to greet him on 5 August were wasted. His special train drew to a halt at one o'clock in the morning on an open stretch of track near the Rollwenzelei inn. The king descended and silently extended his hand to Wagner, who was waiting for him there. The waiting carriage took them both to the Eremitage, where the friends talked until three, when Wagner returned to Wahnfried, charmed and delighted.

The dress rehearsal of *Das Rheingold* was held before an empty auditorium, and was acoustically unsatisfactory, so the guests who had been attending the earlier sessions were allowed in for the remaining three rehearsals. After *Götterdämmerung* the king departed as he had come, in the middle of the night, from the crossing-keeper's house beside the Rollwenzelei, and went back to Hohenschwangau.

'It is impossible for me to describe the impressions with which I came away from the festival at Bayreuth, which afforded me immeasurable ecstasy, and from my happy reunion with you, my revered friend. I came with great expectations and, high as they were, they were all *far, far* surpassed. I was so deeply moved that I may very well have seemed tongue-tied to you! Oh, you understand so well how to shake one's very foundations, to melt with your conquering light the crust of ice which so many sad experiences have caused to form around heart and feelings.' (12 August)

When Wagner went to meet the German Emperor at the railway station on 12 August the building was covered with bunting and the crowd stretched as far as the eye could see. 'I did not believe that you would bring it about,' the emperor replied to his words of welcome, 'and now the sun shines on your work.' Ludwig Schemann recalls that Wagner's face revealed his consciousness that the millennia of human history were speaking through him. The vital clue to understanding Wagner's personality, he adds, was the recognition that as an artist he believed himself a king, and he uses the same comparison as Nietzsche at the beginning of *Wagner in Bayreuth*: no Alexander had ever taken up his daemonic destiny with more profound earnest than Wagner as he assumed the mission that the world spirit had laid upon him. And then, as he climbed into his carriage and drove home through the cheering crowd, shouting hurrah and waving his hat, he was all at once the man of the moment again.[23]

After *Die Walküre*, the emperor sent for him, praised everything he had seen, and expressed his regret at not being able to stay any longer. 'Your graciousness is not to be measured by time and place,' Wagner replied.

Wagner had published a notice asking the audience not to be offended with either the performers or the composer if they did not appear on the stage to acknowledge applause; they had agreed on this act of self-denial, so as not to be seen to step outside the frame of the work. (RWGS, XVI, p. 160) But after *Götterdämmerung* the storm of applause was so prolonged that he felt obliged to appear before the curtain. Gravely, he said: 'It is to your patronage and to the unlimited efforts of my colleagues, the artists, that you owe this achievement. All else that I have to say to you can be summarized in a few words, an axiom. You have now seen what we can do; now it is for you to *want*. And if you want it, then we have an art.' The moment was so impressive that even a dispassionate witness like Dr Strecker, the new director of Schott's, was forced to admit: 'An event of historical importance has taken place, and I can say "I was there".'

The following evening, when seven hundred people gathered for a banquet in the festival restaurant, Wagner, who was sitting with the artists, rose and went to stand on the stairs which joined the upper and lower rooms to make a speech. He wished to refer to what he had said the day before, as he had heard it had been misunderstood. He had not meant that the Germans had had no art until now, but what they had lacked until now was a national art such as the Italians and French possessed. 'Alles Vergängliche ist nur ein Gleichnis' – a work of art, too, is transient, but it is a symbol of what endures, of the eternal. And if what they had presented was still 'inadequate' in some respects, it must nonetheless be recognized as an 'event'. 'My intention is honourable,' he concluded, 'believe me, my intention is really honourable.'

Tumultuous applause and laughter broke out as Signora Giovanna Lucca, his Italian publisher and admirer, produced a 'petit cadeau', a silver laurel wreath which she gracefully pressed upon his brows. But he reverted to a more serious tone, reminding them all of the importance of continuing to have faith in the cause. 'Here is the man who was the first to repose that faith in me, at a time when I was unknown, and without whom you might perhaps today not have heard a note of mine – my dear friend Franz Liszt!' With arms outstretched he walked down the steps and embraced Liszt. Finally, he remarked that so many serious words had been spoken, and an enthusiast had even tried to glorify him in verse: 'So now not one sensible word more!' (GLRW, V, p. 294)

In the midst of all the artistic and social demands on his time Wagner contrived to set the words he had written but not used in Brünnhilde's concluding monologue, beginning 'Verging wie Hauch der Götter Geschlecht', and sent the piece to King Ludwig, who had admired the lines, as a birthday present. It closes in C major with the motive of World Inheritance first heard in the Wanderer/Erda scene in *Siegfried*, where it sounds like 'the proclamation of a new religion'.[24]

At the same time he persuaded the king to come back for the third cycle. 'Nobody will disturb your enjoyment! There will be no "crowned heads" left here for the third performance: perhaps a prince from some little dukedom, but no one with a claim to a seat in the royal box.' (21 August) Before the performance Ludwig spoke a few amiable words to the members of the management committee, but otherwise was accessible to no one except Wagner, since he spent the intervals reading the text. Since it was already apparent that the money they had in hand was not going to be enough, his friends urged Wagner to ask the king personally for more credit, but he vigorously refused to try, saying that he was making every effort to reduce his debts to the king, not to increase them.

At the end of the last *Götterdämmerung* the demonstrations far surpassed everything there had been hitherto. Even Ludwig showed himself at the front of his box and joined in the applause. Wagner appeared before the curtain. His voice shaking, he told them that the festival was now over, and he did not know if it would ever be repeated. He had called this work, which had been so long in the preparing, a 'festival drama', without really knowing what right he had to do so, since there was no festival marked for these days in the calendar of history. Now that it was over and had enjoyed, as the applause indicated, some measure of success, perhaps he could after all claim the right to call it a festival. But credit for the success was due in large part to his colleagues, the artists: 'I wish them to present themselves to me!' The curtains parted; there were the singers and the orchestral players in a broad semicircle with Hans Richter in the middle, waiting to hear the Meister's farewell words: their faith, their dedication had made it possible to keep to the timetable, which nobody had thought beforehand could be done. For the last time he repeated his thanks to them for the long days, and nights too, of work. 'And now that we must part, a heartfelt farewell!' (GLRW, V, pp. 306f.)

But behind the satisfied, confident face Wagner showed the world, he concealed disappointment and despair. Only a few had glimpsed it. The entry in Cosima's diary for 9 September has 'Said goodbye to Mathilde Maier, the last of our friends.[25] Then we discussed the performances and our experiences. Richard does not want the matadors Betz and Niemann again. In his rage at not being allowed to take a bow, Betz's performance was a downright disgrace. Brandt not up to his expectations. Richter not sure of a single tempo [she had remarked at the start of the rehearsals that he had made too much of a meal of beating every crotchet in 4/4 time]. Despondency! Deep distress! Richard very sad, he says he would like to die.' (DMCW, I, pp. 771f.) He may have given some inkling of it to his oldest friend, Anton Pusinelli, with whom he would have liked to retreat to some quiet corner, where they could have enjoyed each other's company. The king was another from whom he did not conceal his mood: the outward success did not serve to hide from him the abyss, from which the last veil had been drawn: 'There is no footing for me and my work in this day and age.' (11

September) He told his Brünnhilde, Amalie Materna, that he was deeply depressed and that he longed only for the moment when he and his family would be able to go to Italy. (9 September) But he revealed himself most unreservedly, to the point of self-forgetfulness, to Judith Gautier, who had come for the second and third cycles and did not leave Bayreuth until 5 September. Her embraces, he confessed a year later, had been a last gift of the gods, who had not wished him to succumb to the 'chagrin de ma fausse gloire des représentations des *Nibelungen*'. (18 November 1877)

The full extent of the financial calamity was one thing he did not yet realize, and he expected to repeat the festival the following year on more favourable terms. What lengthy preparations the Greeks had devoted to their great festivals in honour of Dionysus! Where the ancients had allowed themselves plenty of time, he had to act in all haste. 'Next year we will do everything differently,' he told Richard Fricke. Later, in 1878, when he had recovered from the depression brought on by the immense tension of the preceding years and months, he pronounced a fairer verdict in his *Review of the Festival*: 'A benevolent spell made everything there *good*. And the profound conviction based on that experience is my goodly profit from those weeks.' (*Rückblick auf die Bühnenfestspiele*, RWGS, X, pp 103ff.)

29

Nietzsche in Bayreuth

Wagner had no opportunity to discuss the festival with Nietzsche, for, as he complained, he could not get a single word out of him, even when they spent several hours in each other's company.

By way of explanation the legend offers a sudden insight on Nietzsche's part, the clear recognition of what he had long dimly sensed: that he had deceived himself about Wagner and his work; that Wagner had betrayed his ideal for the sake of quick success; and finally that his music was not really great.

With the thoroughness of the historian and the nose of the detective, Ernest Newman investigated the background and the context of this crisis in three great chapters of his biography: 'Nietzsche in 1876', 'Elisabeth's False Witness' and 'The Realities of the Matter'. (NLRW, IV, pp. 491ff.) No one should forgo the pleasure of reading that masterpiece and model of literary unmasking at first hand. Here I shall do no more than summarize the evidence and supplement it with material from other sources.

As his letters to Gersdorff and Rohde betray, Nietzsche had just gone through a particularly bad year when he went to Bayreuth: violent headaches for days on end, vomiting for hours at a time, general exhaustion, increasing trouble with his eyes. He was so ill at Christmas 1875 that on 18 January 1876 he confided to Gersdorff his fear that he was suffering from a disease of the brain. After a temporary improvement in May, in June he was complaining again that his condition was worsening from day to day.

But he was determined to see Bayreuth through.

After arriving there on 24 July he went to a rehearsal of the first act of *Götterdämmerung*. They were now in the second cycle of rehearsals, with the orchestra but without costumes. Nietzsche had been suffering from a headache for thirty hours without a break and he could not stay in the theatre to the end. The next day he was still so tired, as he told his sister in a letter, that he could hardly write. Nevertheless he went to the rehearsal of the second act that afternoon, and of the third on the following day. On 28 July he reported that he felt better and was now in his element. The third cycle of rehearsals began on 29 July, with the singers in costume; one whole work was taken in a day, but with stops when Wagner had some comment to interpose, and with passages being repeated as necessary. Nietzsche heard *Rheingold*, probably, and, on 31 July, *Walküre*. He was not well, he wrote to Elisabeth the next day: incessant headache and weakness. The day before he had only been able to listen to *Walküre* in the dark: watching had been quite impossible. He wanted to get away, it was absurd for him to stay. The prospect of these long evenings dedicated to art appalled him. This time she would have to see and hear on his behalf. He had had as much as he could stand. He would not even go to the performances, it was such torture for him. He wanted to get away to the Fichtelgebirge or somewhere like that.

Judging by this letter it is improbable that he stayed for *Siegfried* on 2 August. At all events he did not attend a reception at Wahnfried on 3 August, as he had left for Klingenbrunn in the Bavarian Forest because of his continuing headache. He intended to spend about ten days there but not return via Bayreuth – where his sister had arrived in the meantime – as he was running short of money.

It was while he was in Klingenbrunn that he drafted the cutting comments on Wagner and his art that later went into *Human, all too Human*. Cosima had told him, apropos of *Schopenhauer as Educator*, that his writing must 'cut a deep furrow'; it is worth noting that he took up that image and called these notes *The Ploughshare*.

As Newman rightly emphasizes, it would have been impossible even for a person in a normal state of health to judge so vast and novel a work as the *Ring* from such fragmentary acquaintance as Nietzsche had so far had, let alone one in his physical condition, tormented by headaches and eye trouble to the point where he could hardly see.

In fact, he changed his mind and went back to Bayreuth on 12 August. As luck would have it, however, the first cycle of performances took place in a heat wave so enervating, as Schemann recalled, that it was an effort to stand upright. There are no letters by Nietzsche himself to tell us anything about his health during this week, but we have the reliable testimonies of Schuré and Schemann. The former, who also accompanied him on the journey back to Basel, writes that during the performances Nietzsche was gloomy and depressed, and was already suffering from the early stages of the brain disease that later overpowered him. Schemann, who had already known him for some time, visited him on the morning of 18 August, the day after *Götterdämmerung*, and got the impression that he was 'obviously already very ill'.

Back in Basel his condition was so bad that his ophthalmologist reproached himself bitterly for having allowed him to go to Bayreuth. On 27 September Nietzsche wrote to Wagner that he was about to leave for Italy in the hope of putting an end to his suffering. 'It has risen to new heights. . . in these last few years. . . I have put up with incessant pain, as if I had been born for that and no other purpose.'

That these complaints were not just excuses put forward to conceal his disaffection, as has been suggested, is confirmed by the letters written by his physician, Dr Otto Eiser, from Frankfurt am Main to Hans von Wolzogen on 17 October 1877 and to Wagner on 26–7 October 1877.[1] Nietzsche spent a week in Frankfurt in the autumn of that year, to allow Eiser the opportunity to give him a thorough examination, in collaboration with an ophthalmologist. In anamnesis he said that he had been suffering from headaches with paroxysmal intensification for four years. The medical report gave particular emphasis to a 'chronic inflammation of the choroid and the retina (chorio-retinitis centralis)', with morbid alteration of the fundus of the eye, in the right eye reaching as far as the macula lutea; in the absence of any other evidence this optic disorder was taken to be the probable cause of his headaches.

In short, there can be no doubt that Nietzsche was in great pain during the 1876 festival. 'One must really be in good health to receive artistic impressions,' Cosima once wrote to Houston Stewart Chamberlain. 'I almost believe that the whole of this wretched business with Nietzsche arose from the fact that he was tormented by raging headaches in 76.'

Elisabeth Nietzsche did her utmost to conceal this circumstance, which was such as to cast doubt on the objective validity of what Nietzsche later wrote about Bayreuth. In 1895, when she came to the episode in her biography of her brother, she published for the first time extracts from the letters he wrote her from Bayreuth and Klingenbrunn, but suppressing the complaints about his physical suffering which do much to explain his negative response to the *Ring*. Only twelve years later was she able to bring herself to publish the letters in full (ostensibly) in the edition of his collected letters. But even then, as Newman proves, she took the precaution of falsifying the date of every letter, so as to place the greatest possible hindrance in the way of discovery of what her brother really had heard and seen in the crucial days before he left for Klingenbrunn. Newman also demonstrates convincingly that she must have suppressed one letter, if not several, entirely: no doubt they contradicted too blatantly the legend that Nietzsche was in full enjoyment of his receptive and critical faculties during the festival. Newman's suspicions have since been proved absolutely correct by Erich F. Podach and Karl Schlechta.

The very fact that Elisabeth tried to conceal her brother's state of health is the best proof that his condition must have had a decisive influence on his judgement.

There remains the question whether, even had he been in good health, Nietzsche was competent to form a judgement on the music of the *Ring* that would have been in any sense a valuable one. His pronouncements on Beethoven, his adulation of Peter Gast, his high estimation of his own compositions, his later falling away from music to *musiquette*, all make it seem doubtful, to say the least. Newman, at any rate, believed he was swept off his feet for a while by *Tristan*, but 'his natal bias . . . was towards the simple in music'. On the other hand it is probably only fair to the musician in Nietzsche to take his sister's claim that he had expected Wagner to say to him in Bayreuth in 1876: 'Oh, my friend . . . my music will have to change completely, I will return to simplicity and melody!' as yet another of her simplistic fabrications.[2]

There will have been another factor, something human, all too human, of which Nietzsche himself was perhaps quite unconscious. Schuré paints a vivid portrait of Wagner during the rehearsals, commanding the immense assemblage of soloists, chorus, orchestra and stage machinery, and enjoying the well-deserved triumph of bringing the world of his own creation to life. He had to inspire all these beings of flesh and blood with his own spirit. A consummate spellbinder, he pursued his object with a blend of ferocity and friendliness, rage and tenderness, never losing sight of his goal for a moment. In the few hours of relaxation from his superhuman labours he let off steam in a display of high spirits. 'Presented with the spectacle of this artistic miracle that he was performing before our very eyes, every one of us felt . . . Mime's astonishment as he watches Siegfried forging his sword.'

Schuré goes on to speculate whether Nietzsche's self-esteem suffered from a sense of inferiority, and that is undoubtedly a profound psychological insight. It is known that in moods of depression Nietzsche complained of lacking the artist's ability to point to deeds accomplished. And now he sensed the existence of a 'genius that lies in actions', to use Goethe's phrase, that was denied himself.

But even if Nietzsche's later pronouncements on Wagner's music carry little weight today, there is still his charge that Wagner betrayed his ideals and profaned the vision they had shared – in Ernst Bertram's words – 'by its grotesque realization'. 'Utopia had arrived,' Thomas Mann writes, 'and Nietzsche fled.'

He told the story of his flight later in *Ecce Homo*: 'Enough, in the middle of it, on the spur of the moment, I left for a few weeks, in spite of a charming Parisienne's attempts to console me; I made my excuses to Wagner simply by means of a fatalistic telegram. In Klingenbrunn, a little town buried deep in the Bohemian Forest, I carried my melancholia and my contempt for the Germans about with me like an illness – and from time to time I noted down a maxim in my pocketbook, nothing but hard psychological dicta, under the general title *The Ploughshare*.'

But his memory for facts was always poor. He did not leave 'in the middle of it' – 'it', in the context, meaning the festival – but during the rehearsals; it was not 'for a few weeks' but for ten days; he did not make the acquaintance of the 'charming Parisienne' – Madame Louise Ott – until after his return from Klingenbrunn; he makes no reference to the state of his health or to his return to Bayreuth. Both would have contradicted the fiction of his shaking the Wagnerian dust from his feet.

Podach has published an alternative passage from the manuscript of *Ecce Homo* which Nietzsche had pasted over: instead of the story of the 'charming Parisienne' there is one about the old emperor applauding and shouting the while to his adjutant, 'dreadful! dreadful!'[3]

But the heart of the matter is this: has anyone the right to

reproach an artist, in his sixty-fourth year, at last realizing the work
he has struggled for a generation to create – to reproach him for not
having been able to wait? Apart from every other consideration, an
idea achieves life and temporal existence only when it risks taking
the step from concept to action. For Wagner the meaning of
Bayreuth was the giving of an 'active example', and his friends
understood as much: as Schemann says, they saw the true significance of the 1876 festival not in the material accomplishment of the
performance, but in the symbolic act of performing it at all.

'And Nietzsche fled' – not simply into the Bohemian Forest, but
(as we gather from the letter to Mathilde Maier of 15 July 1878
which contains the first version of the legend) to his cherished
Greeks. But how, Newman permits himself to ask,

> would this same Nietzsche have behaved if, instead of
> envisaging his beloved and admired Greeks in the pathos
> of distance bestowed on them by more than twenty
> intervening centuries, he had been in Athens some year
> in the month of Elaphebolion, a studious young Greek
> from Corinth who had been privileged to visit Euripides
> [on Salamis] occasionally and discuss the problems of
> tragedy, myth, ritual and religion with the great artist,
> and who now, for the first time, was to attend one of
> the famous festivals?
>
> What would he have found? Assuredly not the ideal
> spectator dreamt of in *Richard Wagner in Bayreuth*. He
> would have found the streets of Athens and the Attic
> equivalent of Angermann's filled with an excited, noisy,
> garrulous crowd, not all the members of which, perhaps,
> were strictly sober. In the theatre he would have found,
> of course, Sophocles and Agathon and Socrates . . . but
> also the wild Alcibiades, and the crafty demagogic Cleon
> . . . the Sausage-seller and the Lamp-seller . . .
>
> And if in the evening our supposititious young
> Corinthian had called on Euripides and found his idol
> behaving diplomatically to a miscellaneous crowd of
> admirers and flatterers, would he not, especially if he
> had been suffering agonies from headache and eyestrain
> all through the festival, have . . . fled to Delphi or
> somewhere, and there filled his tablets with bitter

reflections on the poet and his devotees and the Hellenes in general? And yet, and yet! these strangely composite audiences . . . bent the knee to an art which they knew to be higher than themselves . . . and placed Aeschylus and Sophocles and Euripides on the pedestals from which all the fluctuations in European taste since then have failed to dislodge them. (NLRW, IV, pp. 527f.)

30

The Nation's Thanks

'Everybody else left soon after you', Cosima wrote to Judith Gautier, 'and a sudden solitude followed the hubbub you witnessed . . . Everything vanished as if by magic, only the silhouette of our theatre in the distance reminded us of what had been, and we seemed to have awoken from a dream. My husband was too exhausted to do any work, and he was even less capable of dealing with the rather complicated business matters arising from the festival; so I had to promise him to put the house in order within a week, and on 14 September we set off on our travels with bag and baggage, that is, four children and their governess and all their paraphernalia.' (Early October 1876)

Wagner hoped to spend a full three months in Italy, 'resting on the laurels of his American march'. Verona reminded him of the melody for *Romeo and Juliet* he had once written down in a dark hour. In Venice he revisited the Palazzo Giustiniani where he had written the second act of *Tristan* eighteen years before. But the 'silhouette of the theatre' pursued him everywhere, looming larger and larger and darkening the Italian skies; a letter from Feustel caught up with them on the road with the news that it was feared that the deficit would be 120,000 marks, an estimate that climbed to 150,000 marks in the next few weeks.

On 29 September they reached Naples and on 5 October they crossed the bay to Sorrento, where they took rooms in a little annexe of the Hotel Vittoria. 'I expect you know that Sorrento is the native city of Tasso,' Cosima wrote to Daniela, who had stayed behind at the Luisenstift; 'this is where he returned to his sister Cornelia, dressed as a pilgrim, after much suffering,' and she reminded her daughter of the anticipation of that return in Goethe's play about the poet, which is suffused with the resignation of a woman's noble heart like a gentler, purer air.

It was her own mood, too, lulled by the beautiful monodic singing of the peasants at the olive harvest, a moonlit evening on the terrace, an excursion to Capri, riding to Tiberius's villa on donkeys, and returning by the light of the stars and the phosphorescent sea. They were both reading Sismondi's *Histoire des républiques italiennes du moyen âge*: just as Wagner had studied Arabian history in the previous winter, now he was instructing her in Italian history, she told a friend. She begged him to forget the whole 'woe of the Nibelungs'[1] and start a new work. But in the midst of all that sunlight and beauty the only thing that came into his mind was a symphony in memory of the fallen. It would have his *Romeo and Juliet* theme as the basis; he imagined biers being carried into a hall, more and more of them, until the sorrow of the individual was subsumed in the general grief.

It was impossible for him to forget the 'woe of the Nibelungs'. He wrote to Feustel on 7 October, outlining ideas for dealing with it: a general appeal to the Patrons; a specific request to some of the foremost Patrons to organize subscription lists with themselves at the head; a petition to the German Emperor to propose to the Reichstag that the government should take over responsibility for the festival.

A rhapsodic letter from King Ludwig, imploring him to banish his lethal worries and preserve himself for many years to come, 'to the glory and loftiest pride of the German nation', encouraged him to write of his scheme to him too. ' "Arise now," I exhort myself, "Arise, despairing soul! Speak now to *Him*!" ' He put very little faith in the patrons, in fact. What had to be done was to bring the matter before the nation as a whole: a proposal could either be moved in the Reichstag by a deputy, or be introduced through the Imperial Chancellery. A third possibility would be for King Ludwig himself to place the matter before the Federal Council, from where it would then go to the Reichstag.

The proposal might be worded something like this: that the Imperial Government should take possession of the Festspielhaus as a national property, against defrayment of the outstanding debts; it should then be assigned to the municipality of Bayreuth with the obligation to promote festivals annually in accordance with the founder's intentions.

It would, of course, be preferable, more seemly and more rational, if Bavaria and her king could execute this plan alone! But there . . .

' "Ah! Fantasia!" that is what the donkeyman kept calling to my wife's mount in encouragement, when we were out for a ride recently. "Fantasia" really was the good beast's name, but she had not the least interest in getting anywhere, so the "Ahs" became more and more exasperated until the donkeyman tried a new ploy: "Corragio, Fantasia! Allegro! Buoni maccheroni, tutto formaggio!" Astonished, we asked him if he would really give his donkey cheese and macaroni; whereupon he answered, oh no, she would be perfectly content with hay; but he liked enticing her with the idea of macaroni. So "Ah, Fantasia!" is what I now say to encourage my weary soul, and perhaps my plan and the motion I drafted have been nothing more than the "buoni maccheroni tutto formaggio" with which that donkeyman spurred on the imagination of his weary animal.' (21 October)

His doubts were confirmed only too soon. He had drawn up and sent off his circular, he told Heckel on 3 November, he had made approaches in Berlin and to the King of Bavaria – and had had no answer. 'So the only thing I can expect now is a truly humiliating issue that will leave me no choice but to demolish everything, quite literally. Without a word or sound I shall assign everything to the creditors, just like a bankrupt . . . In these circumstances my health is not of the best: my inner concern and my anxiety at the uncertainty are too great.'

During October Malwida had arrived in Sorrento, to prepare quarters for the ailing Nietzsche in the Villa Rubinacci, only a few steps from their own lodgings. With characteristic unselfishness, she had undertaken to look after him, together with his friends Brenner and Dr Rée. 'I really do not know how to thank you for what you said and what you offered in your letter,' Nietzsche confessed to her. Later, he found a way, in Aphorism 419 of *Human, all too Human*, where he wrote about the 'dead places' in the head of an old woman who was capable of enthusing in turn over the champions of completely opposing causes.

From a letter Cosima wrote to Daniela on 29 October we learn that the 'quartet', as Malwida described herself and her three charges, had paid their first visit the evening before. Wagner noticed, according to Glasenapp, that Nietzsche, who had already been silent and introspective in Bayreuth, appeared drained and almost entirely wrapped up in his own health. As a consequence, in spite of their proximity, only two or three evenings were spent in each other's company.

On the last of these, according to Elisabeth Nietzsche, the following memorable scene took place. Wagner and Nietzsche went for a marvellous walk along the deserted coast. It was a beautiful autumn evening, mild but with a certain melancholy in the air, hinting at the approach of winter, 'a mood of farewell', as Wagner said. Suddenly he began to talk about *Parsifal* in detail for the first time, in terms not of a projected work of art, but of a religious, Christian experience. While Wagner talked on and on the last ray of sunlight disappeared across the water. 'Have you nothing at all to say, dear friend?' Wagner asked. Her brother explained away his silence with some excuse, but his heart had been full to bursting with his distress at this charade of Wagner's. (EFWN, pp. 262ff.)

This moving story, which Elisabeth paints with such affectionate detail, ought to have been regarded with suspicion from the first. Yet Newman was the first to call it 'highly coloured'. There can be no doubt that the false sentimentality sounds more like Elisabeth Nietzsche than Richard Wagner. It seems very unlikely, too, that the latter would suddenly have made an intimate religious confession to the young friend whose behaviour had been so reserved for so long. In any case the tale can be checked against facts: as we know, Cosima had read Nietzsche the detailed prose scenario of *Parsifal* at Christmas 1869. Schuré, too, tells of their conversation about Wagner's next work when they were travelling together from Bayreuth to Basel after the festival: Nietzsche said that Wagner had told him he was going to read world history before writing the verse text of *Parsifal*. So even if the subject did arise again in conversation in Sorrento it cannot have caused Nietzsche any surprise, and certainly not the disillusion claimed by his sister: that is clearly demonstrated by a letter, first published in 1964, which Nietzsche wrote to Cosima on 10 October 1877, a year after their meeting in Sorrento, where he says: 'The glories *Parcival* promises us can comfort us in all the matters where we need comfort.'[2]

In Elisabeth's glowing painting, it is not only the human figures but the scenery, too, that is imaginary. Instead of the beautiful autumn sunset, with its mood of farewell, which is supposed to have stimulated the fictitious conversation, a cold north wind had been blowing since the beginning of November, the skies were grey, and a blue-black sea hurled foaming waves against the cliffs, so that the Wagners decided on 6 November to leave the very next day.

Should there be any lingering hesitation to accuse Elisabeth Nietzsche of flagrant invention, it will be dispelled in due course when we come to a no less famous scene some six years later which can, by chance, be proved to be an outright lie.[3]

But after the disappointment with Wagner as artist and as champion of an ideal that her brother was supposed to have experienced in Bayreuth, she needed to find a trait that would disappoint him in Wagner the man as well. Since her fictions were only advanced in support of the legend Nietzsche himself propagated in *Ecce Homo*, she can perhaps be excused somewhat, if one is so inclined.

Wagner's troubles continued to follow him through Italy. The honours he was shown there made him all the more painfully aware of his situation in Germany, whence he received no news except the concern of his friends and the denigration of the press.

In Rome, where they spent four weeks, the German ambassador, Herr von Keudell, gave a soirée in his honour in the Palazzo Caffarelli. A deputation from the Regia Accademia di Santa Cecilia informed him of his election as 'socio illustre'. The German artists' colony invited him to a festive gathering in the Palazzo Poli, where he made a stirring reply to a speech of welcome.

At Keudell's reception he met a young Italian composer, Giovanni Sgambati, who was there to take part in one of his piano quintets. Wagner advised him to approach Schott's about publication, and himself wrote to Dr Strecker: he had had Sgambati's two quintets played to him several times, and wanted to recommend them very seriously. For once he had had the pleasure of becoming acquainted with a truly great and original talent, which he would be very happy to present to the wider musical world. 'I advise him to tour Germany, starting with Vienna, as soon as possible, performing his works, which I would expect to have an outstanding success after the tedium of recent *German* chamber music (even Brahms etc.) . . . Please waste no time . . . If he does not suit you, I shall go elsewhere; but I would appreciate a speedy reply, as I am only here for a week.' (23 November) Schott's published not only the two quintets but all Sgambati's later compositions, including a symphony and his fine requiem.

Wagner was able to pass on Schott's affirmative reply to Sgambati before he left Rome, at a reception for Italian artists. Pietro Cossa, whose play *Nerone* Wagner had seen in Venice, was also present and Wagner suggested to them both that they should write an opera on the subject of one of those Italian adventurers he had read about in Sismondi, who might have been an Alexander or a Hannibal on different terrain.

The sights and art treasures of Rome were not neglected. Of the façade of St Peter's Wagner commented that it ought to have been the palace of a Caesar, but in the Sistine Chapel he said: 'This is like being in my theatre, you recognize at once that it was built for a serious purpose.' The tragic lot of genius seemed to him to be epitomized in the life and work of Michelangelo, which he felt were comparable to his own.

He wrote to Feustel that he had to call a halt once and for all and show the world what was involved in entering the financial maze. To stay in it, to be at the mercy of every accident, to be exposed to ever new anxieties – these were things he refused to submit to any longer, since he had never had a financial end in view. If the deficit could not be met in reasonable time, then he would have no alternative but to declare the festival undertaking bankrupt. What belonged to the King of Bavaria would have to revert to him; all other assets would have to go to the highest bidders and the outstanding debts paid with the proceeds. In the suspense of the last few months he had had plenty of time to think about his relationship to the age. 'I have shown what I can do and now feel justified . . . in closing my public career.' (23 November)

This letter brought anxious enquiries from Feustel, to which he replied in clarification that his sole purpose in opting for bankruptcy would be to pay off the debts by selling the material assets. 'The idea of swindling the carpenters and upholsterers of Bayreuth has never entered my head, and if I used the word "bankruptcy" it was intended as a forthright designation of my own position, and I will not hesitate voluntarily to declare myself and my artistic undertaking bankrupt.' He also wanted there to be no doubt that he would, as a matter of course, designate his property in Bayreuth and his income to settling the debts. (29 November)

Having arrived in Florence on 3 December, he went on the very next day to Bologna, which greeted its honorary citizen with a performance of *Rienzi*, at the end of which he was positively buried in flowers, and a banquet, at which he gave thanks for his welcome with a speech on the text of the city's two mottoes: 'Bononia docet' and 'Libertas'.

Back in Florence, he and Cosima made the most of the city's art treasures, and Glasenapp later heard him speak 'with true enthusiasm' of their repeated visits to the Uffizi and the Palazzo Pitti. There were also some inspiriting meetings with the former Jessie Laussot, who now lived in Florence.

His worries continued to hound him in sleepless nights, and he grew bitter and unjust towards those who were loyally looking after his affairs in Germany. He reproached them with being concerned with financial matters to the exclusion of any concern for himself and his well-being. 'I am very sorry to see that even you can find it in your heart to pay me and the position I am in no further attention, and to talk about the business in exactly the same terms as all my other friends,' he wrote to Heckel. If the deficit was not met he was thinking of handing the theatre over to some other agency, perhaps even the court theatre in Munich, and then he would concern himself with it no longer. 'I have reached the end of my strength, my dear friend. Up to this point my undertaking has been a question put to the people of Germany: "Do you want this?" Now I assume that they do not, and so I have come to the end of the road.' (9 December)

Two days later he approached Düfflipp officially with a new suggestion.

Since coping further with the financial side of his undertaking was undermining his health and destroying all further desire to create, he suggested as the most natural and honourable solution that the Hoftheater should take over the enterprise. His works could then be performed in the 'Royal' Festival Theatre in Bayreuth, with the personnel of the Munich court opera. 'For me this solution would also be a release from the pains and torments which make my life a misery, and the continuance of which could easily drive me to surrender all my property and my income in order to pay what must be paid, and to turn my back on Germany.' (11 December)

Arriving in Munich on 18 December, he learned that Düfflipp proposed to visit Bayreuth between Christmas and the New Year, in order to discuss matters with the festival management committee.

For the meantime things remained in the balance. For her birthday Cosima received comforting words from an unexpected quarter: 'Everything on which your life now depends had to happen as it did,' Nietzsche wrote to her from Sorrento, 'and specifically it is impossible to imagine the whole post-Bayreuth present taking any other form than it does, because it corresponds exactly to the whole pre-Bayreuth past: what was wretched and cheerless before is still the same, and what was great remains so, indeed has only now truly become so.' This is another of the three letters first published in 1964, in which he also admits his alienation from Schopenhauer's philosophy, of which, though it must have happened gradually, he had suddenly become aware. (19 December)

Wagner and Cosima, too, took refuge with the Greeks. They read Thucydides' *History of the Peloponnesian War*, and saw a parallel between the fall of the city of Pericles and the defeat of their own work in Bayreuth. Yet at the same time Wagner's mind, which never ceased to dwell on the subject, was at work on a new plan to save it. He wrote to Standhartner that he was rousing himself from the depths of his discouragement to make another experiment. He would shortly be issuing an appeal to the Wagner Societies to form a permanent Society of Patrons, the purpose of which would be to support and maintain the future festivals, to which only the members would be admitted, not the ordinary 'public and the journalistic rabble'. (2 January 1877)

In the appeal, dated 1 January 1877, he said that if there were Germans of discernment to join the ranks of French, English and Americans who had already demonstrated their recognition of the merit of his work, then he would leave it to a Society of Patrons, formed on the lines he envisaged, to lobby the Reichstag for support. To be of any effective use the Reichstag would have to make an annual grant of at least 100,000 marks, and in recognition of this state support free tickets would have to be awarded to deserving applicants. If this plan was put into effect it would be the first time that a theatrical institution received the seal of national importance. (RWGS, X, pp. 11ff.)

Düfflipp arrived at last on 21 January. The next day Wagner made his proposals known to him and the management committee: If the deficit was met by the king or the Reich, then he would be available to resume the festival on this surer basis; alternatively, let the king take over the theatre, and let it be run by the Hofoper, until all the money he had received had been recovered; or, finally, let an impresario like Pollini take on the festivals, with the same end in view of repaying the king. (GLRW, V, pp. 331f.)

Düfflipp made himself very pleasant, recalled his visit to Tribschen ten years previously and expressed his thanks for their hospitality as he left, but said neither yes nor no to the proposals.

Wagner wrote to the king that he would have written long before this, and had only postponed doing so because of Düfflipp's impending visit and his expectation that the king's wishes would be made known then. 'Now that I have discovered he was not to convey any such wishes to me, I shall resort to the course of action I had previously decided on, undeterred by this incident.' He had intended to use the leisure hours of his Italian holiday to write the text of *Parsifal*; but the worries that pursued him there had made his every step a painful one. 'I admit it was an act of great folly to have written my great work "in faith in the German spirit", and I must even fear that I did not serve "the glory of my noble benefactor".' (23 January)

Shortly afterwards he heard from the Court Secretary's office that the king rejected the suggestion that the Munich opera should take over the running of the Bayreuth festivals.

But as Cosima was speaking of the sufferings of genius, Wagner interrupted her with a smile: 'I'm not going to tell you something.' – 'Oh, tell me, tell me!' – 'I'm going to start *Parzival*, and I shan't stop until it is finished.' (DMCW, I, p. 789) Writing a new prose scenario took him until 23 February, and the verse text until 19 April, and all the time his struggle with the overwhelming deficit grew greater. He actually had three concurrent and complementary plans: his 'experimental' proposal for a Society of Patrons, a series of concerts in London, and negotiations with Dr Förster, the director of the Stadttheater in Leipzig.

Förster had made the first approach in August 1876, with the request for permission to stage the *Ring* in its composer's birthplace. At the time Wagner was evasive: 'My work is not yet finished: the actual performances of it have shown me many things that remain unfinished. Give me time to present my work once more in a carefully corrected form next year, here in Bayreuth.' (6 September 1876)

Now Wagner himself turned to Leipzig, primarily in the hope of finding his Siegfried, Georg Unger, a suitable place in a theatre where he would not have to 'go back on the haphazard treadmill of the routine repertory'. In return for this favour he would enter negotiations about the *Ring*, if, as he hoped, Leipzig was still interested. (To Kapellmeister Sucher, 31 January 1877)

The offer was taken up with alacrity, but immediately struck an unexpected difficulty when Düfflipp reminded Wagner that according to the 1864 contract the *Ring* belonged to the King of Bavaria and Wagner had no right to sell it to Leipzig or Vienna. Jauner in Vienna had also announced his interest in producing the *Ring* there, and was putting the thumbscrews on Wagner over the matter of Richter's leave of absence for the London concerts.

In response, Wagner argued, as he had done before, that that contract, which he would in any case like to see revised or cancelled, had only been a form in which a gift from the king had been dressed. It would be sad, he wrote, if – someone – wanted to abuse it! Ever since he had been in receipt of a regular allowance and gifts from the king's bounty, he had voluntarily waived all fees and royalties from performances of his works in the Munich court theatre: he had never asked for anything in return for the fact that *Rienzi*, *Tristan*, *Meistersinger*, *Rheingold* and *Walküre* had been 'of profit solely to the box office of the Royal Hoftheater'. (To Düfflipp, 17 April)

Düfflipp replied that it was not primarily a matter of the 1864 contract but of the one of February 1874, in consequence of which the Cabinet Treasury had advanced the sum of 216,152 marks and 42 pfennigs. If the *Ring* were to be given to Munich, Leipzig and Vienna, it would diminish any hope of recovering anything on that advance, since Bayreuth would then lose its particular pull. 'For years I have made no secret of the fact that His Majesty's building plans make such demands on the resources of the Cabinet Treasury as to exclude expenditure of monies for other purposes.' (20 April)

But these objections were overcome, and coordinated terms were agreed for production in the three 'preferred' theatres: Munich in south Germany, Leipzig in the north, and Vienna in Austria. The contract with Förster seemed to be in the bag at last. In the course of the negotiations Wagner came up with an idea that has a quite modern ring to it, to the effect that the three theatres ought to be able 'in time to mount the festivals [in Bayreuth] by combining their artistic forces as appropriate, and similarly to manage the technical administration of the same'. (To Dülfflipp, 28 April)

'I reaffirm my acceptance of your proposals of last year,' Wagner telegraphed Förster on 24 April, and received by return the reply: 'Regard your telegram . . . as binding agreement.'

The 'proposals' as Wagner had understood them constituted an honorarium of 10,000 marks for the preferential rights to the *Ring*, and a 10 per cent royalty for each performance. He now discovered in the small print of the contract that by 'honorarium' Förster meant an advance to be repaid within a very short term. In spite of attempts to find a compromise the negotiations foundered on this point. Angelo Neumann, whom we have already encountered as a young singer in Vienna, was now Förster's assistant; he revealed that Förster, under the influence of the anti-Wagner faction in Leipzig, was not unwilling to withdraw from the contract. At a dinner in Förster's house in honour of a prima donna, one of these influential people got carried away and proposed a toast to the happy cancellation of the *Ring* contract; when it was Neumann's turn to clink glasses with this enthusiast he instead threw his glass on the floor and smashed it.

Eventually it was Neumann who revived the project that had failed in Leipzig, in an epoch-making new form.

The last two letters to Förster were written from London, where Wagner had gone at the end of April to give a series of concerts. In January he had been approached by the leader of the Bayreuth orchestra, August Wilhelmj, acting on behalf of the concert agents Hodge & Essex, to give twenty concerts in the 10,000-seat Royal Albert Hall, each of which ought to make £500. In spite of this tempting prospect Wagner hesitated: his London experience of twenty-two years before was still a bad memory, and Bülow, who had lost £1500 there, also warned him against it through his American manager Ullmann. But Wagner gave in to the urgings of his Bayreuth friends, in order to show that it was not lethargy or the thought of his own convenience that held him back. Once the matter was agreed he took it up with his usual energy and first of all made sure of the services of some of his Bayreuth artists, who needed some coaxing, apart from the guarantee of high fees: 'You will sing at twenty concerts, nice cosy English affairs, one or two "pièces", and will get 500 marks an evening.'

Finding Hodge & Essex's proposals obscure, he was delighted

when Alfred Jachmann, the husband of his niece Johanna, offered to
go to England to represent him legally. 'Well now, dearest Alfred (a
highly auspicious name for England!), let me wish you the best of
luck! . . . Act for Bayreuth and Wahnfried in the land of Alfred the
Great exactly as your heart inspires you to.' (22 February)

It immediately transpired that the ambitious young agents had
overreached themselves, and the number of the concerts had to be
cut from twenty to six. The contract was signed on 15 March, and
Cosima and Wagner arrived in London on 1 May. She was enthralled – 'If I had to choose a great city it would be London' – while
he got the impression, on a steamer trip on the Thames, that
Alberich's dream had come true: Nibelheim, world dominion,
work, business and everywhere oppressive smoke and fog!

But he could not fail to be struck by the contrast with his 1855
visit. They were welcomed like royalty, and although Wagner did
his best to live quietly he was, in Newman's words, 'dined and
wined and toasted in public and private', and was received at
Windsor on 17 May by Queen Victoria and her youngest son Prince
Leopold. He did not forget to look up his old friends Sainton and
Lüders. Only Judith, whom he had hoped to see again, did not
come. 'Chère âme! douce amie! Et tu n'es pas venue me voir?
Agreed, you would have had little joy at the sight of me, drained
of my strength by incessant strains and bitterness.'[4]

The concerts, employing an orchestra of 169, led by Wilhelmj
and conducted by Wagner and Richter, proved an immense artistic
and social success, and two extra ones had to be given at the end of
the series. But unfortunately Hodge & Essex had overlooked a
factor that had also escaped Jachmann: the fact that *two thousand* of
the most expensive seats in the Albert Hall were privately owned
and the owners either sat in them themselves for nothing or leased
them for their own profit, meaning a loss to the agency of £12,000
over the six concerts. After only three it looked as though the
takings would not even cover the expenses. He had been right to
have doubts, Wagner wrote to Feustel on 13 May. They must at
once find another way of meeting the Bayreuth deficit. He asked the
management committee to open a subscription list and to put his
own name at the head of it for the sum of 3000 marks.

'Should this expedient fail too, I have decided to make a deal with
Ullmann for America, which would also mean putting my house in
Bayreuth on the market, crossing the ocean with all my family and

never coming back to Germany again.' Cosima's diary shows that he spoke in all seriousness; following a reference to the offer he had had from Ullmann, she wrote: 'In that case no return to Germany!'

To redeem the losses in London, Wagner paid the singers' fees, a total of £1200, out of his own pocket. As for the £700 Hodge & Essex were then able to pay him, he sent it at once to Feustel, asking him to put him down for a subscription of 10,000 marks instead of 3000, and to hold the remainder for him for the time being.

The London Wagner festival had a happier epilogue. His friends in London, knowing that he had not only received no fee but had also dug into his own pocket to the tune of £1200, organized a subscription which raised £561. But when Edward Dannreuther, who had been his host in London, called on him in Bayreuth in the middle of August to present him with this sum on their behalf, Wagner, who would gladly have accepted it as a contribution to the festival funds, had to refuse it as a personal gift, courteously but firmly.

Wagner and Cosima left London on 4 June for Bad Ems, where he was going to drink the waters. His two Mathildes came to see him there – 'good, true' Mathilde Maier and Frau Wesendonk, who had acclaimed Brahms in the meantime but returned to the Wagnerian fold after Bayreuth. Kaiser Wilhelm was in Ems at the same time, and when Siegfried gave him a bunch of cornflowers on the promenade he chatted amiably to the boy. But when Feustel urged Wagner to enjoy some dolce far niente, he could only heave a sigh. 'Yes! Yes! Do nothing! No: *accomplish* nothing! That's my holiday. Well, God's will be done!' To satisfy the most pressing of the Bayreuth creditors he authorized the payment of a considerable sum from his and his wife's private means, which, with the fees paid to the singers in London, amounted to 50,000 marks. 'Let's hope that these inroads on my family's existence will at least purchase us the time and leisure to find out how my affairs really stand.' (14 June)

He had noticed that when they had been rejoined by the children all of them, and especially little Siegfried, had greeted him with looks of such 'tender commiseration' as to make him realize that some really bad blow had been struck him while he was away. It turned out that the *Bayreuther Tagblatt* had published the false reports, circulating elsewhere, that the London concerts had been not only financially but also artistically a flop. Just as after the festival, another flood of hatred and scorn washed over Wagner and his work. One has to read at least a selection of the gems published by contemporary critics to gain a notion of the infamy to which journalism can sink.[5]

Now his enemies in Vienna deemed the time ripe to launch a well-prepared attack from the rear. On 16 and 17 June 1877 the *Neue Freie Presse* published 'Richard Wagner's Letters to a Milliner' (Bertha Goldwag) with an ironic commentary by Daniel Spitzer, a colleague of Hanslick. These letters, concerned with the ordering of silk curtains, bedspreads and dressing gowns, would raise, it was hoped, what Newman calls 'a Philistine horse-laugh' at Wagner's expense. This was the experience that made Wagner assure Jauner that he would never darken Vienna's doors again: 'Never! Never!'[6]

When the king heard from Düfflipp that Wagner was thinking of emigrating to America, he wrote imploring him, by the love and friendship that had bound them for so many years, not to entertain the 'horrifying' idea for one moment: it would be an ineradicable disgrace for all Germans, if they allowed their greatest genius to depart from their midst! (Mid-June)

Still completely beset by the 'chaos of demeaning impressions received daily, even hourly', Wagner sent the king a fair copy in Cosima's hand of the text of *Parsifal*, which he had written as a way of escaping disgust and dread. 'There it is! May it give you some pleasure and perhaps strengthen you in your view that preserving me for my art a few years longer was not completely without value.' (22 June)

Now that the Leipzig plan had fallen through, the only course he could envisage was the earlier one of consigning the Bayreuth festival to the Munich theatre. 'As it will be my last effort, I will gladly talk to anybody I am referred to . . . But my fate, grave and heavy, lies in your royal hand!' At the same time he told Düfflipp he would be coming to Munich in the third week in July to discuss matters.

He got there on 20 July, and Düfflipp called on him in his hotel the next morning. He later reported to the king that Wagner had at once got down to business and asked if the king had made any decision about his request. 'When I was obliged to answer that I knew nothing of any such decision on Your Majesty's part, Wagner looked very surprised and shocked, leant back in his chair, drew his hand over his forehead and said in a tone of the deepest emotion:

"Ah! Now I know where I am. So I have nothing more to hope! – And yet the king's last letters were so cordial and showed such good will that I thought the old days were coming back again." '

Since Düfflipp had been commissioned by the king to persuade Wagner to stay in Bayreuth at all costs, he suggested discussing the new plan with the intendant as well. The fact that Wagner agreed, after a little hesitation, to see Perfall, shows how much in earnest he was when he said that he would talk to anybody at all.

Perfall duly worked out a plan, and Wagner agreed to it. But in the end the king rejected it and commanded the production of the complete *Ring* in Munich.

It seemed that what Wagner had predicted in June was already coming to pass, that it would be Bayreuth that would suffer, rather than the *Ring*. 'My work will be performed everywhere and draw huge audiences – but no one will come to Bayreuth again . . . The only charge I can lay against the town is that *I* chose it. But I did it for the sake of a great idea: I wanted to set up a completely independent, new creation, with the aid of the nation, in a town that would owe its importance solely to that creation – a kind of Washington of art. I had too good an opinion of the upper ranks of our society.' (To Feustel, 14 June)

'A great idea': but the king's decision seemed to drive the last nail into its coffin. As to others, so it seemed to Wagner, who had consented to the decision, compelled by circumstances against his will – and yet not solely against his will. When he entered the Festspielhaus for the first time after his return from England the solemn lofty interior struck him once again with the sense of dedication. But the costumes and production photographs filled him with aversion to the idea of ever repeating the festival. Perhaps Rome or Florence had helped to strengthen his dissatisfaction with the visual realization of his drama. He had spoken so emphatically in London of the impression Michelangelo's frescoes had made on him that some of his friends there now sent him a portfolio of reproductions of them.

The idea seemed dead and buried, but it was to rise again, transfigured. He had gradually come to realize the one thing he still had to do, he wrote to Düfflipp. He was now in his sixty-fifth year and had to husband his strength. 'But in extemporized productions like last year's, I squander my strength . . . I have therefore turned my attention to an idea I have long cherished . . . carrying it out will set the seal on my effectiveness and influence. What I have in mind is not a school strictly speaking, but systematic exercises in performance technique under my direction.' (19 September)

Delegates from the Wagner Societies gathered in Bayreuth on 15 September. They met in the Festspielhaus, sitting on the stage in a wide semicircle round Wagner as he gave them a frank report on the festival's affairs.

In 1876 he had believed that it would occur to some of the patrons to ask among themselves: 'Honestly, what are we to do about Wagner?' They would have agreed: 'Don't trouble with him any longer, he is physically done up.' And then they might have asked: 'What about paying the bills?' Whereupon it would have transpired that they could not regard their subscriptions as the end of their contributions, but would take responsibility for the whole affair. 'It didn't happen. Everyone went heedlessly home again. It was all just an entertainment, something out of the ordinary, without any further consequence or significance. I had been shown the greatest honours, afforded the happiness of seeing the best singers and musicians in Germany assemble in a theatre built specially for me to perform one of my works. Emperors and princes had graced the festival with their presence. "What more does the man want?" I was forced to accept that that was the general reaction.'

He went on to tell them about his efforts to cover the deficit. The circular of the previous November had not produced a single subscription – only 'the aunt of Herr Plüddemann from Kolberg' had sent 100 marks. 'Have no fear, gentlemen, that I am losing my thread among unimportant details: you must be acquainted with all this, in order to understand my mood.'

After that disappointment he had decided he was too weak to bear the burden of the theatre. He had turned to the king; he had been given reason to have hopes of the Reichstag. All in vain!

> We must admit, gentlemen, that we are back at the beginning again, though it is true to say that our handicap has been greatly reduced, as they say on the sports field . . . We have the impression made by last year's festival, and we have this theatre. Otherwise, though, we are starting again from the beginning . . .
> You know the goal of all my efforts, of our entire undertaking here in Bayreuth: a style and an art of a

kind that cannot be cultivated in our wretched
present-day theatres. My intention now would be to
build up slowly the means whereby I can make the
festivals here truly enduring, self-renewing, a true
creation. If you like we can call it a 'school', though our
music schools, where the students learn nothing at all,
have given me a strong aversion to the expression! It is
also appropriate to the modest means that are now at
our disposal. We shall achieve much with little in this
way. But it will take resolution, and the support of all
the friends of our cause. So I ask you now, gentlemen, if
you are willing to stand shoulder to shoulder with me in
this, if you are willing to devote patience and tenacity to
an undertaking that is directed towards a great artistic
goal, or whether you would prefer simply to come here
again on some future occasion to see something out of
the ordinary. If the latter is the case, then this had better
be the parting of our ways.

I have had the idea of founding a school here for
training singers, instrumentalists and conductors in the
correct performance of musico-dramatic works of a
truly German style, and I will take the liberty of
explaining to you in a few words the form I envisage it
taking.[7]

He then outlined his plan for building up the school over the next
six years, from the performance of the classics of the instrumental
repertory to the higher reaches of operatic style and the performance of his own works. Like his earlier schemes drafted in Riga,
Dresden, Zürich and Munich, the plan as expounded here and
augmented by further remarks, spoken and in letters to friends, is
distinguished by its firm grasp of the ideal and the practical, and like
them it came to nothing because of the indifference of his contemporaries. The school could have been started for a miserable 20,000
marks, which was not forthcoming.[8]

The only part of the plan that was realized was the founding of
Bayreuther Blätter, originally intended as a newssheet about the
school for circulation among the members of the Wagner Society
who were not actively involved in running it. After the rest of the
plan came to nothing it was published as the monthly magazine of

the Society. His experiences were repeating themselves, Wagner wrote in his preface to the first issue on 1 January 1878: while his sole interest had always been in concrete artistic achievements, he had been obliged all his life to pick up the pen of the theorist to explain himself.

On the day after the meeting Wagner invited the delegates to Wahnfried, where he read them the text of *Parsifal*, the first time he had done so outside his immediate circle. After reading the subtitle, 'a festival drama of dedication', Schemann recalled, he paused and mimicked the foreseeable reaction of his detractors: 'What's Wagner's caper this time?' After the first act he said to Julius Hey, 'well, well, my dear Hey, how are we going to set *that* to music?' and after the second, 'there's a nice little ballet in it, too'. The sun was just setting as he came to Titurel's obsequies in the last act and his vigorous head was transfigured in the light of its last rays.

No performance of any of Wagner's works made a greater impression on him, Schemann avowed, than that reading. Never again did Amfortas's laments so pierce him through and through as they did on that occasion, when Wagner seemed to be consumed in a passionate ecstasy. He returned home afterwards a new man, in a quite different sense from 1876. 'The line "Hört ihr den Ruf? Nun danket Gott, daß ihr berufen, ihn zu hören" had become the truth for me in a quite miraculous way.'

It all made a very optimistic impression. But Wagner was still not a step closer to paying off the deficit. Cosima had a letter from Feustel on 15 January 1878, in which he summarized his calculations that the outstanding debt was still 98,028 marks and 57 pfennigs, not including a certain amount of interest. He was being pressed for the money and although he could delay legal proceedings for a time yet, he would not be able to do so indefinitely.

'I see only one remaining possibility of averting catastrophe, namely that the Hoftheater in Munich guarantee your husband a royalty for his works of 10,000 marks a year for about ten years.'

Cosima wrote a note covering this letter and sent it on to the king: she lacked the courage to go to her husband with this cry of anguish, now that he was caught up in the anguish of Amfortas. 'I beg Your Majesty most humbly to pay heed to these lines which I venture respectfully to lay before my most gracious sovereign.' (16 January)

'Most honoured lady and friend,' Ludwig replied, 'I shall know no peace until I have told you of the great joy it gave me that you turned to me personally in the matter which is the subject of your so esteemed letter. As soon as I had received it I gave instructions in accordance with your wishes to my Court Secretary, who will get in touch at once with Feustel and Perfall, so that the deficit can be met in the said manner, beyond all doubt.' (27 January)

And so on 31 March 1878 a contract was concluded between the management of the Hoftheater and the Court Secretary's office on the one hand and Richard Wagner and the Bayreuth festival management committee on the other, making provision for the deficit to be defrayed by a loan, at 5 per cent interest, repayable in regular instalments. The repayments were to be raised by the payment of a royalty of 10 per cent of the gross receipts from performances of Wagner's works in all the royal theatres.

Wagner had already written to Feustel on 3 February to thank him for the exceptional patience, wisdom and energy he had exercised in their plight. 'The outcome has been this – to me – very satisfactory turn of events, that it will be due essentially to the success of my own works that we shall be given the means to overcome the evil material consequences of 1876. It is honourable.'

He added: 'The profit from all this is that I can now apply myself to a new work with that beautiful equanimity, the disturbance or overshadowing of which drives the good spirits away from us strange "geniuses"!'

His English biographer cannot refrain from making this comment:

> This, then, was the sharply realistic ending to Wagner's dream in 1850 of 'the German spirit' voluntarily 'co-operating' with him in the achievement of his ideal! In the strictest sense of the words, it was he who paid for conferring Bayreuth on a frigid and largely hostile German world. But at any rate, thanks to the only man who really understood him – the 'mad' King of Bavaria – he could now sleep at night unracked by cares of all kinds, and devote what remained of his health to the completion of his *Parsifal*. (NLRW, IV, p. 579)

Part VII: *Parsifal* (1877–1883)

31

'My Farewell to the World'

I

'Oui, il est question de la musique de *Parsifal*. I could not have gone on living without throwing myself into something of the kind,' Wagner wrote to Judith Gautier on 1 October 1877. Cosima had heard the first notes coming from his music room early in August, and he had played her the 'Last Supper' theme on 11 August: he told her that he had written it down all of a sudden when he already had his hat and coat on, ready to go and fetch her. Only the day before he had said a composer should beware of expanding the text for the sake of a melody, and now he had done it after all. In the case of the Prize Song in *Die Meistersinger* he had also written the tune first and shaped the text to fit it, but this new instance was something different again: it was not the beauty of the melody that had tempted him to take this course, but the recognition of the musical fecundity of this central theme coming in the Grail Supper scene, 'the most important scene, the nucleus of the whole'. It contains the anguish of Amfortas,' he told Cosima, and it contains much else besides: specifically the motivic germs of no fewer than five of the principal themes of the work as a whole.[1] It illustrates the principle of motivic development taken to its furthest logical consequences.

He began the composition and orchestral sketches during that September. Each time he sat down to it he felt as though he was writing music for the first time in his life. He was sixty-four years old, harassed by worries and disappointment, and now he was embarking once more on the 'agonizingly difficult work' of creating a completely new world. 'Aidez-moi!' he appealed to Judith, the cry of an ageing man for the youth he has lost, for a renewal of his

527

youth, for the 'recurrent puberty' of genius of which Goethe speaks.

Judith was then thirty-two, in the full flower of her classical beauty. The most celebrated poets and writers of the day praised her dark, deep eyes, the golden tint of her skin, her Grecian profile, comparable to the purest of the reliefs of Aegina. Baudelaire had called her 'petite fille grecque' in her girlhood, Laurent Tailhade wrote of her as 'cette femme au profil de camée, dont le masque faisait penser à la Junon de Velletri'; and in old age Victor Hugo saluted her in his sonnet, 'Ave, dea, moriturus te salutat!'

She and Wagner had been friends since the Tribschen days, but deeper feelings were not aroused until the summer of 1876, when his distress at the 'false fame' that the festival was attracting threatened to overwhelm him. He was disappointed when she did not follow his suggestion that they meet in London: 'Oh, que c'est méchant!' But now commissions for her to buy the surprises he planned for Cosima's birthday created the opportunity for a heady, half-clandestine correspondence, in which Wagner's barber, Bernhard Schnappauf of Ochsengasse in Bayreuth, may be guessed to have played the role of postman as adroitly as his classic colleagues in Seville and Baghdad.

'You behold me in a frivolous mood,' Wagner wrote on 9 November. 'Ah! I am making music, I laugh at life, I laugh at the world. Je me sens aimé, et j'aime. Enfin, je fais la musique du *Parsifal*.' The subject of fabrics and perfumes constantly recurs in the letters: 'There is nothing of the sort here, we live in a desert.' He recalls their stolen embraces: 'C'était un dernier don des dieux.' He asks her to pardon him: he is old enough to be allowed to indulge himself with childish things. And then abruptly he writes about his music, his creation. She wants to translate the text into French, and as she does not know a word of German (though she does know Chinese) Cosima is making a prose translation, which Wagner will annotate for her. He gives the name Parsifal an Arabic derivation after Görres: 'parsi' means 'pure', 'fal', 'fool' in an elevated sense, 'c'est à dire, homme sans érudition mais de génie'. She makes enquiries among noted scholars, who tell her there are no such words in Arabic. Wagner replies that he doesn't know any Arabic, and perhaps Görres didn't either, but he is not worried: he fancies there will not be an excessive number of Orientalists among his future audiences.

And 'les charmeuses de Klingsor'? Those are the flowers that the sorcerer picks in his tropical garden in the spring and which live until the autumn as young girls, 'très gracieusement et naïvement', in order to seduce the knights of the Grail. But he almost despairs of the French language when it comes to translating 'ein furchtbar schönes Weib'. 'Terrible' sounds funny; 'fatal' won't satisfy him; 'terrifiant' is not an approved form, the French have to say 'terrifié'. 'So much for logic! Perhaps there's too much logic, when language is the product of nature and totally irrational, whereas an academy is highly rational, logical and everything else you care to mention – but it is not creative, it merely arranges and lays down conventions. But what is the point of patriotic disputes about languages? It is you, my dear, who make me regret more bitterly than ever that I cannot immerse myself in you entirely through the means of your language!' (4 December)

Judith had obtained a divorce from Catulle Mendès and now lived with her lover Ludwig (né Louis) Benedictus. He was the cause of the only difference between her and Wagner – not jealousy, there was no question of that on either side. But Wagner wrote that Benedictus had fallen greatly in his esteem since he had learned that he composed. Everybody he met was a composer these days and nearly all of them contemptibly weak and idle. 'When I think how much music there is in the world, and how few works have gained my genuine affection, in the sense that these few works comprise everything that I mean by the word "music" – you would be amazed if I told you! But I will not tell you. My heart sinks at your mere mention of "audacious instrumentation": I know all these young people begin with nothing but "audacities", either in the instrumentation or in the harmony – but never in the melody!'

A few days later he explained: 'I did not say that I do not want to see the music of Benedictus, but I am afraid to see it. That's all! I speak from experience. Of late a number of my ardent followers have appealed to me for my opinion of their musical future: against my better judgement I have concealed my despair from them, but they have sensed it and grown cool – or, rather, bitter. That is something that distresses and saddens me.' And to emphasize that his aversion to 'audacities' had not made him an opponent of true innovation in music he added: 'Benedictus qui venit in nomine verae novationis! I embrace him in anticipation!' (23 December)

He imagined her in the room with him as he wrote to her, sitting on the chaise-longue to the right of his desk and looking at him, 'Dieu! avec quels yeux!' To have her there with him and talk to her thus would be an incomparable pleasure. Over and over again, he assured her that she was his only wealth, the 'belle abondance', the 'superflu enivrant' of his life.

Then one day it was all over. 'I have asked Cosima to take those commissions in hand . . . I am so troubled at present by business matters which are not in the least agreeable, that I no longer have the leisure to get on with *Parsifal*. Have pity on me! It will all be over soon, and I shall find again those beautiful moments in which I love to talk to you about myself! . . . Et enfin nous nous reverrons un jour! A vous, R.' (15 February 1878)

What had happened? There is no indication that the relationship had become an issue between Wagner and Cosima. The extracts from her diary for the period available to date (May 1977) report on his work on *Parsifal*, and conversations about Haydn and Mozart symphonies, with which he was much preoccupied at the time. There is nothing to suggest marital discord. Nor, indeed, did the former warm friendship between Wahnfried and Judith fall off at all. She had provided Wagner with a creative impulse, but now that she had played her part passion was converted back into friendship and a grateful memory.

The publication in 1964 of Cosima's letters to Judith also threw a new light on those which Wagner wrote to her. Cosima must have known of the affair at the time, and we can now see it through her eyes. 'She had the wisdom', the editor writes, 'to regard it as passing and unimportant, and the skill to betray nothing to either her husband or her friend and to allow the crisis to run its course.'[2] That is not to say that the experience left no scar on his heart. Two years later, when he was talking to Cosima about Goethe and Ulrike von Levetzow, he said: 'He felt it very deeply – it was a farewell to life.' And perhaps this thought was already in his mind when he asked Judith, in one of his last letters to her, 'shall I forget it?' then goes on: 'No! – But everything is tragic – everything inclines – at best – to elegy' ('tout penche – au melieur [sic] cas – à l'élégie!'). It could well be an allusion to Goethe's *Marienbad Elegies*, the outcome of his passion for Ulrike von Levetzow:

> Wenn Liebe je den Liebenden begeistet,
> Ward es an mir auf's lieblichste geleistet . . .

('If ever love inspirited the lover, it happened to me in the loveliest way.')

Meanwhile the progress of *Parsifal* can be followed in Cosima's diary, almost from day to day. When Wagner played her the prelude from the orchestral sketch he spoke about the attraction of the Grail mystery:'That the blood becomes wine strengthens us and we are therefore able to turn to the earth, while the transformation of the wine into blood draws us away from the earth.' The modulation of the Faith theme to D major in the prelude he compared to the spread of revelation through the whole world. He had been on the verge of giving it all up, he told her one day after he had started the first act. He had picked up his Darwin and then suddenly thrown it down again, 'for while I was reading everything came to me and that put me in such good fettle that I positively had to force myself to stop, so as not to keep lunch waiting. It's an insane state of affairs.' And another evening he played her a marvellous theme for a symphony: he had so many ideas of that kind, new ones occurred to him all the time, but he couldn't use the happy tunes for *Parsifal*.

'When you get the next page,' he said a few days later, 'you'll see that I've had a lot of trouble with it.' He wanted a weighty 3/2 for Amfortas's approach in the first scene, and had had difficulty fitting in Gurnemanz's words: 'Er naht, sie bringen ihn getragen . . .' 'Ingenuity is not what is wanted here, it must sound as though it had to be as it is. But now I've got it!'

One afternoon when he was working, he formed the impression that something that had seemed a good idea that morning now sounded harsh. So he closed the lid of his grand piano, and played it with the soft pedal down, and found it was satisfactory after all. To signal his pleasure to Cosima, who was helping the children with their lessons, he played the lovely theme from the coda of the first movement of Mozart's C major Symphony.

Another day he told her he had had an inspiration that would please her: at the very moment when the esquires were repeating the prophecy, Parsifal would fire his arrow interrupting them at the words 'der reine Tor'.

Sometimes the modulation into another key was what caused him difficulty, sometimes a 'rhythmic battle' he had to win. We learn of his satisfaction with a chromatically descending major third in the transformation music, out of which he then developed the counterpoint in the theme of the lament to the Saviour. When he played her what he had composed of Amfortas's complaint he admitted that the phrase 'nach Ihm, nach Seinem Weihegruße' had occupied him for the whole morning. He had never done anything as 'fantastic' as this before, it was getting greater all the time!

But he had only now come to the most difficult part of all, he told her, and the next day he improvised the Grail Scene from his sketches. In order to represent the spirituality of the words of the Saviour, the complete divorce from all materiality, he wanted to use a blend of voices, 'a baritone solo would make everything material, it must be neither male nor female, neuter in the highest sense of the word'. And so he set the first statement of the Last Supper theme ('Nehmet hin meinen Leib . . .') in the major mode, for altos and tenors, and the second, more urgent statement in the minor, for sopranos and altos. 'The drums will accompany the voices like a soft earth tremor!' He took a look at the scores of Berlioz's Requiem and Te Deum and laughed at all the directions for the tympani: it was like nothing so much as a director in the theatre straightening the actors' wigs.

The work absorbed him completely. He decided not to have Titurel speak again after the Mystery. One afternoon he had a tussle with a modulation and that night, when Cosima was already in bed and on the point of falling asleep, she heard him shout: 'A flat, G flat, F, it must be!' On 22 January 1878 he played and sang her the Grail scene. The words 'Wein und Brot des letzten Mahles' sounded like an age-old story, told by angels. 'But I won't have the old man coming back.' The next evening he told her, 'this will make you laugh', and showed her where he had allowed Titurel to sing again after all.

He was already thinking about the second act before he began to sketch it at the beginning of March. Klingsor was going to be very savage: 'Did you expect him to be brooding?' He was quite clear about how the prelude would be, and Kundry's scream, too. While this was all in his mind he sketched a canon for a 'domestic symphony', lost his temper with one of his adherents who disparaged Mozart's G minor Symphony, and praised Haydn's 'Military' Symphony: 'All our music goes back to these works.' He kept returning to Haydn and Mozart for several days in succession after that. There were things in *Zauberflöte*, he said, that made a chapter in the history of art in themselves: Sarastro introduced an innate, intelligent dignity instead of the conventional operatic kind – and we, the readers, at once recognize the creator of Gurnemanz – and there were things in Mozart, Wagner added, that would never be surpassed. Another evening, Cosima writes, he picked up Haydn's 'Bear' Symphony, and then drew Anton Seidl's attention to the Andante of his G major Symphony [presumably the 'Surprise'], which was one of the most beautiful things ever written – and what a marvellous sound!

While working on Klingsor's scene with Kundry he compared Klingsor to Alberich: at one time, he said, he had felt complete sympathy with Alberich, who represented ugliness yearning for beauty. Alberich possessed the naivety of the pre-Christian world, Klingsor that specific kind of evil that Christianity had brought into the world: 'He does not believe in goodness, like the Jesuits, that is his strength – but also his downfall; there is always *one* individual at any time throughout the ages.' Wagner was glad when he had finished the scene, and had 'thrown Klingsor off the battlements'.

'Ah! Music!' he exclaimed of Parsifal's appearance in the magic garden. 'What could take its place? In spoken dialogue this pause would be impossible. The *speaking pause* is the property of music.' But he was soon dejected again. 'I was so looking forward to my Flower Maidens, and now that's difficult too!' First of all he worked out the contrapuntal vocal writing on four or five staves, and then wrote the words for it: it reminded him of how he had written the words after the music when he was working on the finale of the first act of *Lohengrin* and the street fight in the second act of *Meistersinger*. 'My girls shall rush in with a wail, like children whose toys have been taken away – without anger.' And of the graceful motion of the Ab major passage 'Komm! Komm! Holder Knabe!': 'In the first act I was very sparing with the more sensuous intervals but now I'm using my old paint pot again.'

It was the beginning of April, but the skies were still grey. While he was giving his Flower Maidens something to sing he was thinking about the birds outside: 'Why do the birds sing so? They don't worry about what the sky looks like, they sing as children laugh – for no reason.'

It was in the midst of this happy absorption in writing music, at the beginning of May, that Nietzsche sent them *Human, all too Human*. By a miracle of significance and chance, according to *Ecce Homo*, a copy of the text of *Parsifal* reached Nietzsche at exactly the same time, inscribed 'To his dear friend, Friedrich Nietzsche, from

Richard Wagner, Councillor of the Church'. 'The crossing of these two books – I seemed to hear an ominous note. Was it not the sound of *swords* crossing?'

The truth was less melodramatic: the copy of *Parsifal* had reached him on 3 January 1878. (And the dedication actually ran: 'Cordial greetings and best wishes to his dear friend Friedrich Nietzsche, Richard Wagner (Supreme Councillor of the Church – for the information of Professor Overbeck).' The allusion to Overbeck's book on 'the Christlike-ness of present-day theology' was intended to stress the unecclesiastical nature of the text, as Nietzsche understood very well, but twisted out of malice.)

It reached him, as his sister admits, 'in the middle' of the compilation of *Human, all too Human*, which did not appear until the May of that year. There is no need to go into Nietzsche's allegation of astonishment at the work again, but the publication of *Human, all too Human* had a prehistory that cannot be passed over here. Nietzsche originally wanted to issue it under a pseudonym, but this idea was quashed by the publisher, who did not want to let slip the chance of causing a sensation. Thereupon Nietzsche replaced Wagner's name throughout by 'the artist'. Writers on Nietzsche have claimed that that was all that was necessary to remove any possible cause of offence to Wagner, but this is not borne out by the facts.

Quite the reverse: tempering the text was the last thing he intended. As his confidant Peter Gast told Joseph Hofmiller, he actually added a particularly savage dig after completion. Gast had written three quite long essays, purely atheistic in character – we may assume that they were written in the spirit of Nietzsche's newly adopted positivism, as they met with his approval – and sent them to Hans von Wolzogen for inclusion in the first number of *Bayreuther Blätter*, presumably to serve as a kind of 'programme' for the periodical. Wolzogen rejected the articles in a seven-page letter which, according to Gast, enraged Nietzsche more than Wagner's later reception of *Human, all too Human*, and was the decisive factor in his alienation. It was then that he added to Aphorism 109 the tailpiece probably aimed not only at Wolzogen's letter but also, and primarily, at Wagner's *Parsifal*, which he had since received:

> But certainly frivolity or melancholy of whatever degree
> is better than romantic retreat and desertion of the flag,

an approach to Christianity in any form; for in the
present state of knowledge, no one can have anything at
all to do with that without irredeemably besmirching his
intellectual conscience.

Above all, avoiding Wagner's name concealed absolutely
nothing. Everyone knew at once who was meant, not least Wagner
and Cosima themselves. It would have been one thing if the criticism had been confined only to his ideas and his works, but the
ruthless assault on Wagner's whole personality as man and as artist
– notably in the chapter 'Out of the Soul of Artists and Writers' –
was quite another matter. The climax comes in Aphorism
164:

> It is at all events a dangerous sign when a person is
> overcome with the sense of awe at himself, whether it is
> that famous awe of the Caesars, or the awe inspired by
> genius that is under consideration here; when the scent
> of the sacrifice . . . penetrates into the brain of the
> genius, so that he begins to waver and to believe himself
> more than human. Slowly the consequences follow: the
> sense of not being answerable, of possessing exceptional
> rights, the belief that his very society bestows a blessing,
> insane rage when the attempt is made to compare him
> with others, or even to assess his worth at a lower rate,
> to draw attention to weaknesses in his work . . .
>   In rare individual cases this insane trait may also have
> been the means of holding a nature of this kind together,
> in spite of its tendency to overreach in all directions at
> once: in the life, too, of individuals delusions often have
> the value of those medicines which are in fact poisons;
> but [and now the dagger is thrust home] in the end, in
> the case of every 'genius' who believes in his own
> divinity, the poison reveals itself in exact proportion to
> the ageing of the 'genius'.

(When one reflects on the horrifying way in which Nietzsche
himself was later to succumb to the awe inspired by his own genius,
it is tempting to believe in the working of Nemesis.)
   'I could make a comment on every sentence that I have read,'

Cosima wrote to Countess von Schleinitz, 'and I know that it represents the victory of evil.'

She had not been spared. 'One always loses by too close an intimacy with women and friends; one of the losses is the pearl of one's own life.' (428) But she was most deeply wounded, on her own personal account, by the aphorism on 'the voluntary sacrificial animal' (430):

> There is no way in which remarkable women can so effectively ease the lives of their menfolk, if the latter are great and famous, as by becoming, so to speak, the receptacle of the general disapprobation and occasional resentment of other people. Contemporaries will customarily tolerate a large number of blunders and follies, even acts of crude injustice, on the part of their great men, if only there is someone else to play the part of sacrificial animal, whom they may mistreat and slaughter, and so relieve their feelings.
>
> It is by no means uncommon for a woman to conceive the ambition to offer herself for this sacrifice, and the man can then feel well contented – assuming, that is, that he is enough of an egoist to consent to the presence of such a voluntary deflector of lightning, storm and rain in his vicinity.

Elisabeth Förster-Nietzsche confirmed what is easy enough to guess, that her brother was consciously alluding to Cosima in the aphorism.

Cosima was forced to ask herself what had given Nietzsche the right to parade before the public gaze the most intimate aspects of what she had experienced and suffered for Wagner's sake. She wrote a long letter to Elisabeth in which she expressed herself, as the latter observed, 'with remarkable agitation'. And an extraordinary lack of sensitivity is displayed by the occasion, nine years later, when Nietzsche is supposed to have asked his sister, 'By the bye, why did Frau Wagner take such exception to *this* aphorism in particular that time? On Wagner's behalf? On her own? It's always been a puzzle to me.'

This was the book, then, that Nietzsche despatched to Wahnfried in May 1878. He sent two copies, according to *Ecce Homo*, with a cheerful verse of dedication:

Dem Meister und der Meisterin
entbietet Gruß mit frohem Sinn,
beglückt ob einem neuen Kind
von Basel Friedrich Freigesinnt . . .

('Friedrich the liberal-minded of Basel, rejoicing in his new infant, offers glad greetings to the master and the master's wife.')

The affair of *Human, all too Human* poses more than one psychological riddle. What caused Nietzsche suddenly to lash out at Cosima, almost directly after his last letter of 10 October, in which he had assured her of his sincere devotion 'in good times and in bad'? Charles Andler is probably right in seeing it as the sudden bursting of the dam behind which jealousy had been mounting for a long time: some dark instinct in him had been spoiling for a fight. 'And the decision to attack, long taken in secret and suppressed by his conscience, peremptorily and irresistibly overpowered him on one of his days of crisis, when it was imperative for him to make a clean sweep of things within himself.' Andler considers that Cosima herself may well have been one, and not the least, of the causes of his jealousy of Wagner, and the theory certainly finds confirmation in the aphorism on the voluntary sacrificial animal: reading it we can sense the pleasure Nietzsche is taking at the thought of inflicting pain, sharpening his arrow-point at each word, finally aiming at her heart, at the heart of her heart, her sacrifice of herself for Wagner.

With the aid of references to utterances of Nietzsche from the Tribschen period and to the interpretation of the 'Empedocles' fragments, Erich F. Podach has shown that there is a substantial body of evidence that even at the height of his friendship with Wagner Nietzsche was already planning to 'dethrone' him. He believed Wagner incapable of carrying out their common aim of bringing about the rebirth of Greek culture out of the German spirit and the spirit of music. That role was reserved for himself. Wagner's 'dethronement' was to take place with Cosima's aid, and she was to fall to Nietzsche as the victor's prize.[3]

This plan to reverse the master–disciple relationship shows through in one of Elisabeth Förster-Nietzsche's anecdotes, according to which she once said to her brother at a later date: 'Oh, I wish Wagner had been twenty years younger when you first met him; I

think you might have converted him to your ideas.' Nietzsche
replied: 'I too used to believe and hope the same; but then *Parsifal*
came and destroyed every hope, every possibility.' (EFWN, pp.
266f.)

The role assigned to Cosima is revealed in Nietzsche's 'Ariadne'
fantasy: 'The divine bride Ariadne–Cosima was supposed to turn
away from the inadequate demigod Theseus–Wagner and turn to
the god Dionysus–Nietzsche who alone was worthy of her . . .
Many years later madness presented Nietzsche with the illusion of
fulfilment.'[4] In the first week of January 1889, at the onset of his
madness, Nietzsche sent a number of letters to his friends. To Jacob
Burckhardt he wrote that together with Ariadne he was the golden
equilibrium of all things, and to Cosima, 'Princess Ariadne, my
beloved', he wrote: 'Of late I was . . . perhaps Richard Wagner, too
. . . But this time I come as conquering Dionysus, who will make of
the earth a festival . . .' (3 January 1889)[5]

That was the final act in the tragedy of Dionysus, which had
begun twenty years earlier under Bonaventura Genelli's picture,
and in which the publication of *Human, all too Human* marked the
peripeteia.

The other psychological riddle the book poses is what on earth
was in Nietzsche's mind when he sent Wagner a book with such
contents, with every appearance of innocence and harmlessness.
Did he really think that Wagner would take this blow, dealt him in
full public view, with a smile and in silence? At all events Nietzsche
had no difficulty in laying the blame for the inevitable rupture on
Wagner – at least to the satisfaction of his adherents, who treated as
sacrilege the latter's daring to comment ironically, in the August
1878 number of *Bayreuther Blätter*, without naming names any more
than Nietzsche had, on 'the quite illimitable advance in the field of
criticism of everything human and inhuman'. (*Publikum und
Popularität*, RWGS, X, pp. 79ff.)

'It does me no great honour to have been praised by that man,' he
remarked to Cosima, then added, unable to disguise his hurt, 'one
can't forget it.'

May of 1878 was an eventful month. On 12 May Hödel made his
unsuccessful attempt on the life of the aged Kaiser. Bismarck's
response was to lay the 'Sozialistengesetz' – an emergency bill
containing a number of repressive measures against socialists –
before the Reichstag, where it was defeated by the National Liberal

party under their leader Bennigsen. Amid the public stir, Wagner confessed that he could hear only the voice of indignation, and no note of horror: nobody seemed to be shocked at being a member of a society in which such actions were possible. He condemned the attempt to pass emergency measures, instead of rooting out the causes of the emergency. Bennigsen, normally a weakling, had acted sensibly but had not touched the core of the matter, though he had been close to it when he had spoken of 'our guilt'. To Feustel's admission that, as a deputy, he had voted against the bill with a heavy heart, Wagner replied that reaction was always bad. The leaders of the socialist movement might be muddle-headed and were perhaps a bunch of intriguers, but the future belonged to socialism.

At the beginning of June, as he and his family returned from an enjoyable outing, he was shocked by the news of another assassination attempt: a Dr Nobiling had fired at the emperor on Unter den Linden, and the old man had fainted, covered in blood. If he had anything to do with it, Wagner said, a Day of Repentance would be decreed, so that the whole nation could examine its conscience! In the following days, as details of the event became known, he expressed his admiration for the emperor's unpretentious greatness: his first question had been about his coachman, and his second concern had been with who was to represent him for the time being; not one complaint about what had befallen himself. When Feustel asked him why he did not write to congratulate the old monarch on his recovery, he replied, in a resigned tone: 'What would be the point? The emperor would ask himself: what does *he* want? Ah, he's got that deficit, he wants money!'

There followed the depressing news of mass internments for lèse-majesté, terms of imprisonment of the order of five and ten years, which Wagner predicted would mean the release of an appalling generation in ten years' time! And then the emperor's birthday was celebrated with illuminations, under siege conditions! Wagner turned to Goethe and read the scene in *Egmont* where the hero discusses the same topic with the repressive Spanish general, the Duke of Alba, in purely human terms, far removed from any political commonplaces:

> Doesn't the world, and posterity too, praise kings who
> proved able to forgive offences against their dignity, to

> forgive them, regret them and treat them with disdain?
> Isn't that the reason why they are regarded as being like
> God, who is far too great for any offence to touch him?

Everything about the event struck him as crude and stupid: the socialists, who wanted to gain control of the state in order to organize something impossible, and the government, who couldn't come up with anything but prohibition and repressive police regulations. He disapproved of the socialists making a party matter out of something that concerned all Germans. He hoped that no one believed that the forces at work in the socialist movement were capable of being directed by theories and organizations: if that were so there would be nothing in it. But ethics could be influenced, and human feelings could be prepared to accept the violent changes that would inevitably come with revolution. He had hopes of a new religion issuing from industrialists' love of their workers. He was pleased to hear that Sulzer, his old friend from the days in Zürich, was now at the head of the socialist party there. 'We could do with someone like him in Germany: I'm sure his efforts are directed, not *against* property, but towards property for all.' He re-read the letters he had written to Uhlig a quarter of a century before, and said that then as now he looked forward to the advent of socialism, only now he no longer expected it to happen in the near future. Wagner's political views were in fact far more consistent throughout his life than is commonly realized.

The impression that Bismarck, in his concern with military might, was neglecting cultural and social advances encouraged Wagner in an increasingly urgent private opposition to all forms of militarism in his last years.[6] He admitted now that he had keenly supported the constitution of the army in the past, but the way things were now – the people exhausted, incessant new levies, incessant increase of military strength – it was barbaric. 'Conquering new provinces and never even asking oneself how to win them over; not giving a thought to how to make a friend of Holland, Switzerland etc. – nothing at all – and only the army!'

Schemann tells of an occasion in December 1877 when Wagner had launched a passionate complaint about the distress the German people were in. 'And it's all happening right under the nose of Bismarck, the German of the old school!' Schemann had never seen him flare up in such holy wrath before. After those last words he had rushed out into the wintry night and worked off his agitation in a boisterous game with his Newfoundland dog.

In the same year 1878, which we can regard as marking the climax of the crisis in Wagner's relationship to the empire, he published in the *Bayreuther Blätter*, under the title 'What is German?', the notes he had written for King Ludwig in 1865, the springtime of his German hopes, bringing the article to an abrupt conclusion by asking earnestly whether Constantin Frantz might be able to help answer the question in his title. (*Was ist deutsch?*, RWGS, X, pp. 36ff.)

Frantz answered in an 'Open Letter to Richard Wagner', which was published in the June issue of *Bayreuther Blätter*. To be German, politics needed to have an aim beyond its own immediate ends; it must raise itself to 'metapolitics', which bore the same relationship to ordinary politics as metaphysics to physics. This open letter with its severe criticism of Bismarck, appearing so close in time to the two assassination attempts of the summer of 1878, caused such a shock – 'like a purgative', as Wagner put it – that the members of the Berlin Wagner Society resigned in droves.

Wagner found all his feelings about the Reich expressed in a new book Frantz published the following year, on federalism. 'It's a book I would like to commend in clarion tones to the serious consideration of the entire population,' Wagner wrote to King Ludwig; 'it contains the complete solution to the problems of this world expounded in the clearest and most thorough way, and it is precisely the solution that I myself sense is the only right one.' (7 July 1879)

Constantin Frantz has remained a relevant and controversial figure.[7] He numbers among his champions men like the Austrian historian Srbik, who praised him as a 'national cosmopolitan' in the second volume of his work on German unity, and, in his own time, Jacob Burckhardt, who wrote to Friedrich von Preen in 1872, after reading Frantz's *Das neue Deutschland*, 'That one's got a clear head on his shoulders.'

Once, when Wagner was reading a book by Frantz, a fascinating enough occupation in itself, he remarked that it nonetheless required something of a struggle to occupy himself so much with the 'phenomenal world' when his thoughts were really always with the 'thing in itself'. Even then neither *Human, all too Human* nor political events were able to draw him away from the inner world of

Parsifal. On 29 May, after a boil on his leg had forced him to stop composing for a while, he declared that he felt so well that it was his duty to work. He played Cosima the conclusion of Kundry's narration, which was the most recent passage he had set, up to ' . . . und Herzeleide – starb'. 'Herzeleide dies very simply, like the branch of a tree, she gradually fades.' He wanted to orchestrate some bars straight away, he thought it would help, as when he had written the prelude to *Rheingold* straight out in full score. 'The sound of horns' was something he absolutely had to have in certain passages.

'I'm well away now!' he exclaimed to Cosima on 3 June: Kundry's kiss, 'an instant of daemonic oblivion', and Parsifal's cry: 'Amfortas! Die Wunde! Die Wunde! Sie brennt in meinem Herzen!' 'What I've got myself into! It goes beyond *Tristan*.' Of Kundry's attempt at consolation, 'Die Liebe lerne kennen', he remarked that he had put nothing *Tristan*-like into it: it was not, for instance, like anything Isolde says about love, 'it is something different'. But he had to stop work again at that point, to go to a spa for a cure. 'We are listening to the blackbirds,' Cosima recorded; 'I say that I will miss their song.' 'I shall start then,' Wagner replied, 'now it is the summer that is the composer. I'm thinking about the third act, I prefer not to think about the second.' And a few days later: 'I have written some more of the canon [for the Domestic Symphony], and made up a very pretty figure. This will be the only sort of thing I shall write one day, it needn't be in four movements. I shall ask Lachner for his recipe for suites, I have a great mass of suitable ideas stored away unused.'

Then he suddenly came back to his old idea for a comedy: 'I shall write another piece, *Luthers Hochzeit*, in prose.' (5 July 1878; BBL 1937, p. 7) In other words, he wanted to confront the image of Parsifal, repulsing Kundry because of the danger of forgetting his mission in her embrace, with the contrary image of Luther taking Catharina as his wife, because her gaze brings peace and security to 'the boundless imagination of the striving, desiring male heart'. They represent two variations on the theme of male and female, which measure the full extent of the topic only when placed side by side. Nietzsche's doctrinaire attitude, his inability to understand the composer's multitudinous soul, is never more tellingly revealed than by his playing off the plan of *Luthers Hochzeit*, which Wagner had mentioned to him, against *Parsifal*, as proof of backsliding, of an espousal of 'ascetic ideals'.[8]

Nothing could have been further from the tenor of Wagner's life. In the middle of composing the Good Friday scene he wrote to the king about the happiness the work was giving him, and could not restrain himself from writing, too, about the happiness his wife and children gave him. He expressed his gratitude for the new meaning and new dimension his life had gained with the birth of his son. There is paternal pride in his description of how the boy was developing, and affectionate concern in his outline of the plans he and Cosima had made to bring him up as a free human being. Added to this was the artist's satisfaction with the way *Parsifal* was turning out: 'I feel happier than I have ever been: my work is for me the fountainhead of a life that surrounds me with ever new images arising out of the soul, giving calm and contentment. And there – there, laughing with the joy of being alive, is my son, bonny as a Wälsung; and over and above all my thoughts, presentiments, wishes, a world rises before me, a world not of hope, but of confidence.' (9 February 1879)

Only six weeks after beginning his cure, on 26 July 1878, he took up the composition sketch again, with the great scene between Parsifal and Kundry: the 'duet' in *Die Walküre* was pure joy by comparison, he moaned to Cosima, and in *Tristan* there had at least been the bliss of longing, 'but here there is only the wild suffering of love'. Other remarks he made to her about individual passages illustrate the artistic conscientiousness with which he went about his work. He had thought of a melody for Kundry's words 'Nun such' ich ihn von Welt zu Welt' that had greatly appealed to him but had been too long for the text. He had even begun to think of writing some extra lines when all of a sudden a counter-theme had occurred to him, which had given him everything he needed: the violins got the leaping melody expressing the state of her soul, while she had the theme for her urgent words. But he was still not satisfied. When he came to look at the composition and orchestral sketches again a year later, when he was starting the full score, something in the sequential writing did not please him and he did not rest until it was exactly what he wanted, as we now hear it: 'Nun such' ich ihn von Welt zu Welt, ihm wieder zu begegnen.'

'Oh, my heart sinks at the thought of everything to do with costumes and make-up, when I think that characters like Kundry are going to be impersonated on a stage, it immediately puts me in mind of those dreadful artists' balls, and now I've created the invisible orchestra, I'd like to invent invisible acting too!' (23 September)

When he began the third act on 24 October he talked about the mournful sounds he now had to compose: there must not be a single ray of light, for it would be very misleading. A few days later he asked Cosima to listen to something he had written and give him her advice. He played the prelude, depicting Parsifal's wanderings on 'der Irrnis und der Leiden Pfade', and showed her the pile of manuscript paper he had covered with sketches. 'Improvising like this, having ideas, that's not difficult, my difficulty always is knowing how to cut it down to size.' And when he saw how moved she was he commented: 'So it's good, I'm glad!' He was still not satisfied himself, but the next morning at the moment of waking an idea came to him for an insertion in the middle of the prelude: it only amounted to two bars but made a great difference.

All the time that he was working on *Parsifal*, the evenings were devoted to music: Beethoven, Weber and a lot of Mozart. Then there was Bach: he and Rubinstein went through all the preludes and fugues of the *Well-Tempered Clavier* together, and Cosima's diary contains a wealth of the comments he made.

'This is music *eo ipso*,' he said, 'it's like the root of the word. This is in the same relationship to other music that Sanskrit is to other languages.' Bach's music contained the germ of everything that subsequently ripened in the rich soil of Beethoven's imagination. But then he added: 'That distinction isn't just; he – Bach – is already perfect in himself, incomparable.' Compared with Beethoven and Mozart, Bach was the purest musician, while they had something in common with poets. He played some Italian airs by Bellini: 'This is *pour le monde*'; and then the first part of the C♯ minor Prelude: 'But this here, this *is* the world.'

He started to score the prelude of the first act while he was still sketching the third. More and more, he said, he wanted to avoid anything that sounded strange or jarring; he supposed that what he was attempting was the equivalent of Titian's use of colour. He did not dare give the Last Supper theme to a single instrument, an oboe or a clarinet for instance, so he devised that mysterious, impersonal blend of strings and woodwind, with the addition of the characteristically dry sound of a pianissimo trumpet when the theme is repeated in the higher register. In the orchestral sketch he had anticipated this repeat being accompanied by harps, but in the score the arpeggios are given to the violins and violas, creating a gentle glow (which he liked to compare to the gold background of the mosaics in St Mark's in Venice) by the conjunction of their demi-semiquavers with the triplet chords of the flutes and clarinets. He had already said on an earlier occasion that the instrumentation would be completely different from the *Ring*: 'like layers of cloud, separating and re-forming'.

'I pretended that I was doing nothing but reading (Lecky's *Moral History of Europe* . . . highly recommended!),' he wrote to the king, 'but secretly I was scoring the prelude to *Parsifal* and I decided to surprise Cosima on the morning of her birthday with a performance of it.' The Duke of Meiningen lent him his orchestra for two days, the parts were copied, rehearsals were held in Meiningen and the players arrived in Bayreuth on 23 December in the greatest secrecy. The next day the first rehearsal under Wagner took place in the banqueting room of the Sonne, where it transpired that whenever the Meiningen kapellmeister had been at a loss as to the rhythm of a passage he had doubled the tempo.[9] The rehearsal was chaotic to begin with, according to Anton Seidl; the musicians were thrown into utter confusion by the unaccustomed movements of Wagner's long baton until they grasped that the pre-eminent consideration was the phrase, the melody, not the beat. Later, Bülow was to take over the Meiningen orchestra, but this rehearsal under Wagner raised them to a level they had never reached before. At seven in the morning of 25 December they assembled in the drawing room in Wahnfried, the Christmas tree was moved to one side, the music stands were arranged in the large bay window overlooking the garden. The players hung on Wagner's gaze, while the emotional expression was reflected in his face. Cosima had no chance to give way to her feelings, for he at once told her to prepare the room for a concert that very evening. He had invited about sixty people and played some movements from Beethoven's symphonies, in addition to the *Siegfried Idyll* and the *Parsifal* prelude. Afterwards he himself spoke with satisfaction of the musicians' delight, even ecstasy, when he had shown them how to play the Minuet of the Eighth Symphony, which was normally gabbled. And how beautifully in the end, how exactly as he had wanted, the clarinets had played the Trio, that most charming of all idylls!

Judith had invited them to visit her at her seaside villa in Saint-Enogat near Dinard during the following year, but Cosima wrote on 6 January that they would prefer not to accept: 'All of us, including *Parsifal*, feel so well after our year of complete seclusion that we have promised ourselves to spend 1879 like its predecssor.'

After the 'diversion' of the concert on Christmas Day, which had been like a tonic, on New Year's Day, with Cosima's permission, as Wagner told the king, he returned to *Parsifal* in the best of spirits. By 14 January he was able to sing Gurnemanz's Act III narration to her, up to 'er starb – ein Mensch wie alle'. When she tried to express to him how deeply this simple intensity of feeling moved her, he said: 'Yes, that's something you might call the most German of characteristics, the combination of simplicity with an unshakable faith, and the need to affirm this faith through good deeds.'

'When Parsifal faints – that's where it begins,' he said cheerfully, 'it will be the most beautiful thing – I already have a lot sketched.' And as the melos unfolded, depicting the spring meadow and all its flowers on the 'day of innocence' when nature is 'absolved from sin', with the richest of polyphonic writing, he confessed that he thought it very important that the inner and subordinate parts should sound well, which was why he liked to have a piano handy when he was writing. There were quite often 'squeezed' passages in Beethoven which made him think that if the composer had been able to hear them he would not have written them like that!

'People will ask how it is that Parsifal recognizes Kundry in her altered appearance – but does he recognize her? It is all an unspoken ecstasy, how he comes home and turns to look at this unhappy woman.' He called the end of the Good Friday scene – 'Du weinest – sieh, es lacht die Aue' – an elegy: an awesome transformation takes place in Parsifal's soul, he is wholly man once more before he becomes king.

He finished the composition sketch on 16 April and the orchestral sketch on 26 April. The following day he played through the last scene, from the transformation interlude. He remarked that just as it was the naivety of nature that kept *Siegfried* from sentimentality, so *Parsifal* was saved from it by the naivety of holiness, which was innocent of any of the dross of sentimentality. He illustrated certain intervals on the piano and said: 'That is simply impossible in *Parsifal*.' He turned to Hans von Wolzogen: 'To show you what sort of a fool I am, I will play you something I'm going to alter in the first act.' He failed to find the chord: 'Of course, it's in the prelude; as I heard it I said to myself: that's all very fine, but that chord will have to go.' It was too sentimental. He was talking about bars 99–100; at the performances on Christmas Day 1878 there was only one bar there, in which the Pity motive ended in a colourless imperfect cadence. It was not until he looked through the entire sketch again in August 1879 that he at last decided how to alter it.

On this occasion, too, he gave the ending of the whole work its final form: he said he had gone through the whole thing in his head thirty or forty times before settling on this particular version. Alfred Lorenz has analysed the closing scene as being in three periods: two arch forms (a–b–a) and a Bar (a–a–b), which put together make a larger Bar (A–A–B); to that we may add that, in its final form at least, the structure, building up according to an inner dynamic, was consciously determined by the artist's mind working at its highest level.

'Complete seclusion' – Cosima's words make a motto for the period from August 1879 to January 1882, during which Wagner wrote the score of *Parsifal*. 'What does the man of genius need?' he once asked, when thinking about the lives of Beethoven and Liszt; 'independence shielded by love.' That was what Cosima did her best to give him: an inner world to which he could retire, a world filled with the magical sounds of his own composition, the secret interpretation of the characters of his dramas, daily communion with the masters of music and poetry. It was a state such as he had once described to the king, long before he attained it:

> Only when Jupiter has set his sign on a man's forehead do the storms cease that have dissipated his vital strength until then . . . Now at last he knows blue skies, peace, mild, gentle air, the shady grove; now the man enters into the enjoyment of his divine powers. (30 November 1867)

II

Inevitably some things from the world outside penetrated into Wagner's seclusion, to be met by him with circumspection.

First and foremost was the question of productions of the *Ring* outside Bayreuth, which there was now no way of preventing. In November 1877 Angelo Neumann had made a new approach to obtain the work for the Leipzig opera, of which he was now director. In his reply Wagner consented in principle: since Hamburg had acquired the performance rights in the meantime, Leipzig would no longer be asked to pay a fee for the exclusive right. Neumann came to visit him in Wahnfried in January 1878. 'I am glad you are seeking to renew the arrangements for which the ground was broken last year,' Wagner said; 'I was very sorry at the failure of the plan.' The contract was signed there and then. Leipzig staged *Rheingold* and *Walküre* in April 1878, *Siegfried* and *Götterdämmerung* in the following September, and three complete cycles in January, February and April 1879.

Wagner did not stint his praise and appreciation of Neumann's 'courage, zeal and great skill', but excused himself from going to Leipzig in person on the grounds of his reluctance to become embroiled again in the excitements of musical and scenic direction, which he would certainly be unable to resist if he were there. He meant this to be understood as a reflection of his own 'peculiarity' rather than lack of faith in the capabilities of the Leipzig production team. 'May it prove to be a happy return for me to my home town, from which strange musical circumstances have so long kept me absent!' (23 September 1878)

Munich was eager not to be left behind Leipzig. 'I permit myself to hope', Düfflipp's successor as the king's secretary, Ludwig von Bürkel, wrote to Cosima, 'that Leipzig will not succeed . . . in stealing the honour of the first complete performance from the capital of our gracious sovereign.' (27 June 1878) On the matter of Wagner's participation in the Munich production, Bürkel wrote that His Majesty was most emphatic 'that the Meister was not to be disturbed in his work on *Parsifal*, which he awaits with feverish impatience'. In one of his letters Bürkel enclosed a sketch of the proposed design for Valhalla, on which Wagner commented simply: 'Fasolt and Fafner were not acquainted with this architectural style.' He refused Perfall's invitation to attend the final rehearsals of *Götterdämmerung*. The first performance of the complete tetralogy took place in November 1878, a month and a half before Leipzig. The king did not attend it, but in the following April had a complete cycle performed for himself in private, which aroused his enthusiasm as much as the performances he had seen in Bayreuth. Wagner was embarrassed and vexed by the praise lavished on Therese Vogl, as Brünnhilde, for her 'magnificent equestrian daring' as she jumped on to Grane's bare back in order to leap into (or rather, over) the blazing funeral pyre, making the moment the 'culmination' for many people in the audience: it is perfectly true that this action is in his stage directions and forms part of the whole, but if the audience was distracted by it to that extent, he said, then he would really prefer to cut it.

Schwerin, Vienna, Brunswick, Cologne, Mannheim and Hamburg, too, had all started to build up their own *Ring*s, beginning with productions of the separate parts. Wagner steadfastly refused all invitations to attend these performances so that the audiences could honour the work's author in person. As he wrote to Jauner, he realized that the conditions in normal theatres made cuts necessary, but for him that was a reason both for not attending such performances and for preferring not to learn about the changes in too much detail. 'It is a weakness for which I must be pardoned . . . Oh! how well I appreciate that the Viennese – especially if he is sitting in the stalls – wants his supper and a glass of wine by eleven o'clock at the latest! No, no! I understand that perfectly; and, let's face it, it is absurd to expect a theatre audience to exert itself in any way, even in the interests of its enjoyment; after all, it was in order to obviate such exertions that I invented the Bayreuth festival.' (GLRW, VI, pp. 157f.)

But though Wagner kept aloof from performances of the *Ring* he could not ignore the prospect of staging *Parsifal*. 'I told you once before, my sublime friend,' he wrote to the king, 'that in making the last stroke of the pen on a score like this I consign it to the hell that can turn every bar of it into an instrument of torture for me. I often hear the devilish voice mocking me: "Why did you do it all with such love and joy? Do you want to enjoy it *eternally*?" I believe that anyone who loves me will not grudge my right to keep this one last work of mine from the rough paws of my comrades-in-art and the cawing of that polymorphic monster, our audiences and the public at large, for as long as I can – even, indeed, for ever.' (27 March 1879)

But there were two clauses in the contract of March 1878 that prevented him from doing entirely as he wished with *Parsifal*. One stated that the first performance of his most recent work was to be given at Bayreuth in 1880 and the other that thereafter 'the unconditional right of performance was to be made over to the management of the Hoftheater'. He was determined to free himself from these shackles. He argued that the purpose of the contract had been only to arrange the repayment of his debts, and the schedule about the performance of *Parsifal* constituted 'in no way an integral part of the contract'. His management committee, however, considered it would be more suitable to add a supplementary clause which would leave the date of the first performance to his discretion alone. (7 July 1879) Only three days later Bürkel replied that: 'His Majesty the King . . . had no objection to the postponement of the performance of this work to such later date as seemed fit to the Meister, Richard Wagner.'

With that Wagner was relieved of the pressure of a deadline, and he could now contemplate escaping for a while from the harsh climate of Bayreuth, which he was unable to stand for too long at a time. He took a six months' lease from 1 January 1880 on the Villa Angri at Posilipo above Naples, for a very low rent, as he told the king, which was nevertheless almost beyond the means of a German opera composer. On their way there they celebrated the New Year in Munich with Lenbach, Levi and Bürkel, and Cosima persuaded Bürkel to suggest to the king the establishment of a protectorate over Bayreuth. The suggestion interested Ludwig and he also enquired what he could do to help Wagner fulfil his wish to prolong his stay in the south.

However, the over-enthusiasm of Wolzogen, who on his own initiative proposed a protectorate formed by all the German princes, with the Kaiser at their head, very nearly caused a serious upset. Ludwig was furious at the idea that he should take third or fourth place behind other crowned heads who would have done virtually nothing for the cause. It took all Muncker's diplomacy to make the king understand, through Bürkel, that this was not a new version of the plan proposed by Cosima, but merely the antics of 'our over-eager Wagnerians'.

Wagner and his family arrived in Naples on 4 January. 'The most beautiful scenery in Europe, nothing like it anywhere else . . . then there is our piece of land, the most glorious site in Naples. A Prince Doria once had colossal terraces constructed here and we can now climb from the sea to the level of Posilipo in a garden that is green and full of flowers even at this time of the year . . . All this, which I expect to be able to enjoy until the end of May, already fills me with kindly hope.' (KLRW, III, pp. 167ff.) But then two attacks of erysipelas, recurring for the first time in twenty-four years, confined him to his room until the end of January. In this 'lethargic state' he had obscure dreams that recalled the 'most terrible time in his life, the *Tannhäuser* year in Paris'. A conversation about German current affairs with his doctor, Professor Schrön, brought flooding back the complete hopelessness of his Bayreuth undertaking and made him think seriously once again, as in London in 1877, of emigrating to America. In his imagination he pictured himself turning his back on Europe and building his theatre, his school and his house in Minnesota – after raising a million dollars by subscription. America was the only place on the globe that it gave him any pleasure to think about, he declared: what the Hellenes were among the peoples of Europe, that country was among the nations of the earth. 'Yes, they will outstrip us! We are a hotch-potch destined for ruin.' And he remembered something his uncle, Adolf Wagner, had said: 'Our continent is an overripe fruit that a storm will shake from the branch; the tide of history is moving towards America.' (GLRW, VI, pp. 303f.)

It was in this frame of mind that Wagner wrote on 8 February 1880 to Dr Newell S. Jenkins, an American dentist in practice in Dresden, with whom he had become friendly, and asked him for advice.

> Dear, honoured Sir and Friend!
> I feel as though my patience will soon run out where my hopes of Germany and its future are concerned, and that I may well come to regret not having transplanted the seeds of my artistic ideas to a more fertile and hopeful soil long ago.
> I do not think it impossible that I may yet decide to emigrate for ever to America with my whole family and my last works. As I am no longer young I should require a very substantial accommodation from across the ocean to make it possible. For my moving expenses and to defray all my trouble, an association would have to be formed there which would place at my disposal in a lump sum a capital of a million dollars, half to be paid directly on my settling in a climatically advantageous state of the union, and the other half to be deposited at 5 per cent in a state bank. With that America would have bought me for all time. The association would also have to raise the funds for the annual festivals, in which I would gradually present all my works in model

productions: these would start at once with the *first* performance of my latest work *Parsifal*, which I shall not permit to be performed anywhere else until then. All future work on my part, whether as producer or as creative artist, would, in consideration of the capital sum paid to me, belong unconditionally for all time to the American nation.

I recall that at your last visit you kindly and eagerly offered to make the arrangements for me if I wished to make a so-called artistic tour of America. I hope you will understand why I now turn to you and no one else with these far more drastic ideas. A mere tour, to earn a limited sum of money by giving concerts, and then to return to Germany, would never suit my book. Nothing but a complete move to America would be worth my while!

Would you be so kind as to ponder the matter a little, and, if you think it a good idea, let me know your views! In the greatest friendship and with sincere regards,

Richard Wagner

8 Febr. 1880.   Naples – Villa Angri. Posilipo.[10]

Jenkins, not trusting his own competence in the matter, consulted John Sullivan Dwight, the 'musical sage of Boston', the American Ambassador in Berlin, and other American friends in Germany. 'The consensus was that the plan was not feasible, for both artistic and financial reasons.'

Wagner made no secret of his plan to King Ludwig. 'The news about the performances of my work causes me nothing but concern; I wish I could withdraw permission to give them everywhere, and have already seriously thought about emigrating for good to America, because there I would receive the means to buy back all the performance rights that have been granted. For many other reasons, including my total loss of hope in Germany, I must still look on the project as not yet abandoned; I am waiting for a clear statement of their views, and if I find their account satisfactory then the only thing that could prevent me from the execution of the plan is the consideration of my already advanced years.

'In truth, there is no more ironic fate than mine!' (31 March 1880)

The following day, 1 April, Dr and Mrs Jenkins came to talk to him at the Villa Angri. 'We went to Constantinople by way of Naples expressly to talk with him and Frau Cosima and found they were so full of illusions as to the conditions in America that arguments against this plan had no force.' It took Jenkins another year, with the help of other American friends, to convince the Meister that the place for his future triumphs was in his homeland, and not abroad. 'I rejoiced that that end was attained without a cloud resting upon our friendship.'[11]

But privately Wagner had already begun to think in terms of making his trip to America a concert tour only, starting in September 1880 and going as far as California. He visualized the moment of his arrival in San Francisco. 'It will be the fulfilment of my boyhood wish, for I always had the thought: what? shall I die without having seen this little planet and everything on it? That at least, since we can't go to the stars!' (GLRW, VI, pp. 385f., note)

In the event, as we shall see, another attack of erysipelas forced him to postpone the tour until the next year. But he did not relinquish his determination to have set aside the other clause in the 1878 contract, according to which *Parsifal* was to be placed at the disposal of the Munich theatre after its Bayreuth première.

He had had to surrender all his works, however ideal their conception, to the exigencies of ordinary theatrical practice, he wrote to the king on 18 September 1880, and he wondered whether he ought not to preserve at least this last and most sacred of them from that fate. His allusion to the representation in the work of the Christian mysteries is more likely to have been calculated to influence the king than to be an exhaustive reflection of his own view. 'Was heilig mir' – his criterion of sacredness was the same as Walther von Stolzing's: that in artistic matters it is not the material but the spirit that is decisive.

'Only there [in Bayreuth] let *Parsifal* be performed, only there, in all futurity; never must *Parsifal* be offered to the public as entertainment in any other theatre; that this should be so is the only thought in my head, as I review the ways and means of ensuring my work this destiny . . . I have therefore decided to spend about six months in the United States of North America in the autumn of next year, in order to earn a capital sum which will rid me and my heirs for all time of the necessity of losing control over the performing rights of my works.'

'Although I do not in the least approve of your intention of going to America for six months,' Ludwig replied, 'since the exertions awaiting you there might well undermine your health, on the other hand I am completely in agreement with you that *Parsifal*, your sacred festival drama of dedication, should be given only in Bayreuth and is not to be desecrated on another, profane stage.' (24 October 1880) He had in fact issued the following instructions on 15 October: 'In the furtherance of the great aims of the Meister, Richard Wagner, it is my wish that the orchestra and chorus of my court theatre be placed at the disposal of the Bayreuth festival for two months in the year annually from 1882 onwards;' and, further, 'that all previous agreements about the performances of the festival drama of dedication, *Parsifal*, are herewith annulled.'

The story of how *Parsifal* was accorded this special dispensation, which was so hotly disputed when the copyright expired, has taken our narrative ahead of events. While Wagner was trying to school himself to contemplate the state of affairs in the public sphere of art with 'ironic serenity', other concerns, at first blush completely unrelated, were tormenting him and robbing his nights of sleep.

When Malwida, visiting Wahnfried in 1878, had defended the experiments carried out on living dogs by a certain Professor Goltz, Wagner had turned a thunderous look on her: never, ever, would such bloody methods bring anyone closer to the essence of things. In 1879 he was asked by animal protection societies to raise his voice with theirs against the torture of animals in the name of science.

If he were a young man, he told Cosima, he would not rest until he had raised a general outcry against this barbarism. A religion could be founded on compassion for animals; compassion between humans was more difficult, they were so malicious, they recoiled from each other and it was hard to apply the sublime doctrine of Christianity. But one could make a start with patient, dumb animals, and anyone who was kind to animals would certainly also not be hard on men. (BBL 1937, p. 109)

'Your important pamphlet had already reached me,' he wrote on 14 August 1879 to Ernst von Weber, the author of *The Torture Chambers of Science*, 'and I confess to you my weakness, that I have not had the courage yet to read it properly, since the first glance at it moved me excessively. My son shall be and learn whatever he wants, but I shall urge him to learn enough surgery to be able to

dress simple wounds on humans and animals and – doing
better than his father – to steel himself to the sight of physical
suffering.'

Weber visited him a short time later, and they had some serious
conversations about vivisection. Wagner had hesitated as to how he
could best contribute to the debate, but now decided to write an
'Open Letter to Herr Ernst von Weber', which he published in the
October 1879 issue of *Bayreuther Blätter*, and also as a pamphlet, in
an edition of 3000 copies, printed at his own expense. (*Offenes
Schreiben an Herrn Ernst von Weber*, RWGS, X, pp. 194ff.)

That the anti-vivisectionists wanted to enlist Wagner's support
illustrates, as Newman points out, how great his influence now was
in Germany. It was also his opportunity to prove that his heart was
in the right place. (NLRW, IV, pp. 601f.) The new and distinctive
feature of the 'Open Letter' is its complete rejection of utility as a
criterion and its appeal solely to the ethic of compassion. 'For where
human dignity is concerned, let us agree that the first evidence of it
appears at the point where the human being distinguishes himself
from the animal by showing compassion even for the animal.' In
this unmasking of the cold sophism that pity is only a sublimated
form of egoism, he must have been thinking of Aphorism 46 of
Human, all too Human: 'Compassion Stronger than Suffering'.
Wagner in fact underwent an experience similar to that of his
Parsifal: as the latter's compassion for an animal is the first stage in
his progress towards recognition of a metaphysical guilt in all
existence, so Wagner himself advanced from preoccupation with
the special case of vivisection to a more general problem of modern
civilization which has only increased in earnest since his day:
whether it is right to purchase scientific progress at the cost of
compromising traditional ethics. It is perhaps an insoluble
dilemma, but one that has to be examined frankly.

Early in April 1880 a petition was delivered to the Reichstag,
requesting the abolition or at least restriction of vivisection; the
6000 signatories included 25 generals and 88 staff officers out of a
total of 257 officers – a sign, as Glasenapp remarks, that manliness
and compassion are by no means mutually exclusive. Bismarck
himself later affirmed in a letter to Ernst von Weber: 'Ever since I
learned of the excesses of vivisection, I have shared your sense of
outrage;' although he lacked any legal powers, he would have tried
to use his influence to introduce restraints on experiments with

animals, were it not that the strength that remained to him barely sufficed for carrying out the duties of his office.[12]

The petition was not even presented on the floor of the Reichstag, but was dealt with by a committee, who consulted the expert opinion of only one man, the pathologist Rudolf Virchow. When Wagner was sitting down to lunch with his family on Ascension Day in the Villa Angri, he was unable to prevent himself from blurting out what he had intended to keep from them: the news that the decision in Berlin on the vivisection question had gone against them. 'Things look gloomy in my German heart,' he wrote to Wolzogen, 'and I am thinking more and more of removing myself and my children – by opting for America – from the German empire. But it shall have *Parsifal* first.' He dated the letter: '7 May 1880 (Ascension, whoopee!)'

The household had been joined in the middle of January by the young poet and philosopher Heinrich von Stein, whom Malwida had recommended as a tutor for Siegfried. Fate had brought them a third person, Wagner wrote to the king, who would now share their life for some years as a welcome member of the family. He went on to describe Stein as a man of a kind that he had hitherto encountered only in novels. He came from an old noble family with a wide network of kindred, possessing substantial estates in Thuringia. He was a graduate in philosophy, but would not regard his studies as completed until he had devoted some time to the education of a gifted boy. 'He is slender and blond, like a German youth out of Schiller . . . a very remarkable person, who has come to me like a miraculous gift!' (Naples, 25 January 1880) Nietzsche also had great hopes of Stein, greeting his announcement that he was coming to see him in Sils-Maria in 1884 with '*very* welcome! *Much* wished for – I will not say more today'. And after the visit he dedicated a poem to him, *Einsiedlers Sehnsucht* ('The Recluse's Longing'):

> Der Freunde harr' ich, Tag und Nacht bereit:
> Wo bleibt ihr, Freunde? Kommt! 's ist Zeit! 's ist Zeit!

('I look for my friends, waiting day and night: where are you tarrying, friends? Come! 'tis time!, 'tis time!')

As late as 1888 Nietzsche could still not forgive the dead Wagner for coming between Stein and him even then: 'Oh, that old robber! He robs us of our young men, he even robs us of our women still and carries them off into his cave.' (*The Wagner Case*, postscript) He was referring to Stein – and to Cosima.[13] It is indeed pertinent to wonder whether jealousy of Wagner was not more potent in this than love of Stein. Only a year after the Sils-Maria episode he had written to his sister: 'Do you really believe that Stein's works, which I would not have perpetrated even at the height of my worst Wagnerism and Schopenhauery, are as important as the immense task that is mine?' (Early March 1885)

Soon after Stein's arrival in Naples a young Russian painter, Paul Zhukovsky [Joukowsky], called at the Villa Angri. He had a studio only twenty minutes away, had known Frau Wagner in Munich, and thought it his duty to pay a neighbourly call on her and Wagner. This courtesy visit flowered into an enduring friendship. By an interesting coincidence his father, Vasily Alexandreyevich Zhukovsky, an eminent Russian poet and tutor to the future Tsar Alexander II, had once paid his respects to Goethe more than half a century earlier.[14]

Zhukovsky had hitherto spent most of his life in Italy, but he now decided to make Bayreuth his permanent home. For this reason, Wagner wrote to the king, he had asked him to execute drawings and designs not only for *Parsifal* but for all his works: 'Since it will be done exactly according to my specifications we can expect something to come of it which will be of use to posterity.' They had been to Amalfi together, and visited the Palazzo Rufolo at Ravello high above the bay of Salerno. 'There we discovered splendid motives for Klingsor's magic garden, which were sketched at once with a view to their being adapted for the second act of *Parsifal*.' (31 May 1880)[15]

A third visitor had presented himself at the Villa Angri at the beginning of March: Engelbert Humperdinck, then twenty-six years old. He had received a bursary from the Mendelssohn Foundation 'to pursue his musical studies', but in reality, as he confessed, he used it to traverse 'Italiens holde Auen' with his eyes un-Tannhäuserly wide open. After presenting his visiting card, which bore the resounding title 'Member of the Order of the Grail' – the name adopted by a bunch of young musicians in Munich – Humperdinck was received by Wagner in a large room with half the blinds down. After a searching look, Wagner asked, 'Well, what are you doing here in Naples, you knight of the Grail?' Humperdinck explained about his bursary. 'How extraordinary!' Wagner exclaimed. 'Can a young musician's art still profit today in Italy? Tempi passati!' Then he enquired about his further plans, and when Humperdinck told him he was about to leave for Sicily, he said: 'Now, that's sensible of you. See all the sights, and don't forget Palermo. I shall probably get there again. And when you get back come up and see me again; perhaps you will learn something quite new up here if you do. So, auf Wiedersehen in May!'[16]

The contemporary musical scene in Italy had not made a very good impression on Wagner. His lifelong fondness for Halévy's *La Juive*, which had impressed him by a 'certain spine-chilling sublimity, shot through by an elegiac breath' in 1837 in Dresden,[17] tempted him to see a performance of it in the Teatro San Carlo. '*La Juive* in the evening,' Cosima wrote in her diary, 'delighted by San Carlo – everything an opera house should be, delighted by all the beauties of the work, delighted by the orchestra, especially the playing of the two cors anglais, but horrified by the singing and acting and the production: constant incongruity between the music and the theatrical action. Richard emphasized how this work, from the school of Méhul and Cherubini, is full of life and emotional sensitivity, and not the least Jewish in its emphasis, just rightly delineated.' *La Juive* belonged to the same period as Hugo's *Notre Dame*, he said; Halévy was the first musical genre painter and was more sensitive than Cherubini: 'I liked him very much; his was a yearning, sensual nature.' (BBL 1937, p.154)

But when a Roman prince, a syndic of Rome, sent Wagner a deputation inviting him in the name of the Senate and the Roman people to be the guest of honour at a performance of *Lohengrin* in the Teatro Apollo, he was cautious enough to decline politely. Not even the tempestuous eloquence of Signora Lucca, who came all the way to Naples to persuade him to go, could change his mind. Undeterred, she sent off telegrams to him in both intervals, to report on the tumultuous applause. 'Ah! quel bonheur! j'ai réussi,' he sighed ironically, 'my God, how ungrateful we are!' To King Ludwig he wrote: 'Nobody could understand why I refused the invitation, and I had to hold forth so vehemently and so long that it made me ill . . . Really, my position vis-à-vis this world is so senseless and ridiculous that reminders of it are often our only source of laughter.' (31 March 1880)

On the other hand he had no cause to regret accepting an invitation from the Duke of Bagnara, the president of the Conservatorio di Musica of Naples, to hear a performance of the *Miserere* of Leonardo Leo, a contemporary of Bach. 'The awesome, sublime effect of that music! This is the one, true music, beside which all else is trivial. The composition builds up like a mighty cathedral, meticulously constructed, sublime and necessary, every modulation immensely effective because it follows logically from the part-writing.' According to Cosima, he went on talking long after they got home about this style of church music, 'this most sublime, completely impersonal art'.

On a second, official visit to the conservatory, the 250 pupils saluted him with three 'Evvivas', and then performed for him *La Bataille de Marignan* by the Flemish master Jannequin, as well as an operetta by one of their own number, which earned its composer a hearty 'Bravo!' from the distinguished guest. Wagner also met the aged music teacher, Francesco Florimo, the friend of Bellini, on this occasion. He embraced him, deeply moved, crying 'Bellini! Bellini!' And as he took his leave, with an 'Evviva' for Naples and Italian music, he turned once more to Florimo, who was trembling with emotion, and said, 'Long live the great Bellini!'[18]

Although he had not stinted his applause for the young performers, he could not help but observe the general decline in Italian operatic practice. He felt that the best way he could thank the Duke of Bagnara for his courtesy was candidly to draw his attention to the depredations. 'How are we . . . to get away from trying to achieve results with means that are totally alien to great dramatic art? How are we to impress the feeling for beauty indelibly upon richly talented young natures such as these?' He suggested that the answer lay in deep and sustained study of Mozart's *Figaro*, both versions of Gluck's *Iphigenia*, Spontini's *La Vestale* and the old Italian masters. 'There is in art, just as in life, such a thing as good society.' (RWGS, XVI, pp. 125ff.)

'Perhaps you will learn something quite new up here,' he had told Humperdinck as he was leaving. On the latter's returning now from Sicily, with another of the 'knights of the Grail', Martin Plüddemann, later a well-known composer of ballads, both were at once co-opted to take part in a performance of the Grail scene to celebrate Wagner's birthday. Humperdinck described the occasion. Rubinstein and Plüddemann undertook the task of teaching the four girls the by no means easy choral music sung from the height of the dome. As the sun was shedding its last light over the hills and the coastline, Rubinstein began to play the opening bars of the transformation music. The girls, in their best dresses, stood to the right of the grand piano, their childish faces shining with excitement; Plüddemann and Humperdinck himself stood on the other side, each with a Grail Knight's part in his hand. The audience, across the room, consisted of Cosima, Siegfried, Malwida and Zhukovsky. 'In the middle of the circle sat Wagner, before him on a stand the sketch of *Parsifal*, from which he sang and conducted, soloist, composer and producer in one person. He knew just how to use his voice, which was not large but sonorous and ranged over a wide compass to reach every register, so as to render each passage impressively.' Dusk had fallen as the last notes died away and their rapt attention dissolved in tumults of admiration.

'Well, my children,' Wagner smiled, 'you ought to be pleased with me. I knew what I was doing, all right, when I wrote that. But now, outside, we all need some fresh air!' When Humperdinck took his leave Wagner paused in thought for a moment. 'Young friend, wouldn't you care to come to Bayreuth? There would be all kinds of things for you to do there, which you might enjoy.' While Rubinstein made the vocal score Humperdinck could make a duplicate copy of the autograph full score for everyday use. 'Oh, yes, my dear fellow, the old, great masters of painting had to grind colours, too, before they were allowed to start working on their own.'

As Humperdinck, Rubinstein and Plüddemann were walking away from the house in the mild night, lit by a full moon, they heard a familiar voice singing softly behind and above them:

> Drei Knäblein, jung, schön, hold und weise,
> begleiten euch auf eurer Reise . . .

It was Wagner, on the balcony, sending them on their way with the Three Ladies' song from *Zauberflöte*. The young men burst into Tamino and Papageno's reply, 'So lebet wohl! Auf Wiedersehn!'

Wagner and Cosima kept up their regular practice of reading aloud in the evenings. On 23 June he decided it had to be Aeschylus's *Agamemnon*. 'So he's reading it,' Cosima wrote, 'and I feel as though I've never seen Richard like this, transfigured, inspired, completely at one with what he's reading, the performance could not have been more sublime. Cassandra's first cries were heartbreaking.' A quarter of a century later Zhukovsky confirmed: 'I can still hear her cry of "Apollo! Apollo!" ' Two days later, when he completed the reading with the glorious close of the *Eumenides*, Cosima exclaimed: 'Do you know what work I think has a similar combination of the ideal world and the real, and reminds me of the founding of the Areopagus? In *Meistersinger*, Sachs's address at the end.' – 'That's exactly what I was about to say,' Wagner replied.

He praised Droysen's translation and recalled the impression it had made on him all those years ago in Dresden, when he had immersed himself in the Greek world. And now that, like a sculptor, he had 'worked' his own artistic ideal from the Greek in the intervening years, he experienced that impression anew in the setting of the heroic landscape of the Bay of Naples, where something of the Greek spirit still lives.

Such reliving of earlier experiences – above all of the Ninth Symphony and the *Oresteia* – is characteristic of Wagner's personality, lending it something of the formal integrity, coupled with inner richness, of a Beethovenian symphonic movement.

The time that they had planned to spend in the south really ran out at the end of May, but on 16 June the king ordered: 'To enable the Meister Richard Wagner to prolong his stay in Italy to the benefit of his health, I grant him as a contribution to his costs during the five months June to October inclusive of the current year, the sum of 5200 lire.' Conveying the news of this grant to Cosima, Bürkel was also told to explain that 'the mention of October as the expiry date in no way exercises any kind of pressure to return to frosty Germany'.[19]

'My health gives cause for optimism in this unbelievably wonderful air,' Wagner wrote to Wolzogen early in May, 'but I am idle beyond all measure!' He was referring to a sizeable contribution he had promised for *Bayreuther Blätter*. He wrote regularly for it, not only articles on topics of current interest such as 'Public and Popularity', 'The Public in Time and Place' (1878), 'Shall we Hope?' and 'Open Letter to Ernst von Weber' (1879), but also the essays 'On Writing Poetry and Music' and 'On Writing Poetry and Music for Operas in Particular' (both 1879), which continue the series of writings based on his own unique, personal artistic experience. The 'affinities' that were now looming in his head 'to biblical proportions' related to one of the more important of these works, one of those that encircle the conception and creation of his dramatic works like a philosophical aura; what *The Artwork of the Future* and *Opera and Drama* are to the *Ring*, *Beethoven* (conceived in Venice though not written until later) to *Tristan,* and *German Art and German Politics* to *Meistersinger, Religion and Art,* first published in the October 1880 issue of *Bayreuther Blätter,* is to *Parsifal.* (*Religion und Kunst,* RWGS, X, pp. 211ff.)

He prefaced it with an epigraph from one of Schiller's letters to Goethe: 'I find in the Christian religion *virtualiter* the lineaments of what is highest and noblest, and the various manifestations of the same in real life seem so repugnant and vacuous to me simply because they are failed representations of those ideals.' (17 August 1795) The words are unmistakably Wagner's answer to Nietzsche's assertion that one cannot have anything to do with Christianity 'without soiling one's intellectual conscience beyond redemption'.

A return of his erysipelas at the beginning of July forced him to leave Naples earlier than planned, to seek a change of air in the hills further north, in Siena. He found spacious lodgings in the Villa Torre Fiorentina, outside the city gates; the furnishings included a state bed that Pope Pius VI had slept in and which was big enough, Wagner opined, for a whole schism. When the shadows deepened in the gentle evening light he could trace the graceful outlines of chain after chain of the Umbrian hills, reaching to the horizon. He excused the expense of this brief six-week rental by saying: 'For people like us all extravagances have only one meaning, the achievement of peace and ease, so that the spirit can be free.'

His spirits benefited further from a visit from Liszt, which went off harmoniously, and the completion of the next stage in the composition of *Parsifal.* He had begun what he called 'drawing the bar lines' on 7 August 1879 and now finished it on 24 September 1880; we have Humperdinck's description and explanation of the process. The orchestral sketch, a kind of short score, comprises a complete 'skeleton' of the composition, written down on two or three, occasionally more, staves, while the margins are filled with mysterious symbols and series of numbers, comprehensible only to initiates, pertaining not only to details of the orchestration but also to the planning of the score. By working out the spacing in advance, Wagner was able to paginate the entire full score, already finished in his head, before putting pen to paper. When he finally started to write the work out in full score back in Bayreuth, he worked so fluently that Humperdinck, as copyist, had difficulty in keeping up with him. He writes that it was the spirit of order, creative self-discipline, the logic of his systematic working methods, that led

Wagner to measure with his own hand the depth and width of the trenches and the foundations on which was to arise the miraculous edifice of the Grail Castle. 'That is the reason for the noble architectural line, for the serene sense of proportion in the deployment of the means, not a note too many and not one too few; the reason, too, for the clarity and transparency of the part-writing and the eurhythmic movement that we admire in Richard Wagner's last work.'[20]

In the meantime, while they were still in Naples, Wagner had finished another work that had occupied him on and off since 1865: his autobiography, *Mein Leben*. He was in time to have the fourth part, covering the years 1861–4, printed in Bayreuth, and to send it to the king for his birthday. He sent him a telegram from Siena, saying he hoped the book would arrive in time. (24 August 1880)

'With all my heart,' Ludwig replied, 'I render you, my faithfully loved friend, my deep innermost thanks . . . for the very welcome, much valued gift with which you surprised me.'

'The chief satisfaction, as far as I'm concerned, is the good weather and the beautiful clear skies!' Wagner had recently written to Hans von Wolzogen, not entirely seriously. But he was to owe his most powerful experience in Siena to a work of art. He went to see the cathedral, and after viewing the exterior, at once sumptuous and high-spirited in its decorative use of Gothic style, the lofty, earnest interior, vaulted over by the massive dome, moved him to tears: it was the most powerful impression any building had ever made on him. He lost his temper with Jacob Burckhardt's strictures, in his *Cicerone*, on some irregularity in the lines: 'Where does he find the rules by which to criticize the builders of such a unique work?' Zhukovsky had to make a drawing of the interior, which later served as the basis for the design of the Grail Temple at Bayreuth. It was the solution, for him, to this difficult scenic problem, and all subsequent designs have been variations on it, with greater or lesser degrees of success. Anyone who still remembers seeing Zhukovsky's Grail Temple at Bayreuth will agree that it was distinguished by two features above all else: its obliviousness to conventional theatrical ideas of flats and backcloths and, arising from that but intensified by perspective illusion, the impression that one was not watching from the far side of a proscenium arch but, like Parsifal, attending the ceremony from within the lines of pillars. This effect was helped by the great depth of the stage at

Bayreuth, which enabled the files of knights and esquires to enter down the two aisles on either side of the brightly lit central apse, approaching gradually in the dimmer, bluish light as if from some immeasurable distance.

Making another stop, from 4 to 30 October, in Venice, where they stayed in the Palazzo Contarini dalle Figure on the Grand Canal, Wagner and Cosima renewed their acquaintance with Comte Arthur de Gobineau. 'Diplomate, grand seigneur, courtisan de salon, chroniqueur politique, orientaliste, sculpteur, philologue, feuilletoniste', as a modern biographer, R. Gérard-Doscot, describes him, Gobineau had represented France in three continents, visited Persia, Greece, Brazil, Scandinavia and Russia on ethnological expeditions, and carried out his duties as *maire* of his country community with diplomacy and vigour during the occupation of 1870–1. His writings ranged from political commentary and the history of remote peoples and cultures to authorship of *Nouvelles Asiatiques, La Renaissance* and the tragedy *Alexandre*, to name only three of his best-known works. He took up the chisel in order to conjure to life from stone figures of his imagination – a Valkyrie, a Sonata appassionata. In his versatility he seemed a scion of Renaissance man, such as he had depicted in his *Leonardo da Vinci*. At the same time he loved to preserve an intellectual incognito and once at a party successfully denied his authorship of the later famous *Scènes historiques*.

'Je suis passé par Venise et j'ai vu Wagner, qui voulait m'emmener à Bayreuth où il va donner *Perceval*,' he wrote to Arrigo Boito, one person who admired both Wagner and Verdi. But Gobineau's first visit to Bayreuth did not take place until May 1881.

On the last stage of the journey home, Wagner halted in Munich for two and a half weeks, to give himself and his family the opportunity to see some of his works. He was much moved by *Tristan*, at which he was warmly received by the audience: he told Cosima how he felt for and with each character in turn, with Marke, with Kurwenal – it was as though he was each of them.

On the afternoon of 12 November he conducted for the king a private performance of the prelude to *Parsifal*. He wrote a programme note for the occasion, heading it 'Love – Faith: – Hope?' (RWGS, XII, p. 349) Only a few close friends attended, keeping well in the background. Deeply impressed, the king asked for it to be played again, but when he asked to hear the *Lohengrin* prelude, for purposes of comparison, Wagner handed the baton to Levi. The action was later construed as a sign that Wagner had taken umbrage, and was associated with an outburst in a conversation about politics with Lenbach and some others later the same day, when he referred to 'the great and powerful of the earth': 'whether king, Kaiser or Bismarck, they're all the same!' But this story comes at second hand, and both Glasenapp and Newman doubted its authenticity. The performance had been preceded by a rehearsal and Wagner was tired; his surrender of the baton to Levi for the *Lohengrin* prelude was a matter of no special moment.[21]

After more than ten months away they arrived back in Bayreuth on 17 November. 'We are back among our domestic penates,' Cosima wrote to Judith, 'and it is as though we had never left them. Like all beautiful things Italy has turned into a dream for us, and even if we have left her, she has not left us, and we live on the memories.' Then, referring to Munich, 'in order to forget the sky, the sun and the beauty, we immersed ourselves in the sublime. It proved a good idea, and thanks to it we feel happy to be here, and we are both working in our own way, he for eternity and I for this mortal span. We could go on living like this for hundreds of years!' (28 December 1880)

Wagner resumed work on his score on 23 December. He complained that really he needed more instruments than he had, not to make more noise but to express what he wanted. But by blending the instruments he had, he created completely new timbres, quite distinct from those of the *Ring* or *Tristan*. About to score the passage in the first scene where Amfortas is lifted and carried off to the lake, he told Cosima that he intended to use trombones and trumpets; strange though it might be, it would work well. So it is that we now hear the forest voices of the separate instruments above a soft, warm background of a pianissimo second-inversion B♭ major chord sustained by the trombones and trumpets, as well as woodwind.

In the evenings they read Gobineau's *Nouvelles Asiatiques* and *La Renaissance* together, which gave them great pleasure. Her husband thought it admirable in the latter, Cosima wrote to the count, that he showed the epoch ending with the last evening in the life of its greatest artist, who, while incapable of preventing the decline of the age, was yet seen in the light of his own immortality. 'And how well you have succeeded in representing his temperament!' she added; 'I think one has to have lived with a genius to be able to appreciate the truth of the scene in which you introduce Michelangelo!'

Wagner was even more enraptured with the *Nouvelles Asiatiques*, which Cosima gave him for Christmas. 'That I had to make the acquaintance of this unique, original writer so late! I am consuming the *Nouvelles* slowly, so as to savour them.' In his view that he was discovering completely new delights in the French language, he was far ahead of the writer's compatriots. It was half a century before Jean Prévost called Stendhal and Gobineau 'the two greatest prose writers of the nineteenth century' and Roger Nimier declared: 'Should we put Gobineau and Stendhal on the same footing? Undoubtedly! Indeed, I regard the former as superior, because he is inimitable.'[22]

Otherwise they had the usual miscellany of worries and nuisances to cope with. One source of trouble was Wagner's relationship with his agents, Voltz & Batz of Mainz. When a new copyright law came into force in 1871 this pair recognized it as a sign of the times and offered Wagner their services in negotiating with theatres and collecting his fees – for a consideration of 25 per cent. They relieved him of an immense burden of business correspondence, but on the other hand they involved him in embarrassing difficulties by overstepping their responsibilities. Franz Schott had seen through them at once and refused to countenance their high-handed behaviour. By now Wagner too was ready to dissolve his arrangement with them but since they demanded 100,000 marks by way of settlement, he had no alternative but to contest each one of their officious actions on his behalf as it came up, a constant source of irritation. 'For one last time I want to try to bring home to you the explanation that you apparently need concerning me and my relationship to yourselves. I will keep it short and say no more than this: after a lifetime of experience, I have reached my sixty-ninth year and wish to be treated accordingly. There is no question of "business obligations" or anything of that sort between us; your only obligation is to account, and render an account, for your services, and otherwise to wait until I ask you for them again.' (23 September 1881)[23]

Meanwhile it seemed as though Angelo Neumann's efforts to get the *Ring* produced in Berlin were to be crowned with success after years of haggling. On 28 November 1880 Wagner granted him 'the exclusive performance rights . . . at one of the Berlin theatres in the summer or spring of the coming year, 1881,' which gave him a free hand to negotiate with the Viktoria-Theater and the Royal Opera. After considerable hesitation, Hülsen agreed to have the production in his theatre, under the direction of Neumann and Seidl, 'if', as he telegraphed to Wagner, 'rights for *Walküre* are made available to me afterwards'. Neumann forecast that the message would not even raise a reply, and on Hülsen's commenting that it would be rather rude, Neumann asked him if he thought Wagner would feel flattered by the implication that *Reingold, Siegfried* and *Götterdämmerung* were worthless. Neumann was right; on 7 December the intendant told him: 'The old rascal really has not answered.' The upshot was that Neumann came to an arrangement with the Viktoria-Theater, which had been his original intention.

At the same time he was negotiating with London. 'Rather tempestuous! But I am not disinclined . . .' Wagner replied to his request for approval. That was enough to encourage the impresario to hatch even more ambitious plans. 'To be the herald, abroad and beyond the oceans, of that new musical world your genius has revealed to us all – that sublime mission stirs me to such a degree that I have abandoned all other plans for the future.' (8 January 1881) 'I have no objections to make to all your plans and suggestions,' Wagner answered, 'as I see very well that you are the right man for the business.' (10 January) So was born the idea of a 'travelling Wagnerian theatre'.

In view of the anti-Semitism that was particularly rife in Berlin in those days, George Davidsohn of the *Berliner Börsencourier*, one of the few pro-Wagner journalists, wrote to Neumann to point out the serious threat it would be to the success of the Berlin *Ring* if the idea got about that Wagner had any part in the controversy. Neumann relayed this warning to Cosima and a few days later had the following reply from Wagner: 'Dear friend and patron! I have no connection with the present "anti-Semitic" movement: an essay by me in the forthcoming issue of *Bayreuther Blätter* will testify to this in a way that ought to make it impossible, even, for *people of intelligence* to connect me with that movement.' (23 February)[24] 'We will try to spread the assurance you ask for,' Cosima added, 'but it is all the more difficult because my husband has taken no part in the controversy.' Wagner's desire to dissociate himself from the matter was not, in any event, influenced by fears for his success in Berlin, as emerges from his advice to Neumann, in the same letter, to abandon Berlin altogether: 'It would be the last straw if your – our – enterprise got off on completely the wrong foot as a result of idiocies of the kind that are flourishing in Berlin at the moment.' But Neumann was neither willing nor able to follow that advice.

A year before, indeed, Wagner had refused to sign the mass petition 'against the growing influence of the Jews' which Bernhard Förster, later the husband of Elisabeth Nietzsche, organized for presentation to Bismarck.

After finishing the score of the first act of *Parsifal* on 25 April, Wagner set off with Cosima on 29 April for Berlin, to attend the rehearsals and the first cycle. 'We are here, my heart, when can you come?' Cosima wrote the following morning to Daniela, who had been staying with Countess Schleinitz in the Home Office for some time. 'Frau Wesendonk has just sent this basket of flowers – but they suit you and Mimi better than me, so I am sending them to you.' But she was shocked when she saw her daughter the next day: 'I suffered for you yesterday, for I saw how you trembled, how your speech, your movements, everything had changed.' It so happened that there had been a Liszt festival in Berlin only a few days before, including a concert conducted by Bülow, at which Liszt had presented Daniela to her father, who had not seen her for twelve years. 'Once more, madame,' Bülow wrote to Cosima, 'I thank you on my knees. What an adorable child! What a soul you have formed! I can only weep when I think of it, and I think of it incessantly. This 27 April brought me a revelation. Je remercie la Providence de m'avoir gardé cette indicible joie.' (28 April) But the meeting had aroused a fearful conflict in the heart of his daughter, who was accustomed to regard Wagner's house as her home; Liszt, who had witnessed it, evaded the embarrassment, in the circumstances, of seeing Cosima and Wagner, by leaving Berlin before they got there, but this was enough in itself to draw public attention to a purely family event.

Although the production was not all that Wagner might have desired, and although the Siegfried had not fully recovered from a recent illness, the first cycle was a brilliant success. 'Richard and I, we are – in spite of all the failings in the performance –very moved by it,' Cosima wrote in her diary. 'At Brünnhilde's closing words we were propped up against each other, my head on his arm, and

Richard exclaimed "the things we go through together". He went on to the stage and made a speech.'

Waiting for them in Wahnfried, they found Count Gobineau, who had been made thoroughly at home under the 'petit gouvernement' of Blandine. Animated conversations on every topic under the sun during the next fortnight revealed that happy mixture of agreement and dissent which is the foundation of a creative friendship. Wagner, who had just got to know Gobineau's *Essai sur l'inégalité des races humaines*, read him a section from his chapter on the Germanic races and then played the prelude to *Parsifal*. It was a symbolic act, an attempt to express his desire to override the severity of Gobineau's ideas on race by the spirit of Christianity. This idea was the basis of his last essay, *Heroism and Christianity*: that a true equality needed to be based on what could be gained from a general moral consensus, such as true Christianity was ideally suited to develop. (*Heldentum und Christentum*, RWGS, X, pp. 275ff.)

On 25 May Wagner, Cosima, Gobineau, Zhukovsky and the children set off together for Berlin again, to attend the fourth cycle. 'C'est sublime!' Gobineau wrote to Comtesse La Tour. 'C'est un chef d'oeuvre extraordinaire! C'est le comble de la gloire et du triomphe pour Wagner!'

At the end of *Götterdämmerung*, which was attended by the emperor and his entourage, Neumann had decided to surprise Wagner with a special tribute. When the composer, looking unusually pale, arrived on the stage to thank the artists, Neumann had the curtain raised and began a well-prepared speech, expressing his thanks 'to the gracious members of the imperial family, the art-loving audience and those who represent their views in public'. At these words Wagner turned and left the stage, so that Neumann had to direct his thanks to him into the wings. It was not only the press that interpreted this as an affront to the imperial family: Neumann too would not believe Wagner when he said he had been on the verge of a heart attack. 'It was not until two years later,' he wrote in his memoirs, 'when the news reached us from Venice that the Meister had died of heart failure, that I realized the tragic truth of his words.'[25]

'My husband began scoring the second act today,' Cosima wrote to Judith on 6 June, 'and we're already at work on the sets and costumes.' But the peace that allowed them to work was soon disturbed again. Levi arrived at Wahnfried on 26 June to discuss *Parsifal* with Wagner. As he returned from a walk on the morning of 28 June Wagner received him with a joke about his unpunctuality. 'Well – now let's go and eat,' he went on in a friendly tone, 'but, no, first of all, go and read the letter I've left on your table.' Levi went to his room and found there an anonymous letter from Munich, casting the vilest aspersions on his character and his relations with Wahnfried, and imploring Wagner to keep his work pure and not allow it to be conducted by a Jew. (GLRW, VI, pp. 500ff.)

At table Levi asked Wagner why he had not simply thrown the letter on the fire, to which Wagner replied: 'I'll tell you why: if I hadn't shown the letter to anyone, had just destroyed it, then perhaps something of its contents would have stayed with me, but as it is I can assure you that now I shall not retain the slightest recollection of it.' After the meal Levi packed his bags and went off to Bamberg without saying goodbye, and then sent Wagner a long letter asking to be relieved of the duty of conducting *Parsifal*.

'Friend, you are requested most earnestly to come back to us quickly,' Wagner telegraphed; 'that is the main thing if we are to get the matter straight.' Levi only reiterated his request to be released, so Wagner wrote him the following letter, which succeeded in bringing him back.

> Dear, best friend! I have the greatest respect for your feelings, but you do not make anything easy for yourself or for us. It is precisely your proneness to gloomy introspection that might make our relationship with you a little oppressive! We are quite agreed on telling the whole world this sh—, and your part will be not to run away, leaving people to draw completely nonsensical conclusions. For God's sake, turn round at once and get to know us properly at long last. Do not lose any of your faith, but gain the courage to go on with it!
>
> Perhaps – it will be a turning point in your life – but in any event – you are my conductor for *Parsifal*! (1 July)

So far I have followed Glasenapp's account of the events leading up to this letter, but it lacks one important factor, which we learn from a letter that Julius Kniese, who was later influential in developing the Bayreuth style, wrote his wife on 17 July 1883: the anonymous letter also contained the assertion 'that Frau Wagner was more than kind to Herr Levi, and her relationship with him was perhaps an intimate one'.[26] This is confirmed by Cosima herself, who wrote to Daniela that the day of 28 June had brought 'all manner of unpleasantness . . . namely an anonymous letter to Papa, making such scandalous accusations against poor Levi (and in association with me!) that he completely lost his head and left without warning'. (1 July) It is this element that fully explains both Wagner's attitude and Levi's sensitivity to the charges.[27]

Wagner had never been shy of talking to Levi about his Jewishness. The spirit of their conversations can be deduced from this entry in Cosima's diary: 'When our friend Levi told us his father was a rabbi, the talk came round to the Israelites again, and we discussed the idea that they had impinged on our culture at too early a stage, and that the element of general humanity that should have developed out of the German character, to the benefit of the Jewish character as well, was hindered in its evolution by their premature encroachment on our culture.' (13 January 1879) A short time before that conversation Wagner had said to her that if he ever wrote about the Jews again he would say there was no objection to be made against them, only they had come to the Germans too early, when they (the Germans) were not firmly rooted enough to absorb that element. (BBL 1937, pp. 106, 59)

Levi was far from resenting this frankness, though Newman supposed he must have done. The publication of a letter to his father, who was chief rabbi in Giessen, shows as much:

> You write: 'If only I could really like Wagner' – But of course you can, and you should! He is the best and noblest of men. Of course the rest of the world misunderstands him and slanders him . . . Goethe fared no better. But one day posterity will recognize that Wagner was as great a man as he was artist, which those close to him know already. Even his fight against what he calls 'Jewry' in music and modern literature springs from the noblest motives, and that he's not just narrow-mindedly anti-Semitic . . . is shown by his attitude to me and Joseph Rubinstein and by the close friendship he used to have with Tausig, whom he loved dearly. The most wonderful thing I have experienced in

my life is the privilege of being close to such a man, and
I thank God for it every day. (13 April 1882)[28]

An unpleasant task fell to Cosima immediately after the episode
of Levi's departure and return. She and Wagner wished to adopt her
daughters by Bülow, who were growing up with them. Apart from
the fact that Bülow's itinerant life would have made it impossible
for him to devote the proper attention to his daughters, he did not
possess the temperament for fatherhood. But although he had now
had an opportunity to see for himself how Daniela had prospered in
her mother's care, he refused point-blank to consent to the adoption, so that Cosima decided she must see him and discuss the matter
face to face.

They arranged to meet in Nuremberg in July; but before we
come to that, there is another episode to mention which affected
Bülow's relations with Bayreuth and has often been misrepre-
sented. In view of the loss made by the 1876 festival and the financial
disaster of the London concerts, Bülow made up his mind to do
something for Bayreuth and at the same time to shame his fellow-
countrymen. He had another, purely personal motive, as Newman
points out: not having attended the festival in 1876 had deeply
grieved him, and he wanted to purchase, as it were, by a generous
act, the right to be present, with head held high, at the first performance of *Parsifal*. 'The day after tomorrow I am playing for
Bayreuth again in Berlin,' he wrote to Klindworth on 20 January
1879; '. . . my real concern is not nearly so much with the 10,000
marks as such – which, incidentally, are taking me far more time
and trouble in "shabby Germany" [in English] than I expected – as
with the *moral significance* of my strumming . . . and (egoistically)
with making it possible for me to be present at *Parsifal*!' (NBB, p.
60)

By 10 September 1880 he was able to tell Wolzogen that he had
sent Feustel the 40,000 marks he had set himself as a target, though
since his concerts had brought him only 28,000 marks he had had to
make up the remaining 12,000 marks from his savings, a not incon-
siderable sacrifice. If the Bayreuth school for training musicians in
Wagnerian style failed to materialize, 'then it would be my wish, as
you well know, that the 40,000-mark obolus should be used to
erect a statue of Wagner in B.[ayreuth] – the Bismarck monument
in Cologne cost exactly that'. (BB, VI, pp. 28–31)

There was only one thing Wagner could do, which was to find a
tactful form whereby the money could be, in effect, given back to
Bülow. According to Glasenapp he wanted it to be diverted to
Bülow's daughters instead, though the festival management coma-
mittee were reluctant to lose it. (GLRW, VI, pp. 439ff.) This version
of the story is confirmed by Cosima's letter to Daniela of 16 March
1881: 'Your Papa [Wagner] is sending the fund of 40,000 marks
back to him [Bülow] with the request to invest it for you [the girls],
as I have given my inheritance from my mother to the [festival]
theatre. Papa further wishes to adopt you all.'

Newman is probably right when he comments that this 'palpable
snub' must have played a part in strengthening Bülow's determination not to agree to the adoption.[29]

Cosima's diary contains an account of the meeting in Nuremberg:

> Hans with me from 4 to 6.30, try to subdue his
> violent surges of emotion and overcome his injustice
> towards Daniela. Impossible task! He asks me to stay
> until tomorrow morning, as he has not put the proposal
> he wanted to in the manner he wished. I agree. [The
> next day:] Second interview. Hans tells me he doesn't
> know whether white is black or black white. He no
> longer has a guiding star, he starts to twitch nervously.
> We take our leave! . . . After this meeting I return home
> as if a new life were beginning for me, I am without
> comfort and yet at peace, made happy only by his
> [Wagner's] happiness and deep in my heart the
> consciousness of an inexpiable guilt. God help me to
> enjoy the one and never to forget the other! (DMCW, I,
> pp. 944f.)

The next event in their lives was of a more agreeable kind.
Wagner was working hard every morning and afternoon, and told
Cosima on 28 September that he had reached Parsifal's words in the
second act: 'Ja! Diese Stimme! So rief sie ihm . . .', with an accompaniment featuring alternating figures for solo violin and clarinet.
The next day Judith Gautier and Benedictus, who had been opera-
going in Munich, arrived in Bayreuth. Judith's heart beat fast
as she mounted the steps of Wahnfried: it was to be her first meeting for five years with the 'terrible, gentle master', as she had

addressed him in a sonnet she had written for his sixty-sixth birthday:

> Maître terrible et doux! laisse, de l'humble apôtre,
> l'amour fervent monter vers toi comme un encens.

She found him unchanged or, rather, rejuvenated. 'He received us with the moving sincerity that comes over him in the presence of those of his faithful friends by whom he knows himself truly loved.'

He took her into Zhukovsky's studio to see the designs for *Parsifal*. 'The magical garden created by the sorcerer Klingsor had not been easy to realize. Wagner wanted it to be completely unrealistic, a dream, a vision, a fantastic flowering brought into being by a stroke of a wand, not by earthly increase. Nothing that they tried satisfied him . . . The costumes were no less difficult, because the Meister was not content with approximations: the enchantresses, who are flowers to the extent that sirens are fishes, caused the most trouble. Wagner wanted not seductive young women but flowers with souls – des fleurs animées.'

'He told us about his stay in Naples and Venice, of the joy Italy had given him, and we sensed his homesickness for the sun, his longing for other horizons.'[30]

She left him with the promise to return the next year for *Parsifal*.

His longing for other horizons was not merely the desire for sunshine and health, it was a new stage in his idea of emigrating: 'To go away like Lykurgos and see what they make of my affairs!' But then he would stand by the tall French windows in the drawing room of Wahnfried, look out at the trees tossing in the autumn wind and wonder if he had the right to uproot the children so entirely from their native soil. He had expressed something of his doubt and uncertainty in a birthday poem to King Ludwig that year:

> Wie birgt in Nebeldunst und Dämmergrauen
> vor mir doch immer dichter sich die Welt?

('How obscure the world grows, concealing itself from me in mist and eerie twilight.')

In this dilemma the idea increasingly took the shape of a consoling vision of the future: 'In the expectation of the bad times which will inevitably come, we ought to raise a thousand million by subscription, with which to pay off everything and found a new society over there, but until that time comes we should work to establish the religious basis of this society.' There is something in his visions of the 'wild lyricism' that always appealed so strongly to him in *Wilhelm Meisters Wanderjahre*:

Bleibe nicht am Boden heften,
Frisch gewagt und frisch hinaus . . .

('Don't remain rooted to the spot, up and out!')

While his imagination was working, Cosima had to look for the land of his fantasies on the great schoolroom globe. Zhukovsky captured the significance of the scene in a symbolic drawing: the globe becomes the planet earth, carried by an elephant and a tortoise, the symbols of wisdom and patience. To the left there are a ruined castle, a broken pillar and an antique torso – emblems of the Old World; to the right a ship with sails set, ready to cast off from the quay and sail for the New World. At the top of the drawing there is the motto 'One wingbeat, and aeons lie behind us.'

His own doctor had sent to Erlangen for a specialist in internal ailments, who told Wagner that his organs were perfectly healthy and that he needed only a strict diet and fresh air. That year he set off for the south as early as 1 November. 'Sun! Sun!' he exclaimed in a letter to King Ludwig. 'On the one day that we spent in Naples our eyes could hardly endure the sea of light that flooded over everything! We made a night crossing, staying on deck in glorious moonlight, and in the morning reached Palermo: sun and warmth; everywhere we looked, gardens and groves of orange trees laden with fruit! . . . Oh! My king! And where are *we* living? We've settled ourselves so comfortably – between two gardens of palm trees! [in the Hôtel des Palmes] – that I look forward with complete confidence to full recovery.' (22 November)

He started to score the third act of *Parsifal* immediately after their arrival, and since Rubinstein was staying in the same place he was able to pass each page virtually into his hands for him to prepare the vocal score. He enjoyed pointing out the finer points of the orchestration, for instance the way the first violins cease playing and are replaced imperceptibly by the second. 'For Parsifal's entry I have horns *and* trumpets; horns alone seemed to me too soft, not ceremonial enough; trumpets alone too tinny, too clattery – in such a case one must *invent* something; and on top of that I want it played well.' He thought everyone would marvel at *Parsifal*: especially at the praying to the spear. That was the crux: it would be impossible to express what was happening at that moment with words; it was beyond the scope of concepts or of any other means, nor was any proper impression of it to be gained at the piano: 'At the piano, ah, that's nothing, the instrumentation is all-important there!' (GLRW, VI, pp. 537f.)

(In this instance the strings play an expansive, wide-arching melody that swells and falls away three times; one note in the second phrase is held diminuendo through seven bars plus one beat while the horns announce Parsifal's motive.)

What news they had from the world outside Sicily, such as the thwarting of Neumann's plans to produce *Lohengrin* in Paris by the hostility of the chauvinistic French press, oppressed his spirits and his health. He was already looking forward to the journey up the Nile that they planned to take in twelve months' time: for once he would be free of all such news for three whole months! But in the last analysis he agreed that his work was the principal cause of the recurrence of cramps in his chest, since the excessive concentration of his mind and spirit completely arrested his physical functions. He used to raise his hands to heaven and pray for 'easy pages'.

The thought of the instrumentation of the close of the work worried him: he felt he would need many more instruments than the orchestra actually possessed at the time. Just as he had had an alto oboe built as a substitute for the cor anglais, he would similarly have to augment all the wind sections, to provide him with the 'groups' he needed. Cosima could have no idea, he told her, of *how* the thought tormented him. (20 December)

He looked back over the events of the last few years: the building of the theatre, the rehearsals, the performances and the cares of the months following the festival; how he had written the text of *Parsifal* in order to save himself from despair: and now finishing the work was as difficult as anything he had ever done, because the task demanded concentration such as came only in trance.

All the same he could not help but find it remarkable that he had saved up this work, the subject of which had occupied him from a very early stage of his career and which he called his most 'reconciliatory work', to the highest maturity of his old age: 'I know what I know, and what is in it.'

He had vowed to have finished it entirely by Cosima's birthday:

'Then – predictably, my abdomen started its usual devilish games, rendering me incapable of working for several days: – Adieu, vow! The score will have to wait until the New Year.'[31] It had to wait longer still, in fact: the page including the harps, on which he consulted Rubinstein, took a very great deal out of him and he did not finish the work until 13 January 1882.[32]

The day before, a French visitor to Sicily had left a letter at the Hôtel des Palmes, asking for permission to call on the Meister, so as to give himself the pleasure of taking news of him back to Paris for, among others, M. Lascoux – one of Wagner's devoted French admirers – and Madame Judith Gautier. It was Auguste Renoir, who was touring Italy and had been begged by various mutual friends in Paris to do all he could to get a sketch, at least, of Wagner. When he called at the hotel again the next day, as Wagner was not well, he was received by Zhukovsky, who asked him whether he would not care to stay a little longer in Palermo, as the Meister was just writing the last notes of *Parsifal*, was in a state of nervous debility and no longer able to eat, and so on. Amiably, the young Russian suggested that he return the following afternoon. Renoir wrote a friend a long letter about his attempts to see Wagner, which were at last crowned with success.

> I hear muffled steps approaching across the thick carpets. It is the master in his velvet gown with wide sleeves faced with black satin. He is very handsome and kind and shakes my hand, invites me to sit down again and then we launch into the craziest conversation, interspersed with 'hi' and 'oh', half in French, half in German . . . What a lot of rubbish I must have talked! Towards the end I was burning with embarrassment, I felt quite giddy and red as a turkey cock . . .

Wagner consented to sit for Renoir the next day.

> He was very cheerful, I very nervous and sorry that I was not Ingres. In short, I believe I made good use of my time: thirty-five minutes is not long, but if I had stopped sooner it would have been very good, as my sitter lost some of his cheerfulness towards the end and became stiff. I responded to these changes too faithfully . . .

At the end Wagner wanted to see it. He said: 'Ah! Ah! I look like a Protestant minister.' Which is perfectly true. In short, I was very glad I didn't make too much of a fiasco of it. At least it's some sort of souvenir of that wonderful head.[33]

Wagner's art and personality were probably too alien to Renoir's for any more satisfactory result. One of the other Impressionist masters might have done better – or Van Gogh, who himself once compared his palette with Wagner's orchestra, saying it is only when all the colours are used intensively that the artist recovers repose and harmony. 'The process is comparable to the music of Wagner, the intimacy of which is not impaired in spite of its being performed by a large orchestra.'[34]

Life in a hotel was not without its inconveniences, and early in February Wagner gratefully accepted the offer, from a Prince Gangi, of the use of a house on the Piazza dei Porazzi. One of the last melodies he ever wrote is a souvenir of the time he spent there: it was one he had originally sketched at the time when he was writing the second act of *Tristan*, on which he now improvised until he found the shape he wanted for it. Eva Chamberlain gave the autograph fair copy of it to Arturo Toscanini in 1931, after he had conducted his first *Parsifal* in Bayreuth, and it then came to be referred to as the 'Porazzi theme'.[35]

Like Goethe before him, Wagner discovered that the image of Italy impressed upon his soul became complete only when he came to know Sicily. But while Goethe grumbled at his 'incompetent' guide for spoiling his enjoyment of the scenery by his parade of historical learning – the imagination ought not to be startled out of its peaceful dreaming by such nocturnal alarums – it was precisely the great historical figures and reminiscences that stirred Wagner, from the Greeks to the Normans and Hohenstaufens, right up to the dying Garibaldi, whose passage through Acireale he witnessed.

Stopping in Venice on their way home in the middle of April, Wagner learned by chance the address of his former friend Karl Ritter, whom he had not seen since the year of *Tristan*. A woman with a baby in her arms opened the door to him: Herr Ritter was not at home. When Wagner objected strenuously that he was sure Ritter *was* at home, she ventured in some embarrassment that he must be Herr Wagner. 'Yes, yes!' he replied and asked for a piece of paper,

on which he wrote, 'What sort of a person are you?' It was yet
another experience of friendship to add to his store.

He got back to Bayreuth on 1 May. Gobineau arrived shortly
afterwards for quite a long stay. They had a number of lively conversations about religion, in which the only thing they could not
agree on was the relative merits of Catholicism and Protestantism:
in spite of his Germanophilia the count remained a faithful son of
Rome. All the same, when Wagner offered him a glass of beer,
referring to the invigorating effect that 'Einbecker', from the famous breweries in Lower Saxony, had on Luther, Gobineau was
happy to accept. But he was visibly very tired, as Cosima recalled
in her memoir of him,[36] and it was with great concern that she
saw him leave for Gastein, whither he had been sent by his
doctors. Wagner gave him as leaving present an expensive first edition
of *Faust*.

He finished one of his most important articles on the day
Gobineau left, the *Open Letter to Herr Friedrich Schön of Worms*, in
which he called for the setting-up of a grant-awarding foundation.
Forced by experience to open his festival theatre to audiences that
would pay generously for it, he foresaw that in future, 'though no
camel will go through a needle's eye and no rich man will enter the
kingdom of heaven, we shall have to admit only the rich as a rule to
our theatre'. There was an urgent need for a new foundation 'to
create the means to allow completely free access, and even provid-
ing travel and accommodation costs where necessary, to those who,
in their want, share the lot of the greater number and often the most
deserving of Germany's sons'. (RWGS, X, pp. 291ff.)

Just how seriously Wagner persisted in regarding his artistic
mission, in spite of all the disappointments he had suffered,
emerged in a conversation he had about that time with Schemann
and Wolzogen. The sound of a military band, carrying over to
Wahnfried from the nearby barracks of a light cavalry regiment,
elicited from him a complaint about the 'whores' dances' the military marched to nowadays. Music was dragged in the mud in order
to amuse the crowd, and some charity concerts and conservatory
galas were not much better. 'I renounce everything that is purveyed
as music nowadays: I am no musician; I renounce music for music's
good!' As he went on talking, the words 'I am no musician' recurred
like a refrain; the art, as he understood it, could be saved only if it
were guarded like the most precious of treasures, locked up in a

shrine. And there and then he vowed with a passionate intensity to do what he could to that end.[37]

When Wagner spoke, at moments such as this, of 'the art, as he understood it', he was never referring primarily to his own works; he was exhilarated, he said, by the thought that one's forebears always remained one's criterion of what was highest: it was always the works of others that came into his mind, never his own. (GLRW, VI, pp. 604f.)

In the meantime, thanks to Levi[38] and his assistant Franz Fischer and the chorus master and 'flower-father' Heinrich Porges, the preliminary rehearsals had made good progress: though after a rehearsal of the great scene between Parsifal (Hermann Winkelmann) and Kundry (Amalie Materna), Wagner said privately that it would probably never be performed as he had heard it in his imagination. The performers had simply no conception of all that was inherent in the scene and their roles. And *how* Schröder-Devrient would have delivered the line 'So war es mein Kuß, der welthellsichtig dich machte'!

He had suffered a heavy loss, at the end of 1881, with the sudden death of the resourceful machinist, Karl Brandt. 'To think that this deeply devoted man – for he was that to me – had to die!' His place was taken by his son Fritz, who now had to answer for the fact that the transformation in the first act now took too long. Placidly he asked for so many minutes' more music, as the machine could not run any faster. Wagner's patience was near breaking-point, and Humperdinck volunteered to save the situation. 'I ran home, quickly sketched some transitional bars [to lead into a repeat], orchestrated them and dovetailed them into the score. Then I showed the Meister the manuscript, torn between hope and fear. He looked through the pages, then nodded amiably and said: 'Well, why not? That will do all right.'

Adolphe Appia was to describe the transformations in *Parsifal*, carried out in full view of the audience, as an attempt by Wagner to overcome the limitations of realism by realistic means. But whether the designer works with perspective and movable sets or with what Appia himself called 'active light', the essential factor is that what is seen must correspond to what is heard: the harmonic progressions of the transformation music in the first act clearly prescribe movement in a specific direction, for which fade-out, however visionary, can never be a substitute.

On the rest-day following the dress rehearsal on 24 July a banquet took place in the theatre restaurant. The guests sat at a long, festively decked table. Richard Wagner sat in the middle of one side, talking vivaciously to a young woman who answered him in melodious French, punctuated with peals of laughter. In contrast to the evening dress of the other women she wore a linen blouse *à la matelote*, with a brilliant red cravat round her neck. Word passed that it was the daughter of a French poet called Théophile Gautier. Franz Liszt and Cosima sat across the table from them. After Bürgermeister Muncker had made a speech Wagner leapt to his feet, commanded silence by striking his glass twice and began to speak. He reminded them of the misunderstanding that had arisen from the speech he had made at the end of the previous festival and of the general and inexpungible uncomprehension of his purpose that had resulted from it. 'Now': as he spoke the word his voice broke and he stopped; then he said 'now' again, this time in a whisper, and then again very quietly, unable to control his voice: 'Now I have learned to be silent.'[39]

The murmur of excitement that ran round the room slowly died away, then someone proposed a toast to Liszt. Hardly had his name been spoken than Liszt jumped up and moved quickly along the back of the line of seats, stooping as though he wanted to remain unobserved, until he reached the back of his great friend's chair, where he stopped. Knowing Liszt's reluctance to speak in public, Wagner stood up and thanked the company in his name. Then in simple, sincere words that touched the heart he recalled all that Liszt had done for him. 'To be blunt with you I was a bloke without a hope, and then Liszt came and showed a deep understanding of me and my work that sprang from within himself. He helped my work to become known, he gave me his support, he did more to help me rise than anyone else. He has been the link between the world that lived in me and the other world outside.'[40]

As tongues began gradually to wag more and more noisily, Wagner asked a third time for silence. His brief final words, bubbling over with exuberance, reminded Chamberlain irresistibly of Beethoven: it was like the last movement, or rather the coda of the last movement, of some of his string quartets. 'Children!' Wagner cried emphatically, 'Children, tomorrow is the day we've all been waiting for! Tomorrow the devil's abroad! So make sure, all of you who are taking part, that the devil gets into you, and all of you who are here to listen, that you receive him aright!'[41]

The first two performances, on 26 and 28 July, were reserved for Patrons, and the general public were admitted to the other fourteen. At the first performance the applause that broke out at the end of the first act, and even more at the end of the second, seemed unending. Wagner stepped forward to the front of his box and asked the audience not to insist further on the singers' taking a bow. This was interpreted by some members of the audience as meaning that he did not want to hear any applause, and when it broke out at the end of the third act they attempted to shush it. Once again Wagner stood up and assured them that he had not meant to stop them applauding, only that they should not expect the singers to come out before the curtain to take their customary bows, and with that he gave the signal to renew clapping himself. This was the origin of a tradition that is still observed: silence in the auditorium after the first act, applause after the second and third, while the curtains part to show the final tableau again.

The second performance, the last ever given for the patrons alone, closed a chapter in the history of the festival. At the end the curtains parted and the audience saw Wagner on the stage surrounded by the entire company: the members of that day's cast in their costumes and the two other casts in their everyday clothes, as well as the musical staff, the technicians and stage hands and the machinists in their blue overalls. Wagner stood in the middle with his back to the audience, wearing a black frock coat and a light-coloured overcoat and with his top hat in his hand. Those in the auditorium caught only a few words of his speech of thanks to everyone on the stage, according to Chamberlain. But then he turned round and walked to the edge of the stage and peered down into the orchestra pit: 'You too, my dear minstrels', at which his voice sounded particularly affectionate, even tender. Then he stepped back a few paces, drew himself up and, with a brief flourish of his hat, said in a somewhat harsh tone of voice: 'And with this, meine Herren Patrone, I take leave of you.' The way he pronounced the word 'leave' [Abschied] forcibly reminded some hearers of Gurnemanz's dismissal of Parsifal. According to another eye-witness a trace of proud contempt played on his lips.[42]

It would be impossible to list the names of all the friends who flocked from near and far. But three were absent.

Nietzsche had written to his sister on 30 January that he was very glad to hear she was going to Bayreuth. 'But I – forgive me! – am certainly not going, unless Wagner himself personally invites me and treats me as the most honoured of his guests.' As Newman says, Wagner could have seen no reason why he should humble himself to that extent. He had indeed rid himself of all sentimental feelings towards Nietzsche by then. Lou von Salomé recalls an attempt that was made during the festival to mention Nietzsche's name in Wahnfried, in the hope of bringing about a reconciliation: Wagner left the room in great agitation and forbade the name to be spoken in his hearing ever again.

In contrast to that, we have Elisabeth Nietzsche's tale of how, when she was at Bayreuth for *Parsifal* in 1882, Wagner asked to see her privately. 'We talked about *Parsifal* at first, but as I was leaving Wagner said softly: "Tell your brother, since *he* went from me, I have been quite alone." ' It is a touching story that both Newman and the present author nevertheless ventured to doubt, and the truth emerged as even worse than we suspected. Professor Podach drew my attention to a publication of his, dated 1937, which Newman and I both overlooked, and which establishes that Elisabeth Nietzsche did not exchange a single word with Wagner in the summer of 1882. After his death on 13 February 1883 she wrote to Frau Overbeck on 15 April, from Rome, where she was staying with Malwida:

'How it still grieves me that last summer I did not have the courage to meet Wagner. Malwida reiterates that Wagner positively lamented last summer that he did not see me at all . . . And now I have deprived myself of that last pleasure by my own timidity.'[43]

There could be no more illuminating example of what we are up against when we consider the Nietzsche–Wagner legend.

Bülow, too, who had been one of the first generation of Wagner's disciples, was absent. It is not hard for us to imagine the emotional struggle it cost him. But Adelheid von Schorn, the friend of both Stein and Zhukovsky, received a printed communication from him in Bayreuth during the festival:

Marie Schanzer, member of the Ducal Theatre Company, and
Hans von Bülow, intendant of the Ducal Orchestra,
have the honour to notify you herewith of their marriage,
Meiningen, 29 July 1882.

Bülow also added a handwritten note on the card: 'With a request for your silent commiseration for the sacrifice.'[44]

To Wagner's great distress King Ludwig, too, stayed away: he wrote that he had not felt well for some time and the pure air of the mountains was doing him good. 'And now, to conclude, the *heartfelt request*: let me remain dear to you.' (17 July)

Wagner replied in verse:

> Verschmähtest Du des Grales Labe,
> sie war mein alles dir zur Gabe,
> sei nun der Arme nicht verachtet,
> der dir nur gönnen, nicht geben mehr kann.

('Though you have refused the Grail's consolation, it was all I had to give you; do not now despise the poor man who can only wish you well, having nothing more to give you.' 25 August.)

During the last performance on 29 August Wagner took the baton from Levi's hand during the transformation in the last act and conducted the work to the end. 'I stayed at his side because I was afraid that he might make a mistake,' Levi wrote to his father, 'but my fears were groundless – he conducted with as much assurance as if he had been nothing but a kapellmeister all his life.' He conducted the solemn passages with an impressive breadth, and Amfortas's scene surpassed in power anything that had yet been heard. When the cheering and applauding showed no sign of abating after the reappearance of the final tableau, Levi shouted for silence, whereupon Wagner, still at the conductor's desk, spoke some warm words of farewell to the orchestra and the people on the stage: 'You have done everything perfectly, the greatest perfection of dramatic art above, a continual symphony below.' He concluded with the invitation to return the following year, which met with a thunderous 'Yes!'

32

La lugubre gondola

'Dramatic perfection above, a continual symphony below' – it has the ring of an affirmation of the artistic ideal that had been Wagner's guiding star since his teens, when he saw Schröder-Devrient as Leonora and first read the score of the Choral Symphony. At the end of Chapter 4 I wrote that the whole story of Wagner's artistic endeavours, as theorist and practitioner, was his struggle to synthesize dramatic and symphonic music in symphonic drama; we can now add that the synthesis, the union, is most completely perfected in *Parsifal*. There is even the temptation to say 'most effortlessly', except that we know how hard he found it at the last: but there is no trace of the effort in the finished work.

The 'festival drama of dedication' is a work of old age: not only in the sense of artistic perfection, not only in its inclusion of individual musical and poetic traits that run through his work from *Die Feen* onwards, but above and beyond that in the mysterious way in which it sums up the world's great currents of feeling (philosophies would be already too rationalistic a term) that had moved his heart: echoes of Indian and Greek, Christian and non-Christian ideas are all to be found in it, without any one of them singly dominating the others.

But if the expression 'a work of old age' is taken to imply one in which the creator's powers manifestly slacken their spiritual tension, then *Parsifal* is nothing of the kind. On the contrary, Thomas Mann is absolutely right when he calls it 'the most extreme of his works . . . with a capacity for accommodating the psychological to the stylistic and vice versa that surpasses at the close even Wagner's own usual standards'.[1]

Some perception that this work represents the artistic fulfilment

585

of all that he had struggled for throughout a long life, the sublimation of his completely personal style, struck his contemporaries; even criticism was more moderate and restrained in its expression. People recognized first and foremost that this 'work of farewell to the world' owed its conception to Wagner's recoil, in his own words, from 'this world of murder and robbery, organized and legalized by lies, deceit and hypocrisy'. 'That, in truth, is the meaning and the magic of this last work of the old artist who had seen so much, suffered so much, in his pilgrimage through life . . . We feel in the presence of it as we do in that of the only other music that inhabits the same sphere – the last quartets of Beethoven: the men who can dream such music must have made up their account with time and are ripe for eternity.' (NLRW, IV, p. 705)

It was not a day too soon when Wagner set off for Venice on 14 September. His heart attacks had worsened to an alarming degree as a consequence of the exertions of the last few months, sustained under incessantly grey skies. But on this occasion Italy received him, as it did the first time he and Cosima went there together, with cloudbursts and floods. They set up house on the mezzanine floor of a wing of the Palazzo Vendramin, 'like a puppy in a lion's cage', Cosima joked. One of the double windows of the drawing room gave on to the Grand Canal, the others overlooked a small formal garden in the French style, and Wagner was greatly soothed by looking across the foliage, still a summery green, to the gondolas flitting past 'like elves' on the canal beyond.

'It ought to be possible to close every door behind us and hear nothing more,' he said to Cosima once when they were riding in a gondola. 'In order to endure life, we should be dead in it.' But she had to admit to herself resignedly, 'I cannot hold life at bay, and it always brings disturbances.' There was the correspondence with Bürkel about the private performances of *Parsifal* that King Ludwig wanted to have staged in the Hoftheater in Munich, which upset Wagner profoundly. (1 October) There was the equally tiresome dispute with Signora Lucca, who laid claim to *Parsifal* on the grounds of the expression 'oeuvres inédites' in the 1868 contract. It was an interpretation that the courts might well have endorsed, had things gone so far, and it was only due to the generosity of Dr Strecker that a compromise was reached that did not involve the annulment of the contract giving Schott's the sole right to *Parsifal*. The worst and most persistent disagreement was with the agents

Voltz & Batz, who withheld the fees for performances of *Tristan* on
the grounds of their interpretation of a clause in their contract.
'Whoever thought I had earned a fortune?' Wagner exclaimed.
'Once I was no better than a beggar, glad when somebody gave me
something. Now they all cling to me and suck me dry.' In no event
did he intend to let himself be treated as a fool. 'This pack gives me a
strong desire to sharpen my teeth.' (To Feustel, 27 November) In
the end Adolf von Gross, Feustel's son-in-law, won the case against
Voltz & Batz, and freed Wahnfried from the toils of their contract,
but not until after Wagner's death.[2]

One of the last unwelcome provocations came with the publication of the first four books of Nietzsche's *Gay Science*. Did Wagner
perhaps read the famous Aphorism 279 on 'friendship that is the
will of the stars'? It has been read variously as referring to his
friendship with Paul Rée, Jacob Burckhardt, Franz Overbeck or
Wagner. Nietzsche himself told Lou von Salomé that it was Rée but
he later associated it with Wagner: we can take it as yet another of
those fine-sounding dedications that he so loved to make, capable of
address to any number of different people. His sister finally gave
out that Aphorism 279 was his answer to the message Wagner had
allegedly given her for him in the summer of 1882, which, as
Podach says, is not only one of the most brazen of her fabrications
but one of the stupidest: 'It would not be to Nietzsche's credit if he
had continued to pursue Wagner with hatred after receiving a cri de
coeur like that.'[3]

There was a comet to be seen in the skies above Venice that
autumn, as there had been in 1858, the year of *Tristan*. One clear
night when there was a full moon Wagner and Cosima looked out
of the window and saw it travelling across the sky between the
Plough and Orion, with a fiery tail of shooting stars.

They were deeply shocked by the news of Gobineau's death, on
his way through Turin, alone, on 13 October. 'Barely has one met
such a man, when everything runs away like water through one's
fingers,' Wagner mourned. At his suggestion Cosima wrote a
memoir of Gobineau for *Bayreuther Blätter*, the *Erinnerungsbild aus
Wahnfried* which, as Wagner said, only a woman could have written. Reading it the king would recognize, he wrote to Ludwig, the
lot that had fallen to one of the most excellent of men. Then,
alluding to himself: 'So much lies in ruins about me, all-powerful
death has snatched away almost everything that once had value in

my life: there is just a something in me that remains as young and vital as on the day when a prophetic vision of my life first dawned on me. "Noch losch das Licht nicht aus!" ' (18 November)

Shortly afterwards Liszt arrived to stay in the Palazzo Vendramin. Welcome though he was, he brought with him the particular unrest that was his natural element. 'As a result of his uncommonly rich and restless life, wherever he goes he is surrounded by a tide of acquaintances, who ferret him out, draw him into an incessant life of matinées, dinners and soirées, and thereby completely conceal him from our sight, since we give all that a wide berth and keep ourselves exclusively to ourselves.' (To King Ludwig, 10 January 1883)

Wagner was reading Hermann Oldenberg's recently published *Buddha* at this time. He found it fascinating and talked about it a lot, but in the end it led him to decide once and for all to abandon any idea of writing *Die Sieger*. Oldenberg tore aside the veil of legend and revealed the true face of the Buddha, cool, thoughtful and remote from all our ideas and emotions.

But Wagner's mind was accustomed to be engaged with some great project, and even now it did not rest. On 1 November he finished writing a review of the performances of *Parsifal* that summer, 'a didactic treatise, to further the development of the style I wish to promote'. (*Das Bühnenweihfestspiel in Bayreuth 1882*, RWGS, X, pp. 297ff.) Once more he rehearsed his case for avoidance of trivial operatic effects in words and music, for economy in the control of breath and use of gesture, for movement in stage action never coming completely to a standstill, for noble simplicity of sets and costumes – in short, for the opposite of all that has since been practised in performances of his works under the title of Wagnerian style. He concluded by writing about the 'beauty and intelligence' of the orchestral playing, which all who heard it must have sorely missed when they returned to the usual rough treatment of orchestral music in the world's grandest opera houses.

Heinrich von Stein left them on 15 October, in order to go to Halle and complete his formal qualifications for a university teaching career, at his father's wish. He dedicated his collection of 'dramatic pictures', bearing the title *Helden und Welt* ('Heroes and World'), to Wagner 'in love and respect'.

'There is certainly no happier advance that you could have made than this from musing philosopher to clear-sighted dramatist,'

Wagner replied in a letter, written on 31 January 1883, that was intended to serve as the book's preface, and also turned out to be his last literary utterance. 'Seeing, seeing, truly seeing: that is what is universally lacking. "Have you no eyes?" – again and again one would like to put that question to this world that only ever chatters and hearkens.' The words of Stein's Solon, which he wanted to see emphasized typographically in some way, could serve as his own testament.

> Whatever may be the true nature of the immense, obscure background of things, the only way by which we approach it is here in this poor life of ours, and even our transitory actions have this same earnest, profound and inescapable significance.[4]

For the celebration of Cosima's birthday as a 'family jubilee' he dedicated to her the C major Symphony he had written fifty years before (see vol. I, Chapter 5). He rehearsed it with the students and professors of the Liceo Benedetto Marcello and it was performed before a small audience on the evening of 24 December. He was delighted by his 'old-fashioned' early work, especially by its exclusive concern with the sublime and its lack of sentimentality. 'Young Hercules, taming the serpents', Liszt wrote to Princess Wittgenstein, while Cosima thought 'it was written by someone who has not learned to fear'.

When Wagner walked into the brilliantly lit auditorium in the Teatro La Fenice, briskly climbed the steps to the conductor's rostrum and raised his baton, it was for the last time. After the concert they went back to the Palazzo Vendramin by gondola, gliding along the Grand Canal in the quiet of Christmas Night, bathed in moonlight such as is perhaps seen only in Venice. He was silent, happy, his heart full of memories.

This re-encounter with his early symphony was not an accident. Let us recall that he felt an urge to write orchestral pieces while he was composing Götterdämmerung and Parsifal: the most high-spirited symphonic themes kept coming into his head, he complained, which he could not possibly use then. What increasingly interested him was the form in which to cast his symphonies. He thought of calling them 'symphonic dialogues'. There was no question of his tackling traditional four-movement form, but there had to be two subjects which should be allowed to converse.

'I would go back to the old [preclassical] form of the one-movement symphony with an andante middle section; people cannot write four-movement symphonies any more after Beethoven, they all seem imitative, for instance when they try to write big scherzos like his.' (1 December 1878, BBL 1937, pp. 59f.) 'Last movements are the stumbling block,' he had said more recently, referring to the Pastoral Symphony – only Beethoven could have got away with what was ventured there. 'I shall take care, I shall only write one-movement symphonies.' (17 November 1881)

His idea of symphonic dialogues was still not his last word. Now in Venice, when some beautiful melodies for a symphony came to him he said to Liszt: 'When we write symphonies, Franz, the one thing we must avoid is thematic contrast, Beethoven exhausted the possibilities of that! Instead we must take a melodic thread and spin it out to its furthest extent. *But at all costs no drama*!' (GLRW, VI, p. 752)

He was often to be heard, in these last days, playing the piano softly to himself in his room, a rhapsodic melody in the style of an English folk song that was often in his head. And when he sat down of an evening to improvise on the beautiful grand piano, an Ibach with a particularly soft tone, it was like new blossoms springing up under his fingers from the stems of one lovely melody after another. One recalls something he once said of Beethoven: 'Sometimes it was a Scottish folk tune, sometimes a Russian, or again an old French tune, in which he recognized the kind of nobility of innocence that one dreams of, and at whose feet he laid all his art in homage.'

The first few days in Venice left Wagner feeling refreshed. But there was no let-up in the attacks of cramp, though he surprised everyone by the speed with which he recovered each time and indeed by how well he looked. He had to be especially careful in the mornings: he would say that he had kept his balance well today. Only Cosima suffered from his irritability, which was exacerbated by his old jealousy of her father. 'You must be careful with me, but also considerate,' he pleaded, putting the blame on his 'bad character'.

Humperdinck, who had hastened from Paris to help rehearse the symphony, said goodbye on 3 January. 'It seemed', he wrote, 'as though the setting sun of his life cast a shimmer of transfiguration over the Meister's face, uniquely transforming everything that was astringent and stern into gentleness and kindness. "Auf Wiedersehen, dear Meister," I cried, deeply moved. He looked at me gravely and said softly: "I wish you a good journey, my dear friend." '

Liszt went too, on 13 January, his itinerant life calling him to Budapest. Only the faithful Zhukovsky remained, though he was looked for in Russia to attend his father's hundredth birthday celebrations: an inexplicable anxiety kept him in Venice. Levi arrived on 4 February for a week. He brought news of Nietzsche, who had recommended a 'young Mozart' [Peter Gast] to him, who was an absolute dud as a musician. They discussed all manner of preparations that would be needed for the festival in the coming summer. Wagner said he was thinking of producing *Tannhäuser* next in Bayreuth: a definitive production of that would be more worth while even than doing *Tristan*.

On Shrove Tuesday, 6 February, he and the children went out in the evening to mingle with the carnival crowds streaming from the Riva and the Merceria towards the bright lights of the Piazza San Marco. 'His step was elastic, youthful even, his head was high,' a friend who met them recalled; he was visibly enjoying himself among the jubilant throng. At the stroke of midnight all the countless lights went out, plunging the square into deep darkness. When he got back to the Palazzo Vendramin towards one o'clock, he slapped the old porter who was waiting up for them on the shoulder: 'Amico mio, il carnevale è andato.'

Levi, who was unwell during the last days of his stay, left on 12 February. 'The Meister went with me to the stairs, kissed me again and again – I was very moved.' (To his father, 15 February 1883)

That evening Wagner picked up Fouqué's *Undine* again, which he had started to read the day before. Cosima passed her notebook to Zhukovsky, who made a quick sketch of his face: 'R. reading. 12 Febr. 1883'. Then Wagner played the Porazzi theme and a few bars for a scherzo that he had thought of. 'Children, stay a little while yet,' he pleaded repeatedly. Around eleven o'clock, when everyone else had gone to bed, he struck up the Rhinemaidens' lament on the piano:

> Traulich und treu
> ist's nur in der Tiefe:
> falsch und feig
> ist, was dort oben sich freut!

'To think that I already knew that in those days,' he said to Cosima and then talked about the Undines of legend, water sprites longing for a human soul. 'They are dear to me, these beings of the deep, with their longings. Are you, too, one of them?' He stayed up very late, and she could hear him talking to himself, as if he was writing poetry.

'I must go carefully today,' he said when he got up the next morning, 13 February. He stayed in his study and went on with the essay on the feminine in human nature which he had started two days before. 'In the contrasting opinions held of polygamy and monogamy we encounter the point of contact of the purely human with the eternally natural . . .' (*Über das Weibliche im Menschlichen*, RWGS, XII, pp. 343ff.)

When Zhukovsky arrived as usual for lunch at about two, for the first and only time he found Cosima at the piano, playing Schubert's *Lob der Tränen* to Siegfried, her own tears falling as she did so. Wagner sent word that he did not feel altogether well, there was no need to worry but they were to start the meal without him. Cosima ventured into his study once more and came back with the news: 'My husband has his cramps and rather strongly in fact; but it was better for me to leave him alone.' The maid she left in the room next to his study heard him groan: he sat at his desk, with his cap in front of him and appeared to be waiting for the pain to pass. Suddenly he tugged at the bell: 'My wife and the doctor!' As Cosima ran to him she found him struggling violently. He collapsed in her arms exhausted. She thought he had fallen asleep, but when the doctor came there was nothing he could do but pronounce him already dead.

The sheet of paper he had been writing on lay on the desk. The last two words were 'love – tragedy', then the pen had traced a scrawl across to the edge of the paper.

During his stay at the Palazzo Vendramin, though apparently completely absorbed in the social whirl, Liszt had been strangely impressed by a funeral procession he had seen on the Grand Canal, and it is almost as though a premonition moved him to write, unknown to anyone, the two versions of *La lugubre gondola* for piano, which pushed back the frontiers of harmony. A few weeks later, on 16 February 1883, a procession of gondolas accompanied the boat bearing Richard Wagner's coffin as he set out on his last journey.[5]

The body was embalmed, taken to Bayreuth and interred in the vault in the garden of Wahnfried.

The world was stunned by the news of Wagner's death. He had ended his last letter to King Ludwig, 10 January, with the words: 'So may the circle of my existence close for today . . .' When Bürkel broke the news to him, Ludwig cried out: 'Horrible, dreadful!' Then: 'Now leave me alone.' 'May the Almighty give you the strength to bear this terrible test,' he wrote to Cosima. When Bürkel returned from the funeral in Bayreuth and reported on the attendance and the messages that had poured in from all over Germany and from abroad, he said proudly: 'I was the first to recognize the artist whom the whole world now mourns; I saved him for the world.' (SRLW, II, p. 208)

The news reached Meiningen at a moment when Bülow was just on the verge of recovery from a serious illness. It was not until the evening of the following day that his wife plucked up the courage to tell him, and then in the presence of his doctor. She had had no idea, she wrote to her mother, of the passionate love he still felt for Wagner, in spite of everything, in the very depths of his heart. 'Bülow's life has been so closely interwoven with that name that he now feels, in his own words, spoken with the greatest difficulty, as if his own spirit has died with that spirit of fire, and that only a fragment of his body still remains to wander the earth.'[6]

When he heard that Cosima was refusing all food, to the point that her own life was in danger, he sent her a telegram: 'Soeur, il faut vivre.'

Nietzsche wrote to Cosima and contrived to blend his expression of condolence with that of his admiration for her: 'You have not refused in the past to listen to my voice, too, in grave moments; and now, when the news has just reached me that you have suffered the gravest experience of all, I know of no other way to pour out my feelings but by directing them wholly to you and solely to you . . . I look upon you today, as I have always looked upon you, even from afar, as the woman my heart best honours.'

He had been very ill for several days, he wrote to Peter Gast on 19 February. 'I'm all right again now, and I even believe that Wagner's death was the most necessary relief that could have been granted me at this time.'

'Triste, triste, triste! Wagner è morto!' Verdi wrote to Giulio

Ricordi on 14 February. 'When I read the news yesterday, I may truly say I was crushed. Not a word more! – A great individual has gone from us, a name that will leave a powerful impress in the history of art.' Then, as he read his letter through, he crossed out the word 'potente' and wrote 'potentissima' in its place: 'a *most* powerful impress'.

The most universal, enduring expression of grief for Wagner's passing came from the pen of Anton Bruckner. He was working on the Adagio of his Seventh Symphony at the time, and had just come to the powerful outburst in C major when the news reached him. 'I wept, oh, how I wept!' He went on to write the coda, which he himself called 'Music in mourning for the thrice-blessed master', and in which the C♯ minor of the tubas resolves into the C♯ major of the last bars: 'Non confundar in aeternum.'

Bruckner's biographer Erich Schwebsch wrote: 'This movement was born not of Wagner's *death* but of the awe-inspiring recognition of the *immortal* in a doomed, mortal body.'[7]

APPENDIX I

(cf. p. 444)

Joseph Rubinstein's morbid sensitivity meant that Wagner soon discovered that he had taken on a heavier responsibility than he had expected. In such circumstances, where it was often necessary to restrain the young man's suicidal tendency, he had had to exercise uncommon patience, he confessed to King Ludwig, 'and on the subject of treating the Jews humanely, I think I may claim my share of praise'.

His patience held out for more than ten years, until his own death. He may well have foreseen that Rubinstein would not have survived a separation. He did not disguise his fears from Joseph's father, who wished his son to pursue a career as a concert pianist. After yet another reiteration of this wish, Wagner sent the following letter to Kharkov on 22 January 1882.

> Honoured Sir,
> Pray permit me to write to you briefly once more about your son Joseph, in the hope of persuading you to adopt an attitude towards the young man that I believe would be beneficial.
> Easily though I can grasp your misgivings, as a father, at the way of life your son has adopted, which is certainly open to misinterpretation, yet in my opinion it would take only a determined effort of will to dispel once and for all not only those fears but also the anxiety they cause your son.
> Joseph's honourable efforts to comply with your wishes concerning the exercise of his talent to establish a position in life have been as honourable in intent as they have been rendered useless in effect by his own temperament. Without doubt one reason for this lies in certain morbid dispositions,

595

which, however, I believe I am right in saying, might lead to the most regrettable excess if he was obliged obstinately to persist in those efforts. In him the recognition of the essence and the value of true art has grown to a truly religious belief, rooted in his soul where it has engendered a sensitivity that amounts to a passion. If you will assure him, without opposition, of the modest means he needs for his exceptionally sober and temperate mode of life, you will support him contentedly in the service of a noble cause to which all too few are able to devote themselves freely and unconditionally. By comparison, I venture to ask again, to what nobler use could a substantial fortune, even one acquired only by hard work, be put than, at a time like this, in a case where there are special gifts to be developed and nurtured in tranquillity, to put another human being, one's own son, on a footing of true freedom. Had the King of Bavaria, for instance, not once given *me* the basis for that freedom, I should long ago have subsided in silence, for the necessity of employing my art to earn my living had made it a thing of disgust to me. I am raising my own son in such a way that – should he decide upon any kind of artistic career – he will be able, with the modest means I expect to leave him, to be of use to the world, as a free man, dependent on no one.

If particular temperamental dispositions perhaps prevent your son from attaining to the highest goals, he will nevertheless assist them in the most beneficial possible way as a free man. Not all are able to do everything!

One thing is certain, however, that forcing him to adopt a course alien to his nature will inevitably make him thoroughly unhappy.

Forgive me these utterances, honoured sir, which I have felt compelled to make for no other reason than awareness of the silent conflicts of your son, whom I have grown to value; and permit me to assure you at the same time of my greatest regard. Yours sincerely . . .

Events soon proved the accuracy of Wagner's forebodings. When, after his death, Rubinstein took up a career as a pianist again, he was unable to adapt himself to a world where what he held most sacred was degraded to a commercial undertaking. He was often much in Frau Cosima's thoughts, Du Moulin writes. (DMCW, II, pp. 42ff.) No one gave this lonely man so much encouragement as she. But how was she to offer comfort to anyone after Wagner's death, when she herself was completely without comfort? In spite of that Rubinstein continued to receive a certain life-giving elixir from Wahnfried. He wrote in reply to a letter from Daniela: 'Your letter was once again something for me to cherish and value. Believe me, I could write to you almost every day (I am such a fool), to pour out everything that whirls about in me so violently.' 'The people are so hard,' he wrote to Cosima from London. 'A creature like that. . . thinks that his conscience is clear and truly believes in the maxim "life is business" . . . I believe that maxim is false.'

So he returned to Lucerne, where he had first met Wagner, and took his own life on 22 September 1884.

His father wrote to Wahnfried,

> I see very clearly that my misfortune was incalculable; for where, as with my Joseph, there is a major imbalance of intellect and will, sooner or later – according to Schopenhauer – catastrophe will inevitably ensue. His successes, especially in Rome, while fostering his self-confidence, simultaneously increased his nervousness – a case of monstrum per excessum. The immediate cause is of no importance. 'No one can run away from his fate,' he wrote to me a few years ago. He did not run away from his. According to what they wrote from Lucerne, he went to his death with the lightest of hearts. On his way to an old mill he distributed, it is said, a considerable sum among the poor (which gave rise to the rumour that it was a count who had shot himself) and it was all over in a minute. You see . . . with what premeditation he did it . . . Proof that it was inevitable. I know, too, that it would be in vain for me to seek him on another planet; it is only here that I shall be able to find the traces of his being, which was so dear to me. It is only in memory that I can live on with him. But the heart has no ears and is inaccessible to the promptings of reason. Besides, I am already too old and weak, so I shall not have to wait very much longer for my release. Good old Plutarch, in that famous letter to Appolonius, thought that we should not give way to grief, but honour the memory of the beloved dead instead; well, I mean to do so.

Rubinstein's body was taken to Bayreuth, where he had found his spiritual home under the aegis of Wagner's music. A simple marble obelisk in the Jewish cemetery bears his name.

APPENDIX II

(cf. p. 486)

Draft of a letter to someone in the USA (perhaps Gustav Schirmer, the New York music publisher).

The original manuscript of this draft is in the Wagner Archives; the text is published here by kind permission of Frau Winifred Wagner.

> Dear Sir!
> I have been racking my brains as to what more I can say of particular interest to my friends in America about an undertaking that I believe I can say I have discussed and explained perfectly adequately already in a number of writings and announcements. I prefer, therefore, to send you today my three principal essays along with other documents relevant to my plans, although most of the material is also to be found in the ninth volume of my collected writings, so that you can adapt it as you see fit for communication in detail to your fellow-countrymen. Perhaps they will then grasp my ideas faster than the princes and governments of the German Empire, whose concept of German culture remains a complete mystery to me to this day.
>
> But the main, and perhaps the only necessary piece of advice I have to give Americans is that they should abandon from henceforth Fra Diavolo's maxim, 'Long live art, and above all lady artistes!' for if they cling to it their money is extremely unlikely to attract any but the avaricious, while it cannot possibly furnish them with any notion of what the noblest minds of Europe – and especially of Germany – are struggling, in the teeth of an utterly degenerate culture, to give life to.

The presence of Americans at next year's festival is greatly
to be desired, and you will see that I have taken that into
consideration in the choice of dates in the second half of
August, having taken to heart your request that the
performances should be so late.

I must ask you then to be content with these brief remarks
for today; permit me to hope that what I am sending will be
of use to you in carrying out your good intentions!

Respectfully,

yours most sincerely,

Richard Wagner

Bayreuth, 8 September 1875

APPENDIX III

(cf. p. 538)

Three letters in the Wagner Archives in Bayreuth, addressed to Cosima Wagner by Friedrich Nietzsche when deranged. (First published by kind permission of Frau Winifred Wagner in Westernhagen, *Wagner* (1956), with facsimiles.)

The dots (. . .) do not signify omissions, but are as found in the originals.

(1)

Address: Madame Cosima feu Wagner / Bayreuth / Allemagne
Postmark: Torino / Ferrovia / 3.1.89
They tell me that a certain divine Hanswurst has of late completed the dithyrambs of Dionysus . . .

(2)

Address: Frau Cosima Wagner / Bayreuth / Germania
Postmark: Torino / Ferrovia /3.1.89
To the Princess Ariadne, my beloved.
The belief that I am a man is prejudice. But I have often lived among men and I know everything that men can experience, from the lowest to the highest. I was Buddha among the Indians, Dionysus among the Greeks; Alexander and Caesar are my incarnations, likewise Lord Bakon who wrote Shakespeare. Of late I was Voltaire and Napoleon, and perhaps Richard Wagner too . . . But this time I come as the conquering Dionysus, who will make of the earth a festival . . . Not that I have much time . . . The heavens rejoice at my existence . . . I also hung on the cross . . .

600

(3)

Address: Frau Cosima Wagner / in / Bayreuth / Germania
Postmark: Torino / Ferrovia / 3.1.89
You shall publish this breve to mankind [misspelt] from
Bayreuth, with the title:

The joyful tidings.

APPENDIX IV

(cf. pp. 551–3)

From Dr Newell Sill Jenkins, *Reminiscences*, by courtesy of Professor Klaus Liepmann.

> He [Wagner] was unwilling to speak English, of which he had only a literary knowledge, and was accustomed to say: 'I speak English, but only in the dialect of North Wales.' One day he asked me the origin of my name, saying that it should have a meaning, as German names generally did. Then I told him there was once a great king in Wales, of whom the English 'King Cole' was but a degenerate copy. This king, whose name was Jen, was a model of all a monarch should be, pious, learned, just, generous and, above all, jovial. In his court were assembled all the great artists of his time and they were more honoured than princes. His happy subjects basked in the light of his jolly countenance and lived so happily under his gentle and prosperous reign, that, when at last he died childless, they decided that no successor should bear that beloved name. Only when later a man appeared who in his person and character reminded them of their lamented monarch, they called him 'of the kin of Jen', and so originated the name Jen-kins.
>
> The next morning he gave me a copy of the 'Ring' [in Alfred Forman's translation], which the author had sent to the *Meister* and with which we had all amused ourselves the previous evening. It bore . . . written in Wagner's hand [and in his own English], the following inscription: 'Translated in the dialect of North Wales, in the time of King Jen, forefather of my noble friend, Jenkins.'

Among other 'mementoes of the great *Meister*' Jenkins also had

> Joseph Rubinstein's arrangement for the piano of the great
> Festive March composed by Wagner for the opening of the
> celebration in America of the hundredth anniversary of the
> United States' Declaration of Independence. The flyleaf of the
> book bears these words [in German]:

> My dear Mr Jenkins! In recognition of our mutual hopes, I
> proclaim this dedication to you in friendship: 'Long live
> America!' Yours, Richard Wagner.

> This refers partly to a hope we both entertained that he
> might sometime visit America and partly his sympathy with
> my belief that Europe would eventually become republican
> and not Cossack.

The Wagner Archives possesses the sheet of paper, dated 25 January
1879, on which Wagner drafted the inscription he wrote in Jenkins's copy
of the *Ring*. Forman's version was not a singing translation but intended
for the study; Wagner described it as a 'monument'.

CHRONOLOGY

Summary of Wagner's Life and Work

Specific dates (day and month) are based on the revised version of Otto Strobel's *Zeittafel*.

Part 1 (1813–1849)

1813 Richard Wagner is born in Leipzig on 22 May. His father, Friedrich Wagner, the registrar of police, dies on 23 November.

1814 Wagner's mother, Johanna Rosine née Pätz, marries the painter, actor and playwright Ludwig Heinrich Christian Geyer on 28 August, and the family then moves to Dresden.

1821 Wagner's stepfather dies on 30 September.

1822 Richard enters the Kreuzschule in Dresden.

1826 He displays a particular liking for Greek, and translates the first three books of the *Odyssey* as 'extra homework'.

1828 After moving back to Leipzig he enters the Nicolaischule. He plays truant, writes *Leubald*, 'a great tragedy', and secretly takes lessons in harmony.

1829 He sees Schröder-Devrient in *Fidelio*.

1830 Wagner makes a piano reduction of the Choral Symphony. First essays in composition, including a 'Pastoral', for which he writes words and music 'simultaneously'. Transfers to the Thomasschule.

1831 Wagner enrols as a music student at Leipzig University. Lessons in counterpoint and composition from Theodor Weinlig. Compositions for voice, piano and orchestra.

1832 He begins his first opera, *Die Hochzeit*. He abandons the composition sketch after the first numbers and destroys the text.

1833 A Symphony in C major is performed in the Gewandhaus. Wagner writes his second opera, *Die Feen* (based on Gozzi's *La donna serpente*). He goes to Würzburg as chorus master.

1834 He becomes musical director of the Bethmann theatre company in Lauchstädt, where he meets the actress, Minna Planer. He writes the text for his next opera, *Das Liebesverbot* (based on Shakespeare's *Measure for Measure*). He goes to Rudolstadt and Magdeburg with the company.

1835 On a journey undertaken to audition singers, he sees Bayreuth for the first time; in Nuremberg he witnesses a street fight provoked by a caterwauling carpenter; in Frankfurt am Main he begins making notes for his future biography.

1836 First performance of *Das Liebesverbot* in Magdeburg. Wagner follows Minna to Königsberg, where she has been engaged at the theatre. They are married in the church at Tragheim near Königsberg on 24 November.

1837 Wagner is appointed musical director at the theatre in Riga. He takes back Minna, who deserted him in Königsberg.

1838 He begins the composition of *Rienzi*.

1839 The Wagners do a 'moonlight flit' from Riga, and board the *Thetis* at Pillau for a stormy voyage to London, stopping en route at Sandviken on Boröya. The legend of the Flying Dutchman takes shape. They reach Paris on 17 September. Wagner hears a rehearsal of the Ninth Symphony by the Conservatoire orchestra. Under its impact he composes a *Faust* Overture.

1840 Wagner writes settings of French poems and completes the score of *Rienzi*. Writes arrangements of numbers from French and Italian operas to earn a living. Spends some time in a debtors' prison in October or November. *Eine Pilgerfahrt zu Beethoven* is published in the *Gazette musicale*.

1841 *Ein Ende in Paris* published in the *Gazette musicale*. Conception of Senta's Ballad. Wagner and Minna move to Meudon, where he writes the text and music of *Der Fliegende Holländer*. *Rienzi* is accepted by the Dresden court theatre.

1842 Return to Dresden. On a holiday, Wagner begins the prose sketch of *Tannhäuser* at Schreckenstein near Aussig. First performance of *Rienzi* in Dresden.

1843 First performance of *Der Fliegende Holländer* in Dresden. Wagner is appointed kapellmeister to the King of Saxony. His oratorio *Das Liebesmahl der Apostel* receives its first performance in the Frauenkirche. Holidaying in Teplitz, Wagner reads Jacob Grimm's *Deutsche Mythologie*.

1844 The remains of Carl Maria von Weber are brought from London to Dresden. Wagner composes a funeral march for the occasion.

1845 The score of *Tannhäuser* is finished. Wagner writes the first prose sketch of *Die Meistersinger* and the prose sketch of *Lohengrin* in Marienbad. First performance of *Tannhäuser* in Dresden.

1846 Palm Sunday: Wagner conducts the epoch-making performance of the Choral Symphony. During the summer the Wagners spend three months in Gross-Graupa, where he finishes the composition sketch of *Lohengrin*. Prose sketch for a play about Frederick Barbarossa. Edition of Gluck's *Iphigenia in Aulis*.

1847 While scoring *Lohengrin*, Wagner studies Greek literature and culture; decisive impact of the *Oresteia* of Aeschylus.

1848 The completion of the score of *Lohengrin* is followed by a gap of five and a half years before Wagner writes music again. He addresses the Vaterlandsverein in Dresden on 'Republicanism and the Monarchy'. He tackles the material of the *Ring* for the first time in *Der Nibelungen-Mythus als Entwurf zu einem Drama*, and writes the verse text of *Siegfrieds Tod*.

1849 Prose draft of a play, *Jesus von Nazareth*. The May rising in Dresden, in which Wagner takes part, and during which he has an idea for a play about Achilles.

Part 2 (1849–1883)

1849 Wagner flees Dresden on 9 May, escaping arrest by pure chance. Liszt helps his flight on from Weimar. The Dresden police issue a warrant for his arrest. He reaches Zürich on 28 May. He writes *Das Kunstwerk der Zukunft*.

1850 Wagner goes to Paris and drafts a text for submission to the Opéra, *Wieland der Schmied*. He meets with no success. His plan of going to Greece and Asia Minor with Jessie Laussot is thwarted. He returns to Zürich and to Minna, and begins and abandons a composition sketch for *Siegfrieds Tod*. Liszt gives the first performance of *Lohengrin* in Weimar.

1851 Wagner completes his major theoretical work, *Oper und Drama*, the verse text of *Der Junge Siegfried*, and his autobiographical *Mitteilung an meine Freunde*. The ideas of casting the Nibelung material as a four-part work and of holding a festival to perform it evolve simultaneously.

1852 First visit to northern Italy. Completion of the text of the *Ring*.

1853 Private edition of the text of the *Ring* appears, and Wagner reads it to an invited audience in the Hotel Baur au Lac in Zürich. The scenery of the Julier Pass and Roseg Glacier makes an indelible impression on him, on his way to St Moritz, and is later to leave its mark on the music of the *Ring*. On a second visit to Italy, at La Spezia, the music of the *Rheingold* prelude comes to him in a kind of vision. He returns to Zürich and begins to compose *Das Rheingold*.

1854 Wagner completes the score of *Das Rheingold* and begins *Die Walküre*. He reads Schopenhauer's *Die Welt als Wille und Vorstellung*. First conception of *Tristan*.

1855 Wagner conducts eight concerts in London, but fails to realize any financial profit. Returns to Zürich. *Tristan* takes more definite shape, and Wagner considers introducing Parsifal on his Grail quest.

1856 Completion of the score of *Die Walküre*. Prose scenario of *Die Sieger*. After a cure in Mornex, Wagner resumes the composition of the *Ring* with *Siegfried*. He makes the first musical sketches for *Tristan*.

1857 Good Friday: the first prose sketch of *Parsifal* (then spelt *Parzival*).

The Wagners move into the house Asyl, lent them by the
Wesendonks, on the outskirts of Zürich. Wagner finishes the
orchestral sketch of Act II of *Siegfried*, then lays the *Ring* aside for
twelve years. Begins *Tristan*. Composes the *Wesendonk Lieder*.

1858 Hans and Cosima von Bülow visit Asyl. Crisis in the relationship
with the Wesendonks. Wagner leaves Asyl for ever on 17 August and
goes to Venice. In the Palazzo Giustiniani he resumes the composition
of the second act of *Tristan*. He sketches a song, *Es ist bestimmt in
Gottes Rat*. Draft of a letter to Schopenhauer on the metaphysics of
sexual love.

1859 Wagner leaves Venice on 24 March (after pressure is exerted by the
Saxon government) and goes to Lucerne, where he begins the third
act of *Tristan*. In conversation with the composer Felix Draeseke he
expounds Beethoven's compositional technique, taking the 'Eroica' as
his example. He finishes *Tristan*. In September he moves to Paris,
where Minna follows him.

1860 Three concerts of excerpts from his works in the Théâtre Italien. A
circle of French admirers forms round Wagner. 22 July: a partial
amnesty, permitting him to return to Germany with the exception of
Saxony.

1861 He scores the Paris version of the Bacchanal and Venus's scene in
Tannhäuser. It receives three performances at the Opéra, and is then
withdrawn at the composer's request. The possibility arises of
producing *Tristan*, first in Karlsruhe and then in Vienna. On 14
August Wagner leaves for Vienna, to supervise early rehearsals, but
the whole project falls through. On a train returning to Vienna after
a short trip to Venice he conceives the major part of the *Meistersinger*
prelude, and thereupon writes a second prose sketch. He moves to
Paris, where he writes the verse text and conceives the melody of the
'Wach auf' chorus.

1862 Wagner moves to Biebrich, near Mainz, in order to start the music of
Die Meistersinger. A last brief visit from Minna, who lives apart from
him in Dresden. Wagner's friendship with Mathilde Maier. He
conducts the first performance of the *Meistersinger* prelude in an
almost empty Gewandhaus in Leipzig. He gives a private reading of
the text in Vienna; Eduard Hanslick, believing himself caricatured in
the figure of Beckmesser, becomes Wagner's implacable enemy.

1863 January to April: concerts in Vienna, Prague, St Petersburg, Moscow.
Wagner furnishes an apartment in Penzing, a Viennese suburb, at
great expense. Concerts in Budapest, Prague, Karlsruhe, Löwenberg,
Breslau, Vienna.

1864 In flight from his creditors, Wagner leaves Vienna in haste. After
staying with Frau Wille at Mariafeld near Zürich, he goes on to
Stuttgart, where a messenger from the King of Bavaria finds him.
Ludwig II receives him in the Residenz in Munich on 4 May. Wagner
dedicates the *Huldigungsmarsch* to the king, who commissions the
Ring. Hans and Cosima von Bülow come to live in Munich.

1865 First performance of *Tristan und Isolde* in Munich. Wagner begins to
dictate his autobiography, *Mein Leben*, to Cosima. He writes the
prose sketch of *Parsifal* and a 'diary' for King Ludwig on the subject
'What is German?' A press campaign of mounting hostility and
Wagner's vigorous defence lead to catastrophe: on 6 December the
king asks him to leave Bavaria for the time being. Wagner goes to
Switzerland and rents a villa near Geneva.

1866 Determined never to return to Munich, Wagner searches for a house
in southern France, without success. In Marseilles he receives the
news of Minna's death. He rents the villa Tribschen outside Lucerne,
and resumes the composition of *Meistersinger* with Act II. 22–4 May:
surprise visit from King Ludwig.

1867 Wagner finishes *Die Meistersinger* and takes a brief holiday in Paris.

1868 First performance of *Die Meistersinger* in Munich, with Wagner in the
royal box. He returns to Tribschen, where Cosima follows him after
the denunciation of their relationship to the king. Wagner drafts
scenarios for *Luthers Hochzeit* and a 'Comedy in one act' ('to counter
grave depression'). Cosima and Wagner go to northern Italy and she
decides to stay with him permanently.

1869 Wagner resumes the *Ring* after twelve years, scores Act II of *Siegfried*
and begins the composition sketch of Act III. Nietzsche comes over
from Basel to pay his first call on 17 May. Wagner's son (and third
child) Siegfried is born on 6 June. Serious differences between
Wagner and King Ludwig over the Munich première of *Das
Rheingold*. He begins *Götterdämmerung*, composes *Wahlspruch für die
deutsche Feuerwehr* ('Motto for the German Fire Service'), and writes
Über das Dirigieren.

1870 Recalling his visit to Bayreuth in 1835, Wagner looks it up in an
encyclopedia and learns of the large stage in its opera house, which
gives him the idea of performing the *Ring* there. *Die Walküre* receives
its first performance in Munich, against Wagner's wishes. Judith
Mendès-Gautier and other French friends visit Tribschen. Wagner
and Cosima are married. He writes the centenary essay *Beethoven*,
and the 'comedy in the antique manner' *Eine Kapitulation*, and
composes the *Siegfried Idyll*.

1871 Wagner composes the *Kaisermarsch* and makes his first visit to the
new German Empire. After seeing the Bayreuth opera house he
decides to build his own theatre. He reads his paper *Über die
Bestimmung der Oper* to the Royal Academy of Arts in Berlin, calls on
Bismarck, and conducts a charity concert in the royal opera house, in
the presence of the emperor. He returns to Tribschen. The town
council in Bayreuth decides to let him have a site for the
Festspielhaus. The Wagner Society is founded. Wagner conducts in
Mannheim.

1872 Nietzsche publishes *Die Geburt der Tragödie aus dem Geist der Musik*.
The Society of Patrons of the Bayreuth Festival is founded. Wagner
moves to Bayreuth. 22 May: he lays the foundation stone of the

Festspielhaus, and in the evening conducts the Choral Symphony in
the Margraves' Opera House. He writes the essay *Über Schauspieler
und Sänger*. Cosima is baptized a Protestant. Wagner begins the search
for performers with a tour of Germany.

1873 Concerts in Hamburg, Berlin, Cologne. Wagner reads the text of
Götterdämmerung in Berlin, in the house of Count von Schleinitz,
before an audience including Field-Marshal Moltke and Adolf
Menzel. Anton Bruckner visits Wagner in Bayreuth and dedicates his
Third Symphony to him.

1874 Financial crisis of the festival undertaking. King Ludwig guarantees a
credit of 100,000 talers. The Wagner family moves into Wahnfried.
21 November: Wagner completes the score of *Götterdämmerung*
(having started *Das Rheingold* on 1 November 1853). Composes
Kinderkatechismus for four girls' voices and small orchestra.

1875 Concerts in Vienna, Budapest (jointly with Liszt), Berlin. The
preliminary rehearsals for the *Ring* are held in Bayreuth.

1876 Composition of the Festival March in celebration of the centenary of
the American Declaration of Independence: while working on it
Wagner gets the idea for the Flower Maidens' 'Komm', komm'
holder Knabe'. The first Bayreuth festival, with three complete cycles
of the *Ring*. The emperors Wilhelm I of Germany and Pedro II of
Brazil are present at the opening performances (while King Ludwig
attends the dress rehearsals and the third cycle).
September–December: the Wagners are in Italy, spending a month in
Sorrento, where Wagner and Nietzsche meet for the last time. News
of the festival's deficit of 147,851·82 marks reaches Wagner. They
return to Bayreuth just before Christmas.

1877 Wagner writes the second prose sketch and the verse text of *Parsifal*.
He gives eight concerts in the Royal Albert Hall in London, in aid of
the Bayreuth deficit, and is received at Windsor Castle by Queen
Victoria. He discloses his plan for a school of music in Bayreuth
(never realized) to delegates of the Wagner Societies. He begins the
composition of *Parsifal*.

1878 *Bayreuther Blätter* begins publication, edited by Hans von Wolzogen.
The prelude to *Parsifal* is performed in Wahnfried for the first
time.

1879 While continuing to work on *Parsifal*, Wagner writes a number of
articles for *Bayreuther Blätter*. Heinrich von Stein joins the household
as Siegfried's tutor.

1880 January–October: residence in Italy (Naples, Siena, Venice). Wagner
writes *Religion und Kunst*. On the way home, Wagner stops in Munich
and conducts the *Parsifal* prelude at a private concert for King
Ludwig.

1881 Angelo Neumann produces the *Ring* at the Viktoria-Theater in
Berlin. Wagner, his family and Count Gobineau, a guest in
Wahnfried, attend the fourth cycle. From November: residence in
Italy (Palermo, Acireale).

1882 Wagner finishes the score of *Parsifal* on 13 January in Palermo. May:
      return to Bayreuth, where Count Gobineau again visits.
      Establishment of the Bayreuth Stipendiary Fund. Sixteen
      performances of *Parsifal* in Bayreuth. Wagner and his family leave for
      Venice on 14 September and take up residence on the mezzanine
      floor of the Palazzo Vendramin. On Christmas Eve Wagner conducts
      his C major Symphony (first performed in the Gewandhaus in 1833)
      in the Teatro La Fenice.

1883 12 February: before going to bed, Wagner plays the Rhinemaidens'
      lament: 'Traulich und treu ist's nur in der Tiefe: falsch und feig ist,
      was dort oben sich freut!' 13 February: while working on the essay
      Über das Weibliche im Menschlichen, Wagner is struck by another heart
      attack and dies in Cosima's arms. The last words he writes are 'Love
      – tragedy'. 18 February: Wagner's burial in the garden of Wahnfried.

THE WORKS

The author's article on Wagner in *Die Musik in Geschichte und Gegenwart*, XIV, incorporates a list of the works, compiled by Gertrud Strobel, with notes on their first performances and first publication.

1. The Operas and Music Dramas

Die Hochzeit (Fragment, 1832)

Die Feen (1833–4)

Das Liebesverbot, oder Die Novize von Palermo (1834–5)

Rienzi, der Letzte der Tribunen (1838–40)

Der Fliegende Holländer (1841)

Tannhäuser und der Sängerkrieg auf Wartburg (1843–5) (Act III finale rewritten 1847; Bacchanal and Venus's scene in Act I rewritten 1860–1)

Lohengrin (1845–8)

Tristan und Isolde (1857–9)

Die Meistersinger von Nürnberg (1861–7) (First sketch 1845)

Der Ring des Nibelungen. Ein Bühnenfestspiel für drei Tage und einen Vorabend (First prose sketch, *Die Nibelungensage (Mythus)*, 4 October 1848; complete score finished 21 November 1874)

  – *Das Rheingold* (Text 1852; music 1853–4)

  – *Die Walküre* (Text 1852; music 1854–6)

  – *Siegfried* (Original title *Der Junge Siegfried*; text 1851; music: Acts I and II 1856–7 (Act II orchestrated 1869), Act III 1869–71)

  – *Götterdämmerung* (Original title *Siegfrieds Tod*; text 1848, revised 1852; music 1869–74)

  – Composition sketch for *Siegfrieds Tod*, scenes 1 and 2 (1850; abandoned)

Parsifal. Ein Bühnenweihfestspiel (First prose sketch 10 April 1857; first prose draft 1865; verse text and music 1877–82)

2. Plays, Fragments, Sketches: including operatic texts written but not composed by Wagner

Leubald. Ein Trauerspiel (1825)

Die Hohe Braut (1836 and 1842; libretto, set by Johann Kittl as *Bianca und Giuseppe, oder Die Franzosen vor Nizza*)

Die Glückliche Bärenfamilie (Männerlist größer al Frauenlist) (1837; libretto; some music written)

Die Sarazenin (Prose draft 1841–2, verse text 1843)

Die Bergwerke zu Falun (Prose draft for an unwritten libretto, 1841–2)

Friedrich I. (Sketch for a play, 1846 and 1848)

Alexander der Große (Sketch for a play, 184?; does not survive)

Jesus von Nazareth (Draft of a play; 1849)

Achilleus (Sketch for a play, 1849)

Wieland der Schmied (Prose draft of a libretto, 1850)

Die Sieger (Sketch for a music drama, 1850)

Luther / Luthers Hochzeit (Sketch for a play in prose, 1868)

Lustspiel in 1 Akt (Draft, 1868)

Eine Kapitulation. Lustspiel in antiker Manier (1870)

Lessing und Friedrich der Große (Idea for a comedy, 187?; mentioned GLRW, V, p. 381, Correspondence 16, p. 47)

Hans Sachs / Hans Sachs' zweite Ehe (Idea for a play, 187?; mentioned Correspondence 16, p. 47)

Herzog Bernhard von Weimar (Idea for a play, 187?; mentioned KLRW, II, p. 7; Correspondence 16, p. 47)

3. Orchestral Works

Overture in B♭ major ('Drumbeat') (1830)

Overture to Schiller's *Die Braut von Messina* (1830)

Overture in C major (1830)

Concert overture in D minor (1831)

Overture to Raupach's *König Enzio* (1832)

Concert Overture in C major (1832)

Symphony in C major (1832)

Symphony in E major, first movement (1834)

Beim Antritt des neuen Jahres (cantata, five numbers; 1835)

Overture to T. Apel's *Columbus* (1835)

Polonia Overture (1836)

'Rule Britannia' Overture (1837)

Overture to Goethe's *Faust* (Originally intended as the first movement of a *Faust* Symphony; first version 1840; revised as a *Faust* Overture 1855)

Trauermusik nach Motiven aus 'Euryanthe' (1844)

Träume for small orchestra and solo violin (Arrangement of one of the *Wesendonk Lieder*; 1857)

Huldigungsmarsch (1864)

Romeo und Julia (Sketch for a symphony in A♭ minor; 1868)

Siegfried Idyll (1870)

Kaisermarsch (1871)

Großer Festmarsch (Celebrating the centenary of the American Declaration of Independence; 1876)

4. Vocal Compositions

Seven Compositions for Goethe's *Faust*: *Lied der Soldaten, Bauern unter der Linde, Branders Lied, 'Es war einmal ein König', 'Was machst du mir vor Liebchens Tür', 'Meine Ruh' ist hin', 'Ach neige, du Schmerzensreiche'* (melodrama) (1831)

'Dein ist das Reich' (Four-part vocal fugue, exercise; 1832)

Abendglocken (Text by T. Apel; 1832)

Scene and Aria for soprano (1832)

Tenor aria for insertion in Marschner's *Der Vampyr* (1833)

Bass aria for insertion in Karl Blum's *Maria, Max und Michel* (1837)

Bass aria for insertion in Joseph Weigl's *Die Schweizerfamilie* (1837)

Nicolay-Volkshymne for chorus (Text by H. von Brackel; 1837)

Der Tannenbaum (Ballad by G. Scheurlin; 1838)

La Descente de la Courtille for chorus (Text by Dumanoir; 1840)

Bass aria for insertion in Bellini's *Norma* (1840)

'Tout n'est qu'images fugitives' (Text by J. Reboul; 1840)

Les Adieux de Maria Stuart (Text by Béranger; 1840)

'Dors entre mes bras, enfant plein de charmes' (Poet unknown; 1840)

Mignonne (Text by Ronsard; 1840)

L'attente (Text by Victor Hugo; 1840)

Les deux grenadiers (Setting of Heine's poem in a French translation made at Wagner's request by Professor Loeve-Veimars; 1840)

Gesang zur Enthüllung des Denkmals Sr. Majestät des hochseligen Königs Friedrich August der Gerechte, for chorus (1843)

Das Liebesmahl der Apostel. A biblical scene for men's voices and large orchestra (Text by Wagner; 1843)

Gruß seiner Treuen an Friedrich August den Geliebten, for chorus (Text by Wagner; 1844)

'Hebt an den Sang' for chorus (Text by Wagner; 1844)

Fünf Gedichte für eine Frauenstimme: Der Engel, Stehe still, Im Treibhaus, Schmerzen, Träume (Texts by Mathilde Wesendonk; 1857-8)

Wahlspruch für die deutsche Feuerwehr (Text by F. Gilardone; 1869)

Kinder-Katechismus zu Kosels Geburtstag, for girls' voices (Text by Wagner; first version with piano, 1873; second version, with the accompaniment arranged for small orchestra, 1874)

5. Works for the Piano

Sonata in D minor (1829)

Sonata in F minor (1829)

Sonata in B♭ major for piano duet (1831)

Sonata in B♭ major, opus 1 (1831)

Polonaise in D major for piano duet, opus 2 (1831)

Fantasia in F♯ minor, opus 3 (1831)

Große Sonate in A major, opus 4 (1832)

Albumblatt in E major, for E. B. Kietz (1840)

Polka in G major, for Mathilde Wesendonk (1853)

'*Eine Sonate für das Album von Frau M. W.*', in A♭ major (1853)
'*Züricher Vielliebchen / Walzer, Polka oder sonst 'was*', in E♭ major (1854)
'*Notenbriefchen für Mathilde Wesendonk*', in G major (1857)
Albumblatt in C major, for Princess Pauline Metternich (1861)
Albumblatt, '*Ankunft bei den schwarzen Schwänen*', in A♭ major, for Countess
   Pourtalès (1861)
Albumblatt in E♭ major, for Betty Schott (1875)
'Porazzi' Theme, in A♭ major (1858 and 1882)

6. Performing Arrangements

Rossini, *I Marinari*, duet, orchestrated by Wagner (1838)
Gluck, *Iphigenia in Aulis* (1846–7)
Palestrina, *Stabat mater* (1848)
Mozart, *Don Giovanni* (1850)

A complete edition of the works of Wagner is in process of publication at the
   present time, under the auspices of the Munich Academy of Fine Arts
   Gesamtausgabe der Werke Richard Wagners, Mainz, (1970–).

THE CORRESPONDENCE OF RICHARD AND COSIMA WAGNER

Letters are quoted from the following editions:

Wagner, Richard, *Briefe in Originalausgaben.* Leipzig, 1912:
  vol. 1/2 An Minna Wagner
  vol. 3 Familienbriefe
  vol. 4 An Theodor Uhlig, Wilhelm Fischer, Ferdinand Heine
  vol. 5 An Mathilde Wesendonk
  vol. 6 An Otto Wesendonk
  vol. 7 Briefwechsel mit Breitkopf & Härtel
  vol. 8 Briefwechsel mit B. Schott's Söhne
  vol. 9 Briefwechsel Wagner–Liszt
  vol. 10 An Theodor Apel
  vol. 11 An August Röckel
  vol. 12 An Ferdinand Praeger
  vol. 13 An Eliza Wille
  vol. 14 An seine Künstler
  vol. 15 Bayreuther Briefe
  vol. 16 An Emil Heckel
  vol. 17 An Freunde und Zeitgenossen
- *Gesammelte Briefe (1830–50)*, see RWGB, p. ix
- *Briefe nach Zeitfolge und Inhalt*, ed. by Wilhelm Altmann. Leipzig, 1905
- *Briefe*, selected and ed. by Wilhelm Altmann, 2 vols. Leipzig, 1925
- *Briefe. Die Sammlung Burrell,* see RWBC, p. ix
- *Lettres françaises*, see TWLF, p. ix
- *An Hans von Bülow.* Jena, 1916
- *An Judith Gautier*, ed. by Willi Schuh. Zürich, 1936
- and Cosima Wagner, *Lettres à Judith Gautier*, see LJG, p. viii
- 'Richard Wagner und Judith Gautier. Neue Dokumente', ed. by Willi Schuh, in *Schweizerische Musikzeitung* 1963 / 3
- *Zwei unveröffentlichte Briefe an Robert von Hornstein*, ed. by Ferdinand von Hornstein. Munich, 1911
- 'Briefe an Dr Theodor Kafka', ed. by Wilhelm Kienzl, in *Die Musik*, 1906–7 / 19

615

- and King Ludwig II, *Briefwechsel*, see KLRW, p. viii
- *An Mathilde Maier (1862—78)*, ed. by Hans Scholz. Leipzig, 1930
- 'Fünf neu aufgefundene Briefe . . .' [to Princess Pauline Metternich], ed. by Maria Ullrichowa, in *Beiträge zur Musikwissenschaft*, 1964 / 4
- 'Fünf ungedruckte Briefe . . . an Meyerbeer', ed. by Georg Kinsky, in *Schweizerische Musikzeitung*, 15 November 1934
- *The letters to Anton Pusinelli*, see RWAP, p. ix
- *Briefe an eine Putzmacherin*, ed. by Daniel Spitzer. Vienna, 1906
- *und die Putzmacherin, oder Die Macht der Verleumdung*, ed. by Ludwig Kusche. Wilhelmshaven, 1967
- 'Briefe . . . an Editha von Rhaden', ed. by Wilhelm Altmann, in *Die Musik* 1924 / 10
- *An Hans Richter*, ed. by Ludwig Karpath. Berlin, Vienna, Leipzig, 1924
- *An Frau Julie Ritter*, ed. by Siegmund von Hausegger. Munich, 1920
- *Die Briefsammlungen des Richard-Wagner-Museums in Tribschen bei Luzern*, ed. by Adolf Zinsstag. Basel, 1961

Other letters are published in:

Fehr, Max, *Richard Wagners Schweizer Zeit*, see FWSZ, p. viii

Förster-Nietzsche, E., *Wagner und Nietzsche*, see EFWN, p. viii

Fricke, Richard, *Bayreuth vor dreißig Jahren*

Hey, Julius, *Richard Wagner als Vortragsmeister 1864–76*

Kapp, Julius, *Wagner und die Frauen*, see JKWF, p. viii

Kapp, Julius, and Hans Jachmann, *Richard Wagner und seine erste Elisabeth*. Berlin, 1927

Lippert, Woldemar, *Richard Wagners Verbannung und Rückkehr*, see LWVR, p. viii

Neumann, Angelo, *Erinnerungen an Richard Wagner*

Niemann, Gottfried, and Wilhelm Altmann, *Richard Wagner und Albert Niemann*. Berlin, 1924

Röckl, Sebastian, *Ludwig II. und Richard Wagner*, see SRLW, p. ix

Schemann, Ludwig, *Lebensfahrten eines Deutschen*

Weissheimer, Wendelin, *Erlebnisse mit Richard Wagner, Franz Liszt und vielen anderen Zeitgenossen*

Westernhagen, Curt von, *Richard Wagner* (1956)

Wille, Eliza, *Fünfzehn Briefe von Richard Wagner*

Wagner, Cosima *und Houston Stewart Chamberlain im Briefwechsel 1888–1901*, ed. by Paul Pretzsch. Leipzig, 1934
- *Briefe an ihre Tochter Daniela von Bülow 1866–85. Nebst 5 Briefen Richard Wagners*, ed. by Max von Waldberg. Stuttgart and Berlin, 1933
- 'Lettres à Gobineau', ed. by C. Serpeille de Gobineau, in *La Revue Hebdomadaire* 1938, pp. 263ff., 400ff.
- *Briefwechsel zwischen C. W. und Fürst Ernst zu Hohenlohe-Langenburg*. Stuttgart, 1937
- *Briefe an Friedrich Nietzsche*, see CWFN, p. viii
- *Briefe an Ludwig Schemann*. Regensburg, 1937

Other letters by Cosima Wagner are published in:
Du Moulin Eckart, Richard, *Cosima Wagner*, see DMCW, p. viii

A complete edition of Wagner's letters in fifteen volumes is in process of publica-
tion at the present time, commissioned by the Richard-Wagner-
Familien-Archiv Bayreuth and edited by Gertrud Strobel and Werner
Wolf. The first volume appeared just before the first edition of the present
work and is cited herein as RWSB (Richard Wagner, *Sämtliche Briefe*,
Leipzig, 1967–).

Chapter 25. Munich

1 Pfistermeister transmitted this message by word of mouth and not, as Wagner says in *Mein Leben*, in a letter from the king. (KLRW, I, pp. xxxiv f.)

2 Ludwig's diary was published in 1925. Newman calls the editing and commentary of Edir Grein 'a deplorable exhibition of pseudo-psychiatry'. (NLRW, iii, p. 244)

3 On the Brown Book see note 9 of this chapter.

4 The painting (oil on canvas) disappeared until it was identified in the Metropolitan Museum, New York, by Martin Geck, who published it in colour in his book *Die Bildnisse Richard Wagners*. See Vol. I, pl. 16b.

5 The Annals twice refer to 'Schwabe–Schwind'. At the time Wagner suspected that the painter Moritz von Schwind, who was hostile to him, was behind the presentation of the bill, but this appears not to have been the case. Cf. KLRW, V, pp. 229f.

6 Otto Wesendonk remained a generous friend to Wagner, in spite of everything. At Wagner's request he even surrendered the autograph score of *Das Rheingold* to King Ludwig, who wrote him a cordial letter of thanks in his own hand (28 August 1865).

7 Schuré, *Souvenirs sur Richard Wagner*.

8 Wagner's account of the incident in a letter to the king of 9 June 1866 is slightly different. 'Curtly and brusquely they asked her if she wanted to carry the sacks of silver coin herself. When she asked them in amazement to give her notes they explained that they did not have enough in paper, and she would have to take at least half in silver. In the face of this discourtesy she drew some consolation at least from having spared me similar humiliation.' (KLRW, II, p. 57)

9 The Brown Book is kept in the Wagner Museum in Bayreuth. Extracts from it had been published, principally in BBL and KLRW, but it was first published in full in 1975, edited and with a commentary by Joachim Bergfeld (*Das Braune Buch*, Zürich). At some time Eva Chamberlain, the daughter of Richard and Cosima Wagner, unfortunately took it upon herself to interfere with the

manuscript, removing and destroying seven pages and pasting blank paper over five more sides. These last have now been uncovered and rendered legible, and their content reveals that Eva's filial piety was excessive; the conclusion is that the seven pages she destroyed probably did not contain any 'sensations' either. The text of the Brown Book, as now made available, sheds new light on the events of the following weeks in Wagner's life (10 August to 11 September 1865), so this section of the present biography has been revised and expanded for this edition.

10 *Les Misérables*. Hugo's treatment of social, economic and communal questions extends even to the drainage system, a considerable problem in Paris. Reading the book made such an impression on Wagner that he made it the starting point of his 'comedy in the antique manner', *Eine Kapitulation*, in 1870.

11 The suburb of Vienna where Wagner had lived from May 1863 to March 1864.

12 The Hindu epic by Valmiki. On that occasion, at least, Wagner was reading it in the French translation by Fauche, which was later in his library at Wahnfried.

13 'unvermerklich': this should perhaps be read as 'unvermeidlich' ('unavoidable').

14 'The visit to Venice that we had planned had unfortunately to be abandoned for various reasons.' (BB, IV, p. 59)

15 Part of this was published in the second issue of BBL in 1878 and so made its way into the complete *Schriften* (RWGS, X, pp. 36ff.). Published in full in KLRW, IV, pp. 5ff.

16 Wagner was later to look back on his own situation during Cosima's journey to Pest: 'He . . . spoke about the despicable position for a lover of knowing that his beloved is in the power of another, who governs her life. It is endurable in the first raptures of love, but in time the situation becomes thoroughly dishonourable.' (5 April 1873; CT, I, p. 667)

17 Cosima wrote to Auguste de Gaspérini on 14 December: 'Ils auraient bâti des palais et six théâtres pour un à W., s'il avait voulu se faire leur agent auprès du roi; je le sais par les tentatives qu'ils ont faites.'

18 Cf. KLRW, I, pp. lxvi f., and IV, pp. 116f.; SRLW, II, pp. 1f.; GLRW, IV, pp.51ff.; NLRW, III, pp. 396ff.

19 Remarkably, in 1937 Otto Strobel found it impossible to track down the complete text of this article, since *the relevant pages were missing* from the Bavarian State Library's copy of the *Volksbote*! (KLRW, IV, pp. 106f.)

Chapter 26. Die Meistersinger

1 The text as given in *Richard Wagner an Freunde und Zeitgenossen* is incomplete; it is supplemented here from KLRW, I, pp. 257f.

2 In Friedrich Herzfeld, *Minna Planer*, pp. 330f.

3 The text is published in KLRW, IV, p. 124; a draft of it in RWBC, p. 565. Light is shed on the methods adopted by Wagner's enemies by further reference to the *Volksbote*: on 6 February the paper claimed to have learned from a person of some rank in Dresden that Minna Wagner had been receiving poor relief; it could therefore be assumed that her denial had been extorted from her. On 21 February the paper had to publish an official statement from the Dresden Commission for the Welfare of the Poor that Frau Wagner had by no means lived in straitened circumstances and had neither claimed nor received any relief. (KLRW, IV, pp. 128f.)

4 Herzfeld, *Minna Planer*, p. 354.

5 Published in Westernhagen, *Vom Holländer zum Parsifal*, pp. 132f.

6 Peter Cornelius, *Ausgewählte Briefe*, II (Leipzig, 1905), pp. 370ff. The editor of his correspondence, his son Carl Maria Cornelius, dated this letter '(12 May)', which Otto Strobel later showed to be incorrect; it must be '13 May'. (KLRW, V, p. 194, note 3)

7 The departure took place on 12 May, not on 11 May as planned. (KLRW, V, p. 194)

8 Editing his father's correspondence in 1904, Carl Maria Cornelius evidently decided he ought to make certain omissions so as to prevent identification of the author of the letter to Cosima that Bülow opened, out of consideration for the house of Wittelsbach. At all events, his editing of the letter of 13 May allowed Kapp to invent the legend of 'the great lie of the last two years', and it has taken the combined efforts of Strobel, Newman and myself to refute it.

9 This improbable story is to be found in KLRW, II and IV. A relative of Malvina Schnorr, C. H. N. Garrigues, took up her cause in his book *Ludwig und Malvina Schnorr* (Copenhagen, 1937), in which he put Wagner's version of the events in a bad light. Otto Strobel annihilated the charges in 1939 in KLRW, V.

10 Westernhagen, *Vom Holländer zum Parsifal*, p. 136.

11 Each stanza in Bar-form has three sections: the first two (the Stollen) are musically identical or nearly so; the third (the Abgesang) is different but shows some resemblance to the Stollen.

12 According to KLRW, II, p. 134, note, the text of the letter as given in *Richard Wagner an Freunde und Zeitgenossen* is incomplete. The full text was published in the *Münchner Neueste Nachrichten* of 19/20 May 1929.

13 *Denkwürdigkeiten des Fürsten Chlodwig zu Hohenlohe-Schillingsfürst*, I (Stuttgart and Leipzig, 1906), p. 211.

14 Newman's refusal to see anything more in this than the 'tirade' of a political amateur concerned only with his own interests illustrates the limits of his treatment of his subject. He did not appreciate that this letter related to a quite specific occasion and that Wagner was quite obviously inspired by Hohenlohe to champion his pro-Prussian policies. (Cf. NLRW, IV, pp. 71ff.)

15 On Eva's first birthday, 17 February 1868, Cosima was in Munich, and Wagner sent her a telegram to mark the day:

Was die Weise mir gebar,
mehr als Morgentraum nur war;
vom Parnaß zum Paradies
sie den Weg dem Leben wies.

('What the song bore me was more than a morning dream; it showed me the path of my life, from Parnassus to Paradise.')

He also recorded in the Brown Book: 'Eva sat on the piano and listened to the birth-song and then the Apprentices' Dance: very attentive and pleased.'

16 Otto Strobel gives a further illustration of the noble Freiherr's mentality by quoting a poem Völderndorff wrote and recited at a social gathering in Munich a few days after Wagner's death. (KLRW, II, p. 209, note)

So bist du hin, du Schwindler sondergleichen,
Hat dich der Teufel endlich doch ergriffen,
Du hast dein letztes Leitmotiv gepfiffen,
Dem Himmel Dank, jetzt mußt du einmal schweigen . . .
Fahr hin, du schlechter Mensch und schlechter Dichter,
Und sei der Teufel dir ein strenger Richter!

('So you've gone, you incomparable swindler, Old Nick's collared you at last, you've warbled your last leitmotiv, heaven be thanked, you must be quiet now . . . Good riddance, bad man and bad poet, and may the devil judge you severely.')

17 Strauss (ed.), *Instrumentationslehre von Hector Berlioz*.
18 First version 21 April, second draft 7 May 1868. Published in facsimile and transcription in Westernhagen, *Wagner* (1956), p. 57. A transcription is also to be found in *Das Braune Buch*, p. 175.
19 W. Weissheimer, *Erlebnisse*, p. 391.

Chapter 27. From Tribschen to Bayreuth

1 O. Strobel, 'Flucht nach Tribschen', *Bayreuther Festspielführer* 1937, pp. 77ff.
2 Andler, *Nietzsche, sa vie et sa pensée*, II (Paris, 1921), pp. 219ff.: 'Les sources du livre sur la naissance de la Tragédie'.
3 The various documents relating to the *Rheingold* affair are to be found, according to date, in KLRW II, IV and V.
4 From the *Revue Wagnérienne* (Paris), February 1887 (abbreviated).
5 Furtwängler, *Ton und Wort,* p. 11.
6 This letter is printed in two parts in KLRW, II, the *latter* half on pp. 287f., correctly dated 22 October, and the *first* part on p. 290, speculatively dated mid-November, as though it were a separate letter. I am indebted to Herr Erich Neumann of East Berlin for drawing my attention to Strobel's correction in KLRW, IV, p. 261.
7 Westernhagen, *Wagner* (1956), p. 154.

8 The 'Pine Forest Mountains' to the east of Bayreuth. Wunsiedel (mentioned in the next paragraph) is one of many small spas in the district.

9 'There is no braver nation in the world, if they have the right leaders.' (*Wilhelm Meisters Lehrjahre*, Book 4, chapter 16.)

10 Leprince, *Présence de Wagner,* pp. 45, 72.

11 In TWLF this letter of Wagner's is wrongly dated 12 August, instead of September, 1870, which reverses the order of the two letters and makes nonsense of the sequence.

12 Zuckerman, *The first hundred years of Wagner's 'Tristan',* pp. 100f.

13 Cf. Podach, *Ein Blick in Notizbücher Nietzsches,* pp. 72f. CT. I, pp. 375f., confirms the doubts as to Elisabeth's version of events. Wednesday, 5 April 1871: 'Professor Nietzsche reads to me from his work (origin and goal of Greek tragedy), which he wishes to dedicate to Richard; greatly delighted by it; it reveals a very gifted man who has absorbed Richard's ideas and made them his own.' 6 April : 'Further reading.' 7 April: 'The last reading from the essay.'

14 DMCW, I, pp. 583f. has two differences here: 'a great chorus' instead of 'a Greek chorus' and 'those themes' instead of 'these serious themes'. In answer to my enquiries, Dr Dietrich Mack, the co-editor of the diaries, has assured me that in this instance there can be no doubt as to the correctness of the reading in CT. The obvious conclusion to be drawn is that on 29 September 1871 Wagner was talking about a preliminary sketch which has not survived and in which the funeral music was not yet conceived as a march, but as a passage of reminiscence, comparable to a Greek *stasimon*, and concluding with the statement of Siegfried's theme, instead of going on to the Hero theme. Further evidence that this sketch was not identical with the composition sketch of the third act is offered by the fact that in the latter the Funeral March follows straight on, on the same page, from the setting of Siegfried's dying words (cf. my *Forging of the 'Ring',* p. 226). Du Moulin could not have known this, and evidently thought Cosima was in error.

15 Later, in an edition of the text of *Götterdämmerung,* he could speak of other, less personal reasons for the decision. (Cf. vol. I, p. 219)

Chapter 28. The First Festival

1 Erwin Rohde, too, his 'beloved philologist of the future', wasted no time in coming to Nietzsche's defence, in *A philologist's letter to Richard Wagner: Pseudo-philology.* The title itself ('*Afterphilologie*': 'hideous word', in Wagner's view) was coined by Nietzsche's friend Professor Overbeck of Basel, who therewith aligned himself in their camp. (Cf. Erwin Rohde, *Kleine Schriften,* Tübingen, 1901.) Wilamowitz followed up with a *Second part: a rejoinder to the attempts to salvage Friedrich Nietzsche's 'Birth of tragedy'* (Berlin, 1873).

2 The anniversary of Luther's nailing of the Ninety-five Theses to the church door in Wittenberg, celebrated as Reformation Day.

3 *Erinnerungen an Auber*, RWGS, IX, pp. 42ff.

4 Of the other works that she and Judith discussed, Wagner asked the Mendès, in a letter of 12 December 1873, to get him the following: Anquetil Duperon's *Oupnekhat* (the Persian version of the Upanishads, in a Latin translation favoured by Schopenhauer), E. L. Burnouf's translation of the Bhagavad-Gita and H. Fauche's translation of the Maha-Bharata. All are in the library at Wahnfried.

5 An entry in Cosima's diary indicates that though the king now denied it by implication, he had indeed been angry. 'Thursday, 29 January 1874. After dinner, Richard went to see Herr Feustel, who was very puzzled by what the king said about Dahn's poem, since when he was at Hofrat Düfflipp's he had seen telegrams from Secretary Eisenhart saying that the king was extremely displeased with Richard!' (CT, I, p. 787)

6 Nietzsche, *Die Unschuld des Werdens. Der Nachlaß*, selected and ed. by Alfred Baeumler, I (Leipzig, 1931), pp. 97ff.

7 C. A. Bernouilli, *Franz Overbeck und Friedrich Nietzsche*, I (Jena, 1908), p. 137.

8 Andler, *Nietzsche*, II, p. 400.

9 Anton Bruckner, *Gesammelte Briefe*, Neue Folge (Regensburg, 1924), p. 166; *Richard Wagner an Emil Heckel* (Leipzig, 1899), p. 99; *Bayreuther Festspielführer*, 1938, pp. 35f.; G. A. Kietz, *Richard Wagner . . . Erinnerungen*, pp. 182ff.; H. v. Wolzogen, *Erinnerungen an Richard Wagner*, pp. 28f.; Peter Raabe, *Bruckner* (Regensburg, 1944).

10 Wagner lived in Bayreuth, at no. 7 Dammallee, from the end of September 1872 to 28 April 1874.

11 Cf. Franz Stassen, 'Wahnfried', in *Bayreuth* (Munich, 1943). During the Second World War the books and pictures were placed in safe keeping. Some of the pictures are now in the Siegfried-Wagner-Haus, but the books were returned to the drawing room, to their original places on the shelves, in 1976.

12 GLRW, V, pp. 151f., 390ff.; MWKS, II, pp. 130ff.; *Richard Wagner an seine Künstler* (*Briefe in Originalausgaben*, vol. 14), p. 349, note 1: 'The very detailed discussions and clarifications of the Meister's intentions necessitated various alterations in the execution of the Hoffmann designs; there was not time enough in the end to meet the Meister's wishes in everything.' (Max Brückner to the editor)

13 The original painting is now in the Siegfried-Wagner-Haus.

14 MWKS, II, pp. 141ff.; DMCW, I, pp. 722ff.; GLRW, V, pp. 164ff.

15 KLRW, IV, pp. 214f.; also published in full in Nietzsche, *Werke*, ed. by Karl Schlechta, III, pp. 1105ff.

16 Kietz, *Richard Wagner . . . Erinnerungen*; Hey, *Richard Wagner als Vortragsmeister*; Fricke, *Bayreuth vor dreißig Jahren*.

17 Leprince, *Présence de Wagner*, pp. 90f. There can be no doubt as to the reliability of Vidal's statements.

18 Neumann, *Erinnerungen an Richard Wagner*.

19 Material from Mottl's diary was published by Willy Krienitz in *Neue Wagner-Forschungen* [I].

20 Kapp, *Wagner und die Berliner Oper* (Berlin, 1933), pp. 56ff.

21 The translator is inclined to adapt Andrew Porter's version of the Spring Song: 'Winter storms have vanished at your command.' The telegram went on to quote Brünnhilde's apostrophe to Siegfried: 'O Heil der Mutter, die Dich gebar!' etc.

22 Mottl kept a record in his diary (cf. note 19 of this chapter); Porges's *Die Bühnenproben zu den Bayreuther Festspielen 1876* was first published in instalments in BBL, from 1880 onwards, and appeared later in four booklets, published variously by Schmeitzner in Chemnitz and Siegismund und Volkening in Leipzig, 1881–96.

23 Schemann, *Meine Erinnerungen an Richard Wagner*.

24 Published in facsimile in KLRW, III, facing p. 88.

25 'Abschied von Mathilde Maier, der letzten Freundin'; 'der letzten Fremden' ('the last stranger') in CT, I, p. 1001 is obviously an erroneous reading of the manuscript: Cosima would never have referred to Mathilde Maier as a stranger. Cf. also GLRW, V, p. 308: 'Their close friends, such as . . . Mathilde Maier . . . remained until the first week in September.'

Chapter 29. Nietzsche in Bayreuth

1 Published in Westernhagen, *Wagner* (1956), pp. 524ff.

2 Cf. Martin Vogel's reference to Nietzsche as a 'music-lover who persisted in his dilettantism' in his essay 'Nietzsches Wettkampf mit Wagner'.

3 Podach, *Friedrich Nietzsches Werke des Zusammenbruchs*, pp. 274ff.

Chapter 30. The Nation's Thanks

1 A mild pun: apart from its obvious meaning, 'die Nibelungen-Not' is the alternative title of the medieval *Nibelungenlied*. [Tr.]

2 Joachim Bergfeld, 'Drei Briefe Nietzsches an Cosima Wagner', in *Maske und Kothurn*, 10 (1964), 3/4, pp. 597ff.

3 CT, I, pp. 1011ff. now proves beyond doubt that the 'walk' and the 'confession' *cannot* have taken place.

4 This undated letter must have been written in London in May 1877. It reveals that Wagner still hoped she would come over for the two additional concerts.

5 See Max Chop, 'Richard Wagner im Spiegel der Kritik seiner Zeit'.

6 The letters ended up in the possession of Brahms, who bequeathed them to the Gesellschaft der Musikfreunde, but since he only initialled his will instead of signing it, his relatives contested it. The letters later turned up in the catalogue of a dealer in Boston, Mass., and were bought by the Library of Congress. The prehistory of their publication in the *Neue Freie Presse*, including the role Brahms is alleged to have played, will be found in an appendix, 'The Putzmacherin Letters', in NLRW, III, pp. 567ff. In 1967 Ludwig

Kusche published more letters he had found in the Wagner Museum in Eisenach, in *Richard Wagner und die Putzmacherin, oder die Macht der Verleumdung* ('Richard Wagner and the Milliner, or The Power of Calumny'). Kusche appears not to be acquainted with Newman's account. (The siglum KBMG, which Newman uses on p. 569, is omitted from his own key: it refers to Ludwig Karpath's *Begegnung mit dem Genius*, Vienna, 1934.)

7 The speech was taken down in shorthand by Franz Muncker and is to be found in RWGS, XII, pp. 326ff. The editor, Richard Sternfeld, remarks that the rare pleasure of reading an authentic transcript of one of the Meister's longer oral pronouncements surely justified its publication there.

8 The plan is published in full, with the statutes of the Society of Patrons, in RWGS, X, pp. 16ff.

Chapter 31. 'My Farewell to the World'

1 Alfred Lorenz, *Das Geheimnis der Form bei Richard Wagner*, IV: *Der musikalische Aufbau von Richard Wagners 'Parsifal'*, pp. 13ff.

2 Cf. the present author's review in *Die Musikforschung*, 1966 / 2.

3 Podach, *Friedrich Nietzsche und Lou Salomé*, pp. 96ff.

4 Ibid.

5 The text of the three letters to Cosima is given in Appendix III. They were first published in Westernhagen, *Wagner* (1956), pp. 470ff., where they were given both in transcription and in facsimile, reproduced from the originals in the Wagner Archives. Karl Schlechta's edition of Nietzsche's works has a version based on an erroneous oral tradition: 'Ariadne, I love you, Dionysus.' (5th, rev. edn, 1966, III, p. 1350) Cf. also Podach, 'Nietzsches Ariadne', in *Ein Blick in Notizbücher Nietzsches*, pp. 115ff., and Westernhagen, 'Nietzsches Dionysos-Mythos, im Lichte neuer Dokumente', in *Neue Zeitschrift für Musik*, 1958, pp. 419ff.

6 Wagner no doubt took note of the 'Imperial Message' of 17 November 1881 announcing new social measures, but he did not live to see its implementation.

7 Cf. Eugen Stamm, *Ein berühmter Unberühmter. Neue Studien über Constantin Frantz* (Konstanz, 1948).

8 *The genealogy of morals, 3: What is the meaning of ascetic ideals?*

9 The prelude to *Parsifal* is the only composition of Wagner's for which there is a record of the playing-time under his direction. He conducted it twice at one sitting in a private concert for King Ludwig in Munich on 12 November 1880, and Dr Strecker, who was also present, timed both performances at exactly $14\frac{1}{2}$ minutes. (Strecker, *Richard Wagner als Verlagsgefährte*, p. 299)

10 From the text published in facsimile in *High Fidelity*, December 1975: Klaus Liepmann, 'Wagner's proposal to America' (by kind permission of Professor Liepmann).

11 Jenkins had the satisfaction of witnessing such a triumph when he

attended the first performance of *Parsifal* in Bayreuth in 1882. 'I can recall nothing of the close. I do not remember if we applauded or not, for even like those who had the ability to understand the music, I was overwhelmed with the sublime effect of this magnificent drama.' (Dr Newell Sill Jenkins, *Reminiscences*, privately published; communicated to me by Professor Klaus Liepmann and quoted here by kind permission of Dr Jenkins's grandson, the musicologist Newell Jenkins jr.) See also Appendix IV.

12 Bismarck's letter is published in *Bisher ungedruckte Briefe von Richard Wagner an Ernst von Weber* (Dresden, 1883).

13 Cf. H. von Stein, *Gesammelte Dichtungen*, 3 vols. (Leipzig, n.d.), and *Goethe und Schiller* (Leipzig, n.d.); Günter Ralfs, *H. von Stein, Idee und Welt* (Stuttgart, 1940). When I mentioned Stein in my first book, *Wagner* (1956), somebody objected that his name was by now completely unknown in Germany. So far as I know, nobody had anything to comment on what I said. But in 1965 Iwao Takahashi, lecturer in aesthetics at Keio University, Tokyo, wrote to me: 'The "Wagnerian" H. von Stein, who died young and about whom I once published an article in a Japanese periodical, remains my ideal of an aesthetician.'

14 *Goethes Unterhaltungen mit dem Kanzler von Müller*, 5–7 September 1827.

15 Wagner wrote in the visitors' book in the Palazzo Rufolo: 'Klingsor's magic garden has been found! 26 May 1880. RW.'

16 Humperdinck, *Parsifal–Skizzen*.

17 *Halévy and French opera* (1842), RWGS, XII, pp. 131ff., 423.

18 Florimo, *Riccardo Wagner ed i wagneristi* (Ancona, 1883).

19 King Ludwig's gifts, in cash and other forms, to Richard Wagner over the period – little short of nineteen years – from 1 May 1864 to 13 February 1883 amounted to a total of 521,063 marks. Anyone who feels driven to tot up the other side of the account should bear in mind the valuable manuscripts Wagner gave the king, including, for instance, the autograph scores of *Die Feen, Das Liebesverbot, Rienzi, Meistersinger, Rheingold* and *Walküre*. Cf. Otto Strobel, 'Richard Wagner und die Königlich Bayerische Kabinettskasse', *Neue Wagner-Forschungen*, [I] pp. 101ff.

20 Humperdinck, *Parsifal–Skizzen*, pp. 7f.

21 The other version purports to be that told by Lenbach to Heinrich von Poschinger, who published it (only in 1903) in his book *Bausteine zur Bismarckpyramide*.

22 'Cosima Wagner: Lettres à Gobineau', in *La Revue Hebdomadaire* 1938, pp. 263ff., 400ff.; Arthur Gobineau, *Nouvelles Asiatiques*, ed. R. Gérard-Doscot (Paris, 1963).

23 Some of Wagner's letters to Voltz & Batz (though not this one) were listed and selectively quoted for the first time in RWBC, pp. 737ff. Cf. also Strecker, *Richard Wagner als Verlagsgefährte*, pp. 234ff., and GLRW, V and VI, passim.

24 The essay in question was *Know Thyself.* (*Erkenne dich selbst*, RWGS, X, pp. 263ff.)

25 Neumann, *Erinnerungen*, pp. 188f.

26 *Der Kampf zweier Welten um das Bayreuther Erbe. J. Knieses Tagebuchblätter aus dem Jahre 1883* (Leipzig, 1931), pp. 95f.

27 The grounds for this calumny were presumably the numerous letters exchanged between Cosima and Levi while the Wagners were in Naples: cf. DMCW, I, pp. 886–918. In Du Moulin's opinion her letters to Levi were among the most beautiful and expressive she ever wrote, and he adds: 'That may well be because it was there that Levi had bade farewell, for ever in this life, to the woman he had hoped to make his wife.'

28 Bayreuth Festival programme, *Parsifal*, 1959, p. 9.

29 Cf. NLRW, IV, pp. 641ff. Newman's account of the episode is illuminating as a whole.

30 From Judith Gautier, *Richard Wagner et son oeuvre poétique*. Liszt was visiting at the same time and told Princess Wittgenstein that Judith remained in an incessant state of 'heavenly rapture'; Cosima's diary betrays her own jealousy (CT, II, pp. 798f.), but it did not prevent her from writing to Schott's on Wagner's behalf to recommend Judith's translation of *Parsifal* as 'excellent in every respect'. (14 October 1881)

31 To Albert Niemann, 16 December 1881. Wagner wrote the last page of the score in time for 25 December, which he was able to do in consequence of his working out the pagination in advance. (KLRW, III, p. 232, note.)

32 Schott's paid Wagner 100,000 marks for *Parsifal*, the highest fee ever paid by a German music publisher at that date. There is a detailed account of the negotiations in Strecker, *Richard Wagner als Verlagsgefährte*, pp. 308ff.

33 Willi Schuh, *Renoir und Wagner*.

34 Van Gogh, *Briefe an die jüngere Schwester und an die Mutter* (Munich, 1961), pp. 52f.

35 *Bayreuther Festspielführer 1934*, pp. 183ff., with a facsimile.

36 *Graf Arthur Gobineau. Ein Erinnerungsbild aus Wahnfried* (2nd edn, Stuttgart, 1916).

37 Schemann, *Meine Erinnerungen an Richard Wagner*, pp. 14, 22; *Lebensfahrten eines Deutschen*, pp. 110f.

38 'To me he [Wagner] remarked that if he was in the orchestra he wouldn't like to be conducted by a Jew.' (CT, II, p. 983) On the other hand he had earlier told Levi that he had had the idea of getting him baptized, and taking Holy Communion with him.' (CT, II, p. 755) And there is his emphatic statement in the letter to Levi of 1 July 1881: 'In any event – you are my conductor for *Parsifal*!'

39 Taken from the eyewitness account by Houston Chamberlain in *Lebenswege meines Denkens*, pp. 237ff.

40 Ibid., and GLRW, VI, p. 632.

41 Chamberlain, op. cit., and Friedrich Eckstein, *Alte unnennbare Tage* (Vienna, 1936), quoted in MWKS, II, p. 208.

42 Ehrenfels, *Richard Wagner und seine Apostaten,* p. 55.

43 Podach, *Friedrich Nietzsche und Lou Salomé.*

44 A. von Schorn, *Zwei Menschenalter* (Stuttgart, 1920), pp. 342f.

Chapter 32. La lugubre gondola

1 *An einen Opern-Spielleiter* (1927).

2 Cf. GLRW, VI, p. 716; DMCW, II, pp. 67f.

3 Podach, *Ein Blick in Notizbücher Nietzsches,* p. 159 (apropos of a draft of *Nietzsche contra Wagner*); p. 212. The germ of the aphorism lies in a letter to Overbeck of 14 November 1882.

4 Stein, *Gesammelte Dichtungen,* II: *Solon und Krösos.* Wagner, *Brief an H. von Stein,* RWGS, X, pp. 316ff.

5 Cf. Westernhagen, 'Wagners Beziehungen zu . . . Liszt'. 'With Béla Bartók, we hold the view that Liszt hit upon new possibilities without exploiting them.' (English summary, p. 332.)

6 Marie von Bülow, *Hans von Bülows Leben,* 2nd edn (Leipzig, 1921), pp. 389f.

7 Schwebsch, *Anton Bruckner* (Stuttgart, 1923), pp. 299f.

BIBLIOGRAPHY

(See also the Summary Bibliography on pp. viii–ix, which has a key to the abbreviations used in the text, and the bibliography of published correspondence on pp. 615–7. Readers are also referred to *The New Grove Dictionary of Music and Musicians* (London, 1979), which includes a fuller bibliography than is appropriate in a book of this compass.)

Periodicals are listed separately at the end.

Abraham, Gerald, *A hundred years of music*, 4th edn. London, 1974

Adler, Guido, *Richard Wagner. Vorlesungen gehalten an der Universität Wien.* Leipzig, 1904

Adorno, T. W. *Versuch über Wagner*. Frankfurt am Main, 1952

Appia, Adolf, *Die Musik und die Inszenierung*. Munich, 1899

Arnswaldt, W. K. von, *Ahnentafel des Komponisten Richard Wagner*. Leipzig, 1930

Bailey, Robert, 'The genesis of *Tristan* . . . a study of Wagner's sketches and drafts for Act I'. Unpublished dissertation, Princeton University

Barth, Herbert, *Internationale Wagner-Bibliographie*. 2 vols: 1945–55 and 1956–60. Bayreuth, 1956, 1961

Barth, Herbert, Dietrich Mack and Egon Voss, compiled and ed. *Wagner. Sein Leben und seine Welt in zeitgenössischen Bildern und Texten*. Vienna, 1975

 – *Wagner; a documentary study* [translation of the foregoing]. London, 1975

Baudelaire, Charles, 'Richard Wagner et *Tannhaeuser* à Paris', *Revue Européenne*, 1 April 1861. Reprinted in *Oeuvres Complètes*, vol. 2, *L'Art Romantique*, ed. by Jacques Crépet. Paris, 1925

Beeson, Roger, 'The *Tristan* chord and others: harmonic analysis and harmonic explanation', *Soundings*, 5 (1975), p. 55

Bekker, Paul, *Wagner. Das Leben im Werk*. Stuttgart, 1924

 – *Richard Wagner: his life in his work* [translation of the foregoing]. London and Toronto, 1931

Bergfeld, Joachim, *Wagners Werk und unsere Zeit*. Berlin and Wunsiedel, 1963

Blunt, Wilfrid, *The Dream King: Ludwig II of Bavaria*. London, 1970

Bory, R. *Richard Wagner. Sein Leben und sein Werk in Bildern*. Frauenfeld and Leipzig, 1938
  – *La vie et l'oeuvre de Richard Wagner par l'image* [French edn of the foregoing]. Lausanne, 1938

Boulez, Pierre, 'Time re-explored' (German–English–French). *Rheingold* programme, Bayreuth Festival, 1976

Bournot, Otto, *Ludwig Heinrich Christian Geyer, der Stiefvater Richard Wagners*. Leipzig, 1913

Braschowanoff, Georg, *Richard Wagner und die Antike*. Leipzig, 1910

Burrell, Mary, *Richard Wagner: his life and works 1813–34*. London, 1898

Chamberlain, Houston Stewart, *Das Drama Richard Wagners*. Leipzig, 1892
  – *Lebenswege meines Denkens*. Munich, 1919
  – *Richard Wagner*. Munich, 1896 [and later edns]
  – *Richard Wagner* [English translation of the foregoing]. London and Philadelphia, 1897 [and later edns]

Chop, Max, 'Richard Wagner im Spiegel der Kritik seiner Zeit', *Richard-Wagner-Jahrbuch*. Leipzig, 1906

Dahlhaus, Carl, ed. *Das Drama Richard Wagners als musikalisches Kunstwerk*. Studien zur Musikgeschichte des 19. Jahrhunderts, vol. 23. Regensburg, 1970

Dahlhaus, Carl, 'Wagner, Richard: musical works', in *The New Grove Dictionary of Music and Musicians*. London, 1979

Daube, Otto, '*Ich schreibe keine Symphonien mehr'*. *Richard Wagners Lehrjahre*. Cologne, 1960

Deathridge, John, *Wagner's 'Rienzi': a reappraisal based on a study of the sketches and drafts*. Oxford, 1977

Donington, Robert, *Wagner's 'Ring' and its symbols*. 3rd edn. London, 1974

Drews, Arthur, *Der Ideengehalt von Richard Wagners dramatische Dichtungen, nebst einem Anhang Nietzsche und Wagner*. Leipzig, 1931

Du Moulin Eckart, Richard, *Cosima Wagner*, see DMCW, p. viii
  – *Cosima Wagner* [English translation of the foregoing]. 2 vols. New York, 1931

Ehrenfels, Christian von, *Richard Wagner und seine Apostaten*. Vienna and Leipzig, 1913

Einstein, Alfred, *Music in the Romantic era*. New York, 1947
  – *Die Romantik in der Musik* [German edn of the foregoing]. Liechtenstein and Munich, 1950
  – *Von Schütz bis Hindemith*. Zürich and Stuttgart, 1957

Ellis, William Ashton, *Life of Richard Wagner*. 6 vols. London, 1900–8. (The first three volumes are mainly a translation of Glasenapp's biography.)

Engelsmann, Walter, *Erlösung dem Erlöser. Richard Wagners religiöse Weltgestalt*. Leipzig, 1936
  – *Wagners klingendes Universum*. Potsdam, 1933

Faerber, Uwe, *Der Jubiläums-Ring in Bayreuth 1976*. Berlin, 1976 [English edn: Berlin, 1977]

Der Fall Bayreuth, with contributions by S. Skraup, E. Stradler, H. Altmann, W. Abendroth, P. O. Schneider. Munich, 1962

Fehr, Max, *Richard Wagners Schweizer Zeit,* see FWSZ, p. viii

Fricke, Richard, *Bayreuth vor dreißig Jahren. Erinnerungen . . .* Dresden, 1906

Fries, Othmar, *Wagner und die deutsche Romantik.* Zürich, 1952

Fuchs, Eduard and Ernst Kreowski, *Richard Wagner in der Karikatur.* Berlin, 1907

Furtwängler, Wilhelm, *Briefe,* ed. by Frank Thiess. Wiesbaden, 1965
- *Gespräche über Musik.* Zürich, 1949
- *Ton und Wort. Aufsätze und Vorträge, 1918–54.* Wiesbaden, 1954
- *Vermächtnis. Nachgelassene Schriften.* Wiesbaden, 1956

Gautier, Judith, *Richard Wagner et son oeuvre poétique.* Paris, 1882
- *Richard Wagner and his poetical works* [translation of the foregoing]. Boston, 1883

Gautier, Judith, *Le troisième rang du collier.* Paris, 1909

Geck, Martin, *Die Bildnisse Richard Wagners.* Studien zur Kunst des 19. Jahrhunderts, vol. 9. Munich, 1970

Glasenapp, Carl Friedrich, *Das Leben Richard Wagners,* see GLRW, p. viii
- *Wagner-Encyklopädie,* 2 vols., Leipzig, 1891. (Reprint: Hildesheim, New York, 1977)

Glasenapp, C. F. and Heinrich von Stein, *Wagner-Lexikon.* Stuttgart, 1883

Gollancz, Victor, *The 'Ring' at Bayreuth . . .* with an afterword by Wieland Wagner. London and New York, 1960

Golther, Wolfgang, *Richard Wagner als Dichter.* Die Literatur. Berlin, 1904
- *Die sagengeschichtlichen Grundlagen der 'Ring'-Dichtung.* Charlottenburg, 1902

Grand-Carteret, John, *Wagner en caricatures.* Paris, 1891

Gregor-Dellin, Martin, *Wagner-Chronik. Daten zu Leben und Werk.* Munich, 1972

Grimm, Jacob, *Deutsche Mythologie.* 2 vols. Göttingen, 1844. (Reprint, 3 vols. Darmstadt, 1965)
- *Teutonic mythology* [translation of the foregoing by J. S. Stallybrass]. London, 1882

Guichard, Léon, *La musique et les lettres en France au temps du wagnérisme.* Paris, 1963

Gutman, Robert W. *Richard Wagner: the man, his mind and his music.* London, 1968

Halm, August, *Von Grenzen und Ländern der Musik.* Munich, 1916
- *Von zwei Kulturen der Musik.* 3rd edn. Munich, 1947

Hanslick, Eduard, *Musikalische Stationen.* Berlin, 1880
- *Vom Musikalisch-Schönen.* Vienna, 1854
- *The beautiful in music* [translation of the foregoing by G. Cohen]. New York, 1957

Herzfeld, Friedrich, *Königsfreundschaft,* see FHKF, p. viii
- *Minna Planer und ihre Ehe mit Richard Wagner.* Leipzig, 1938

Hey, Julius, *Richard Wagner als Vortragsmeister 1864–76*, ed. by Hans Hey.
  Leipzig, 1911

Holloway, Robin, 'The problems of music drama', *Music and Musicians*
  (April–July 1973)

Hopkinson, Cecil, *'Tannhäuser': an examination of 36 editions*.
  Musikbibliographische Arbeiten, vol. 1. Tutzing, 1973

Humperdinck, Engelbert, *Parsifal-Skizzen. Persönliche Erinnerungen an Richard
  Wagner*. Siegburg, n.d. (Reproduced from ms.)

Indy, Vincent d', *Richard Wagner et son influence sur l'art musical français*. Paris,
  1930

Jacobs, Robert L. *Wagner*. The Master Musicians. London, 1947

Jäckel, Kurt, *Richard Wagner in der französischen Literatur*, vol. 1, *Die Lyrik*; vol.
  2, *Die Prosa*. Breslau, 1931–2. (A projected vol. 3, *Das Drama*, was
  not published.)

Jung, Carl Gustav, *Symbole der Wandlung*. Zürich, 1962, etc.
  – *Symbols of transformation* [translation of the foregoing by R. F. C.
  Hull]. Coll. Edn, vol. 5. London 1956

Jung, Ute, *Die Rezeption der Kunst Richard Wagners in Italien*. Studien zur
  Musikgeschichte des 19. Jahrhunderts, vol. 35. Regensburg,
  1974

Kapp, Julius, *Richard Wagner. Eine Biographie*. Rev. edn. Berlin, 1929
  – *Richard Wagner und die Frauen*, see JKWF, p. viii
  – *The women in Wagner's life* [translation of the foregoing]. London,
  1932

Katz, Adele T. *Challenge to musical tradition*, chapter 6: 'Richard Wagner'. New
  York, 1972

Kietz, Gustav Adolf, *Richard Wagner in den Jahren 1842–9 und 1873–5*.
  Erinnerungen, aufgezeichnet von Marie Kietz. Dresden, 1905

Koch, Max, *Richard Wagner*. 3 vols. Berlin, 1907–19

Kurth, Ernst, *Romantische Harmonik und ihre Krise in Wagners 'Tristan'*. Bern and
  Leipzig, 1920

Lange, Walter, *Richard Wagner und seine Vaterstadt Leipzig*. Leipzig, 1933
  – *Richard Wagners Sippe*. Leipzig, 1938

Leprince, G. *Présence de Wagner*. Paris, 1963

Leroy, Maxime, *Les premiers amis français de Wagner*. Paris, 1925

Liess, Andreas, *Beethoven und Wagner im Pariser Musikleben*. Hamburg, 1939

Lindau, Paul, *Nüchterne Briefe aus Bayreuth*. Breslau, 1876

Lippert, Woldemar, *Richard Wagners Verbannung und Rückkehr*, see LWVR, p.
  viii

Liszt, Franz, *Richard Wagner (Tannhäuser, Lohengrin, Holländer, Rheingold)*.
  Gesammelte Schriften, vol. 3, pt 2. 2nd edn. Leipzig, 1899

Loos, Paul Arthur, *Richard Wagner. Vollendung und Tragik der deutschen
  Romantik*. Munich, 1952

Lorenz, Alfred, *Das Geheimnis der Form bei Richard Wagner*. Vol. 1: *Der
  musikalische Aufbau des Bühnenfestspiels 'Der Ring des Nibelungen'*; vol.
  2: *Der musikalische Aufbau von Richard Wagners 'Tristan und Isolde'*; vol.
  3: *Der musikalische Aufbau von . . . 'Die Meistersinger von Nürnberg'*;

vol. 4: *Der musikalische Aufbau von . . . 'Parsifal'*. Berlin, 1924–33. 2nd edn. Tutzing, 1966

Ludwig, Emil, *Wagner oder die Entzauberten*. Berlin, 1913

Machlin, Paul S. 'Genesis, publication history and revisions of Wagner's *Flying Dutchman*'. Unpublished dissertation, University of California, Berkeley
- 'A sketch for the *Dutchman*', *Musical Times*, 117 (1976), p. 727

Magee, Bryan, *Aspects of Wagner*. London, 1968

Mann, Thomas, *Leiden und Größe Richard Wagners*. Various edns
- *Wagner und unsere Zeit. Aufsätze, Betrachtungen, Briefe*, ed. by Willi Schuh. Frankfurt am Main, 1963

Mayer, Hans, *Richard Wagner in Bayreuth, 1876–1976*. Zürich, Stuttgart and London, 1976. [English and German edns]

Meyerbeer, Giacomo, *Briefwechsel und Tagebücher*, ed. by Heinz Becker. Berlin, 1960–

Meysenbug, Malwida von, *Memoiren einer Idealistin*. 2 vols. 3rd edn. Berlin, 1881. [English translation: New York, 1936]

Millenkovich-Morold, Max, *Cosima Wagner. Ein Lebensbild*, see MMCW, p. viii

Mitchell, William J. 'The *Tristan* prelude: techniques and structure'. *Music Forum*, vol. 1. New York, 1967

Morold, Max, *Wagners Kampf und Sieg*, see MWKS, p. viii

Moser, Max, *Richard Wagner in der englischen Literatur des 19. Jahrhunderts*. Bern, 1938

Neumann, Angelo, *Erinnerungen an Richard Wagner*. 3rd edn. Leipzig, 1907

Newman, Ernest, *The life of Richard Wagner*, see NLRW, p. ix
- *Wagner nights*. London, 1949. [Reprint, London, 1977; American edn: *The Wagner operas*, New York, 1949]

Nietzsche, Friedrich, *Richard Wagner in Bayreuth* (*Unzeitgemäße Betrachtungen*, 4), 1876. *Der Fall Wagner*, 1880. *Nietzsche contra Wagner*, 1901. Various edns
- *Werke*, ed. by Karl Schlechta. 3 vols. 5th, rev. edn. Munich, 1966
- *The Complete Works*, ed. Oscar Levy. New York, 1924

Österlein, Nicolaus, *Katalog einer Wagner-Bibliothek*. 4 vols. Leipzig, 1882–95 [Modern reprint, Wiesbaden and Liechtenstein]

Pfitzner, Hans, *Die Ästhetik der musikalischen Impotenz*. Munich, 1920
- *Werk und Wiedergabe*. In *Gesammelte Schriften*, vol. 3. Augsburg, 1929

Podach, Erich F. *Ein Blick in Notizbücher Nietzsches*. Heidelberg, 1963. (Includes accounts of the writing of *Die Geburt der Tragödie* and the origins of the 'Ariadne' myth.)
- *Friedrich Nietzsche und Lou Salomé. Ihre Begegnung 1882*. Zürich and Leipzig n.d. [1937] (Contains Elisabeth Nietzsche's account of the 1882 Bayreuth Festival.)
- *Friedrich Nietzsches Werke des Zusammenbruchs*. Heidelberg, 1961. (Contains authentic texts of *Nietzsche contra Wagner* and *Ecce homo*.)
- *The madness of Nietzsche*. London, 1931

Porges, Heinrich, *Die Bühnenproben zu den Bayreuther Festspielen des Jahres 1876*. Leipzig, 1896

Pourtalès, Guy de, *Wagner. Histoire d'un artiste*. Paris, 1932

Preetorius, Emil, *Wagner. Bild und Vision*. 3rd edn. Godesberg, 1949

Redlich, H. F. 'Wagnerian elements in pre-Wagnerian operas', in *Essays presented to Egon Wellesz*. Oxford, 1966

Röckl, Sebastian, *Ludwig II. und Richard Wagner*, see SRLW, p. ix

Roeder, Erich, *Felix Draeseke. Der Lebens- und Leidensweg eines deutschen Meisters*. Vol. 1: *Richard Wagner in der Schweiz*. Dresden, n.d. [1931]

Rolland, Romain, *Musicians of today*. New York, 1915

Schemann, Ludwig, *Meine Erinnerungen an Richard Wagner*. Leipzig and Hartenstein, 1924

– *Lebensfahrten eines Deutschen*. Leipzig and Hartenstein, 1925

Schrenck, Erich von, *Richard Wagner als Dichter*. Munich, 1913

Schuh, Willi, *Renoir und Wagner*. Erlenbach–Zürich and Stuttgart, 1959

– 'Renoir und Wagner (neue Folge)', in *Umgang mit Musik*. Zürich, 1970

– *Richard Strauss, Lebenschronik 1864–98*. Zürich, 1976

Schuré, Edouard, *Le drame musical. 2: Richard Wagner. Son oeuvre et son idée*. Paris, 1875

– *Souvenirs sur Richard Wagner*. Paris, 1900

Schweitzer, Albert, *J. S. Bach*, chapter 20: 'Dichterische und malerische Musik'. Various edns. [English translation: New York, 1911]

Shaw, George Bernard, *The Perfect Wagnerite*. Various edns

Silège, H. *Bibliographie wagnérienne française*. Paris, 1902

Sitwell, Sacheverell, *Liszt*. London, 1934

Skelton, Geoffrey, *Wagner at Bayreuth*. London, 1965

Spengler, Oswald, *Der Untergang des Abendlandes*. Vol. 1: *Pergamon und Bayreuth*. Munich, 1923

Staehelin, Martin, 'Wagners Persönlichkeit im Urteil eines Zürcher Freundes, Jakob Sulzer', *Neue Zürcher Zeitung*, 20/21 March 1976

Stein, Herbert, *Dichtung und Musik im Werke Richard Wagners*. Berlin, 1962

Stein, Jack, *Richard Wagner and the synthesis of the arts*. Detroit, 1960

Strauss, Richard, *Betrachtungen und Erinnerungen*. Zürich, 1949

– *Briefe an die Eltern*. Zürich, 1954

– *Briefwechsel mit Joseph Gregor*. Salzburg, 1955

– *Briefwechsel mit Hugo von Hofmannsthal*. 4th edn. Zürich, 1975

– *Briefwechsel mit Willi Schuh*. Zürich, 1969

– ed. *Instrumentationslehre von Hector Berlioz*. Leipzig, 1904

Strecker, Ludwig, *Richard Wagner als Verlagsgefährte*. Mainz, 1951

Strobel, Otto, 'Eingebung und bewußte Arbeit im musikalischen Schaffen Richard Wagners', *Bayreuther Festspielbuch*, 1951

– ' "Geschenke des Himmels": Über die ältesten überlieferten Tristan-Themen', *Bayreuther Festspielführer*, 1938

– *Richard Wagner. Leben und Schaffen. Eine Zeittafel*. Bayreuth, 1952

– *Richard Wagner über sein Schaffen*. Munich, 1924

– ed. *Skizzen und Entwürfe zur 'Ring'-Dichtung*, see SERD, p. ix

- 'Über einen unbekannten Brief Richard Wagners an Mathilde Wesendonk', *Bayreuther Festspielführer*, 1937
- 'Unbekannte Dokumente Richard Wagners', *Die Sonne*, February 1933
- 'Die Urgestalt des *Lohengrin*', *Bayreuther Festspielführer*, 1936
- 'Wagners Prosaentwurf zum *Fliegenden Holländer*', *Bayreuther Blätter*, 1933
- 'Zur Entstehungsgeschichte der *Götterdämmerung*', *Die Musik*, February 1933

Stuckenschmidt, H. H. *Schönberg*. Zürich, 1974

Tappert, Wilhelm, *Richard Wagner im Spiegel der Kritik. Wörterbuch der Unhöflichkeit*. 2nd edn. Leipzig, 1903 [Reprint, Munich, 1967]

Turing, Penelope, *New Bayreuth*. St Martin, Jersey, 1969

Vanselow, A. *Richard Wagners photographische Bildnisse*. Munich, 1908

Vogel, Martin, *Apollinisch und Dionysisch*. Studien zur Musikgeschichte des 19. Jahrhunderts, vol. 6. Regensburg, 1966
- 'Nietzsches Wettkampf mit Wagner', in Salmen, Walter, ed. *Beiträge zur Geschichte der Musikanschauung im 19. Jahrhundert*. Studien zur Musikgeschichte des 19. Jahrhunderts, vol. 1. Regensburg, 1965

Voss, Egon, *Studien zur Instrumentation Richard Wagners*. Studien zur Musikgeschichte des 19. Jahrhunderts, vol. 24. Regensburg, 1970

Wagner, Cosima, *Die Tagebücher*, see CT, p. viii

Wagner, Richard, *Das Braune Buch. Tagebuchaufzeichnungen 1865–82*, ed. by Joachim Bergfeld. Zürich and Freiburg im Breisgau, 1975
- *Mein Leben*, see ML, p. viii
- *My life* [translation of the first edition of the foregoing]. London and New York, 1911
- 'The work and mission of my life', *The North American Review*, 1879
- *Lebensbericht* [back translation of the foregoing]. Hanover, n.d.
- *The Ring of the Nibelung*. A new translation by Andrew Porter. [Parallel German and English texts.] London, 1977

Wagner, Siegfried, *Erinnerungen*. Stuttgart, 1923

Wagner, Wieland, ed. *Richard Wagner und das neue Bayreuth*. Munich, 1962

Wagner, Wolf-Siegfried, *Die Geschichte unserer Familie in Bildern*. Munich, 1976
- *The Wagner Family Albums* [translation of the foregoing]. London, 1976

Wagner-Archiv, Bayreuth, *Katalog der Bibliothek von Richard Wagner in Wahnfried*. [Ms., compiled 1888]

The Wagner companion, ed. by P. Burbidge and R. Sutton. London and New York, 1979.

The Wagner companion, ed. by R. Mander and J. Mitchenson. London, 1977

Wagner 1976: a celebration of the Bayreuth Festival, ed. by Stewart Spencer. The Wagner Society. London, 1976

Warrack, John, *Carl Maria von Weber*. 2nd edn. Cambridge, 1976

Weissheimer, Wendelin, *Erlebnisse mit Richard Wagner, Franz Liszt und vielen anderen Zeitgenossen nebst deren Briefen*. 2nd edn. Stuttgart and Leipzig, 1898

Westernhagen, Curt von, *Die Entstehung des 'Ring'*. Zürich, 1973
- *The forging of the 'Ring'* [translation of the foregoing]. Cambridge, 1976
- *Gespräch um Wagner. Discussion on Wagner. Entretiens sur Wagner.* Bayreuth, 1961
- *Richard Wagner. Sein Werk, sein Wesen, seine Welt.* Zürich, 1956
- 'Richard Wagner und das Ausland' [German–French–English], *Rheingold* programme, Bayreuth Festival, 1972
- *Richard Wagners Dresdener Bibliothek 1842–1849.* Wiesbaden, 1966
- *Vom Holländer zum Parsifal. Neue Wagner-Studien.* Zürich, 1962
- *Wagner.* Zürich, 1968. [First edn of the present work. Italian translation, Milan, 1973; Japanese translation, Tokyo, 1973. Second German edn, Zürich, 1978.]
- 'Wagner, Wilhem Richard', in *Dictionnaire de la Musique*, ed. by Marc Honegger, vol. II, Paris, 1970
- 'Wagner, Richard: biography; literary works', in *The New Grove Dictionary of Music and Musicians.* London, 1979
- 'Wagner, Wilhelm Richard', in *Die Musik in Geschichte und Gegenwart*, vol. 14. Kassel, 1968. [Includes a list of the works, compiled by Gertrud Strobel.]
- 'Wagner, Wilhelm Richard', in *Sohlman's Musiklexikon.* Stockholm, 1977
- 'Wagners Auswanderungsutopie' [German–French–English]. *Götterdämmerung* programme, Bayreuth Festival, 1976
- 'Wagners Beziehungen zu dem Komponisten Liszt' (with English summary 'Wagner's connection with . . . Liszt'), in Bonis, Ferenc, *Magyar Zenetörténeti Tanulmányok.* Budapest, 1973
- 'Wagners Dresdener Studien über unbekannte Quellen von *Tristan und Isolde*' [German–French–English], *Tristan* programme, Bayreuth Festival, 1970
White, Chappell, *An introduction to the life and works of Richard Wagner.* Englewood Cliffs, N.J., 1967
Wille, Eliza, *Fünfzehn Briefe von Richard Wagner mit Erinnerungen und Erläuterungen.* 3rd enl. edn. Munich, Berlin and Leipzig, 1935
Wolzogen, Hans von, *Bayreuth.* Die Musik, ed. by R. Strauss. Berlin, n.d.
- *Erinnerungen an Richard Wagner.* Leipzig, n.d.
- *Musikalisch-dramatische Parallelen.* Leipzig, 1910
Zuckerman, Elliott, *The first hundred years of Wagner's 'Tristan'.* New York and London, 1964

Defunct Periodicals

Bayreuther Blätter, see BBL, p.viii
La Revue Wagnérienne, ed. by Edouard Dujardin. Paris, 1885–8
Richard-Wagner-Jahrbuch, ed. by J. Kürschner. 1 vol. Stuttgart, 1886
The Meister. The quarterly journal of the British Wagner Society, ed. by W. A. Ellis. London, 1888–95
Bayreuth. Handbuch für Festspielbesucher, ed. by F. Wild. Bayreuth, 1894–1930

Bayreuther Festspielführer (various titles). Bayreuth, 1901–39
Richard-Wagner-Jahrbuch, ed. by Ludwig Frankenstein. 5 vols. (Various
    publishers) 1906, 1907, 1908, 1912, 1913
Neue Wagner-Forschungen. Veröffentlichungen der Richard-Wagner-
    Forschungsstätte Bayreuth, ed. by Otto Strobel. 1 vol.
    Karlsruhe, 1943
Das Bayreuther Festspielbuch, published by the administration of the
    Bayreuth festivals. Bayreuth, 1950–1

Current Periodicals
'*Bayreuth*'-*Jahreshefte*, published by the administration of the Bayreuth
    festivals. Bayreuth, 1954–
Programmhefte der Bayreuther Festspiele [Bayreuth Festival programmes].
    Bayreuth, 1953–
Newsletter (untitled) of the Österreichische Richard-Wagner-
    Gesellschaft. Graz
Tribschener Blätter, Zeitschrift der Schweizerischen Richard-Wagner-
    Gesellschaft. Lucerne, 1956–
Bulletin de Cercle National Richard Wagner. Paris
Bulletin de L'Association Européenne pour la Musique Wagnérienne. Paris
Feuilles Wagnériennes, Bulletin d'Information de l'Association
    Wagnérienne de Belgique. Brussels, 1960–
Wagner, The Wagner Society. London, 1971–
Periodical (untitled) of the Wagner Genootschap, Amsterdam, 1961–
Monsalvat. Revista Wagneriana. Barcelona, 1973–

INDEX

Compiled by G. M. Tucker

Note:
pp. ix–xx = preliminary pages of Vol. I; pp. 1–327 = Vol. I; pp. 329–628 = Vol. II.
Wagner's literary and musical works are indexed under their respective titles.

Abt, Franz, 170, 174
Achilleus (Wagner), 127, 139
Aeschylus, 98–9, 110, 274, 412, 423, 505, 560
Agoult, Comtesse Marie d' (Cosima Wagner's mother), 248, 334, 469
Alexander II, Tsar of Russia, 312, 557
Alexander der Große (Wagner), 127
Alexander the Great, 447
America, 164, 212, 256, 344, 470, 486–7, 493, 517–18, 519, 551–3, 556, 598–9, 603
Ander, Alois, 295, 296, 298, 310, 311
Anders, Gottfried Engelbert, 52, 54, 70
Anderson, G. F., 200
Andler, Charles, xiii, 411, 464, 492, 537
Apel, Theodor, 32, 35, 37, 39, 42, 51, 61, 62
Appia, Adolphe, 580
Ariosto, Ludovico, 20
Aristophanes, 100
Art and Revolution (Wagner), 143, 145
Artwork of the Future, The (Wagner), 143, 144–6, 332, 468, 469, 561
Assing, Ludmilla, 214
Auber, Daniel François, 47, 273, 453
Augusta, Princess, of Prussia, 280, 282
Avenarius, Cäcilie, *see* Geyer, Cäcilie

Bach, Johann Sebastian, 4, 29, 38, 317, 319, 355–6, 381, 559; influence on W, 31, 262; works, 31, 237, 262, 544
Bagnara, Duke of, 558–9
Bailey, Robert W., xi, 322
Bakunin, Mikhail, 133, 137

Balzac, Honoré de, 393
Banck, Carl, 83, 155
Barthou, Louis, 322
Baudelaire, Charles Pierre, 111, 273, 275, 290–1, 528
Baumgartner, Wilhelm, 172, 175
Bayreuth, 10, 425, 557, 560, 562, 565; Margraves' Opera House, 423, 433, 447, 459; W's early visits to, 379, 423; W's move to, 443–4, 623; *see also* Wahnfried
– festival, 78, 116, 232, 432, 435–7, 451, 474, 485, 488–98, 503–4, 515–16, 549, 563, 572, 576, 579, 582–4, 591; finance of, 454, 460–4, 480, 485–6, 487–8, 506, 507–8, 511–14, 517–18, 519–24; management committee, 441, 454, 463, 469, 513, 517, 524, 550, 573; theatre, 340, 437, 439, 441, 445, 446–7, 449, 460, 462, 466, 471–3, 506–7, 512, 520–1, 563–4, 576; Wagner Societies and Society of Patrons, 82, 141, 245, 436, 437, 439, 444, 454, 461, 463, 469, 507, 513, 514, 521, 522, 541, 582
Bayreuther Blätter, xii, 160, 522–3, 534, 538, 541, 555, 561–2, 567, 587
Bechstein, Carl, 360, 405
Becker (Justice), 304
Becker, Dr Heinz, 321
Beethoven, Ludwig van, 32, 62, 112, 207, 296, 331, 356, 381, 411, 420, 437, 457, 459, 468, 469, 476, 490, 502, 544, 546, 547, 581, 590; conducted by W, 48, 86–90, 133, 170, 172–3, 203, 204, 241–2, 434, 439, 447, 545;

Beethoven, Ludwig van—*cont.*
  influence on W, 22–6, 28, 31–3, 38, 81,
    173, 174, 180, 189, 262, 265; W's planned
    biography of, 54
  – works, 22, 25, 48, 148, 172, 184, 186, 204,
    262, 419, 427, 478, 486; *Fidelio*, 22–3, 132,
    144, 170, 274, 585; symphonies, 25, 32, 33,
    48, 62, 172–3, 194, 203, 204, 242, 265, 392,
    434, 439, 545, 590, Ninth Symphony, xiii,
    22, 24–6, 53–4, 62, 86–90, 105, 107, 133,
    145, 184, 197, 242, 276, 420, 426, 447–8,
    456, 467, 468, 489, 561, 585
Beethoven (Wagner), 425–6, 427–8, 430, 561
Bekker, Paul, 32
Bellini, Vincenzo, 47, 459, 544, 559; influ-
    ence on W, 39; works, 38–9, 170
Benedictus, Ludwig, 529, 573
Bennigsen, Rudolf von, 539
Bergfeld, Joachim, x, xiv, 350, 618
Berlin, 116, 129, 191, 429, 430; Court Opera,
    68, 70, 73, 141, 204, 282; Königstadt
    theatre, 41, 44; Royal Academy of Arts,
    432, 433, 436; W's visits to, 44, 49, 70,
    119–20, 335, 433–6, 441, 455, 478, 487–8,
    568, 569; W's works performed in, 70, 117,
    118, 119–20, 121, 128, 152, 180, 204–5,
    256, 487–8, 566–9
Berlioz, Hector, 63, 87, 110, 114, 153, 207,
    272, 273, 278, 327; meeting with W, 208;
    on W's works, 274; W on, 62; works, 62,
    274, 288, 532
Berthold (schoolteacher), 139
Bertram, Ernst, 503
Bethmann, Frau Heinrich, 40
Bethmann, Heinrich, 40, 404
Betz, Franz, 414, 472, 480, 497
Beust, Friedrich Ferdinand von, 282
Biebrich, 303–6, 308
Bischoff, Professor, 146
Bismarck, Otto von, 362, 367, 378, 386,
    434–5, 460, 485–6, 538, 540–1, 555, 565,
    568, 572
Bissing, Harriet von, 314–15
Bizet, Georges, 483–4
Blasewitz, 45–6
Bleichröder, Gerson von, 455
Böcklin, Arnold, 472
Boieldieu, François, 47, 170
Boito, Arrigo, 181, 564
Bonfanti, G. A., 492
Bote & Bock (publishers), 191
Bourget, Paul, 96

Bournot, Otto, 8
Brahms, Johannes, 39, 86, 193, 200, 308, 310,
    327, 462, 477, 510, 518, 624
Brandt, Fritz, 580
Brandt, Karl, 414, 473, 497, 580
Breitkopf & Härtel (publishers), 31, 81, 94,
    114–15, 122, 159, 173, 190–1, 209, 220,
    227, 254, 256–7
Brendel, Franz, 146, 264
Brenner, Albert, 508
Brockhaus, Clemens, 440
Brockhaus, Friedrich, 12, 27, 94
Brockhaus, Heinrich, x, 94, 102, 117
Brockhaus, Hermann, 45–6, 94
Brockhaus, Luise, *see* Wagner, Luise
Brockhaus, Ottilie, *see* Wagner, Ottilie
Bruckner, Anton, xiii, 465–8, 594
Brückner, Gotthold, 473
Brückner, Max, 473, 623
Brussels, 277, 486
Bruyck, Karl Debrois von, 77
Buch, Marie von, *see* Schleinitz, Marie von
Bucher, Lothar, 434–5
Bülow, Blandine von, 333, 373, 381, 426,
    569, 572
Bülow, Cosima von, *see* Wagner, Cosima
Bülow, Daniela von, 215, 333, 364, 370, 373,
    381, 426, 477, 506, 508, 568, 571, 572
Bülow, Franziska von, 15, 169–70
Bülow, Hans von, xii, 14–15, 83, 106, 135–6,
    141, 149, 171, 173, 194, 198, 201, 256, 259,
    264, 268, 280, 287, 290, 307, 340, 354, 360,
    411, 415, 451, 516, 583, 593; and Bayreuth,
    493, 572–3, 583–4; and his children, 568,
    572–3; and Ludwig II, 331, 335, 375, 377,
    387, 422–3; as conductor, 169–70, 342,
    343, 389, 397, 410, 420, 545; as husband to
    Cosima, 233, 247, 249, 334, 340, 347, 349,
    352; kapellmeister in Munich, 341, 373,
    377–8, 384, 387, 410; on the Cosima/W
    affair, 373–4, 388, 396, 405–7, 493; on W's
    works, 48, 77, 262, 381; on the Wesen-
    donk affair, 252
Bulwer Lytton, Edward George, 46
Buol-Schauenstein, Karl Graf von, 257–8
Burckhardt, Jacob, 127, 538, 541, 563, 587
Burk, John N. (editor of the Burrell Collec-
    tion), 41, 48, 183, 277
Bürkel, Ludwig von, 548, 550, 586, 593
Burnouf, Eugène, 212, 395, 623
Burrell Collection, ix, 41, 47, 61, 72, 75, 148,
    149, 183, 214, 243, 277, 289

Burrell, Mary, 10, 28, 41, 48, 243
Büsching, Johann Gustav Gottlieb, 35

Calderón de la Barca, Pedro, 239, 413
Capitulation, A (Wagner), 428, 429, 430, 432, 619
Carl Alexander, Grand Duke of Saxe–Weimar–Eisenach, 176–7, 217–18, 250, 257, 263
Carlyle, Thomas, xi, 319
Chabrol de (pseudonym Lorbac), 271
Challemel-Lacour, Paul, 271, 283
Chamberlain, Eva, *see* Wagner, Eva
Chamberlain, Houston Stewart, xvi, 9, 208–9, 270, 293, 501, 581, 582
Champfleury, Jules, 270, 273–4, 297
Charnacé, Claire (half-sister of Cosima Wagner), 405–6
Cherubini, Luigi, xviii, 47, 148, 170, 558
Chopin, Frédéric François, 277
Chorley, Henry, 206
Communication to my Friends, A (Wagner), 43, 104–5, 112, 132, 143, 159, 160
Constantin, Prince Friedrich Ferdinand, of Weimar, 9–10
Cornelius, Carl Maria, 620
Cornelius, Peter (composer), 296, 298, 300, 302, 303, 308, 314, 316, 340, 343, 364, 373–4, 396, 402, 459, 476
Cornelius, Peter (painter), 94, 133, 473, 474
Cossa, Pietro, 511
Crespi, Angelo, 258
Creuzer, Professor Friedrich, 20, 412
Curtis, Mary, 243

Dahlmann, F. C., 95
Dahn, Felix, 462–3
Dangl, Frau, 360–1
Dannreuther, Edward, 29, 319, 518
Dante Alighieri, 20, 207, 242
Daru, Count Pierre Antoine Bruno, 254
Darwin, Charles, 531
Daube, Otto, xi, 24, 28, 30, 31
Davidsohn, George, 567
Davison, J. W., 206
Delacroix, Eugène, 304
Delbrück, Rudolf von, 485
Devrient, Eduard, 135, 140, 231, 232, 257, 272, 321, 325, 326, 407
Devrient, Emil, 340
Dietrich (lover of Minna Wagner), 45, 47, 320

Dietsch, Pierre Louis, 64, 289
Doepler, Karl Emil, 474–5
Dolci, Carlo, 71
Dolgoruki, Prince, 251
Donizetti, Gaetano, 60
Doré, Gustave, 270
Dorn, Heinrich, 28, 49, 50, 433
Draeseke, Felix, 264–5, 325, 396
Dresden, 171, 178; court theatre, 11, 12, 22, 62, 67, 91, 135; Kreuzschule, 19, 21; Liedertafel choral society, 84, 115; revolution in, 15, 130, 137–40, 175, 213, 257; Vaterlandsverein, 122, 130–2; W kapellmeister in, 75, 80–92, 113, 119, 121–2, 150; W's flight from, 94, 118, 123, 139–49; W's friends in, 115; W's library in, xi, 94–5, 103, 117, 133, 136, 145, 219, 233, 235, 320, 326; W's residence in, 11, 18–20, 23–4, 71–4, 94, 97–8, 106, 340, 522, 561; W's visits to, 45, 308, 344, 433; W's works performed in, 14, 67, 70, 73, 78, 116, 178
Drews, Arthur, 136
Droysen, Johann Gustav, 98, 127, 143, 561
Düfflipp, Lorenz von, 382, 387, 394, 414–15, 422, 433, 436, 446, 460, 461–2, 463, 488, 512–14, 515, 516, 519–20, 548, 623
Dumba, N., 426
Du Moulin Eckart, Richard, xii, 493, 596, 622, 627
Duncker, Lina, 213, 223
Duparc, Henri, 426
Duperon, Anquetil, 623
Dürer, Albrecht, 420
Dustmann, Luise, *see* Meyer-Dustmann, Luise
Dwight, John Sullivan, 552
Dysart, Lord, 208

Echter, Michael, 474
Eckermann, Johann Peter, xv, xviii
Eckert, Karl, 329–30
Eckstein, Friedrich, xvii
Eger, Manfred, 327
Eichel, Gottlob Friedrich, 4
Eichelin, Johanna Sophie, *see* Wagner, Johanna Sophie
Einsiedel, Ernst Rudolf von, 41
Einstein, Alfred, 49
Eisenhart (Secretary), 623
Eiser, Otto, x, 501
Elisabeth, Empress of Austria, 296, 309
Ellis, William Ashton, 324

Engels, Friedrich, 133
Enzenberg, Karl Graf, 377
Erard, Mme, 241
Erlanger, Emile, 294, 326
Esser, Heinrich, 276, 295, 298, 380, 485
Ettmüller, Ludwig, 95, 219
Eugénie, Empress of France, 280
Euripides, 107, 423, 504, 505

Fauche, H., 619, 623
Feen, Die (Wagner), 36–8, 42, 43, 76, 453, 585
Fehr, Max, ix, 202, 205
Ferreira-Franca, Ernesto, 232
Ferry, Jules, 271
Fétis, F. J., 267
Feuerbach, Ludwig, 145
Feustel, Friedrich, 439, 441, 453, 454, 460, 461, 482, 485, 506, 511, 517, 518, 523–4, 539, 572, 587, 623
Fischer, Franz, 580
Fischer, Wilhelm, 67, 71, 75, 135
Flaubert, Gustave, 60
Flaxland (publisher), 326
Fliegende Holländer, Der (Wagner), 132, 271; composition of, 63–5; conception of, 51, 59–60; musical language of, 49, 65, 66, 109, 174, 189; performances (projected and actual), 67–8, 70, 73–4, 114, 117, 174, 177, 204, 273, 487; publication of, 114–16, 118, 122–3, 159; revisions of, 65–6; sources, 60
Florence, 148, 511–12, 520
Florimo, Francesco, 559
Forman, Alfred, 602–3
Förster, August, 514, 515–16
Förster, Bernhard, 568
Förster-Nietzsche, Elisabeth, *see* Nietzsche, Elisabeth
Fould, Achille, 280, 286
Fouqué, Friedrich Heinrich Carl, 591
Franck, Dr Hermann, 104, 106, 120
Franco-Prussian War, 426–8, 429–31, 434
Frantz, Constantin, 356, 367, 370, 377, 395, 541
Frauenstädt, Julius, 199, 200
Frederick the Great, 4, 317, 459, 460
Freiligrath, Ferdinand, 214
Fricke, Richard, 481, 489, 498
Friedrich I, Grand Duke of Baden, 232, 257, 295, 304, 325, 326, 462
Friedrich I. (Wagner), 127–8

Friedrich August I, King of Saxony, 84
Friedrich August II, King of Saxony, 72, 75, 84, 86, 91, 121, 129, 132, 137, 176, 204, 258
Friedrich Wilhelm III, King of Prussia, 40
Friedrich Wilhelm IV, King of Prussia, 120–1, 152
Fritzsch, Ernst Wilhelm, 32
Fröbel, Julius, 359, 360–1, 384, 389–90, 394
Frommann, Alwine, 55
Fürstner, Adolf, 78, 123
Furtwängler, Wilhelm, xv, 77, 187, 420

Gade, Niels, 88
Gaillard, Karl, 76, 101, 105, 113
Gangi, Prince, 578
Garibaldi, Giuseppe, 578
Garrigues, C. H. N., 620
Gaspérini, Auguste de, 268–9, 270, 272, 273, 276, 287, 297, 619
Gast, Peter, 484, 491, 502, 534, 591, 593
Gautier (Mendès), Judith, ix, xiii, xvi, xvii, 17, 56, 270, 393, 410, 416–18, 425, 426–7, 442, 444, 448, 498, 506, 517, 527, 528–30, 545, 565, 569, 573–4, 577, 581, 623, 627
Gautier, Théophile, 277, 410, 416, 581
Geck, Martin, xi, xix, 618
Genelli, Bonaventura, 144–5, 411, 433, 459, 473, 538
Georg, Mitalis, 175
Gérard-Doscot, R., 564
Gersdorff, Karl Freiherr von, 338, 441, 444, 455, 456, 461, 484, 491, 499
Gevaert, François Auguste, 273
Geyer, Benjamin, 9
Geyer (Avenarius), Cäcilie (W's half-sister), 7, 11, 13, 18, 71, 270
Geyer, Christian Gottlieb (Ludwig Geyer's father), 6
Geyer, Ludwig Heinrich Christian (W's stepfather), 6–9, 11, 12, 17–18, 19, 67, 459, 469
Gfrörer, August Friedrich, 476
Glasenapp, Carl Friedrich, xi, xii, 121, 278, 369, 423, 488, 508, 512, 555, 565, 570, 573
Gluck, Christoph Willibald, 38, 296; works, 80, 106–7, 121, 204, 454, 481, 559, conducted by W, 80, 106, 204
Gobineau, Comte Joseph Arthur de, ix, xvi, 564, 565–6, 569, 579, 587
Goethe, Johann Wolfgang von, xv, xviii, 4, 7, 9, 10, 20, 69, 95, 98, 138, 199, 224, 254, 279, 304, 323–4, 390, 411, 413, 420, 425,

428, 469, 476, 486, 503, 528, 530, 557, 562, 571, 578; influence on W, 23, 284; works, 5, 106, 140, 320, 343, 468, 470, 539, *Faust*, xv, 90, 243–4, 284, 304, 424, 579, *Tasso*, 237, 255, 260, 271, 324, 506–7, *Wilhelm Meister*, 19, 296, 338, 575, 622

Golther, Wolfgang, 236

Goltz, Professor, 554

Görres, Joseph, 103, 528

Götterdämmerung (Wagner), 19, 421, 427; compared with *Siegfrieds Tod*, 151–2, 162–3, 418; completion of, 468, 470, 475; composition of, 231, 418–19, 424, 425, 426, 437–9, 441–3, 449, 451, 465, 468, 470, 475, 589; motives in, 202, 419, 438, 442; new ending for, xiv, 219, 442–3, 622; orchestration, 458–9, 475, 479; performances, 426, 477–8, 479; readings of, 455–6; sketches for, 442–3, 476, 622

Gottfried von Strassburg, 232

Gounod, Charles, 270, 273, 292

Gozzi, Carlo, 36

Grahn, Lucile, 396

Grässe, J. G. T., 94

Gregor, Joseph, 343

Grein, Edir, 618

Grimm, Jacob, 93–6, 103, 152, 158, 161, 185, 284, 320

Grimm, Wilhelm, 94, 96, 103, 158, 193

Grisi, Ernesta, 416

Gross, Adolf von, 294, 587

Gruben, Baron von, 359

Gutzkow, Karl, 91–2

Habeneck, François Antoine, 51, 53, 87

Hagen, F. H. von der, 94, 233

Hagenbuch, Franz, 142

Haimberger (violinist), 175

Halévy, Jacques Fromental, 60, 71, 558

Hallwachs, Reinhard, 414

Halm, August, 186

Handel, George Frideric, 477

Hanslick, Eduard, 28, 107, 295–6, 301, 308, 402, 426, 484, 489, 519

Härtel, Dr Hermann, 220–1, 227, 240–1, 263

Härtel, Raymund, 114, 220–1, 227, 263

Hartenfels (impresario), 256

Hatzfeld-Wildenburg, Paul Graf von, 280

Hauser, Franz, 38

Haussmann, Georges Eugène, 285

Haydn, Joseph, 530, 532–3

Hebbel, Friedrich, 310

Heckel, Emil, 437, 439, 460–2, 463, 467, 485, 487, 508, 512

Hegel, Georg Wilhelm Friedrich, 145

Heine, Ferdinand, 62, 67, 71, 72, 92, 103, 114, 135–6, 177

Heine, Heinrich, 51, 53, 60, 61, 64, 65

Heinse, Wilhelm, 39

Helene Pavlovna, Grand Duchess, 312, 314, 315, 396

Hellmesberger, Joseph, 478

Helmholtz, Hermann, 478

Herbeck, Johann, 415

Herder, Johann Gottfried von, 99

Hermann, Gustav, 322

Hermann, Paul, 94

Herwegh, Emma, 241, 245, 248, 334

Herwegh, Georg, 163, 165, 179, 180, 197, 198, 334

Herwegh, Marcel, 214

Herzen, Alexander von, 292

Herzen, Olga von, 292

Hettner, Hermann, 214

Heusler, Andreas, 95

Hey, Julius, 472, 481, 483, 487, 489, 523

Hiebendahl (oboist), 115–16

Hillebrand, Karl, 148

Hiller, Ferdinand, 103, 117, 119

Hindemith, Paul, 238

Hochzeit, Die (Wagner), 35–6

Hödel, Max, 538

Hodge & Essex (concert agents), 516–18

Hoffmann, E. T. A., 5, 61, 72, 281; influence on W, 19, 24; works, 10, 19, 29, 70, 215, 477

Hoffmann, Joseph, 473–4, 623

Hofmann, Julius von, 339, 362, 363, 380

Hofmannsthal, Hugo von, 108

Hofmiller, Joseph, 534

Hohe Braut, Die (Wagner), 49, 73, 128

Hohenlohe, Prince Konstantin von, 183

Hohenlohe-Schillingsfürst, Prince Chlodwig, 361–2, 379–80, 384, 385–7, 389–90, 620

Hohenzollern-Hechingen, Prince of, 313

Holtei, Karl von, 46, 50

Holtzmann, Adolf, 207

Homer, 20, 211, 407, 413, 424, 473

Hornstein, Robert von, 198, 199

Hugo, Victor, 96, 348, 431–2, 528, 558, 619

Hülsen, Botho von, 141, 204–5, 256, 434, 487–8, 567

Hülsen, Helene von, 487

Humboldt, Wilhelm von, 98, 254
Hummel, Johann Nepomuk, 25, 27
Humperdinck, Engelbert, 82, 289, 557–8, 559–60, 562, 580, 590
Hürlimann, Dr Martin, 319
Hurn, Philip Dutton, 243

Jachmann, Alfred, 517
Jahn, Otto, 81, 191, 221
Janin, Jules, 271, 291
Jannequin, Clément, 559
Jauner, Franz, 482–3, 484, 515, 519, 549
Jenkins, Dr Newell Sill, x, 551–3, 602–3, 625–6
Jesus von Nazareth (Wagner), 136–7, 145
Jewry in Music (Wagner), 153, 407
Joachim, Joseph, 308, 433
Johann, King of Saxony, 217–18, 264, 282
Joly, Anténor, 52
Joly, René, 426
Joukowsky, *see* Zhukovsky
Junge Siegfried, Der (Wagner), 46, 158, 161, 163

Käfferlein (Bayreuth lawyer), 441
Kalergis (Muchanoff), Marie, 277–8, 406, 407, 476
Kant, Immanuel, 390
Kapitulation, Eine (Wagner), see *Capitulation, A*
Kapp, Julius, 90, 243, 271, 277, 291, 325, 373–4, 488, 620
Karl, Prince of Bavaria, 363
Karl August, Grand Duke of Saxony, 9–10
Kaulbach, Wilhelm von, 391
Keller, Gottfried, 172, 175, 213–15, 223, 241, 280
Kempen von Fichtenstamm, Johann, 257–8
Keudell, Robert von, 510
Kietz, Ernst Benedikt, 52, 70, 71, 73, 74, 105, 113, 116, 150, 156, 163, 176, 178, 294
Kietz, Gustav Adolf, 105–6, 133, 135–6, 467, 469, 480
Kittl, Johann, 128, 322
Kleist, Heinrich von, 199
Klemm, Gustav, 79
Klepperbein, Wilhelmine, 394
Klindworth, Georg Heinrich, 277, 281, 359–60
Klindworth, Karl, 149, 189, 208, 209, 222, 227, 247–8, 256, 271, 278, 326, 407, 572
Knebel, Karl von, 9

Kniese, Julius, 570–1
Köhler, Louis, 189
Königsberg, 13, 44, 47
Köppen, C. F., 255
Kossak, Ernst, 128, 199
Kranz, Walter, 98
Krausse, Robert, 469
Kriele, Hans,. 115–16
Krug, Gustav, 441
Kummer, Friedrich August, 87
Kurth, Ernst, 186–7, 237
Kurtz, Hermann, 233
Kusche, Ludwig, 624–5
Küstner, Theodor, 67, 70, 120

Lachmann, Karl, 103
Lachner, Ignaz, 542
Lalas, Demetrius, 471
Lamprecht, Pfaffe, 128
Lanckoronski, Count, 296
Langlois, Alexandre, 459
Lascoux, M., 577
Lassen, Eduard, 415
Laube, Heinrich, 36, 39, 52–3, 54, 296, 402
Laussot, Eugène, 147–8, 149
Laussot, Jessie (Taylor), 147–50, 222, 381, 396, 512
Lecky, William Edward Hartpole, 545
Lehrs, Samuel, 52, 70, 71, 75, 80, 93, 97, 99, 153
Leipzig, 117; Battle of, 6; Euterpe Society, 33; Gewandhaus, 6, 33, 53, 77, 307; Nikolaischule, 27, 144; theatre, 22, 28, 33, 37, 402, 514; Thomaskirche, 4, 6, 29; Thomasschule, 4, 27; University of, 4, 7, 27–8, 29; W born in, 5–6; W's residence in, 20, 27, 35; W's visits to, 102, 307–8, 406, 410, 433, 436, 452; W's works performed in, 515, 519, 547–8
Lenbach, Franz von, 453, 472–3, 476, 550, 565, 626
Leo, Leonardo, 559
Leonardo da Vinci, 259
Leopold, Prince (son of Queen Victoria), 517
Leprince, G., xi, 428
Leroy, Adolphe, 270
Leroy, Léon, 268, 270
Leroy, Maxime, 268, 283
Lessing, Gotthold Ephraim, 5
Leubald (Wagner), 21, 28
Levetzow, Ulrike von, 304, 530

Levi, Hermann, 415, 423, 550, 565, 570–2, 580, 584, 591, 627
Lewald, August, 50
Liebesverbot, Das (Wagner), 40, 42–3, 50, 52, 76, 102; performances, 12–13, 42, 43–4, 272, 453
Lindau, Paul, 326
Lindau, Rudolf, 281, 326
Lipinski, Karl, 81
Lippert, Woldemar, 258
Liszt (Ollivier), Blandine, 240, 271, 278, 298
Liszt, Eduard, 315, 327
Liszt, Franz, 73, 109, 122, 141, 142, 146, 147, 148, 152, 153, 156, 158, 160, 164, 175, 176, 185, 189, 191, 194, 200, 217, 227, 250, 257, 264, 267, 277, 343, 354, 356, 385, 438, 469, 547, 627; and his daughter Cosima, 334, 335–6, 350, 354–5, 405–6, 450–1, 475, 590; as conductor of W's works, 151, 154–5, 204; friendship with W, 178, 198, 216, 220, 231, 241, 248, 259, 278–9, 297, 442, 445–6, 496, 581; meetings with W, 140, 178–9, 183–4, 221, 222–4, 336, 391–2, 450–1, 460, 477–8, 496, 562, 581, 588–91; on the Cosima/W affair, 336, 355, 374, 391, 418, 568; on W's works, 104–5, 111, 267, 589; W on the music of, 225, 465, 477; works, 148, 207, 222, 225, 261, 322, 347, 373, 465, 477, 592
Lobe, J. C., 155
Logier, Johann Bernhard, 28
Lohengrin (Wagner), 66, 267, 340, 464, 467, 473, 488; alternative endings for, 104–5; as romantic opera, 111–12; composition of, 98, 102, 105–6, 107, 113, 127, 129, 533; influences on, 86, 107; Ludwig II and, 109, 329, 331–2, 333, 565; motives in, 108–9; musical language of, 55, 108–11; orchestration in, 110–11; performances (projected and actual), 103, 120, 135, 151, 154–6, 159, 177, 191, 256, 271, 272, 273, 277, 295, 311, 332, 374, 389, 402, 434, 439, 482–3, 484, 558, 576; publications of, 122, 190, 485; sources, 93, 101–3; text, 107–8, 119, 271; W's first hearing of, 177, 295
London, 140, 149, 514, 567; W in, 87, 114, 206–10, 516–18, 520, 528, 551, 572
Lorenz, Alfred, 109, 186, 201, 259, 380, 383, 547
Louis Napoleon, Prince, *see* Napoleon III
Louis Philippe, King, 129
Lucas, C. T. L., 70, 103

Lucca, Giovanna, 402, 404, 496, 558, 586
Lucerne, 154, 260–6, 413; *see also* Tribschen
Lüders, Karl, 208, 517
Ludwig I, King of Bavaria, 358
Ludwig II, King of Bavaria, xi, 63, 139, 227, 316, 353, 370–1, 469; and Bayreuth, 436, 438, 446, 460, 461–3, 470, 488, 494–5, 496–7, 507–8, 511, 513–14, 519–20, 523–4, 553–4, 584; and the Bülow/W scandal, 374, 377–8, 382, 388, 402, 405–6, 422–3; and his ministers, 340–1, 345–6, 358–9, 380; and W's banishment from Munich, 363–4, 366, 370, 385–6; artistic plans, 339, 345, 384–5, 387, 389–91, 394–5, 438, 460; as W's patron, 332, 339, 346, 365–6, 371, 463, 470, 471, 477, 488, 524, 550, 561, 596, 626; engagement to Princess Sophie, 330, 385; first meeting with W, 119, 330, 332; intrigues concerning, 341, 359–63, 366, 385–6; performances ordered by, 409–10, 414–17, 422–3, 425, 433, 520, 548, 565, 586, 625; plans to abdicate, 374–6, 379, 386; relationship with W, 330–2, 341, 358, 363, 366, 389, 394, 397, 421–2, 427, 519, 593; W's works dedicated to, 43, 397–8, 459; W's works owned by, 438, 446, 515, 549–50, 618, 626; W's works written for, 338, 354, 356, 357–8, 496, 519, 541
Luther, Martin, 9, 317, 340, 579, 622
Luthers Hochzeit (Wagner), 403, 542
Lüttichau, Ida von, 104, 140
Lüttichau, Wolf Adolf August von, 67, 73, 74, 85, 87, 91–2, 118, 120–2, 131, 135, 258
Lutz, Johann von, 346, 361–2, 363, 365, 376

Mack, Dietrich, 622
Magdeburg, 12–13, 40, 43, 51, 67, 113, 452–3, 459
Magnan, Bernard Pierre, Marshal of France, 273
Maier, Mathilde, xvii, 304, 305, 308, 310, 311–13, 315, 333, 350, 361, 380, 396, 497, 504, 518, 624
Mainz, 294, 301, 302, 304, 315, 452, 566
Makart, Hans, 473, 478
Mallarmé, Stéphane, 283
Mann, Thomas, 111, 112, 164, 193, 214, 236, 324, 503, 585
Mannheim, 82, 437, 439, 452, 549
Marbach, Dr Oswald, 13
Maria Pavlovna, Grand Duchess of Saxony, 140

Marienbad, 102, 295, 299–300
Marschner, Heinrich August, 39, 66
Martini, Giovanni Battista, 29
Marx, Karl, 133
Massmann, H. F., 233
Materna, Amalie, 482, 498, 580
Maurin-Chevillard Quartet, 184
Mauro, Seraphine, 298, 302
Maximilian, Archduke, 258
Maximilian II, King of Bavaria, 316, 332
Maximilian, Prince of Thurn und Taxis, 359–60
Méhul, Etienne, 47, 170, 558
Mein Leben (Wagner), xv, 8, 9, 41, 47, 51, 85, 93, 94, 121, 137, 147, 153, 327, 335, 492; dictation of, 137–8, 232, 242, 357–8, 370, 379, 381, 407; written for Ludwig II, 138, 242, 357–8, 563
Meistersinger von Nürnberg, Die (Wagner), 409, 489, 515, 562; completion of, 66, 393; composition of, 299–302, 304–6, 313, 318, 329, 365, 367–8, 369–70, 374, 377, 379, 380–3, 386, 389, 392, 527, 533; conception of, 102, 294, 299; ending of, 383–4; influences on, 30, 255, 561; musical language of, 110, 231, 297; orchestration in, 308, 392–3; performances (projected and actual), 307, 309, 338, 391, 395, 396–8, 401, 402, 439, 465, 488; readings of, 301, 302–3, 304, 308, 312; rehearsals, 395–7, 401; sketches for, 305, 380, 382, 384
Mendelssohn-Bartholdy, Felix, 77, 120, 206, 477, 557
Mendès, Catulle, xii, 270, 393, 416–17, 427, 430–2, 529, 623
Mendès, Judith, *see* Gautier, Judith
Menzel, Adolf, 478, 480
Meser, C. F., 115–17, 123
Metternich-Sándor, Princess Pauline, 280–1, 286, 291, 296, 300–1
Meyendorff, Baroness, 446
Meyer, Friederike, 308
Meyerbeer, Giacomo, 36, 47, 52, 63–4, 67–8, 117–18, 121, 273, 280, 291, 321, 322, 330, 369, 453; influence on W, 48, 55; meetings with W, 51, 119–20, 208; W on, 50, 152–4, 281; works, 73, 147, 153, 154
Meyer-Dustmann, Luise, 82, 296, 301, 308
Meysenbug, Malwida von, 61, 208, 270, 271, 286, 290, 291–2, 301, 342, 454, 461, 508, 554, 556, 560, 583
Michaelson (agent), 191

Michelangelo Buonarotti, 511, 520, 566
Milan, 259, 404
Millenkovich-Morold, Max, 374, 388
Mitterwurzer, Anton, 89
Moltke, Helmut Graf von, 455
Mottl, Felix, 484, 489, 624
Mozart, Wolfgang Amadeus, 30, 38, 62, 107, 191, 199, 296, 453, 544; conducted by W, 47, 80, 82, 171, 203–4, 439; influence on W, 31, 81–3; works, 82, 203–4, 213, 237, 530, 531, 532, *Don Giovanni*, 40, 41, 80, 82–3, 171, 213, 329, *Le Nozze di Figaro*, 82–3, 559, *Die Zauberflöte*, 82, 171, 439, 472, 473, 532, 560
Muchanoff, Marie, *see* Kalergis, Marie
Müller, Alexander, 142
Müller, Christian Gottlieb, 29
Müller, Franz, 155, 219
Müller, Karl Otfried, 143, 412
Muncker, Theodor, 441, 454, 456, 474, 550, 581, 625
Munich, 177, 557, 573; court opera, 67, 116, 256, 300, 401–2, 512, 513–14, 515, 519–20, 523–4, 549, 553, 586; W's residence in, 263, 329–64 *passim*, 522; W's visits to, 144, 316, 386, 389, 393, 395, 406, 415, 462, 512, 519, 550, 564–5; W's works performed in, xiii, 38, 66, 341–3, 391, 396–8, 414–17, 422–3, 426, 465, 473, 474, 515, 548, 564
Music of the Future (Wagner), 283, 332

Naples, 550–62, 563, 574, 575, 626
Napoleon Bonaparte, 4, 6
Napoleon III, Emperor, 162, 272, 280–1, 286, 386
Nerval, Gérard de, 155
Neue Zeitschrift für Musik, 107, 146, 153, 155, 173, 225
Neumann, Angelo, 484, 516, 547–8, 566–8, 569, 576
Neumann, Erich, 621
Newman, Ernest, ix, x, 7, 9–10, 20, 31, 47, 50, 52, 77, 91, 107, 113, 115, 123, 133, 155, 179, 191, 236, 238, 245, 276, 308, 324, 331, 336, 362, 373–4, 396, 450, 461, 477, 491, 492, 499, 500–5, 509, 555, 565, 571, 572, 583, 618, 620, 625
Niemann, Albert, 55, 247, 286, 287, 289, 292, 298, 481–2, 487, 497, 627
Nietzsche, Elisabeth (sister of Friedrich), x, . 410–11, 432–3, 457, 477, 479, 491, 500,

501–2, 509–10, 534, 536, 537–8, 568, 583, 587, 622

Nietzsche, Friedrich, ix, x, xvi, 28, 99, 427, 562, 591, 593; alienation from W, 368, 464–5, 477, 494, 508–9, 534–5, 537–8, 556–7, 583; and the Bayreuth festival, 425, 461, 491, 499–505, 513; friendship with W, 423–4, 433, 440–1, 449–50, 454–5, 456–7, 459, 479–80, 491–2; illness, 428, 499–502, 508; influenced by W, 412, 433, 440, 622; on W's works, 96, 259, 338, 421, 439–40, 451, 538, 542; visits to W, xiii, 410–11, 421, 424, 432, 444, 456–7; works, 423–4, 432–3, 440, 446–7, 454, 457–8, 461, 465, 476, 491–2, 500, 503, 510, 587, *The Birth of Tragedy*, 411–12, 440, *Human all too Human*, 500, 533–8, 541, 555, *The Wagner Case*, 8, 464, 484, 508, 557

Nimier, Roger, 566
Nobiling, Karl, 539
Nordmann, Johannes, 100
Nottebohm, Gustav, xiii
Novalis (pseudonym of Friedrich von Hardenberg), 235

Oehme (brassfounder), 138
Offenbach, Jacques, 429
Oldenberg, Hermann, 588
Ollivier, Blandine, *see* Liszt, Blandine
Ollivier, Emile, 240, 271, 281–2, 298, 426
Opera and Drama (Wagner), 143, 153–4, 156–7, 173, 332, 395, 432, 452, 561
Ott, Louise, 503
Ott-Imhof, Konrad, 178
Overbeck, Franz, 464, 534, 587, 622
Overbeck, Frau Ida, x, 583
Overbeck, Johann Friedrich, 473

Pachta, Jenny, 32–3
Palermo, 575–8
Paris, 49, 140, 577, 590; Conservatoire orchestra, 53, 87, 172, 184, 420; Grand Opéra, 51, 52, 62, 64, 272, 276, 281; Jockey Club, 283, 290–1; Opéra Comique, 50; revolution in, 128–9, 132, 163; Théâtre de la Renaissance, 52, 272; Théâtre Italien, 272–3, 275; W's friends in, 52–3, 59–60, 62, 70, 282, 292–3; W's residence in, 51–4, 60–70 *passim*, 121, 129; W's visits to, 143, 147, 149, 184, 238, 240–1, 267–94 *passim*, 296–7, 301–2, 393, 551; W's works performed in, 290–2, 416, 576

Parsifal (Wagner), xvii, 16, 18, 324, 338, 421 468, 509, 538, 556, 562, 627; as W's last work, 354, 563, 585–6; composition of, xii, 403, 468, 470, 484, 486, 514, 524, 527–30, 531–3, 541–7, 548, 562–3, 568, 569–70, 573, 575–7, 589; designs for the staging of, 557, 563–4, 574, 580; earliest conceptions of, 216, 226–7, 254–5, 262, 279, 355, 451; musical language of, 84–5, 288, 527, 542, 546–7, 585; orchestration in, 16, 544–5, 565, 575–6; performances (projected and actual), x, xvi, 545, 549–50, 552, 559–60, 564, 570, 572, 578, 582–4, 586, 625, 626; prose scenario, xiv, 139, 354, 421, 509; readings of, 523; rehearsals, xvi, 580; restricted to Bayreuth, 553–4; sources, 102, 476, 482; text, 519, 528–9, 533, 576, 627

Pasdeloup, Jules Etienne, 402
Patersi, Madame, 184
Pätz, Johanna, *see* Wagner, Johanna
Paul, Prince, of Thurn und Taxis, 360, 380
Pecht, Friedrich, xi, 52–3, 59, 304, 341
Pedro II, Dom, Emperor of Brazil, 232
Perfall, Karl von, 373, 396, 401–2, 414, 415–16, 520, 524, 548
Perrin, Emile, 271
Pestalozzi, Salomon, 203
Petipa, 285
Petrarch, 20
Pfister (Police Assessor), 359
Pfistermeister, Franz Seraph von, 329, 341, 345–6, 359–62, 363, 366, 375, 376, 380, 384, 415, 421, 618
Pfitzner, Hans, 77, 108, 259
Pfordten, Ludwig von der, 340, 362, 366, 370, 378, 384
Pilgrimage to Beethoven, A (Wagner), 26, 54
Pillet, Léon, 64
Planer, Amalie, 46–7, 49
Planer, Minna, *see* Wagner, Minna
Planer, Natalie, 41, 61, 144, 243, 303, 369
Plato, 100, 331, 424
Pleyel, Ignaz Joseph, 31
Plüddemann, Martin, 521, 559–60
Plutarch, 279, 594
Podach, Erich F., x, 502, 503, 537, 583, 587
Pohl, Richard, 84, 238, 391, 493
Pollini, Bernhard, 514
Porges, Heinrich, 109–10, 111, 246, 296, 308, 315, 323, 340, 364, 390, 416, 479, 489–91, 580, 624

Porter, Andrew, 624
Poschinger, Heinrich von, 626
Pourtalès, Albert, Count, 280
Pourtalès, Countess, 297
Pourtalès, Guy de, 274
Praeger, Ferdinand, 208–9
Prague, 19, 33, 128, 137, 311, 313
Preen, Friedrich von, 541
Preller, Friedrich, 473
Prévost, Jean, 565
Proudhon, Pierre Joseph, 143, 163
Puschmann, Theodor, 450
Pusinelli, Anton, 115–16, 117, 118, 122–3,
    217, 252, 269–70, 307, 342, 368, 433, 497

Raabe, Peter, 467
Rackowitz, Baron Joachim, 312
Raff, Joachim, 384
Rahl, Carl, 473
Raumer, Friedrich, 69
Redern, Wilhelm von, 68, 70, 119
Redwitz, Oskar von, 341
Rée, Paul, 508, 587
Reissiger, Gottlieb, 67, 73, 86, 121, 128, 129,
    198, 321
Renoir, Auguste, 577–8
Reutter, Isidore von, 381
Reyer, Ernest, 271, 273
Rhaden, Editha von, 312, 314, 315, 396
Rheingold, Das (Wagner), 193, 202, 239, 419,
    515, 618; composition of, 181–2, 184–90,
    266, 542; conception of, 180, 183; form in,
    186, 188, 225; musical language of, 55,
    109, 187–8, 265; musico-poetic synthesis
    in, 185–6, 188–9; performances, xiii, 232,
    248, 271, 309, 409–10, 414–17, 422, 473,
    474; publications of, 276, 402; scoring of,
    189–90, 221; sketches for, 159, 161, 163,
    184–7
Richter, Hans, 277, 391–2, 427, 429, 471,
    474, 485, 489, 515, 517; as a conductor of
    W's works, 414–15, 480, 497
Richter, Jean Paul Friedrich, 10, 317
Ricordi, Giulio, 593–4
Riehl, W. H., 439
Riemann, Pastor, 356
Rienzi (Wagner), 71, 115, 132, 294, 515;
    composition of, 46, 48–9, 51, 54, 60, 67;
    influence of grand opera on, 48–9, 55; in
    relation to later works, 55; performances
    (projected and actual), 14, 55–6, 67, 70, 73,
    113, 114, 119–20, 121, 128, 152, 177, 204,

256, 416, 512; publication of, 116, 122–3;
    rehearsals, 72–3; sources, 46
Rietz, Julius, 191
Riga, 13, 45, 60, 178, 522; theatre in, 46; W's
    flight from, 51
Ring des Nibelungen, Der (Wagner), 149–50,
    157, 223, 417, 426, 430, 488, 561, 565; and
    Schopenhauer, 197, 199–200; composi-
    tion of, 66, 172, 218, 227, 263, 339, 346,
    368; conception of, 98–9, 123, 128, 134,
    150; designs for the staging of, 470, 472–5;
    leitmotiv in, 169, 174; musical realization
    of, 74, 136, 169, 176–7, 179; performances
    (projected and actual), 177, 179, 338, 339,
    423, 425, 437, 438, 462–4, 495–8, 514–15,
    516, 520, 547–9, 566–9; publication of,
    220–1, 257, 263–4; readings of, 165, 176,
    179, 214, 312; rehearsals, 190, 195, 471–2,
    475, 480–2, 489–91, 492–4, 499–500, 502,
    503; sources, 93–7; text, 94, 160–5, 199,
    214, 235, 310–11, 332, 602–3; see also Göt-
    terdämmerung, Junge Siegfried, Rheingold,
    Siegfried, Siegfrieds Tod, Walküre
Ritter, Alexander, 287, 290
Ritter, Julie, 147–8, 150, 160, 164, 169, 176,
    190, 194, 205, 211, 222, 223–4, 226
Ritter, Karl, 135–6, 147, 149–50, 155,
    169–71, 198, 199, 200, 217, 223, 247,
    248–9, 251, 578–9
Roche, Edmond, 269, 281, 292
Röckel, August, 129, 132–2, 137, 138, 145,
    188, 198, 378, 386, 387, 402
Röckel, Eduard, 208
Rohde, Erwin, 410, 411, 412, 424–5, 427,
    432, 439, 441, 456, 458, 464, 491, 499, 622
Rollett, Hermann, 194
Rome, 510–11, 520, 558, 583, 597
Root, Waverly Lewis, 243
Rossini, Gioacchino, 42, 47, 181, 199, 275
Royer, Alphons, 281, 286, 289
Rubinstein, Joseph, 443–4, 471, 481, 484,
    544, 560, 571, 575, 577, 595–7, 603

Saburoff, General (director of St Petersburg
    theatre), 285
Sainton, Prosper, 208, 517
Saint-Saëns, Camille, 415, 426
St Petersburg, 285, 294, 311, 314, 396
Salis-Schwabe, Julie, 342
Salomé, Lou von, 583, 587
Samuel, Lehmann, 175
Sanctis, Francesco de, 242, 243

San Marte (pseudonym of A. Schulz), 103
Sarazenin, Die (Wagner), 69–70
Sardou, Victorien, 281
Sayn-Wittgenstein, Caroline, Princess, *see* Wittgenstein, Caroline
Sayn-Wittgenstein, Princess Marie, *see* Wittgenstein, Princess Marie
Schack, Adolf Friedrich von, 144
Schanzenbach, Dr Oscar, 361, 385–6
Schanzer (von Bülow), Marie, 583, 593
Scharf, Anton, 473
Schauss, Friedrich von, 342–3, 395
Schade, John H., 189
Schelle, Eduard, 426
Schelling, Friedrich Wilhelm, 145
Schemann, Ludwig, xviii, xx, 495, 500–1, 504, 523, 540, 579
Scheuerlin, Georg, 49
Schiller, Johann Christoph Friedrich von, 69, 224, 254, 323, 332, 343, 361, 363, 390, 411, 425, 469, 476, 490, 556, 562; influence on W, 23, 279; works, 5, 7, 33, 160, 279, 413
Schirmer, Gustav, 598
Schladebuch, Julius, 155
Schlechta, Karl, 502, 625
Schleinitz, Alexander, Count, 455
Schleinitz, Marie (von Buch), Countess, 335, 433, 434, 436, 462, 482, 487, 536, 568
Schlesinger, Maurice, 60–1, 71
Schletter, Heinrich, 117
Schmitt, Friedrich, 340
Schnappauf, Bernhard, 528
Schnorr von Carolsfeld, Julius, 474
Schnorr von Carolsfeld, Ludwig, 343, 344–5, 347, 381, 438
Schnorr von Carolsfeld, Malvina, 343, 381–2, 620
Schobinger (student), 426
Schoenberg, Arnold, 325
Schön, Friedrich, 579
Schönaich, Gustav, 296, 315, 316
Schopenhauer, Arthur, xv, 304, 343, 384, 438, 476, 480, 513, 557, 597, 623; influence on W, 105, 162, 197–201, 211–12, 231, 236, 254, 269, 279–80, 367; views on W, 198–9; works, 148, 162, 196, 197, 200, 426
Schorn, Adelheid von, 583
Schott, Betty, 26, 301, 304
Schott, Franz, 24–6, 27, 276, 298, 300, 301, 304, 306–7, 401, 416, 422, 425, 468, 471, 476, 566

Schott's Söhne (publishers), 276, 392, 396, 487, 510, 586, 627
Schrenk, Erich von, 234
Schröder-Devrient, Wilhelmine, 22–3, 38, 67, 69, 72–4, 100, 113, 115, 118, 144, 155, 321, 420, 436, 580, 585
Schrön, Otto von, 551
Schubert, Franz, 592
Schuh, Willi, xi
Schumann, Clara (Wieck), 28, 33, 34
Schumann, Robert, 33, 51, 77, 120, 199, 477
Schuré, Edouard, 344, 365, 494, 501, 502–3, 509
Schwebsch, Erich, 594
Schwind, Moritz von, 618
Scott, Walter, 220
Scribe, Eugène, 49–50, 73
Seebach, Albin Leo von, 282
Seelisberg, 211
Seidl, Anton, 471, 533, 545, 567
Semper, Gottfried, 135, 213–14, 242, 339, 340–1, 355, 384, 390, 394–5, 478
Sgambati, Giovanni, 510–11
Shakespeare, William, 413, 456, 490; influence on W, 21, 22, 23, 28; works, 21, 40, 48
Shaw, George Bernard, 133
Sieger, Die (Wagner), xiv, 218–19, 224, 255, 338, 354, 395–6, 409, 588
Siegfried (Wagner), 15–16, 17, 139, 219, 220, 340, 411, 419, 446, 464; completion of, 414, 425, 430; composition of, xiv, 221–2, 224, 225, 227–8, 232, 266, 337, 347, 349–50, 363–4, 365, 407–9, 412–13, 418; form in, 413; motives in, 237, 407, 409, 413–14; musical language of, 225, 409, 413–14, 474; performances, 426, 433, 477; resumption of, 263, 269, 272, 339, 407; sketches for, 337; see also *Junge Siegfried*
Siegfried Idyll (Wagner), 336, 429, 430, 439, 441, 476, 545
Siegfrieds Tod (Wagner), 150, 151, 156, 158, 219, 220; readings of, 135, 136, 143, 148, 184, 481; sketches for, xi, 151–2, 157, 169, 188, 322; text, 135, 161–3
Siena, 82, 562–3
Sillig, Julius, 20, 97
Simmerl (advocate), 394
Simrock, Karl, 103
Singer, Otto, 24
Sismondi, Simonde de, 507, 511
Smart, Henry, 206

Sophie Charlotte, Duchess in Bavaria, 330, 385

Sophocles, 20, 504, 505

Sorrento, 506–10, 513

Speidel, 484

Spengler, Oswald, 96, 321

Spitzer, Daniel, 519

Spohr, Louis, 39

Spontini, Gasparo, 483; influence on W, 48–9, 55, 86; works, 49, 85–6, 172, 559

Srbik, Heinrich Ritter von, 541

Stahr, Adolf, 104, 155

Standhartner, Josef, 296, 298, 299, 305, 308, 313, 315, 513

Stein, Heinrich von, xviii, 181, 556–7, 583, 588, 589, 626

Stendhal (pseudonym of Marie Henri Beyle), 566

Stern, Professor Adolf, 461

Sternfeld, Richard, 50, 90, 154, 271, 325, 615

Stocker, Jakob, 404, 412, 426

Stocker, Verena, see Weidmann, Verena

Strauss, David Friedrich, 457

Strauss, Richard, 28, 108, 110, 207, 261, 265, 288, 343, 364, 392, 486

Strecker, Ludwig, 495, 510, 586, 625

Strecker, Ludwig (son of the above), 300

Street, Agnes, 277, 326, 360

Strobel, Gertrud, 321

Strobel, Otto, 219, 331, 619, 620, 621

Strousberg, Bethel Henry, 455

Stuttgart, 294, 318, 329, 452

Suarès, André, 283

Sucher, Josef, 515

Sulzer, Jakob, 142, 143–4, 173, 175, 192, 209, 213–14, 215, 217, 260, 323, 540

Tacitus, 474

Tailhade, Laurent, 528

Tannhäuser (Wagner), 66, 84, 89, 93, 102, 103, 118, 241, 295, 340, 464, 473, 488; and Catholicism, 76; ballet in, 283, 285; completion of, 101; composition of, 75, 78–9, 93, 127; conception of, 69–72; for Paris, 70, 78, 280–93 *passim*, 416, 551; musical language of, 43, 77; performances (projected and actual), 15, 77, 78, 148, 155, 172, 177, 180, 190–1, 204–6, 207, 267, 272, 273, 276, 277, 285, 290–2, 385, 389, 482–3, 484, 591; publication of, 116, 122–3, 159, 485; rehearsals, 281, 286–90; revisions/alterations, 76, 78, 283–5, 286–9, 297, 483; sket-ches for, 72; text, 76–7, 102, 235; translation of, 269, 271, 281–2

Tasso, Torquato, 20, 506

Taubert, Karl Gottfried Wilhelm, 433

Tauler, Johannes, 318

Tausig, Karl, 245, 247, 262, 264, 296, 308, 310, 315, 396, 433, 435–6, 437–8, 571

Taylor, Jessie, see Laussot, Jessie

Teplitz, 7, 15, 39, 71, 75, 93, 96

Tessarin (piano teacher), 251

Thomas, Theodore, 486

Thucydides, 513

Thum, Professor, 139

Tichatschek, Joseph, 67, 72–3, 78, 155, 247, 298, 389

Tieck, Ludwig, 70

Titian, 299, 544

Toscanini, Arturo, xii, 578

Tribschen, 17, 94, 208, 263, 371–444 *passim*, 477, 491, 492, 514, 528

Tristan und Isolde (Wagner), xi, 36, 55, 66, 98, 269, 274, 340, 354, 409, 411, 417, 464, 488, 502, 515, 562, 587; and Schopenhauer, 236, 254; completion of, 266, 274; com-position of, xiv, 224, 233, 237, 239, 241, 244–6, 247, 253–6, 258–66, 506, 542, 543, 578; earliest conceptions of, 200, 216; intention to write, 232; musical language of, 31, 110, 231, 237–8, 258, 261–2, 265–6, 279, 288, 344, 565; performances (pro-jected and actual), 257, 271, 272, 273, 276, 278, 280, 295, 296, 326, 337, 341–3, 360, 409–10, 439, 465, 487–8, 564, 587; publica-tion of, 241, 257, 270; readings of, 236, 407; rehearsals, 298, 300, 310, 340, 342; scoring of, 265; sketches for, 242, 246, 263, 325; sources, 233; text, xiv, 233–6, 260, 271

Truinet, Charles (pseudonym Nuitter), 271, 281, 292, 297, 302, 393

Tunis, Bey of, 421

Uhlig, Theodor, 66, 109, 130, 142, 146, 151, 153, 155, 157, 158, 160, 163, 165, 171, 173–4, 176, 540

Ulibishev, Alexander, 81

Ullmann, Bernard (impresario), 516, 517–18

Unger, Georg, 515

United States, see America

Vaez, Gustav, 147

Vaillant (W's doctor), 219–20

Van Gogh, Vincent, 578
Venice, 545, 619; W in, 250–9, 299, 506, 511, 561, 564, 574, 578, 586–91; W's death in, 6, 569, 583, 587, 591–8
Verdi, Giuseppe, 42, 483, 564, 593–4
Verona, 506
Viardot-Garcia, Pauline, 278
Victoria, Queen of England, 207, 517
Vidal, Paul, 484, 623
Viel Castel, Horace de, 281
Vienna, 171, 183, 191, 519; court opera, 296, 392, 482, 484; revolution in, 129, 132; W in, 132, 294, 295–6, 298–301, 308, 312–16, 444, 458, 467, 477–9, 482–4, 619; W's works performed in, 295, 482–3, 515–16, 549
Villiers de l'Isle-Adam, Philippe Auguste, 416–17, 427
Villot, Frédéric, 270, 283
Virchow, Rudolf, 556
Vogel, Martin, xi, 624
Vogl, Heinrich, 410
Vogl, Therese, 410, 548
Völderndorff, Otto Freiherr von, 391, 621
Voltaire, François Marie Arouet de, 317
Voltz & Batz (W's agents), 566, 587, 626
Voss, Johann Heinrich, 20

Wagenseil, Christoph, 300
Wagner, Adolf (W's uncle), 20, 82, 97, 469, 551
Wagner, Albert (W's brother), 12, 37, 74, 102, 118, 204, 476
Wagner, Cosima (Liszt, von Bülow), 189, 200, 215, 241, 289, 294, 461, 469, 560; and Hans von Bülow, xvii, 233, 247, 249, 336, 340, 347, 349, 352, 388, 404–7, 451, 493, 572–3; and Judith Gautier, ix, xiii, xvii, 417–18, 506, 530, 546, 565, 569, 627; and Ludwig II, 346, 358, 370, 371, 375, 385, 389, 394, 397, 409, 523–4, 550; and Friedrich Nietzsche, ix, 414, 416, 419–20, 420–1, 425, 428, 440–1, 443–4, 448, 453, 454, 461, 465, 509, 513, 536–8, 600–1; diaries of, xi–xiv, xvi–xx, 323, 406, 531, 622; divorce from Hans von Bülow, 404, 405, 418, 426; first meetings with W, 184, 236, 334–5; marriage to W, 427, 433; on W's music, 42, 383, 425, 449, 479, 546, 589; on the Wesendonk affair, 248; permanent residence with W, 406; visits W, 333–5, 337, 370–1, 373–88 passim, 395,

402; W's love for, 331, 347–57, 373–4, 388, 395, 476, 619; writings of, 358, 587
Wagner, Emanuel (schoolmaster and organist), 3
Wagner (Chamberlain), Eva (W's daughter), xii, xiv, 350, 354, 357, 388, 406, 578, 618–19, 621
Wagner, Friederike (W's aunt), 4
Wagner, Gottlob Friedrich (W's grandfather), 4–5
Wagner, Isolde (W's daughter), 342, 352, 381, 406
Wagner, Johanna (W's niece), 78, 118, 204, 517
Wagner, Johanna (Pätz) (W's mother), 5–10, 11–16, 17, 18, 27, 29, 30, 42, 70, 395, 469
Wagner, Johanna Sophie (Eichel) (W's grandmother), 4–5
Wagner, Karl Friedrich (W's father), 5–7, 10
Wagner (Wolfram), Klara (W's sister), 12, 243, 307, 308
Wagner (Brockhaus), Luise (W's sister), 12, 14, 117, 307, 433, 476
Wagner, Martin (schoolmaster), 3
Wagner, Minna (Christiane Wilhelmine Planer) (W's first wife), xvii, 15, 142, 147, 176, 192, 204, 236, 267; alienation from W, 141, 143–4, 158; death of, 368–9; deserts W, 13–14, 45–6; early life, 41; first meeting with W, 40–1, 42; illness of, 244, 342; last meeting with W, 308; marriage, 44; on the Laussot affair, 148–9, 150; on the Wesendonk affair, 242–3, 245, 247, 251, 260, 303–4; reconciliations with W, 46–7, 151; separation from W, 251, 297, 304; W in love with, 41–2; W's relationship with, 140, 154, 158, 183, 251–2, 269–70, 271, 297, 306–7, 310, 312, 333, 368–9
Wagner, Moritz (silver-miner), 3
Wagner (Brockhaus), Ottilie (W's sister), 21, 45–6, 406, 410, 439
Wagner, Richard:
– ancestry and paternity, 3–10
– and the Gesamtkunstwerk, 26, 54, 79, 146–7, 585
– and the press, 81, 114, 117, 155, 174, 206, 213, 267, 272–3, 291, 310, 341, 402, 481, 483, 493, 510, 518–19, 569, 576, 620
– as conductor, 13, 41, 48, 80–4, 87–90, 170–3, 174–5, 177, 203–4, 206–7, 273, 307–11, 313–14, 419–20, 433–4, 437, 439,

Wagner, Richard—*cont*.
   444–5, 447, 454, 458, 477–9, 484–5, 517,
   545, 584, 589
  – as exile, 15, 118, 130, 152, 155, 175–6,
   177–8, 191, 199, 204–5, 217–18, 250,
   257–8, 264, 267, 282
  – as orchestrator, 49, 85, 110–11, 120, 187,
   189–90, 202, 207, 265, 309, 364, 392–3,
   458–9, 475, 479, 544–5, 565, 575–6, 578
  – as poet, 21, 36, 65, 77, 95, 108, 199, 214,
   233–6, 260
  – as revolutionary, 91, 128–33, 137–41, 143,
   150, 157, 159–60, 162–4, 340
 –birth and childhood, 4, 5–6, 11, 15, 17–21,
   23, 144
  – creative technique of, 37, 51, 65, 75, 78–9,
   184–6, 189, 221, 254, 302, 442, 527, 533,
   562–3
  – earliest compositions, 21, 28, 30–4, 35–6
  – education, xi, 19–20, 27–31, 82, 97, 198,
   319
  – financial problems, 13, 28, 45, 50, 60–1,
   66, 71, 73, 94, 97, 113–23, 145, 179, 190–2,
   204–5, 217, 256, 275–8, 285–6, 294, 310,
   315–16, 327, 342–3
  – harmony, use of, 75, 109–10, 186, 201–2,
   237, 288, 546–7
  – illness, 17, 157, 176, 211, 215, 219–20, 287,
   346, 347, 350–1, 357, 550, 553, 561–2, 569,
   575–7, 586, 590, 592
  – influenced by:
    German opera, 63
    German and Nordic mythology, 93–7,
     99–100, 134, 219, 407
    grand opera, 48–9, 55
    Greek history, mythology and tragedy,
     19–20, 93, 97–100, 101, 107, 110, 127,
     134, 143, 284, 370, 407, 451, 513,
     560–1, 585
    Indian literature and philosophy, 105,
     207, 211, 218, 236, 255, 269, 347, 349,
     395, 459, 585
    Italian opera, 39, 42
    mediaeval literature and history, 35,
     69–70, 94, 101, 103, 112, 127, 233
    other composers, *see* Bach, Beet-
     hoven, Bellini, Berlioz, Meyerbeer,
     Mozart, Spontini, Weber
    philosophers, *see* Feuerbach, Hegel,
     Nietzsche, Schelling, Schopenhauer
  – isolation of, 15, 105, 136, 183, 209, 231,
   270, 313, 333, 407

  – leitmotiv, use of, 36, 38, 43, 65, 108–9,
   152, 169, 174, 179–80, 187–9, 193, 202,
   261–2, 419, 527
  – marriages, 13, 44, 427, *and see* Wagner,
   Cosima; Wagner, Minna
  – plans for a music school, 341–2, 345, 359,
   467–8, 520–2, 551
  – plans for a new theatre, 156, 177, 339–41,
   345, 355, 387, 401, 439, 551
  – plans to emigrate, x, 517–18, 519, 551–3,
   556, 574–5
  – plans to write a symphony, 54, 395,
   429–30, 468, 507, 531, 532, 542, 589–90
  – residences in: Biebrich, 303–6, 308;
   Blasewitz, 45–6; Königsberg, 13, 44, 45,
   47; Lucerne, 154, 211, 260–6; Magdeburg,
   12–13, 40–1, 43–4, 51, 453; Riga, 13, 45,
   46–51, 60, 522; Würzburg, 37, 142, 453; *see
   also* Bayreuth, Dresden, Munich, Paris,
   Tribschen, Venice, Vienna, Wahnfried,
   Zürich
  – sweethearts and mistresses, *see* Gautier,
   Judith; Laussot, Jessie; Maier, Mathilde;
   Wagner, Cosima; Wagner, Minna;
   Wesendonk, Mathilde
  – views on:
    Christianity and Catholicism, 136, 355,
     417, 442, 484, 533, 562, 569, 579
    concert performances and orchestral
     reform, 47–8, 74, 90–1, 178, 309
    drama, 99, 101, 157, 432, 436, 451–2
    France and the French, 62, 393, 428, 431,
     484
    German art, 39, 342, 390, 396, 445
     496
    himself as artist, 76, 114, 210, 220, 254,
     317, 344, 350–1, 408, 480, 495, 511
    Italian opera, 39, 559
    Jews, 153, 245, 390, 407, 436, 438, 558,
     567–8, 570–1, 595, 627
    politics, 130–3, 163–4, 361–2, 367, 377,
     378–80, 386–7, 390, 427, 430–1,
     539–41
    Protestantism, 403, 451, 579
    theatrical reform, 47, 129–30, 132,
     171–2
    vivisection, 554–6
WORKS:
    arrangements, 24–5, 49, 60, 71, 106–7,
     276
    journals: Annals, 162, 200, 216, 226,
     253, 254, 335, 336, 360, 365, 385, 391,

393, 394, 395, 396, 401, 402, 403, 404, 405, 406, 407, 619; Brown Book, xiv, 336, 347–57, 367–8, 369–70, 388, 395, 403, 423, 428, 618–19, 621; Red Book, 59, 320, 358; Venetian Diary, 236, 240, 251, 252, 253, 254, 256

operas, *see individual titles*

orchestral works, 28, 31–3, 36, 49, 51, 54, 55, 85, 203, 310, 338, 395, 396, 430, 434, 439, 446, 459, 486–7, 506, 589, 603; see also *Siegfried Idyll*

piano works, 26, 31–2, 297

prose works, 23, 28, 39, 50, 61–2, 96, 123, 129–30, 133, 134, 161, 172, 206–7, 275, 319, 338, 384, 395, 407, 419–20, 429, 432, 434, 436, 437, 449–50, 451–2, 453–4, 456, 460, 498, 541, 561–2, 579, 592; see under their titles *Art and Revolution, Artwork of the Future, Beethoven, Communication to my Friends, Jewry in Music, Mein Leben, Music of the Future, Pilgrimage to Beethoven*

songs and choral music, 36, 49–50, 51, 84–5, 115, 238–40, 253, 260, 389, 459

texts, scenarios and sketches, *see individual titles*

Wagner (Marbach), Rosalie (W's sister), 12, 13–14, 22, 36, 37, 38, 40, 46

Wagner, Samuel (I) (schoolmaster), 3

Wagner, Samuel (II) (W's great-grandfather), 3–4

Wagner, Siegfried (W's son), xviii, 410, 425, 470, 518, 543, 554, 556, 560, 592

Wagner Societies, *see under* Bayreuth

Wahnfried, 23, 82, 208, 232, 294, 393, 432, 456, 466–7, 468–71, 477, 479, 481–2, 489, 494, 500, 523, 530, 545, 548, 554, 569, 570, 573–4, 579, 583, 587, 593, 597, 623; library in, xi, 20, 81, 94, 213, 235, 469, 619, 623

Walewski, Count, 292

Walküre, Die (Wagner), 419, 515; completion of, xiv, 216–17, 218, 266; composition of, 192–6, 200–2, 207, 211, 215–16, 543; musical language of, 31, 49, 82, 193, 225; performances, xiii, 222, 248, 271, 309, 422–3, 425, 426, 434, 445, 478, 482; scoring of, 202, 221; sketches for, 159, 161, 163, 193–5, 201–2, 323

Warnkönig, Leopold August, 321

Weber, Carl Maria von, 33, 66, 544; conducted by W, 47, 81, 170, 172, 204; influence on W, 18, 22, 33, 38; reburial, 85; works: *Euryanthe*, 39, 73, 81, 85, 172, *Der Freischütz*, 18, 22, 24, 62–3, 170, 204, 473

Weber, Caroline von, 75, 81

Weber, Dionys, 33, 83

Weber, Ernst von, 554–5, 561

Weidmann (Stocker), Verena, 263, 373, 404, 478

Weimar, 160; theatre, 10, 158, 159; W in, 140, 297, 441, 450–1, 465; W's works performed in, 103, 151, 154–6, 177, 426

Weinlig, Theodor, xi, 28, 29–31, 33, 36, 84, 198, 319

Weissheimer, Wendelin, 248, 303, 308, 309, 310, 329–30, 396

Welcker, Friedrich Gottlieb, 412

Wesendonk, Guido, 215, 253

Wesendonk, Mathilde, xvii, 66, 105, 177, 203, 205, 221, 225, 226, 233, 238, 241, 269, 279, 315, 318, 327, 343, 427, 518, 568; W's affair with, 194, 201, 215, 236–7, 238–44, 246–9, 251–3, 260, 299, 303, 314

Wesendonk, Otto, 160, 179, 180, 192, 205, 215, 217, 221, 225–6, 233, 239–40, 241, 246, 249, 253, 260, 263–4, 276, 299, 343, 398, 618

Widmann, Professor, 140

Wieck, Clara (Schumann), 28, 33, 34

Wieck, Friedrich, 28

Wieland der Schmied (Wagner), 147, 148

Wigand, Otto, 143

Wilamowitz-Moellendorff, Ulrich von, 449, 622

Wilbrandt, Adolf, 478

Wilhelm I, German Emperor, 433–4, 464, 485, 487–8, 495, 507, 518, 538–9, 569

Wilhelmj, August, 297, 471, 516, 517

Wille, Eliza, 75, 165, 198, 231, 241, 247, 252, 253, 255, 314, 315–18, 343, 435

Wille, François, 165, 179, 198, 253, 316, 318, 343, 435

Winckelmann, Johann Joachim, 145, 413

Winkelmann, Hermann, 580

Winkler, C. T., 67

Winterberger (pupil of Liszt), 251

Wittgenstein, Caroline, Princess, 178, 183, 198, 222–3, 336, 343, 355, 445, 450, 465, 589, 627

Wittgenstein, Princess Marie, 183, 222, 224, 266, 274

Wolfram, Heinrich, 139, 476
Wolfram, Klara, *see* Wagner, Klara
Wolfram von Eschenbach, 101
Wolzogen, Hans von, xii, xviii, 22, 65, 82,
    465, 467, 534, 546, 550, 556, 561, 563, 572,
    579
Wüllner, Franz, 415, 416, 423
Würzburg, 37, 142, 452–3

Zhukovsky, Paul, xix, 557, 560, 563, 569,
    574, 575, 577, 583, 591, 592
Zhukovsky, Vasily Alexandreyevich, 557

Zukunftsmusik (Wagner), see *Music of the
    Future*
Zumbusch, Caspar, 469
Zumpe, Hermann, 471
Zürich, 37; municipal theatre, 169; Music
    Society, 172, 177, 190, 202–3, 212; W con-
    ducts in, 169–73, 174–5, 177, 202–4; W's
    friends in, 143–4, 149, 175–6, 213, 264;
    W's residence in, 75, 142–5, 147, 151, 159,
    178–9, 184, 221–2, 225–6, 522; W's visits
    to, 294, 316; W's works performed in
    205–6